DAVID O. McKAY

David O. McKay, 1934

DAVID O. McKAY

Apostle to the World, Prophet of God

Francis M. Gibbons

Deseret Book Company
Salt Lake City, Utah

Books by Francis M. Gibbons

Joseph Smith: Martyr, Prophet of God
Brigham Young: Modern Moses, Prophet of God
John Taylor: Mormon Philosopher, Prophet of God
Lorenzo Snow: Spiritual Giant, Prophet of God
Joseph F. Smith: Patriarch and Preacher, Prophet of God
Heber J. Grant: Man of Steel, Prophet of God
David O. McKay: Apostle to the World, Prophet of God

All photographs used courtesy of Church Archives, The Church of Jesus Christ of Latter-day Saints, Salt Lake City, Utah.

First printing April 1986

Library of Congress Cataloging-in-Publication Data

Gibbons, Francis M., 1921–
    David O. McKay : apostle to the world, prophet of God.

    Bibliography: p.
    Includes index.
    1. McKay, David Oman, 1873-1970.   2. Mormon Church—Presidents—Biography.   3. Church of Jesus Christ of Latter-day Saints—Presidents—Biography.   I. Title.
BX8695.M27G53   1986   289.3'32'0924 [B]   86-4564
ISBN 0-87579-036-4

To the grandchildren

Contents

Preface

The diaries (in eighty-four binders), scrapbooks (in two hundred and fifteen large folio volumes), and extensive correspondence of President David O. McKay comprise perhaps the most comprehensive known record of any individual member of The Church of Jesus Christ of Latter-day Saints. These documents, which are housed in the Historical Department of the Church, formed the core for the biography which follows. The author expresses heartfelt thanks to Elder G. Homer Durham, deceased, former Church Historian and to Elder Dean L. Larsen, his successor, for giving him unrestricted access to these records. He is also indebted to Earl E. Olson, Assistant Managing Director of the Historical Department; Donald E. Schmidt, former Director of the Church Library-Archives and his successor, Glenn M. Rowe, for their uniform kindness and helpfulness.

A special debt is acknowledged to Clare Middlemiss, deceased, President McKay's loyal and efficient personal secretary, who supervised the preparation of the scrapbooks and who transcribed the diaries as dictated by President McKay during the many years she served him.

Thanks also go to Richard Davis, who assisted with the research; to many family members and others who provided important insights into President McKay's character and service; to the editorial staff of Deseret Book Company, especially Jack Lyon; and, as usual, to my Mentor.

Key to Abbreviations

Chapter One

East of Eden

Had David and Jennette Evans McKay lived a stone's throw northwest of the family home on September 8, 1873, their third child and first son, David O. McKay, would have been born in Eden on that day. As it was, the wee one had to settle for Huntsville, a rural community, which, in his maturity, David O. McKay seemed to equate with the original home of our first earthly parents.

The Eden of which we now speak is Eden, Utah, which, with its neighbor, Huntsville, shares the spectacular Swiss-Alpine setting of the Upper Ogden Valley. The McKays first came to this remote area in 1860 when, in June of that year, Isaac and David, ages twenty and sixteen, accompanied by their eleven-year-old sister, Williamena, harvested hay there for the use of the family livestock. This trio, children of William McKay and Ellen Oman McKay, then lived in Ogden, where the family had arrived in 1859 following a three-year odyssey from their ancestral home in Thurso, Scotland. This industrious clan, which included two other children, Isabella, age eighteen, and Catharine, age nine, had promptly established a rustic home on a small acreage in Ogden. And, learning of the lush grass growing in the upland valley, the father had sent the three children there in the family wagon to harvest supplemental feed for the animals. Winding their way up the narrow canyon, which connects the lower and upper valleys, these natives of Thurso, located on the northern tip of Scotland, who were accustomed to the treeless, peat hills of the Pentland Firth with their blanket of Scottish heather, were treated to the contrasting sight of rugged, mountainous terrain, dotted with towering pines, through which, in a meandering channel, roared a clear mountain stream.

Using scythes, the two powerful young Scotsmen harvested while their young sister, whose chief function was to prepare and serve the meals, helped cock the hay they left to dry.

Although the Indians later burned the hay, William was so pleased with the report of the harvest and so impressed with the glowing accounts of his children about the wondrous valley with its heady, invigorating atmosphere, that the following year, 1861, he purchased a tract of land there. Soon a small log cabin was erected on the site, which was used for several years as a family headquarters during the valley's comparatively short growing season. The harsh winters, with their biting winds and drifting snow, the lack of adequate housing, and the absence of school and church facilities, precluded year-round living in those early years.

This, then, was the genesis of the McKay presence in the Upper Ogden Valley and, more particularly, in Huntsville. It was a beginning that, though inauspicious, would produce significant results. It was the starting point from which the seed of William and Ellen Oman McKay would grow into a numerous progeny of productive and talented men and women, one of whom would give them and their name worldwide recognition. But, of more immediate and mundane importance, this marked the opening of the door of economic opportunity for these immigrants who had found a congenial place to profitably wield the farming and livestock skills learned on the Scottish highlands.

A year before his introduction to the Upper Ogden Valley, David McKay first met the young girl who would

2

David McKay and Jennette Evelyn Evans McKay, the parents of David O. McKay. The picture of David hung for many years in the old Huntsville church, where he was bishop from 1885 to 1905.

become his bride and who would help assure the perpetuation of the McKay clan. It was in 1859 in Ogden that fifteen-year-old David McKay first saw ten-year-old Jennette Evans, whose parents, Thomas and Margaret Powell Evans, had recently migrated to Utah from their ancestral home near Merthyr Tydfil, South Wales. Pert and pretty, Jennette was seated on the tongue of the family wagon when David first saw her. At that young age, there would appear to have been little in the way of female allurement to evoke feelings of matrimony, especially in a fifteen-year-old adolescent; still, David reported later that at this moment he knew that Jennette Evans was to be his bride. He never forgot the emotional impact of the young girl's large brown eyes peering at him from beneath a pink sunbonnet.

Eight years after this first encounter, when Jennette had blossomed into a young woman of stunning beauty, twenty-three-year-old David McKay courted and won her, as he won the respect and approval of her parents. Their marriage and sealing were performed in the Salt Lake Endowment House on April 9, 1867, by Wilford Woodruff of the Quorum of the Twelve Apostles.

3

The struggling pioneer community in which David and Jennette elected to establish their home, Huntsville, took its name from Captain Jefferson Hunt, veteran commander of Company A of the Mormon Battalion. Captain Hunt and his three sons, Joseph, Hyrum, and Marshall, and their families began settling in the valley in the early fall of 1860. These pioneers left a strong imprint on the community, including their name, which is still a memorial to them and their rugged spirit of enterprise.

Following the example of their father, Isaac and David McKay purchased land in the Huntsville area as their finances allowed and eventually formed a ranching and farming partnership that continued until David returned from his mission. The brothers raised hay for winter feed for their livestock, and grain. A garden and a small orchard supplied them with fruits and vegetables, the excess from which was canned for winter use. These, in addition to milk, butter, cheese, and eggs from their own cows and chickens and meat from their own herd provided the families with ample food and a good diet. The sale of their livestock, part of which went to their father, William, who owned a butcher shop in Ogden, was a chief source of liquid income.

It was a healthy, happy, and hard life, hard in the sense that constant toil was necessary to keep the operation running smoothly. And vagaries of the weather and the unpredictable fluctuations of market prices for their cattle and grain were recurring sources of uncertainty and concern. Moreover, the lack of modern farm implements placed a premium on manual labor, which, for an operator without robust sons or the means to hire laborers, raised the threat of utter failure in the event of his death or disability.

In such circumstances, sons were an especially blessed event to a young farmer-rancher and his wife. So the birth of David Oman McKay on September 8, 1873, was cause for special celebration in his family, not only because it provided his father with a male heir and namesake, but also because it provided a potential worker for the future. It was

4

hoped and expected that he would, in time, help to shoulder the heavy burdens of labor, thereby giving a sense of security to parents who were struggling to wrest a living from the soil.

But the physical role the new son was expected to play in the family was overshadowed by the spiritual implications of his birth. David and Jennette had accepted without question the teachings of their parents' adopted religion. From that, and from the blessings conferred upon them at the time of their own temple marriage and sealing, they were convinced that this son, as well as two daughters who had preceded him in birth, Margaret and Ellena, and any children who would follow, would be theirs in a family relationship through eternity, conditioned upon their obedience to heavenly principles.

The significance of these concepts in the lives of the children of David and Jennette McKay can hardly be overemphasized. They were impressed upon their minds repeatedly from the first moments of consciousness. From their days as toddlers to the time of their departure from the parental home, words expressed in daily family prayers, in Sunday School classes, or over the pulpit reinforced and elaborated upon these seminal ideas.

As David O. emerged from infancy to childhood, he began to reveal the physical characteristics that would be the distinguishing features of his mature years. He had inherited the thick, wavy hair of his father and the pleasant expression of his mother. The eyes also seemed to be a maternal inheritance, although they were not as deeply brown as were Jennette's. And the rangy, powerful physique he would develop in maturity was an obvious gift from the McKay clan, moulded and toughened by years of hard labor on the farm.

At a very early age, the son showed a marked interest in animals and pets, a quality that would remain with him until the moment of his death. From childhood, he had a pet dog. When he was old enough to ride it, he had his own pony. Pigeons, rabbits, and magpies from time to time also became part of the menagerie over which this youngster presided.

Next to his family, the most powerful influence on this growing boy was the Church. Soon after Jefferson Hunt arrived in the valley, a branch was established with the captain as its first president. At the outset, the membership of this small unit was comprised mostly of Hunts—the families of the branch president and his sons. In 1865, when Captain Hunt moved to Marsh Valley, Idaho, his replacement was F. D. Hammond, who called the young twenty-one-year-old bachelor, David McKay, as his second counselor. So, at the time of his marriage two years later, this promising young man was already a seasoned Church leader who carried into his home the dedication to duty that his ecclesiastical calling inspired and required. And six years later, by the time of David O.'s birth in 1873, the pattern of David and Jennette's family life was firmly fixed with regular family prayer as its keystone. From his infancy, therefore, the eldest son of this pioneering couple was exposed to the fervent prayers of parents who poured out their souls to the Lord daily for help in raising their family, in managing their temporal affairs, and in striving for exaltation.

In 1877, when David O. was four years old, the Huntsville branch was organized into a ward, and his father then became the president of the Eden Branch, a position in which he served until 1881 when he was called on a mission. During this four years, the father frequently traveled the several miles between his home and Eden to discharge his Church duties, often taking David O. and other members of the family with him in the McKay buggy or on horses. Also at a very early age, the son accompanied his father on outings to gather firewood or to check on the family's animals. Not infrequently this required overnight stays. On one such occasion, father and son camped in an area where a nearby pack of coyotes howled during most of the night. A mature David O. McKay related how the presence of his manly father made him feel perfectly safe and secure against any danger from these predators. (RSM, October 1953, p. 602.) On another occasion young David O. became terribly frightened during a violent storm when neither of his parents was there to comfort him. But, following a practice they taught him, he prayed for protection; then there came into his mind the calming thought, "Don't be afraid. Nothing will hurt you." David O. later reflected upon the influence David and Jennette McKay had upon him during his growing years: "It was this realization of mother's love, with a loyalty to the precepts of an exemplary father, which, more than once during fiery youth, turned my steps from the precipice of temptation. If I were asked to name the world's greatest need, I should say unhesitatingly wise mothers; and the second exemplary fathers." (Morrell, *Highlights*, p. 34.) And in that same reflective mood, he wrote of the comforting realization that came to him as a growing boy that he was loved and appreciated: "Among my most precious soul treasures, is the memory of mother's prayers by the bedside, of her affectionate touch as she tucked the bed clothes around my brother and me, and gave each a loving good night kiss. We were too young and roguish, then, fully to appreciate such devotion, but not too young to know that mother loved us." (Ibid.)

The impact on a growing boy of the example of selfless service by the father and the love and concern of the mother is difficult to gauge, although we can make an educated guess from the exemplary lives of David O. McKay and the other children who came from that home.

The economic growth of Huntsville in its early years kept pace with the growth of its family and church life. Soon after the first settlers came to the valley, Thomas Bingham established a hand-driven shingle mill that was later superseded by a power-driven sawmill owned by the Ferrin brothers, Jacob and Samuel. Soon the area could boast a grist mill, a flour mill, and a tannery; and in due course, these were followed by shops for a blacksmith, a shoemaker, a milliner, a cloth and carpet weaver, a printer, a butcher, and a basket weaver.

David and Jennette Evans McKay with their four eldest children (left to right): Ellena, David O., Thomas E., and Margaret. Photo taken in 1877.

The other essential element of a successful community—a school for the children—was established not long after families began to settle in the valley. On March 3, 1861, the County Selectmen organized Ogden Valley into a precinct and designated an area within the precinct, which included Huntsville, as School District No. 14. Later, funds were appropriated to construct a modest building and to hire a teacher who, in the beginning, taught children of all ages.

By the time of David O. McKay's birth, Huntsville was, therefore, a well-organized, thriving, and, for the most part, self-sustaining community. Although its residents traced their ancestry to several different countries, the town was surprisingly homogenous, a result produced by the influence of The Church of Jesus Christ of Latter-day Saints. The terms *brother* and *sister* were used routinely to identify those outside an immediate family, suggesting the fraternal bond that welded Huntsville together. And some in the community were regularly called "aunt," "uncle," "father," and so on by persons who bore no blood relation-

The Old McKay home in Huntsville. David O. once wrote to his brother Thomas E.: "It is only an old country home, but no palace ever was filled with truer love and devotion on the part of parents, brothers, and sisters than that which pervaded the hearts of the loved ones in that family circle."

ship to them. The midwife, for instance, who officiated at the birth of David O. McKay, Mary Heathman Smith, was fondly called "Grandma Smith" by one and all.

It is difficult to conceive of a society better calculated to create a sense of security and self-worth in growing children than the one into which David O. McKay and his brothers and sisters were born. In their infancy and young childhood they were shielded, for the most part, from the trials and traumas of the parents who intermittently suffered from drought, insect invasion, a declining livestock market, and illness. What concerns may have filtered down to the children over such alarming events were soon shrugged off as they returned to their insular world of friends, pets, games, and the grandeur of their mountain home.

The first concerns that appear to have penetrated the shield of David O.'s childish indifference were the deaths of his two elder sisters, Margaret and Ellena. To see them lifeless in their caskets taught the seven-year-old brother a grim lesson about the reality of death and the tenuous nature of life. Margaret, the eldest sister, had contracted rheumatic fever in the fall of 1879, preventing her from attending school that year. Her condition deteriorated over the following months as the inadequately trained doctors in the area were unable to stem the tide of her baffling illness. She died on March 28, 1880. Four days later, the day of Margaret's funeral, Ellena passed away unexpectedly from pneumonia.

These deaths cast a pall of grief over the McKay household for many months. The stunned parents found it difficult to face the reality of what had happened. And David O. and Thomas E. and their younger sister became disconsolate and moody.

A year later, when the cloud of depression had begun to lift, the McKays received another shock in the form of a letter from Box B in Salt Lake City. It contained a call from President John Taylor to the father to serve a mission in his native Scotland. To thirty-seven-year-old David McKay, married with three living children and another expected soon, this was the ultimate test of his faith and commitment. To leave a wife in these circumstances with the eldest child, David O., being only eight, and with a farm and livestock operation to manage, seemed beyond reason. In these circumstances, it is understandable why the father showed some reluctance to accept the call at first. And at that moment of hesitancy, had his wife voiced any complaint or shown any uncertainty, it is likely he would have declined, which would have radically altered the direction and aspirations of the McKay family. As it was, Jennette spoke with firmness and finality: "Of course you must accept; you need not worry about me. David O. and I will manage things nicely." (L. R. McKay, *Home Memories*, p. 6.) Still not convinced it was timely to go, and thinking, perhaps, that his wife, carried away by an excess of zeal, had not counted the cost of his acceptance, David counseled with some of the brethren in the ward. Many of them, fully aware of the business and domestic implications of his departure, sided with the husband and encouraged him to decline. But one of them, Uncle John Grow, correctly appraising the situation, gave the advice David eventually followed: "You may be right, and you may be wrong," said Uncle John, "but if Jennette has set her mind that you should answer the mission call, you might as well give in!" He then offered this postscript, which was a source of comfort and encouragement: "I'll keep an eye on things and help out when I can." (Ibid.)

With that assurance, which was seconded and reinforced by other neighbors, David McKay willingly accepted the mission call. He left for Scotland on April 19, 1881, less than three weeks after he had received the letter from President Taylor. The parting word to his namesake, "Take care of Mama," was the signal to eight-year-old David O. McKay that he had prematurely entered the world of adulthood. No longer was he merely one of the children. He was the man of the house, bearing the weight of a special stewardship conferred by his departing father.

Reason convinces us that this eight-year-old boy was incapable of actually filling the role assigned by his father. He was too small, too inexperienced, and too lacking in the manly discipline necessary to direct a farming and ranching operation. The father knew this. And so did the son. Yet, by conferring the title on him, David had shown confidence in the boy that could not have failed to give him a sense of competence and dependability.

Later events demonstrated that the missionary could not have left home at a more inopportune time. Ten days after his departure, Jennette gave birth to their sixth child, Ann. Moreover, this occurred in the midst of spring planting. The neighbors pooled their resources to help. The men brought the equipment and animals necessary to complete the planting. And the women came to clean and wash, to help prepare meals, and to tend the older children. Although he was not yet eight years old, David O. was a help rather than a hindrance and cooperated to assist with the housework and with the lighter chores outside, helping the men.

The change in his attitude wrought by the father's charge to the son to take care of his mother was extraordinary. Only a few years before, an aunt, who had come to help at harvest time, complained to Jennette about her eldest son, "If you will just take care of this boy, I'll gladly cook for the threshers." Now he was all business, anxious to help in any way possible and to demonstrate his sudden manliness. However, there were times of discouragement when David O.'s boyishness showed through this veneer of maturity. On one such occasion he tired of carrying hay to feed two huge oxen. Annoyed at their ravenous appetites, he said in exasperation to his mother who had come to help, "Now, let's give them two large armsful of hay and run to the house before they eat it." (Morrell, *Highlights*, p. 24.)

The harvest in 1881 was bounteous. But, as usually happens in years of plenty, the market prices were depressed. In fact, the price of grain had fallen so low as to erase all hope of profit. Using her good sense, and following the obvious advice of neighbors, Jennette decided to store the grain, hoping for a better market in the spring. Her hopes were realized and she turned a neat profit. The following year's crop was equally profitable, producing an impressive surplus, which Jennette decided to use in a way that would surprise her missionary. She went forward with plans she and her husband had previously discussed to enlarge their home. Without consulting or notifying him, David's resourceful wife completed the plans for the addition, negotiated the contract with the builders, and supervised the construction. When the missionary returned from Scotland, he was incredulous at what Jennette had accomplished, proudly referring to her as "the greatest miracle that one could ever find." (L. R. McKay, *Home Memories*, p. 6.)

The dedication David McKay had shown in the mission field marked him as one in whom the leaders of the Church could place implicit trust and confidence. This was demonstrated when, on November 20, 1883, just a few months after returning from Scotland, he was called as bishop of the Eden Ward. This calling lasted only sixteen months. On March 29, 1885, he was called to replace Francis A. Hammond as the bishop of the Huntsville ward, a service that would extend for two decades until his ordination as a patriarch in 1905 by President Joseph F. Smith.

Chapter Two

The Bishop's Son

David O. McKay was almost twelve years old when his father was called as the bishop of the Huntsville Ward. From then until he left the parental home, his status was largely one of reflected distinction. To those who resided in the valley, and to those who came to visit, David O. was known in those days chiefly as "Bishop McKay's oldest boy" or as "one of the Bishop's sons." The father, measured by any standard of that day, was the most prominent man in the valley. Almost all of the residents there were members of The Church of Jesus Christ of Latter-day Saints. And as such, those in the Huntsville Ward fell under the jurisdiction of Bishop McKay, who was their spiritual guide and the one to whom they paid their tithes.

Most of the ecclesiastical activities of the community revolved around the ward chapel, where the bishop presided, or around the bishop's large home, where members often came for counsel or to pay their offerings. And since there was no hotel in Huntsville, prominent visitors who stayed overnight would invariably enjoy the hospitality of David and Jennette McKay in their lovely home. These included General Authorities of the Church who came occasionally to instruct and inspire the people. One such visit, to which the family attached special significance, was when all three members of the First Presidency—Wilford Woodruff, George Q. Cannon, and Joseph F. Smith—stayed under the McKay roof. That the Prophet, Wilford Woodruff, was the one who had performed their temple sealing many years before added another dimension to the excitement of the bishop and his wife on this occasion. And had their thoughts been prophetically attuned to the future, they would not only have been excited but amazed to learn that within a few years President Woodruff's tall and taciturn second counselor, Joseph F. Smith, would call their eldest son to the apostleship, a call that would carry the seeds of his ultimate elevation to the prophetic office.

Aside from his prominence as an ecclesiastical leader, Bishop McKay also played a key role in civic affairs. He served as a trustee of the Huntsville school district, county commissioner, justice of the peace, and member of the board of education of the Weber Stake Academy. He was also elected to the lower house of the Utah Legislature, where he helped spearhead the movement for women's suffrage; and later he served as a Utah state senator.

In these varied roles, David McKay met and exerted a positive influence on many people. He was looked upon as a man of wisdom and good judgment, wise in counsel, and prompt in execution. Many sought his advice on matters ranging from the rotation of crops to the conditions of exaltation. And the advice he gave was always to the point and expressed in clear, understandable terms. It is questionable whether, in life, he realized the full extent of his favorable impact on others. Certainly he could have assessed this to an extent from the distinction that came to his eldest son, who grew to maturity under his tutelage. But he would never know about countless others who were inspired by his words or example, as in the case of Ernest L. Wilkinson, who became a prominent and successful attorney and was later president of Brigham Young University. Once, when he was a young boy, the future university president rode to Salt Lake City on the Bamberger electric train going to general conference. In front of him was Bishop McKay, who was conversing with a friend about the gospel. Young Ernest, who overheard the conversation, wrote of the incident: "At that time he recited . . . the advice given in the Doctrine and Covenants 'to retire to thy bed early, that ye may not be weary; to rise early that your bodies and your minds may be invigorated.' " The enthusiastic and positive manner of the bishop had a profound effect upon the impressionable boy, who was anxious to claim the rewards offered by obedience to this scripture. "What little success I have had in my profession," President Wilkinson wrote later, "has been due, I am sure, in large part to the fact that I generally get started much earlier in the morning than most men in my profession." (L. R. McKay, *Home Memories*, p. 24.)

David O. McKay and his brothers also learned the lesson of rising early from their father. But they learned it by example, not by precept, as in the case of Ernest L. Wilkinson. Bishop McKay ordinarily arose at four o'clock in the morning. The signal to his sons that he was up and stirring was the squeaking of the old pump under the sleeping porch where the boys slept. From the moment the sons were awakened by that irritating noise, further sleep was impossible, either because of David's racket as he went about the other chores, or because of guilt feelings in the sons, who were uncomfortably reminded of their sloth compared with their father's diligence.

The remedy, of course, was to get up and to go to work like the father. While at first it was difficult for the growing boys to arise that early, as the months and years wore on, it became a deeply ingrained and, ultimately, an enjoyable habit. Through all of his adult life, David O. McKay was an early riser, thanks to the example of his hardworking father. And as with Ernest Wilkinson, there can be little doubt that this habit was a principal ingredient in David O.'s success by giving him the edge of a few productive hours at the top of the day, hours that most others spent in blissful slumber.

In time, as he grew and as his muscles hardened, David

O. took his place alongside his father in the farming and ranching enterprise. But before he had reached the stage of physical maturity that made this possible, he engaged in less arduous activities. After the father returned from his mission, the son took a job delivering a newspaper, the *Ogden Standard Examiner*. Most of his customers were in LaPlata, a mining town several miles up Middlefork Canyon. Each weekday during the summer, the boy would saddle his horse, securing the newspapers in his saddle bags, and, bidding good-bye, would usually be on his way by 7:00 A.M. Ten hours later he would return, having made the long round trip and having delivered the papers to the miners who, hungry for news from the outside, always welcomed him with enthusiasm and gratitude. He made many friends among these hardworking men, some of whom shared his sturdy Welsh heritage.

During these long, solitary trips and at other times, the boy's mind was often called up to serious reflection about life and its meaning and about the nature and the very existence of God. Repeatedly through the years he had knelt in prayer with his family, joining them in imploring the Lord for guidance and assistance and in expressing gratitude for the many blessings He had conferred upon them. Although he had never seen God, nor had he enjoyed a spiritual experience that had demonstrated to him the reality and power of His being, David O. had accepted the testimonies and teachings of his parents about these matters. But a time came when he desired to know for himself, not in a secondhand way from others. At home and in his Sunday School classes, he had often heard the story about Joseph Smith, who as a young boy had received heavenly answers to similar questions through secret prayer. So on one occasion during those formative years, young David O. McKay, while riding alone outside Huntsville looking for cattle, decided he would make a similar attempt to receive divine confirmation of the things he had been taught by his parents and instructors. "I dismounted, threw my reins over my horse's head," he wrote of the incident, "and there under a serviceberry bush prayed that God would declare to me the truth of his revelation to Joseph Smith." He said he prayed "fervently and sincerely and with as much faith" as he could muster. When he had finished, the young boy waited expectantly for some spiritual response to his prayer. Nothing happened. With a sense of disappointment, David O. mounted his horse and rode slowly away. He later recalled saying to himself at the time, "No spiritual manifestation has come to me. If I am true to myself, I must say I am just the same 'old boy' that I was before I prayed." (*New Era*, January 1972, p. 56.)

The candor with which he acknowledged the failure to receive an answer to his prayer on this occasion lends added strength to a testimony David O. McKay later bore of a powerful spiritual experience he had while serving as a young missionary in Scotland. And, as we shall see, that spiritual experience, which lighted the way to his future, also gave illumination to the earnest prayer he had offered years before on an isolated hillside near Huntsville.

Although he was oblivious to its meaning at the moment, this earnest young boy received prophetic guidance about this same time. It occurred on July 17, 1887, when the Church patriarch, John Smith, conferred a patriarchal blessing on Bishop McKay's eldest son, who was then within a few weeks of his fourteenth birthday. With the solemnity characteristic of his calling, the benign, white-haired patriarch laid his hands on the boy's head, saying: "Brother David Oman McKay, thou art in thy youth and need instruction, therefore . . . be taught of thy parents . . . that at an early day you may be prepared for a responsible position, for the eye of the Lord is upon thee. . . . The Lord has a work for thee to do, in which thou shalt see much of the world, assist in gathering scattered Israel and also labor in the ministry. It shall be thy lot to sit in council with thy brethren and preside among the people and exhort the Saints to faithfulness." (DOMP.)

Viewing this extraordinary blessing from the perspective of David O. McKay's entire life, it would be difficult to formulate a statement of equal brevity that would more accurately outline the salient features of his remarkable career. Here we see foreshadowed his early call to the Twelve; his extensive world travels; his prominence in missionary work; his administrative labors "in the ministry"; his role in counseling with the Brethren; and his ultimate mission to "preside among the people."

The astonishing impact of what he had just said may account for what the inspired patriarch told Bishop McKay's fourteen-year-old son when the blessing was completed. Placing his hands on the boy's already muscular shoulders, he looked intently at him, saying: "My boy, you have something to do besides playing marbles." (Morrell, *Highlights*, p. 26.) That the blessing as yet had little real meaning for him is evident from what followed. Going to his mother, who was preparing dinner in the kitchen, David O. said defensively, perhaps defiantly, "If he thinks I'm going to stop playing marbles, he is mistaken." (Ibid.)

Such a frank response from one so young who had been reared in a home of devoted orthodoxy provides significant insight into the character of this prophet-to-be. It did not matter that the counsel came from the Church patriarch, one of the General Authorities. He was prepared to reject it as not conforming with his own views of the matter. Here, then, we see in embryo the man whom this boy was to become, self-confident, positive in his views, and determined to be guided by his own lights.

But another facet of character is revealed by the incident. When the wise mother explained that the patriarch's statement was merely a figure of speech and that he meant only that the boy's juvenile obsession with marbles or other games was insignificant compared with his ultimate purpose in life, he understood it and accepted it. So this youngster was teachable and would yield to reason, a quality that grew with his sense of boldness and independence.

That David O. McKay did not readily grasp at an early age what his mission in life was to be is not difficult to understand. Even the Savior's true identity and purpose were withheld from him during early childhood. It was only as he matured, encountering and surmounting the trials of life, that the full import and scope of his role were impressed upon his consciousness. So it was with Bishop McKay's eldest son. It would be many years after the event, before the significance of what the patriarch had told the young man would be made plain to his understanding.

Meanwhile, he had many lessons to learn, both about Church organization, procedure, and doctrine and about the challenges of disciplining his mind and the powerful impulses of a healthy, growing body. As to the formalities of Church organization and procedure, his education began early as he watched his father discharge his duties as a branch president and bishop. The son's personal involvement commenced at an early age when, in 1888, the year after he received his patriarchal blessing, he became the second counselor in the second quorum of deacons in the Huntsville Ward. And the following year he became the president of this quorum. At that day, the present practice of ordaining young men to offices in the Aaronic Priesthood at an early age had not been adopted. So the bishop's son was not ordained a priest until August 4, 1893, when he was almost twenty. Excellent minutes of meetings of the Huntsville second quorum of deacons in the Church Archives reveal the developing leadership skills of David O. McKay. He periodically gave talks on gospel themes to his quorum and now and then admonished its members to "do better." He led out in providing work parties to help maintain the chapel and grounds and in performing chores—cutting wood, milking, and so on—for widows or infirm members.

During this same period, he served as the secretary of the Huntsville Ward Sunday School, and, at about the time of his ordination as a priest, he was called as a Sunday School teacher, thus beginning a long association with the Church auxiliary to which he would devote much time and effort throughout his life.

The studying required to teach Sunday School or to in-

David O. McKay as he appeared when he was sustained as secretary of the Huntsville Sunday School on January 27, 1889.

struct his priesthood brethren broadened the budding leader's technical knowledge of the gospel. And alongside that, he learned about the practical application of its principles from the lives of his family and neighbors. A vivid lesson on the principle of tithing was taught to him by his father during an autumn harvest. At this time tithing was usually paid in kind. David O. and his brother, Thomas E., then affectionately called Tommy, were helping their father harvest the hay. They had taken the ninth load from a low area of the field where there was wire and slough grass. When they had deposited that on the "family" stack, the boys started again for the low area for the tenth load, which all understood would go to the "tithing" stack representing the family's contribution to the Lord. They were deterred, however, by the father. "No, boys, drive over to the higher ground," he said, directing them to an area with quality hay, timothy, and redtop. The eldest son remonstrated with the father, "No, let us take the hay as it comes." The response drove home a gospel truth neither son ever forgot, and which has served and will serve as an object lesson to untold thousands: "No, David, that is the tenth load, and the best is none too good for God." (*New Era*, January 1972, pp. 55-56.) The example of a bishop-father who served his people faithfully without compensation and who, in addition, gave the very best of what he produced to the Lord as a tithe was a clinching demonstration of principle welded to practice and a powerful example of dedication and commitment to the emerging prophet and his brother.

But the life of a bishop's son living in a remote rural community was not an endless, mirthless procession of work, study, and Church meetings. These were intermingled with an astonishing variety of recreations and diversions. Dramatic presentations, debates, choral singing, and dancing vied with horseback riding, swimming, and baseball for the attention of David O. McKay and his young friends. It was a lively and exciting social whirl that ordinarily found the bishop's handsome and friendly namesake at the vortex.

David O. played the piano for Huntsville's band, an ensemble that enlivened things at town dances. And its talents were occasionally exported to Eden and other neighboring communities. Members of the band, who, in addition to the pianist, included a cornet player and a fiddler, took their turns dancing with the exuberant, shapely, fresh-faced young ladies from around the valley. Given his virility and his ruggedly handsome appearance, not to discount the prominence of his family, David O. McKay would have been considered a fair catch by designing mothers intent on promoting an advantageous marriage for their daughters. And some of the girls themselves doubtless were not unwilling participants in ploys designed to attract this impressive young man into matrimony. So, as David O. McKay reported later, during these years of his "fiery youth" he was turned more than once "from the precipice of temptation" by the teachings and chaste example of his parents.

One can only speculate about the ultimate end of his

life had David O. McKay yielded to forbidden romantic enticements during these crucial years of adolescence. He most likely would have lived a useful and productive life. But it is highly unlikely he would have ascended to the prophetic office as he ultimately did.

Chapter Three

The Student

Bishop McKay and his wife were anxious that their children have opportunities for formal education, which they had been denied by the excessive demands of migration and pioneering. So when David O. had exhausted all the educational possibilities of Huntsville, they counseled together about his future schooling. The decision was to send him to the Weber Stake Academy in Ogden, which had opened its doors on January 9, 1889. Since the lack of adequate transportation made commuting impossible, it was necessary for the son to live in the city during the school year. The problem of board and room was easily solved when his Grandmother Evans happily invited him to live with her.

To say that the academy had opened its doors on the date indicated is a euphemism, because at that time the school had no doors to open. During the first year of its existence, the academy used the facilities of the old Ogden Second Ward chapel at Twenty-sixth and Grant Streets. From there it moved to another temporary home in the Ogden Fifth Ward. And on November 23, 1891, it settled into its new permanent quarters, the Moench Building, located on East Jefferson between Twenty-fourth and Twenty-fifth Streets. The building took its name from the academy's first principal, Louis F. Moench, an immigrant from Wurtemberg, Germany, who had brought to his adopted country the love for scholarship that permeated the great universities of his native land. He also brought to Ogden a great fervor for his adopted religion, Mormonism, even as his countryman Karl G. Maeser had transmitted a similar fervor to the students of another struggling Utah school that later evolved into Brigham Young University.

David O. McKay's intellectual powers were first challenged and stimulated by this stern but kindly German professor, he with the piercing eyes, the luxuriant beard, and the bald pate with bushy fringes of hair above the ears. Professor Moench was didactic and demanding in his classroom demeanor. He brooked no nonsense from his students and expected and received their undivided attention and their all-out performance. But behind this facade of professorial militance lay a genial spirit whose sole aim—as stated in the address he gave upon accepting the principalship and as inscribed on a monument on campus erected to his memory—was "to lay a true foundation in the hearts of the pupils upon which they may build their education." (See *Ogden Standard Examiner*, January 7, 1964.)

The new facilities the Huntsville student found at the academy were also conducive to a pursuit of academic excellence. The Romanesque entry of the main building displayed three sculptured figures in bas-relief, the central figure representing astronomy, with a spy glass in the left hand and the right resting on a globe. On its right was Agriculture, with a sickle and bunch of wheat; and the left figure represented art, with an easel and brush. The classrooms were new and well-appointed; the library, though comparatively small, was adequate; and the combined assembly and recreation room was spacious and comfortable.

David O. spent two years at the academy, years during which the future course of his life began to emerge. It was during this period that his desire for an academic career was aroused. He found that he enjoyed dealing with ideas and concepts more than he enjoyed farming and ranching. He was stimulated by great literature and by the power of the written and the spoken word to affect lives and to influence the course of human events. So, upon completing his studies in Ogden, he took advantage of the teaching accreditation he had earned there by accepting a contract to teach in the Huntsville grade school. He remained there a year, living at home and, in his off hours, helping his father on the farm. It was a rewarding life and held the prospect of a satisfying future by combining the intellectual challenge of teaching (and the study and reflection that entailed) with the satisfactions of husbandry that farming and ranching afforded.

There seemed to be a consensus in the family, however, that this was not enough, that there was more for the McKay children than Ogden and the upper valley could offer. The parents, conscious of their immigrant status and of the educational deprivations they had suffered as a result, were anxious that their children enjoy the advantages they had missed. Moreover, these devoted Latter-day Saints truly believed that the glory of God is intelligence, as their scriptures taught, and that any knowledge or skills ac-

The Huntsville School, built in 1891. David O. McKay was teacher and principal here from 1891 to 1894.

quired in life would inure to their benefit hereafter. These incentives, added to the desire for learning with which the oldest son had become imbued at the Academy—a desire that ultimately infected all the children—created a family attitude and purpose that only awaited the maturing of events to come to fruition.

The catalyst that brought reality out of hope and expectation was an unexpected gift of $2,500 Jennette received from her mother. A brother and sister who had received similar gifts urged Jennette to invest this windfall so as to provide a nest egg for her old age. She ignored this counsel with the same sense of certitude with which her husband had been confronted when he wavered momentarily about accepting his mission call to Scotland. The money, she declared unhesitatingly, would be used entirely to help educate her children.

The growth of a family or an individual can often be traced to decisions made at moments of critical importance. Surely Jennette's decision about the expenditure of her gift falls in this category in respect to the McKay family. The election she made at this time to invest in her children rather than in stocks, bonds, or real estate, produced results that are still beyond calculation. The successful career of her eldest son, for instance, is assignable in large part to the special skills he acquired or honed while he was a student at the University of Utah. It was this education that qualified him to serve as the principal of the Weber Stake Academy; and it was in the showcase of that service, and the related service with the Ogden Stake Sunday School superintendency, that, as we shall see, he was called to the favorable attention of the General Authorities of the Church.

While $2,500 was a substantial gift by the standards of that day, it was hardly enough to finance a student's entire university education. And the significance of the amount dwindles even more when measured against the needs of several students, not one. The fact is, it was decided to send four McKay children to the university at the same time—David O., his brother Thomas E., and their sisters Jeanette and Annie. So plans for their sustenance in Salt Lake City and the payment of their tuition and fees had to be made with meticulous care. The ingenuity the family exhibited in the circumstances is impressive: "My brother, my father, my sisters Jeanette and Annie, and I rolled over the sand ridge from Huntsville," David O. recorded, "with horse and wagon, a cow in the trailer, with a sack of flour milled from wheat we had grown, with jars of fruit which mother had put up, going down to start our schooling at the University." (L. R. McKay, *Home Memories*, p. 9.) At Farmington, where the caravan stopped for the night, it was decided to sell the cow when a ready buyer was found, because the animal had created special problems of transport as it shifted weight in the trailer. A replacement was purchased later in Salt Lake City. "We were assured of bread, milk and fruit," David O. wrote optimistically. (Ibid.)

With a basic food supply assured, the most pressing need of the students on arriving in Salt Lake City was housing. This problem was solved when the bishop, with the concurrence of the children, rented a small house near the university campus, which was located on what was then called Union Square, a site now occupied by Salt Lake City's West High School on north Third West. The campus was not moved to its present location on the east bench until several years after David O. completed his studies at the university.

The main building on the campus, University Hall, was a sprawling, four-story structure with an attic that housed several small lecture rooms. The building looked like the product of an architectural committee that had been in constant, irreconcilable disagreement. Its hodgepodge appearance was also traceable in part to the fact that it was ten years in construction. The delays were the handiwork of an irascible, stingy governor, Eli H. Murray, who vetoed several university appropriation bills passed by the legislature, thereby earning the title "Murray-atic acid" among the disenchanted faculty.

During the years David O. McKay attended the University of Utah (whose name had been changed from the University of Deseret in 1892, two years before he enrolled), the campus was enlarged by the addition of two major buildings—the West or Normal Building, which originally housed the State School for the Deaf; and the Physical Science Building, which was originally the Deseret Museum Building. For its dramatic productions and graduation exercises, the university used the Salt Lake Theatre, which then stood on the northwest corner of the intersection of State and First South streets.

The director of the school's speech and drama department at the time was Maude May Babcock, one of Utah's most noted dramatists. Other faculty members who exerted a strong and positive influence on young David O. McKay were George M. Marshall, an honors graduate of Cornell University who was professor of English literature; George R. Mathews, a Yale University graduate, professor of modern languages; and Byron Cummings of Rutgers, professor of ancient languages and literature.

There were two other instructors with whom the Huntsville student became acquainted at the time and with whom he would later associate in the Quorum of the Twelve: Joseph F. Merrill, whose specialties were chemistry and physics; and Richard R. Lyman, who lectured in engineering. The new president of the university, James E. Talmage, who was installed the same year David O. first enrolled, was another future apostle. And among his classmates were three young men who would also join him later in the apostleship: J. Reuben Clark, Stephen L Richards, and George Q. Morris. These three were key members of the staff of the *Chronicle*, the school's newspaper, during David O.'s last year at the university, Reuben Clark serving as the editor. It is doubtful that there will ever again be brought into such close association during their formative years an equally large number of men destined to fill roles of distinctive leadership in The Church of Jesus Christ of Latter-day Saints.

Despite the obscurity of his beginnings and his lack of urban wealth or social polish, the young Huntsville native immediately entered into the mainstream of university life. He was thrust into prominence during his first year because of his athletic ability. He played right guard on the school's football team, where the brawn and toughness developed during his years on the farm enabled him to survive in the no-holds-barred warfare that then characterized football line play. The team picture for 1894 shows a group of fourteen grim, somber young men, with their manager; they seem intent on intimidating any opposition by their poised stance and by their cool, aloof, and self-confident expressions. However, they labored under the handicap of having no regular coach. A Russian student named Maximilian Lipenov, who understood the rudiments of the game, undertook to teach them what he knew. Maximilian also sought to give the team a psychological edge by organizing what was descriptively called a "yelling brigade," the forerunner of the modern "pep club." It was during this year that organized cheering, or, as was then preferred, yelling, was heard at university athletic events. The team also suffered from a lack of equipment and found it necessary to borrow gear from neighboring schools or groups, the Fort Douglas Athletic Association being a chief donor. And, without a coach or trainer, their conditioning was not the best. But these deficiencies were compensated for by the spirit, enthusiasm, and good sportsmanship with which they played against their opponents—Brigham Young College, Brigham Young Academy, Fort Douglas, a city team called the Crescents, and the Salt Lake High School, which usually included on its roster a knot of mature non-students.

The effect upon David O. McKay of this exposure to university football was deep and lasting. The camaraderie, the teamwork, and the physical and mental discipline associated with the sport seemed to strike a responsive chord with some of his inherent qualities of character. The athletic friendships he established during these years endured

The University of Utah football team, 1894. David O. McKay is second from the left on the back row.

throughout his life. In later years, he had intermittent contact with his teammates when reminiscences of football days revived the feelings and attitudes that dominated their thinking during this important period. And because of his longevity, David O. outlived all the members of the team, which, in a sense, constituted him the unofficial team chaplain as he spoke at the funerals of his fallen teammates.

This exposure to football also gave him a genuine interest in other sports that continued through the years. And when his days as a participant ended, he retained an avid interest as a spectator, cheering on "his" team, the University of Utah. He never lost that bias for the school that had nurtured him, and, in later years, though admittedly he had mixed feelings, he usually cheered on his alma mater in athletic contests with its arch-rival, Brigham Young University.

The athletic prowess of the student from Huntsville automatically and speedily elevated him into an exclusive social realm. The notoriety given to the team and its members soon brought home to the entire student body and faculty the identity of David O. McKay. And his outgoing personality, his skill at the piano, and his tall, rugged good looks made him a favorite with the students of both sexes. His prominence in student affairs is shown by his election as the president of his class. And the proof that he was more than a one-dimensional student appears from his selection as the class valedictorian, a role reserved for one who has excelled academically.

It was these years at the university that first marked David O. McKay as a leader of extraordinary ability and a young man to watch. He was an athlete but not a professional. He was studious but not pedantic. He was sociable but not a socialite. And he accepted his roles of leadership with natural dignity and good grace without fanfare or posturing.

Yet, with all this, he was a private person who kept his own counsel and who did not easily admit someone into his inner circle of confidentiality. It was this unusual combination of qualities that produced what to some was an anomaly in the personality of David O. McKay. On the one hand his friendly and outgoing demeanor reached out to embrace everyone. On the other hand, those with whom he shared his innermost thoughts and aspirations and in whom he placed implicit trust comprised a small, select circle. And once such a friendship had been formed, it was never severed, except temporarily by death. Two young men with whom David O. formed such a relationship at the University were Stephen L Richards and George Q. Morris. Unlike the Huntsville native, whose roots grew out of a rustic, rural setting, these students were the product of a comfortable, even luxurious, urban environment, the sons of prominent, well-to-do families. Stephen L's father was a skilled and successful physician, while George Q.'s family operated a thriving business. Their Huntsville friend, fondly called "Dade" by his close university friends, was a frequent visitor in these homes of culture and refinement, whose rich appointments were in stark contrast with the modest, sparsely furnished apartment he shared with his brother and sisters. In these homes he was accepted as if he were a member of their families, the trusted friend of their sons.

As already noted, this trio would later share the apostleship; and the two city-bred boys would be honored by calls extended by their friend from the farm who, in the meantime, would be elevated to the prophetic office. Stephen L Richards would be called as President David O. McKay's first counselor in the First Presidency; and George Q. Morris would be called by President McKay to the Quorum of the Twelve at age eighty, the oldest man ever inducted into this distinctive body.

However, it is doubtful that thoughts of ecclesiastical distinction ever crossed the minds of these young students. They were too much obsessed with professors, books, journalism, athletics, dramatics—and girls. It was only natural that at this time of life, healthy young men would give avid attention to members of the opposite sex, appraising their attractions and qualities and speculating about the standard one might apply in seeking or recognizing a life's companion. Interestingly enough, while speaking at the funeral of his eighty-eight-year-old friend, George Q. Morris, the eighty-seven year old Prophet, David O. McKay, reminisced about a conversation these two had shared while they were university students as to the criteria for selecting a wife: "George Q. and I were members of the Zeta Gamma Fraternity," related President McKay. "I remember one night following a meeting of the Zeta Gamma we were walking toward home . . . and boy-like, George and I were talking about how we should know when we would fall in love. I shall never forget the advice George Q. offered at that time on a moonlit night. Said he: 'My mother once told me that when I met a girl who awakened in me the highest and noblest feelings of manhood, who inspired in me a desire to be worthy of a woman such as she, then that would be a feeling of true love.'" (*Church News*, May 5, 1962.)

It is a curious circumstance that at the moment this con-

David O. and Thomas E. McKay, 1895.

versation took place, young David O. McKay was walking toward the home on north Second West in Salt Lake City where his future bride, Emma Ray Riggs, lived. David O. was then boarding with Ray's mother, Emma Robbins Riggs. He was, therefore, well acquainted with the stylish and pretty daughter, who could not have failed to draw the attention of this young man whose thoughts, now and then, dwelt on the subject of girls and matrimony, as his conversation with George Q. Morris intimates. At the moment, however, there was no romantic attachment between the pair as David O. was dating a classmate and Ray was all but engaged to a young businessman. Their acquaintance would not ripen into affection, love, and then matrimony until several years later, when, as if by fate, they were brought together in Ogden, Utah, following David O. McKay's mission to Scotland.

As the young scholar approached the end of his university career in 1897, a mission was not the top item on his agenda for the future. This is not to say that his commitment to the Church and its goals was any less fervent than it had been. Indeed, it would appear that the faith of his parents loomed even larger in his estimation than when he left their home. He had maintained a high level of activity in the Salt Lake ward he and his brother and sisters attended, and his exposure to the personal influence of the General Authorities of the Church, many of whom lived in close proximity to the university and who spoke often in the local wards or at the nearby Tabernacle and Assembly Hall on Temple Square, would have had a positive effect on the religious attitudes of one as orthodox in his upbringing as was Bishop McKay's son. But a combination of factors had relegated a mission to a subordinate position on this athlete's agenda. First, it was not the customary thing at that time for all young men to be expected to fill missions. So the failure to go would not have cast a reflection on one's level of faith and commitment. Also, David O. felt an obligation to start working soon to replenish the McKay family's meager education fund so that his younger brother and sisters could receive university schooling. And the prospect of immediate employment arose at the time of his graduation when Professor William M. Stewart, who was the head of teacher training at the University of Utah, offered him a position to teach in Salt Lake County.

It was an exciting prospect for a young man with a university education. Salt Lake City and Utah were then positioned for a period of extraordinary growth and prosperity. Utah had at last attained its long-held goal when it was admitted to statehood on January 4, 1896. The economy appeared to be working out of the doldrums into which it had fallen a few years before. And the social and political problems created by the Church's advocacy and practice of polygamy had been largely resolved by the announcement of the Manifesto.

It was against this background that David O. McKay received a startling letter from Box B in Salt Lake City—a call to serve as a missionary in the British Isles, the ancestral home of his Scottish and Welsh forebears. In a sense, the turmoil the call created was a repetition of the turmoil through which his father had passed years before when he had been called to Scotland.

Chapter Four

The Missionary

Once David O. McKay had decided to accept the mission call from President Wilford Woodruff, he was filled with a kind of anticipation he had not known before. He had heard his father relate his experiences while serving in Scotland. And since this land of the McKays was within the British Mission, there was the possibility he would be privileged to serve there also, which doubtless aroused feelings of excitement, expectation, and ancestral longing. Moreover, the thought that David O. McKay, native of tiny Huntsville, who had never been outside Utah, would soon be traveling across the continent and thence over the Atlantic to Great Britain was incredible.

The reality of what lay ahead began to come into focus when he reported to Salt Lake City the first week in August 1897 for a brief indoctrination by the General Authorities. Unlike missionaries today, who receive several weeks of intense instruction, Elder McKay and his associates received only a bare preview of what to expect or of how to go about their work. Essentially they were told to be humble, prayerful, and studious; to rely upon the Lord; and to work. That counsel was appropriate for any missionary, but its brevity left large areas of uncertainty and perhaps created not a little concern for the new proselyters.

The tall elder from Huntsville was ordained a seventy and was set apart to labor in Great Britain by Elder Seymour B. Young of the First Council of Seventy on August 6, 1897. Two days later he received the sacred endowment in the Salt Lake Temple, which for the first time opened to his view the higher ordinances of his religion, ordinances that he, as the president of the Church, would first make readily available to Saints living abroad.

Twenty-one elders destined for Great Britain, including David O. McKay, left the Salt Lake train depot a few days after receiving their endowments. The milling crowd at the depot, the noise and bustle of the red caps with their baggage carts, the cries of the newsboys and conductors, and the well-wishes and good-byes to the departing passengers intermingled to produce an aura of excitement and festivity. This, however, could not mask the sadness that brooded in the hearts of the missionaries as they waved farewell to family and friends. "My trip from Salt Lake to Philadelphia was a very pleasant one," Elder McKay told George Q. Morris in a letter dated August 25, 1897, written from Liverpool, "that is, after the gloomy feelings caused by that sad word 'good-bye' had begun to wear away." (DOMP.) Soon the attention of the elders was diverted from thoughts of separation by their absorption in the panoramic view of America as it flashed by outside their train window. David O., whose life on the Huntsville farm had sensitized his perceptions of agriculture and growing things, was impressed by the vast fields of corn and grain in Nebraska and Iowa and the verdant forests of Illinois and Ohio. And he was quite unprepared for the din and chaos of smoke-filled Chicago and for the contrasting beauty and orderliness of Washington, D.C.

Crossing the Alleghenies, the missionaries spent a day in metropolitan New York, traveling thence to the city of brotherly love, Philadelphia, where on August 17 they boarded their ship, the S. S. *Belgenland,* a well-traveled old craft that had confronted and survived the storms and gales of the Atlantic for many years. Moving slowly down the Delaware River past Wilmington, Newcastle, and Delaware City, and through Delaware Bay, the *Belgenland* headed into the open sea for its eight-day voyage to Liverpool, England.

The passengers from inland Utah, whose idea of waves was conditioned by the modest breakers on the Great Salt Lake, were hardly prepared for the turbulence of the Atlantic. Sharing with George Q. Morris his amazement at the grandeur—and the beauty—of the sea in commotion, Elder McKay wrote: "The water was a dark blue, and, as a strong gust of wind would throw a wave as high as the ship, one might see the crest of it white with ocean foam. At one moment, we would be on the top of a high wave, then plunge 'below the sea' while behind us rose another mighty heave." (Ibid.)

How did the young elder from the farm in Huntsville fare in this new marine environment? He reported to George Q. that he was seasick only once during the voyage but then was so nauseated he feared he would part with his "principal digestive organ . . . and all its appendages." (Ibid.) Aside from this, and from the frivolous conduct of a few of the missionaries, the passage was a pleasant and enlightening experience. Yet David O. and his companions were overjoyed when they heard the cry of "land" as the *Belgenland* approached the southwest coast of England. Angling up St. George's Channel, the old ship rounded the point at Anglesey and, heading due east, sailed into the harbor and thence up the Mersey River to the Liverpool wharf. As the ship moved slowly upriver between New Bristol and Liverpool, the young missionaries from a newly settled land were treated to their first sights of a truly ancient civilization. Elder McKay graphically described its impact on him and his companions: "We looked with *open eyes* first at one city then the other. There was plenty there to not only arouse one's interest but also to hold it; yet every now and then one might see their eyes assume their natural size, their mouths close and heads droop just a little as a short sigh escaped from the breast." The correspondent attributed this reaction to a touch of homesickness as the elders were "awakened by the thought that, here we are about 7,000 miles from home landing in a strange city without even the hope of meeting a friend." (Ibid.) This mood of loneliness and alienation was heightened by the polluted atmosphere, the dull aspect of the weathered buildings along the waterfront, and the unfamiliar rhythm of human life at dockside: "Then, too, the cloud of fog and smoke hanging around," observed Elder McKay, "the dim light from the *blood like* sun, the long stretch of dismal looking warehouses, the strange faces on the dock, the queer looking cabs, together with the bustle and noise, all helped to make us aware of the painful fact that we were not *home.*" (Ibid.)

These graphic descriptions by David O. McKay, who celebrated his twenty-fourth birthday two weeks after arriving in Liverpool, reveal an innate poetic quality as well as a basic grounding in English prose and sentence structure, acquired from his university training and from reading the masters of English literature. And they also convey the awe, anticipation, and uncertainty that possessed this native of rural Utah who had suddenly been thrust into an environment whose history was measured in centuries, not decades.

The loneliness and homesickness that took hold of the missionaries as the *Belgenland* made its meandering way up the Mersey were largely dispelled when they reached the headquarters of the European and British Missions at 42 Islington in Liverpool. There they were greeted and made welcome by the mission president, Rulon S. Wells, and members of his staff, all of whom hailed from Utah or surrounding areas in the western United States. Here, then, was a small island of Mormon culture where, for the moment, at least, Elder McKay and his traveling companions could relax from their arduous journey amidst understanding and helpful friends.

But the period of relaxation was short lived. A brief postscript to the letter to George Q. Morris dated August

*David O. McKay,
missionary to Great
Britain, 1897.*

26, the day after David's arrival in Liverpool, tells the story: "Received my appointment this morning. Glasgow Conference. Take the next train for Scotland. Good bye, George, for this time. Kind regards to all."

The alacrity with which President Wells acted to assign him to his field of labor taught Elder McKay a basic lesson for success in missionary work—promptness. And the new elder from Huntsville would learn many other valuable lessons from this forty-three-year-old leader and his counselors, especially Joseph L. McMurrin. At the time of David's arrival in the field, Rulon W. Wells had been a member of the First Council of Seventy for four years. A son of Daniel H. Wells, who had served two terms as the president of the same mission, President Wells had preceded Elder McKay into the field by thirteen months and would leave Great Britain several months before the young elder, to be replaced by Platte D. Lyman. It is an interesting and instructive commentary on the operation of the Mormon priesthood to note that in less than a decade after David O. McKay arrived in the mission field, a somewhat homesick young man, he would be elevated to the Quorum of the Twelve, a quorum with higher ecclesiastical authority than that exercised by his former mission president. And in 1941 when Elder Wells passed away, one of those who eulogized him was President David O. McKay, then a member of the First Presidency.

Assigned to the Glasgow Conference with Elder McKay were John T. Edward, Joseph Mitchell, and Thomas Gilchrist. Boarding the train at the Liverpool station, the four new missionaries crossed into the land of Elder McKay's Scottish ancestors within a few hours. Glasgow was then, as it is now, the largest city in Scotland and the industrial and commercial capital of the country, with the suburban satellites of Paisley, Rutherglen, and Clydebank. Sitting astride the Clyde River, Glasgow, which takes its name from the Celtic words *glas ghu* (the dear, green glen), was famed in its early days for its large catches of salmon. Here the new missionary from Huntsville and his companions found another ancient, dingy city whose buildings bore a thick mantle of smoke, which had billowed for centuries from Glasgow's chimneys. And the forests and heath that once abounded in the surrounding countryside had been denuded, exposing large areas of gently undulating terrain, mostly covered with thick grass.

The elders' arrival coincided with one of the more favorable seasons of the year in Glasgow. Being late summer, it was pleasantly warm, which minimized the burning of fuel, thereby improving the atmosphere that, in midwinter, was usually choked with coal smoke. And the improved atmosphere allowed intermittent sunshine, a comparative novelty.

Elder McKay's first residence in Glasgow was at 130 Barrack Street, where he shared small, modest quarters with several elders in what was called the "Conference House." There a Mrs. Noble did the washing and cooking for the missionaries, each one contributing a share of her modest wage. This enabled the elders to devote themselves exclusively to their proselyting, which consisted mostly of tracting, interspersed with cottage and street meetings. Elder McKay soon learned that active participation in missionary work is the best way to become skilled in proselyting. "I have had three or four lively discussions with women during the last two weeks," David O. wrote to his Aunt Mary on October 29, 1897, two months after he arrived in Glasgow, "and really, Aunt Mary, they have done me more good than twice that time spent in studying." (DOMP.) He was impressed by the extent of their scriptural knowledge: "You know the women here seem to know the Bible as well as I know the *Lord's Prayer*." This had been a goad for him to sharpen his scriptural skills. He soon learned how to counter the oft-heard affirmation that one had been "saved": "When they begin to quote *Paul* on the saved question, I tell you it makes one think, and hurriedly turn over leaves to *James* in order to try to convince them that mere belief alone is not sufficient." The new missionary then appraised the scriptural writings of several of the early apostles, ranking James first in terms of plainness and clarity, followed closely by Peter. The apostle Paul, he opined, outranked all others in "ardour and enthusiasm."

After a season of training in Glasgow under the experienced eye of the conference president, Elder McKay was assigned to labor with Peter G. Johnston in Stirling, on the right bank of the Forth, forty miles northeast of Glasgow. David was pleased with this assignment because of the fine qualities of his new companion, who was from Idaho, "an experienced, wealthy man, a lover of all things beautiful," (Talk on September 13, 1957, DOMP) and because of the ancient Stirling Castle, which crowned the hill overlooking the Forth and whose history reached back at least seven centuries. Moreover, this place had special significance for a university graduate whose academic emphasis had been on English literature because of the allusion to Stirling in Sir Walter Scott's "The Lady of the Lake." Here, then, was a place where one could not only fulfill a missionary responsibility but could also pursue one's literary and cultural interests. Elder McKay was soon to learn, however, that he could not serve two masters during his consecrated missionary service. And the lesson he learned in Stirling radically altered the perceptions he had of himself and of his duty toward the Lord and His church.

The day Elder McKay and his companion chose to explore Stirling Castle did not start well. While tracting in the morning, an outspoken Scotchwoman had said to David O. as she accepted a piece of Church literature, "Better gae to your hame; ye canna have any o' oor lassies." (Ibid.) This rebuff served to intensify a gnawing feeling of homesickness with which he had arisen. And it was in this mood that the Utahn accompanied Elder Johnston to the castle.

As they walked up the broad esplanade leading to the massive structure, the missionaries admired the colossal statue of Robert Bruce, scion of a noble family, whose first progenitor in Scotland was Robert de Bruce, a Norman knight who came to England with William I. This set the stage for several hours of sight-seeing during which the two elders were immersed in the sights and smells of the massive structure, the most ancient building David O. had ever entered. As they were conducted through the building, the visitors were made aware of the turbulent history of the castle, which had served as a royal residence and as a fortress for several centuries. They were treated to a special insight into the bitter enmity that existed between the English and the Scots before the union of the crowns in 1603 as the possession of the castle fortress had passed back and forth between the two battling nations. They were also instructed in the unusual architectural features of the building, which, despite the ravages of war and the elements, had stood intact through the intervening centuries.

There can be little doubt that this had been one of the most interesting cultural experiences David O. McKay had ever had. And the impact on him would have been heightened because of his Scottish ancestry. Here, in a sense, stood a symbol of the strength, tenacity, and talents of his countrymen as well as a reminder of the futility of war and of the evils of monarchical reign. But despite the many insights he had received and the intellectual value of the tour, Elder McKay felt uneasy as he and Elder Johnston walked back to town.

"I saw on my right an unfinished dwelling," he said of the return to the city, "over the front door of which was a stone on which there was carving. That was most unusual, so I said to Elder Johnston, 'I'm going to see what that is'. I was half way up the graveled walk when there came to my eyesight a striking motto as follows, carved in stone: 'What e'er Thou Art, Act Well Thy Part'. . . . I said to my-self, or the Spirit within me, 'You are a member of the Church of Jesus Christ of Latter-day Saints. More than that, you are here as a representative of the Lord Jesus Christ. You accepted the responsibility as a representative of the Church.' Then I thought what we had done that fore-noon. We had been sightseeing; we had gained historical instruction and information, it is true, and I was thrilled with it. . . . However, that was not missionary work. . . . I accepted the message given to me on that stone, and from that moment we tried to do our part as missionaries in Scot-land." (Ibid.)

The catalytic effect of this incident was extraordinary. It marked the point when David O. McKay became truly imbued with the spirit of his work. The import of the motto would strongly influence him during the remainder of his mission and thereafter would color his attitudes and actions, at length becoming a fixed quality in his character. It is not difficult to see how this concept was translated into the habit President McKay developed of giving care-ful, concentrated attention to those whom he engaged in conversation. He became noted for his ability to wall out every distraction and competing influence in order to focus his full attention on the one to whom he was speaking. And similarly, he developed the habit of directing all his powers of concentration on the issue or problem of the moment. And the fruit of this characteristic can also be seen

in President McKay's deliberate, measured pulpit style;
in the easy cadence of his conversation; and in the un-
hurried tempo of his step and movements. These aspects
of his demeanor bespeak a sense of contentment and self-
confidence and complete satisfaction with the role providence had assigned to him and with the activities or opportunities of each day.

Whether these elements of his personality were innate
and were merely ignited by the incident, or whether it was
the motivating cause that produced them, there can be no
doubt that this experience, which planted the motto in his
mind under such unusual circumstances, was one of the
major factors in the growth and development of David O.
McKay. He referred to it often during his long and productive life, always under circumstances that reflected the importance of the concept to him, or to anyone else who
might elect to apply it.

Following this mountaintop experience, we see Elder
McKay in various places in the mission and in association
with various missionaries: Wm. Pender; Robert Hogg, Jr.;
John T. Edwards; Malcolm McKinnon; and others. And
while, during the early months of his service, he was subordinate to the elders with whom he labored, he was,
nevertheless, a marked man. His credentials for ultimate
success and recognition as a missionary were impeccable.
He was intelligent, personable, handsome, cooperative,
and diligent. He came from a solid, faithful family that was
known and admired by the leaders of the Church. He was
a university graduate and he had excelled in his studies, in
athletics, and in university politics. Therefore, he spoke
and wrote well, was widely read, and acquitted himself
well in personal conversation on a wide variety of subjects.
And despite these impressive qualifications, he was approachable and devoid of arrogance. Therefore, it came as
no surprise to those who knew him when the *Millennial
Star* for June 9, 1898, carried this news item: "David O.
McKay has been appointed to preside over the Scottish

Conference." Although he had been in the mission field a scant nine months, he was appointed to preside over missionaries older and more experienced than he and to direct the affairs of nine branches within the conference.

With this appointment, Elder McKay was charged with heavy administrative responsibilities in addition to his proselyting activities. It was now his duty to instruct the new missionaries as he had been instructed, to assign and reassign the elders as the circumstances required, to oversee the compilation of statistics and the preparation of reports, and to supervise all the ecclesiastical and temporal activities of the missionaries and members in Scotland. He also became the spokesman for the Church in his area. So the December 21, 1898, issue of Glasgow's *Daily Record* carried a "vigorous rebuttal," written by Elder David O. McKay, to an attack on the Latter-day Saints in the Glasgow press. "He gives credit to his associates for sacrifice, devotion and purpose," wrote the editor of the *Millennial Star* in reviewing the article, "and claims that their only object is to preach the Gospel, obedience to which 'will make bad men good and good men better'. As to the home life of the people in Utah, he refers to 'the testimony of unprejudiced intelligent men' whose communications and writings ought to be familiar to all who write for and control the press in this country from which so many have been drawn into the fold of Christ and to the gathering place in Utah." (MS 60:82.)

Had the young conference president, who had so ably defended his people and their motives, been able to see clearly into the future, he doubtless would have been surprised to discern that in little more than half a century he, as the president of The Church of Jesus Christ of Latter-day Saints, would be the chief instrument in altering the concept of Utah as "the gathering place" and in substituting the concept of a "gathering" to stakes of the Church located all over the world. And he likely would have been astonished to see that the first symbolic act of this radical change in proselyting and administrative strategy would be his dedication of a beautiful new chapel in Glasgow, Scotland.

In addition to jousting in the public press with critics of the Church, the Scottish Conference president also made literary contributions to the *Millennial Star*, the official news organ of the European Mission. In the November 24, 1898, issue, for instance, there appeared a report filed by Elder McKay about an unusual spiritual experience enjoyed by two elders who were laboring in Ayr. There the missionaries met an investigator who, on being shown a picture of the Prophet Joseph Smith, told them "I saw in a dream that man praying in the woods, a long time ago." (MS 60:746.) She also told the two elders, "I saw you two men coming from America to preach the gospel." (Ibid.) On March 16, 1899, the *Star* carried a report from President D. O. McKay about the illness and impending departure for home of an Elder Edwards (MS 61:173); and the April 17, 1899, issue carried an optimistic report from President McKay about a new hall that had been rented by the Glasgow Branch: "Several Elders from surrounding districts attended the opening services," wrote he, "the Saints were out en masse, and, as all were united and gratified with their new surroundings, a rich outpouring of the Spirit was manifested." (MS 61:244.)

The "Spirit" alluded to here brought the comforting, confirming feeling David O. McKay had experienced many times since his childhood in Huntsville. The fervent prayers offered by his parents in the family circle, or the sermons or lessons he had heard over the years in the Huntsville Ward, or under the tutelage of Professor Moench, or from the pulpit in the Salt Lake Tabernacle, had struck a responsive chord with his spiritual being and had given him strong convictions about the truth of the gospel message and the divinity of the Church he represented. Yet to this point in his life, as he approached age twenty-six, David O. McKay had only a hearsay testimony of the kind referred to in verse 14 of the 46th section of the

Doctrine and Covenants. He believed, and he had strong and good feelings about the Church, but he did not *know* that it was divine from any personal, spiritual revelation.

It was in this state of conviction that Elder McKay neared the end of his missionary service in Scotland. On May 29, 1899, a special priesthood meeting of the Scottish Conference convened in Glasgow at 53 Holmhead Street. Present, in addition to the missionaries laboring in the conference and certain local priesthood brethren, were James L. McMurrin and Henry W. Naisbitt, counselors in the European Mission presidency; Charles Woolfenden, president of the Leeds Conference; T. L. Allen, president of the Irish Conference; and Elder Joseph McFarlane of the mission office in Liverpool.

Being the conference president, Elder McKay conducted the meeting under the direction of President McMurrin. After the opening song, "O My Father," and the invocation of Elder N. M. Stewart, President McKay "stated his pleasure in meeting with the brethren, suggested that brief concise remarks be made by the elders in making their reports. He also requested that all express themselves freely regarding the work of the Lord, and their feelings toward each other and the Priesthood of God." (See copy of minutes by William Nisbet, DOMP.)

The first part of the meeting went according to the usual pattern, with progress reports being intermixed with expressions of conviction and testimony. However, following an intermediate song rendered by a missionary quartet, "Your Mother Is Praying for You," and testimonies by Elders D. C. Eccles, William Cameron, and John Young, something extraordinary and electrifying happened: "After Bro. Young had taken his seat," recorded Elder Nisbet, "President Woolfenden testified that he saw two Holy Beings standing beside Bro. Young. . . . The heavenly beings remained some length of time, and the Spirit of God pervaded every bosom to an unexpressible degree." (Ibid.)

This incident radically altered the spirit of the meeting as the room became charged with excitement and expectancy. Elder William Worthington "said he was unable to express his feelings, for the manifestation of the power and spirit of God in our midst." President T. L. Allen "testified that the Spirit of God had borne record to him when coming into the room, that he would see a manifestation of the power of God, which had been literally fulfilled." (Ibid.)

When President McMurrin rose to speak, he "bore testimony to the presence of the Holy Beings, seen by Bro. Woolfenden." He also "exhorted the Brethren to be faithful, virtuous and energetic. Related some instances where men had allowed themselves to be overcome with the devil principally through women." (Ibid.) It was at this point that the speaker turned to Elder McKay, saying: "Brother David, Satan hath desired you that he may sift you as wheat, but God is mindful of you. If you will keep the faith you will yet sit in the leading councils of the church." (Statement of October 27, 1934, DOMP.)

President McKay thought at the time this statement "was more of a caution than a promise. . . . At that moment there flashed into my mind temptations that had beset my path, and I realized even better than President McMurrin, or any other man, how truly he had spoken." (Ibid.)

This unquestionably was a watershed experience in the life of David O. McKay, marking the point at which he ceased living on borrowed light and acquired, through spiritual means, a personal witness of the reality and power of God. "Never before had I experienced such an emotion," he said later. "It was a manifestation for which as a doubting youth I had secretly prayed most earnestly on hillside and in meadow. It was an assurance to me that sincere prayer is answered 'sometime, somewhere.' " (Ibid.)

But the experience not only shed light on the past, revealing the goodness and power of God in answering the fervent prayers of a puzzled youth; it also illuminated the path ahead for a chosen servant who was to become God's earthly spokesman.

"With the resolve then and there to keep the faith," wrote President McKay, "there was born a desire to be of service to my fellowmen, and with it a realization, a glimpse at least, of what I owed to the elder who first carried the message of the restored gospel to my grandfather and grandmother who had accepted the message years before in the north of Scotland." (Ibid.)

Like the enormous thrust generated by a soaring rocket that hurls a spacecraft into orbit, this experience was a major force in propelling David O. McKay through more than six decades of dedicated service as an apostle of the Lord Jesus Christ. This we may infer from the frequency with which he related the experience and from the confirming comments he made about it. The incident was a moment of illumination that transformed him from an able, amiable, respectable, industrious man to a wholly converted, concerned Saint, committed to a life of service to God and to his fellowmen.

We may wonder why the Lord delayed so long in answering the prayers of one so faithful and promising. Without presuming to delve into the purposes and designs of Deity, it is apparent that there was no urgent need for young David O. McKay to receive a prompt answer to his inquiries. And, judging from his own comments, the admonition and prophecy, coming when it did and under the favorable conditions that existed at the time, provided a powerful impetus toward a life of Christian service. This impetus could have been significantly dissipated had the spiritual confirmation of God's reality and power come in his boyhood. The conclusion seems inescapable that the circumstances were not ripe when he first began as a boy to pray fervently for a spiritual witness. It was only when, in the providence of God, the outward conditions and his own spiritual perceptions had matured, that the much-sought-for revelation came. And the long wait doubtless taught the prophet-to-be a valuable lesson in patience and subservience, a lesson that has been and will be shared vicariously by thousands.

Before the end of his first mission, Elder McKay enjoyed two special experiences that were unrelated to missionary work. These were pilgrimages to the birthplaces of his parents. Since Thurso, on the northern shore of Scotland, lay within his ecclesiastical jurisdiction, he was able to visit there without special permission from his leaders. It aroused powerful feelings to inspect the quaint, ancient village and the humble cottage where some of the missionary's progenitors had lived and to visit with neighbors who had known his grandparents and who remembered his father when he had served in Scotland.

Later it was planned that David O. would accompany President McMurrin to Cardiff, Wales, to attend the International Eisteddfodau, which would enable him to make an easy side trip to Merthyr Tydfil, his mother's birthplace. An illness prevented President McMurrin from attending this annual festival of music and the arts, so Elder McKay went alone as the official representative of the Church. He carried with him a letter of introduction from Evan Stephens, director of the Salt Lake Tabernacle Choir, to Dr. Parry, the administrator of the festival. Here for the first time Jennette Evan's son was introduced to the rich cultural inheritance from his Welch ancestry. The haunting melodies and lively tunes of the choirs and solo vocalists; the energetic numbers played by the instrumentalists, the harpists, the crowders, and the pipers; the displays of the painters and sculptors; and the poetic, prosaic, and dramatic competitions enjoyed there would have given David O. McKay important insights into the ancestral origins of some of his innate characteristics—his love for music, literature, and beautiful decor.

His pilgrimage to Merthyr Tydfil produced feelings hardly equaled by any other experience he had enjoyed. Seeing the small room where his mother had been born filled him with love and gratitude—love for the saintly woman who had given him birth and nurtured him through childhood, and gratitude that she had been caught in the gospel net and ultimately been led to Ogden, Utah, and into contact with his noble father. While dominated by these nostalgic feelings, Elder McKay sat down in the tiny bedroom and wrote his mother a loving letter, which doubtless became one of her most treasured possessions.

The missionary from Huntsville received his formal release on August 24, 1899, just two years lacking one day from his arrival in Liverpool. And two days later he departed from Glasgow for home aboard the *City of Rome* in charge of a group of twenty-two Latter-day Saints, including five returning missionaries, six returning tourists, and eleven British immigrants. Behind him lay a record of solid missionary achievement, including fifteen months as the president of one of the largest conferences in the British Mission. And he now had the unqualified endorsement of those with whom he had labored in the mission field. President James L. McMurrin, who had uttered the startling prophecy about the young elder, included this appraisal of David O. McKay in his journal: "On June 4 [1899], I attended conference in Belfast, Ireland; but I must first record the Glasgow Conference. On the 27th of May I went to Glasgow where I met President D. O. McKay, one of the finest young men it has ever been my lot and privilege to become acquainted with." (See CC JLM journal in DOM papers.) And the president of the mission who served at the time of Elder McKay's release, Platte D. Lyman, gave the young elder an equally impressive endorsement with the following answers on his release form: "As a speaker: Good." "As a writer: Good." "As a presiding officer: Very Good." "Has he a good knowledge of the gospel? Yes." "Has he been energetic? Very." "Is he discreet and does he carry a good influence? Yes sir." "Remarks: None better in the mission."

Accolades such as these, comments that were never intended for his own eyes, speak eloquently of the achievements of David O. McKay as a missionary and of the impact on others of his personality and demeanor. When added to the impressive credentials he carried with him into the mission field, these endorsements placed the departing elder in a class by himself, a distinction that would be acknowledged in a few years by the president of the Church, who would call David O. McKay to the Quorum of the Twelve Apostles at age thirty-two.

Meanwhile, there remained one exciting incident connected with the released elder's missionary service—the return voyage. The smooth passage of the *City of Rome* downriver through the Firth of Clyde and the North Channel to the open sea gave no inkling of the terrifying incident that lay ahead. Indeed, the first five days on the Atlantic were routine in every respect. The sea was comparatively calm, and the mild temperature and relatively clear skies made the passage almost idyllic. On the night of August 31, however, the passengers were rudely jarred out of the placidity of sleep by a loud crash that hurled loose furnishings against the bulkheads, unceremoniously dumped the slumberers on the deck, and created a scene of chaos and terror unlike anything David O. had ever experienced. When the initial panic subsided and reason replaced panic, it was discovered that the ship had collided with an iceberg. As the crew and passengers peered into the murky darkness, bobbing pieces of white ice could be dimly seen alongside the ship, ominous sentinels of the huge ice mass that lay below.

A hasty inspection revealed that the ship had sustained no serious damage. At reduced speed and with a beefed-up watch, the *City of Rome* gingerly inched its way through the ice field off the Grand Banks of Newfoundland. Near this place, thirteen years later, another collision would not end so happily. Then the 46,000-ton White Star liner, *Titanic*, cruising at twenty-two knots on its maiden voyage, would crash into a submerged iceberg, ripping a 300-foot gash in its starboard hull and carry 1,513 passengers to an icy grave.

In a later account of the *City of Rome*'s collision with the iceberg, Elder McKay, after reciting the details, saw in his safe return home the fulfillment of a promise Elder Seymour B. Young had made in setting him apart as a missionary. (DOM papers.) And now that he was safely home, there remained other prophetic promises yet to be fulfilled.

Chapter Five

The Husband-Father-Educator

Before leaving Scotland, David O. McKay had received a welcome letter from the board of education of the Weber Stake Academy, offering him a teaching position. He accepted the offer with alacrity, and within weeks after returning home he was teaching classes there in pedagogy and literature. And within a few months after assuming his teaching duties, this newest member of the faculty was appointed the head of the Preparatory Department, a step up the administrative ladder that in a very short time would lead him to the principalship of the academy.

The future looked bright and promising to the young Huntsville native. He had just turned twenty-six, had distinguished himself at the University of Utah, and had completed an outstanding mission. And now he occupied a position of honor and respect in a thriving community with an adequate income, good health, and excellent prospects for the future. Moreover, he was near his large, close-knit family and in the midst of a host of loyal friends and associates, many of whom he had known since childhood. Yet he lacked one thing. And that missing ingredient had become of overriding importance to him as his understanding of the gospel had grown with his physical and emotional maturity. David O. McKay was ready for marriage.

And as subsequent events proved, the woman intended for him had recently moved to Ogden to begin her teaching career at the Madison School. Emma Ray Riggs, the petite daughter of Emma Robbins Riggs, David O.'s landlady during the latter part of his schooling at the university, had graduated in 1898. She had then studied at the Cincinnati College of Music, returning to Utah shortly before the release of the tall Scottish conference president.

Because of their prior acquaintance, which had been essentially platonic, the courtship was easily initiated. As we shall see, however, the courtship, though rather short, did not actually end at marriage, for David O. McKay ardently courted this choice woman throughout his life. Within a year they had decided on marriage and had begun to lay plans for their nuptials the early part of 1901. These culminated with their sealing in the Salt Lake Temple on January 2, 1901, the first couple sealed there in the new century.

Although Elder McKay was well aware of fine qualities in Emma Ray Riggs even before their marriage, he learned that what he had observed beforehand was but a hint of the scope and depth of her character, personality, and achievements. She was the product of a home where spirituality and intellectuality went hand in hand. Both O. H. Riggs and Emma Louise Robbins Riggs, the parents, had taught at the University of Utah. And the father had been the first territorial superintendent of schools in Utah. The name "Ray" had been added to her mother's name, Emma, when the daughter was blessed, because she was to her parents a "little Ray of sunshine." As this child grew to maturity, she reflected in her demeanor an innate poise and dignity, characterized by a certain reticence, a demure detachment from the events around her. Yet there was no element of conceit or arrogance in her conduct. On the contrary, Emma Ray was friendly and genuine in her personal relationships.

The special training Emma Ray received at the University of Utah and the Cincinnati College of Music added important credentials to her future role as the wife of a prophet and the mother of a large, active, and accomplished family. There she learned homemaking skills; acquired a taste for good literature, drama, and the arts; and became a fine amateur musician. With all this, she was practical, hard working, and companionable.

Although neither the bride nor the groom had inherited wealth, other than the treasure of good ancestry, healthy bodies and minds, and moral upbringing, they were not subjected to some of the economic stresses that afflict many newlyweds of this day. They had been frugal with their means during the engagement. And when Emma Ray left teaching to devote herself fully to the role of wife and mother, her husband's income at the academy was adequate. This was due, in large part, to their ready accessibility to the products of the McKay farm and ranch in nearby Huntsville. By assisting his father there on weekends and during the school off-season, David O. was able to obtain fruits, vegetables, meat, and dairy and poultry products to supplement their diet.

This couple was an alluring addition to Ogden's educational, social, and religious life. They had an aura of enthusiasm and success that tinged everything they did and the organizations with which they became affiliated. The husband's role at the academy brought them into an immediate and favorable relationship with the intellectual leaders of the community; and their commitment to the Church, David's outstanding performance as a missionary, and the influence of Bishop McKay among the local and general leadership brought them instant prominence in their ward and stake. Soon, therefore, Emma Ray was called into service in the Relief Society and as a teacher of religion classes, while her husband found himself involved in a Church assignment that, because of his extraordinary performance, would bring him to the favorable attention of the president of the Church, thereby laying the foundation for the fulfillment of President James L. McMurrin's prophecy.

Shortly after assuming his duties at the academy in Sep-

David O. McKay

Weber Stake Sunday School board, 1900. David O. McKay, second assistant in the Sunday School superintendency, is third from the right in the second row.

tember 1899, the returned missionary was called to the Weber Stake Sunday School board. And within weeks after the marriage, he was called as the second assistant to Thomas B. Evans, the superintendent of the Weber Stake Sunday Schools. Brother McKay's assignment was to supervise Sunday School class work. It was an assignment peculiarly suited to his tastes and training, combining the methodology of his schooling as a teacher and the spirit and enthusiasm generated by his missionary service.

As the new assistant analyzed the content and procedures of the stake's Sunday School classes, he was struck by the absence of consistency and order and by the lack of training among the faculty. To remedy these defects, he devised a system and procedure that would revolutionize the Sunday Schools of the Weber Stake—and ultimately of the entire Church. His first step was to hold weekly meetings with the stake board. There the leaders were drilled in the fundamentals of lesson preparation—the selection of an objective; the orderly arrangement of the subject matter; the gathering of interesting enrichment materials; and the practical application to the lives of the students. Next came

David O. McKay as principal of the Weber Stake Academy.

the monthly union meeting where the stake board taught these concepts to their ward counterparts and outlined the lessons for the coming month. And finally, the ward Sunday School leaders were trained to hold a weekly faculty meeting where the plans for the ensuing week were reviewed and polished.

Meanwhile, superintendent McKay was making equally significant progress in his work on the faculty at the academy, so much so that on the resignation of Professor Louis F. Moench, he was appointed its principal. The ascension to its leadership of David O. McKay on April 17, 1902, marked the beginning of an era of significant development at the Weber Stake Academy. With the guidance of the new principal, the school soon found its voice with the organization of the *Acorn*, the academy's official newspaper. In its excitement at breaking into print, the *Acorn* staff unaccountably failed to indicate the name of the originating school, whereupon a quizzical reader asked, "Where does the little Acorn grow?" Everyone within earshot was soon to know the answer to this question, as they were to become aware of a creative force at the helm of the Weber

Stake Academy. Aside from his laudable work in giving strong administrative leadership to the school, improving curriculum, and strengthening and motivating the faculty, David O. McKay was the generating force behind numerous initiatives that broadened the scope of the academy, created a strong esprit de corps among the student body, and attracted the interest and support of the community. Early in his administration, the new principal encouraged the development of a lecture course that featured educators, dramatists, and now and then a politician. This series, which attracted the townspeople as well as the student body, became so popular over the years that it was ultimately moved to the Orpheum Theatre off-campus, where the larger audiences could be comfortably seated. Professor McKay also spearheaded the organization of the student body and, as one might expect, of the academy's first football team. He also encouraged the formation of the school's first track and baseball teams and gave unqualified support to its basketball team, which competed for several years before he became the principal. On the academic side, David O. McKay's administration started the departments of Domestic Arts and Domestic Science and the Conservatory of Music.

As the size of the student body grew with the spawning of new departments and activities, the principal became acutely aware of the need to enlarge the school's physical plant. When he approached the board of education, of which his father, Bishop David McKay was a member, the progressive young administrator was told the board had no money for this purpose. However, the door was left open, provided he raised the funds himself! The principal immediately organized his faculty for an aggressive fund-raising campaign. Every ward within the stakes served by the academy was visited by a faculty representative who explained the needs of the school and solicited contributions. Special contacts were made to business and professional leaders in the community. And publicity of the drive found its way into the press. Within a comparatively short time,

Emma Ray Riggs McKay as she appeared when David O. was president of the Weber Academy.

$40,000 was collected or pledged, and work went forward on the new facility. When completed, it provided space for geological and chemical laboratories, additional classrooms, a vocational training shop, and a spacious auditorium.

It was during this period of professional achievement and maturity in his Church calling that David O. McKay became a father and, with Emma Ray, laid the foundation of what was of overriding importance to him—his family. The first child, David Lawrence, who was born in Ogden on September 30, 1901, was joined three years later by another son, Llewelyn Riggs. Over the next sixteen years, five more children, all born in Ogden, joined the family.

From its inception, the family life of David O. and Emma Ray McKay was ideal. They were mature adults when Lawrence was born, the father being twenty-eight and the mother twenty-four. Their mutual love of music, good books, and beautiful decor gave assurance that their home would be one of culture and refinement. And their shared convictions about the divinity of the restored Church and their faith in God introduced a spiritual quality into the home that manifested itself in regular family and personal prayers and in love, kindness, and forgiveness. That these are not mere platitudes is best evidenced by the conduct of this family throughout the years. In public and in private, the husband was unfailing in his consideration of the wife. And she reciprocated in kind, creating in the home a place of peace and quiet. The children imbibed these influences from their infancy and reflected them in their many relationships.

The family poetry, which became a tradition, usually composed for special events and anniversaries, best reflects the spirit of the McKay home. On their fifty-fourth wedding anniversary, President McKay greeted his wife with this rhyme:

> Fifty-four years! How the years speed away!
> But each makes more precious our own "Mama Ray."
> This morning I greet you with prayers in my heart
> That through Time and Eternity ne'er shall we part.

And a few years before, when she celebrated her seventy-seventh birthday, he wrote:

> Three score years plus ten and seven!
> Children around her—a score plus eleven!
> And I whom she's blessed will love her alway.
> The sweetest of sweethearts our own "Mama Ray."
> (L. R. McKay, *Home Memories*, p. 174, 175.)

In wishing her husband a happy Father's Day, Emma Ray expressed her feelings in verse:

> How much have I remembered you? As much as night
>   and day!
> Not any thoughtful moment have you ever been away.
> From sunlight to moonlight and from darkness to dawn,
> Your image and my love for you have always lingered
>   on.
> What more could I have done, dear one, to show my feel-
>   ing true?
> What more is there in life, my love, that I can offer you?
> (Ibid.)

The children, too, were the recipients of similar poetic pieces from their parents. Emma Rae, the youngest daughter, was buoyed up in McCammon, Idaho, where she was teaching school, on receiving a seven stanza poem from her father. It began:

> Lonesome seems the home today, yet four of us are here!
> The sun is shining brightly, yet there's an absence, sure,
> of cheer!
> Mother—tearful—still is smiling, and the boys pretend
> to play,
> But home is not the same—now that Emma's gone away!
> (Ibid.)

And when the father repurchased for him a violin Lawrence had sold to help defray the expenses of law school, the son received the bonus of a poem from which this has been excerpted:

> This viol I know isn't the best of its kind,
>   but it's won a place in my heart and mind
>   which no Stradivarius can fill.
> So I've bought it again for connoted joy,
>   and the tones it gave forth at the touch of our boy—
>   I recall them e'en now with a thrill. (Ibid., p. 179.)

It was this violin that Lawrence played over the years in the family's three-piece orchestra, joined by Llewelyn on the clarinet and Lou Jean on the piano. This trio frequently performed at family nights—or family home evenings as they are now called—and on other occasions. The clarinetist reported: "One of father's joys was to sit (sometimes for hours) and listen to the trio. . . . It seemed to relax him to listen to strains from Il Trovatore, Schubert's Barcarole, Angel's Serenade or the Sextet from Lucia." (Ibid., p. 178.) And the music provided by these three was augmented by the parents and by other family members who also shared their talents.

While the growth and maturity of the family of David O. and Emma Ray McKay lay mostly in the future as the year 1906 approached, important first steps had been taken. Lawrence was going on four and Llewelyn was approaching two. By any standard of the day, the McKays of 1905 would have been regarded as a special young family. But they were much more than that. They were marked for distinction, largely because of the growing reputation and prominence of the husband and father. His performance at the academy and his work in revolutionizing the Weber Stake Sunday Schools had drawn the attention of the leading brethren in Salt Lake City. Particularly impressed was President Joseph F. Smith, who not only headed the entire Church, but who was also the general superintendent of the Church's Sunday Schools. So impressed was he with the intelligent order that had been introduced into the Ogden Sunday Schools in the preparation of lessons that he invited the young professor who had initiated the change to prepare an article for publication in the Sunday School's magazine. The result was a paper written by David O. McKay entitled "The Lesson Aim: How to Select It, How to Develop It, How to Apply It," which appeared in the April 1905 issue of the *Juvenile Instructor* (pp. 242-45). The Prophet was also intrigued by the fact that under David O. McKay's leadership, the Weber Stake Sunday Schools had experimented for two years in holding adult Sunday School classes. Until this time, attendance at Sunday School had been restricted to children, as the name of the magazine the *Juvenile Instructor* implies. This experiment would later become a standard practice in the Church's Sunday Schools throughout the world.

It is a matter of great interest that within six short years after his release as a missionary, David O. McKay's abilities and qualifications had been brought to the favorable attention of the president of the Church. And it occurred not because of any personal influence he or his family had with the Prophet, but because of the exceptionally able job he had performed in a subordinate position in a Church auxiliary away from the headquarters of the Church. He had, indeed, acted well his part. And once his performance had been noticed by those in authority, an examination of his overall qualifications revealed that here was a man possessing every qualification to fit him for high office in The Church of Jesus Christ of Latter-day Saints.

Chapter Six

The Apostle

At the time David O. McKay's article appeared in the April 1905 issue of the *Juvenile Instructor*, there were no vacancies in the Quorum of the Twelve Apostles. Within ten months, however, there would be three such vacancies. On October 28, 1905, the leaders of the Church were saddened when John W. Taylor and Matthias F. Cowley resigned their apostolic offices. These handsome, articulate men, both only forty-seven years of age, had been caught up in the problems that followed the publication of the Manifesto in 1890. And, in 1905, finding themselves out of harmony with their brethren on this issue, they had voluntarily stepped down from these high offices. The third vacancy occurred when seventy-four-year-old Marriner W. Merrill passed away on February 6, 1906.

The resignations of John W. Taylor and Matthias F. Cowley had not been announced publicly before April 1906. So, as the general conference approached, the membership of the Church was aware of the possibility that one new member of the Twelve would be called—but not three. As the conference opened on Friday, April 6, there was the usual air of excitement and expectancy with not a little speculation about who the new member of the Twelve would be. Through the Friday, Saturday, and Sunday morning sessions, nothing was said about filling the vacancy. And the veil of silence shrouded the Sunday afternoon session as well—until the very end. Francis M. Lyman, president of the Twelve, was called upon by President Joseph F. Smith to deliver the concluding address. He spoke at some length about the educational institutions in the state, both religious and secular, and about the development of the physical resources of the state. He then noted with regret the passing of Elder Marriner W. Merrill, following which he made this brief statement: "Also to announce to you the resignation of our beloved brethren, John W. Taylor and Matthias F. Cowley, from their positions in [the Twelve] because they found themselves out of harmony with the Presidency of the Church and the quorum to which they belonged. Their resignations, you may well appreciate, caused us the deepest sorrow." (CR, April 1906, pp. 93, 94.) President Lyman then presented the General Authorities and officers of the Church for sustaining vote. In presenting the Quorum of the Twelve Apostles, he read out the names of the three new members—George F. Richards, Orson F. Whitney, and David O. McKay.

The first two of the new apostles were well known in the Church. Forty-five-year-old George F. Richards was the son of Franklin D. Richards, deceased, a former member of the Twelve. He was also the second counselor in the Tooele Stake presidency and an ordained patriarch. The second one named among the new apostles, fifty-one-year-old Orson F. Whitney, was even better known than Elder Richards. For over twenty-five years Elder Whitney, a descendant of both Newell K. Whitney and Heber C. Kimball, had served as the bishop of the Eighteenth Ward in Salt Lake City. This is the ward in which the headquarters of the Church were located (and still are) and in which many of the General Authorities resided. Moreover, Elder Whitney had earned a solid reputation as a writer and historian, having written a multivolume history of the state of Utah that had been widely circulated in the area.

Compared with these two, the new junior apostle, thirty-two-year-old David O. McKay, was unknown. Except for the small circle of acquaintances he had made while attending the University of Utah, or the General Authorities who knew him through his father, or through his own work in the mission field or in Ogden, or for the subscribers to the *Juvenile Instructor* who had read his article, the new leader was practically unknown in Salt Lake City. "Who is this new leader from remote Huntsville?" the conference attenders may well have asked themselves when his name was read from the Tabernacle pulpit. They would not know of his background until they read about it later in the newspapers or the Church magazines. And most of them were unable to appraise his speaking style until the following October as the April general conference was adjourned shortly after he and the others had been sustained.

What the members later learned was somewhat astonishing. His call was not unlike that of David of old who was called from his shepherding chores to be king of Israel. Except for the short periods when he served as a deacons quorum president or as the conference president in Scotland, this young man had never acted in a Church administrative office. He had never served in a bishopric or on a high council or in a stake presidency. Therefore, he had never been ordained a high priest and held only the office of a seventy in the Melchizedek Priesthood. Yet at a very young age he had been called to the second governing body of the Church and placed in a position from where, ultimately, he would be elevated to the prophetic office.

But his call at such a young age, in preference to hundreds of men of wider experience and equal dedication, was not without precedent. Indeed, the man who called him, Joseph F. Smith, had been ordained to the apostleship at age twenty-eight. And a few years before Elder McKay's call, Hyrum Mack Smith and George Albert Smith had been inducted into the Twelve at ages twenty-nine and thirty-three, respectively. Moreover, there sat in the circle at this time a forty-nine-year-old leader, Heber J. Grant, who was called at age twenty-five. Notwithstanding this, it was extraordinary that one so young and so relatively inexperienced would be called to such a high position in preference to so many who, on the surface, appeared to be better qualified. But while, from an objective point of view, an uninformed onlooker may have wondered about the call, those acquainted with the conferral of divine authority would have seen in it a repetition of an ancient precedent. In calling David of old, the Lord said to the prophet Samuel: "The Lord seeth not as man seeth; for man looketh on the outward appearance, but the Lord looketh on the heart." (1 Samuel 16:7.)

Elder McKay was ordained both a high priest and an apostle on April 9, 1906, by President Joseph F. Smith. And on October 6, 1906, at the following general conference, he was called to serve as the second assistant to President Smith in the general superintendency of the Sunday Schools of the Church. With this last call, a chief reason for Elder McKay's elevation to the Twelve and a harbinger of the principal role he would play during the early years of his apostleship were made manifest.

As a member of the Twelve, David O. McKay was automatically inducted into the Council of the First Presidency and the Quorum of the Twelve. This council, which ordinarily consists of fifteen men—the three members of the First Presidency and the twelve apostles—is the body that considers and is the ultimate authority as to all matters of doctrine, policy, and procedure affecting the Church. While the Prophet, who holds all the keys, or his quorum, the First Presidency, possess the inherent authority to act independent of the Twelve, this occurs only infrequently and then, usually, only in cases where urgent necessity requires prompt action. And in such cases, the customary practice is to bring these exceptional matters to the Twelve later for discussion and ratification. It was to this council, then, the most prestigious and powerful council in the Church, that Elder David O. McKay was introduced shortly after he was sustained at the April 1906 general conference. Its meetings were—and still are—held in the upper room of the Salt

Lake Temple, where the Brethren gather weekly to pray and to counsel together about the international interests of the Church. Mere entrance into this sacred room, of itself, is sufficient to induce feelings of humility, feelings that would be greatly magnified to one who entered not as a mere spectator, but as a member of the circle, jointly responsible for the actions taken there and individually empowered and charged to speak and to act as a special witness of the Savior in all the world.

It is not difficult to imagine the combined sense of exhilaration, excitement, anticipation, and inadequacy that must have dominated David O. McKay's thoughts when he first entered the upper room as a member of the council on April 9, 1906, and took his place at the end of the semicircle, ranged around the three chairs of the First Presidency placed against the west wall of the room. He was the junior member of the body, both in age and length of service. President Joseph F. Smith was the dean of the group in apostolic tenure, having functioned in that role for forty years. And to the Prophet's right sat John R. Winder, the spry eighty-five-year-old first counselor, who had lived more days than any of his brethren. On the other side of President Smith sat his sixty-two-year-old second counselor, Anthon H. Lund. At the head of the semicircle was the president of the Twelve, Francis M. Lyman, sixty-six, who had been a member of the Twelve for twenty-six years. And seated in order of their seniority were the other members of the Twelve: John Henry Smith, fifty-eight, who would later be called as a counselor in the First Presidency; the seventy-five-year-old Englishman, George Teasdale; Heber J. Grant, age fifty, a future president of the Church; Rudger Clawson, who had once been called and sustained as a member of the First Presidency, but who was never set apart to that office because of the intervening death of President Lorenzo Snow; Reed Smoot, only forty-four, who would later serve with distinction as a United States senator; Hyrum M. Smith, the thirty-four-year-old son of President Joseph F. Smith, who was widely thought to be a future president of the Church, but who died unexpectedly in 1918; George Albert Smith, thirty-six, another future president of the Church; Charles W. Penrose, age seventy-four, a future counselor in the First Presidency; and the three new members of the quorum. The average age of this distinguished group of men was fifty-five.

As he was inducted into the council, Elder McKay and the other two new members were given, and willingly accepted, a charge that imposed upon them irrevocable duties of unity, dedication, and confidentiality. From that moment to the time of his death almost sixty-four years later, David O. McKay labored diligently under the yoke of the apostolic mandate, traveling the earth to proclaim the gospel of Jesus Christ and to set the affairs of the Church in order, and then returning again and again to the council room to report to and to receive instruction and motivation from his brethren. It was in the environment of this room that Elder McKay underwent a forty-five-year prophetic apprenticeship during which he received the most intensive kind of instruction to prepare him for the time when he would be elevated to the presidency of the Church.

Although the Church was comparatively small at the time of his call to the Twelve—approximately 330,000 members divided into fifty-five stakes and twenty-one missions—Elder McKay was surprised at the scope and volume of matters brought before the council for discussion and decision. The decisions made here would affect thousands of people around the world. This applied not only to the members of the Church but to nonmembers as well, some of whom would be affected by its decisions relating to proselyting methods, or decisions such as the one made a week after Elder McKay's induction when it voted to donate $10,000 to Governor George C. Pardee of California to aid those affected by the terrible earthquake and fire in San Francisco. And it was here that the council received regular reports of the progress of the Church in its various ecclesiastical units, which provided an important overview and barometer from which needs could be assessed and appropriate action taken.

At this time in Church history, the General Authorities usually traveled to stake conference assignments in pairs. Elder McKay's first such assignment was to Blackfoot, Idaho. His companion was Hyrum M. Smith of the Twelve. With the two apostles was Andrew Kimball, a stake president from the Gila Valley in southeast Arizona, who also had duties with the Lamanites and who was along to check into the status of Lamanite members in the vicinity of Blackfoot. President Kimball, who had come to Salt Lake City for the general conference, had left his family at home in Thatcher, Arizona. One member of his family was an eleven-year-old, ruddy cheeked boy named Spencer who one day would occupy the prophetic office.

Attesting to the durability of both the members in Blackfoot and their conference visitors, three meetings were held on Saturday and three on Sunday, all of which were interspersed with counseling sessions with local leaders and members.

The members of the Church living in outlying areas doted on the General Authorities, especially on the Twelve, more so than in Salt Lake City, where it was common to see and hear them. So in communities like Blackfoot, the members looked forward, weeks in advance, to their visits. And after the conference, there would be frequent references to their sermons and counsel and to their appearance and demeanor. And the young people, especially, almost idolized them, sought to be like them, and yearned for some incident or circumstance to effect a personal relationship with them. The most common means of doing this was to invite one of the brethren to perform a temple sealing. That a General Authority had performed one's marriage in the temple became a mark of distinction, pointed to with pride and commented on frequently over the years. This perhaps was more true of Elder McKay than most of the General Authorities because of the special appeal to youth that his personality and achievements engendered. So ten days after his apostolic ordination, Elder McKay performed the first of thousands of temple sealings at which he would officiate over the years. The bride and groom to share this distinction were from Ogden, as one might have expected, Fred May and the daughter of Mr. and Mrs. Francis Brown.

Family members were equally anxious to have David O. perform their sealings. So on June 19, 1907, he performed the ceremony for his sister Jeanette in the Logan Temple: "At 11 A.M. Dr. Joseph Morrell and Jeanette McKay knelt at the altar," the apostle recorded, "and were united in the bonds of wedlock for time and for all eternity. I officiated." That evening the bridal party had dinner at the Ogden home of David O. and Ray, 676 21st Street, and the following day the entire clan gathered at the "auld hous" in Huntsville. The memories, some sad, some happy, this reunion evoked were poignantly recalled by Elder McKay: "It was delightful to meet all together once again in the dear old house of our youth," he wrote. "But there was a vacant chair that reminded us of one who is gone—vacant chair did I say? Everything seemed vacant. Mama was not there. I missed her kiss at the doorway, her smile in the parlor, her laugh at the table by Papa's side, and the evening talks before going to bed."

Occasionally circumstances made it necessary for a general authority to be assigned alone to attend a stake conference. When this happened to Elder McKay, he usually tried to take a member of the family with him. In later years, after the children were all married, Emma Ray almost invariably was his companion on such occasions. But during the years when her domestic responsibilities required her presence at home, the children were invited, alternately, to accompany their father. So on June 29, 1907, just a few days after Jeanette's marriage, young Lawrence, who was not yet six, accompanied his father to LaGrande, Oregon, on the train. It was a memorable experience for this lad, whose

David O. McKay

amazement at the conveniences and comforts of railway travel was doubtless overshadowed by the awe in which he held his powerful and kindly father.

While the eager, inquisitive son was avidly absorbing the beautiful scenery along the route of the train and sampling the delicacies dispensed by the vendors, the apostle devoted the leisurely trip mostly to reading, reflection, and writing. The theme that dominated his thoughts and that found its way into his journal carries a pronounced contemporary tone, though written almost eighty years ago. "Search for the gospel in the world," he began. "The newspapers publish the bad; [but] the people should seek the good in order to arrive at a just estimate of the world." There followed this perceptive appraisal of why the press was dominated by bad news: "But why does the press give such publicity to evil and sensationalism? Because the public is demanding it."

A few days after returning from Oregon, Elder McKay was able to enjoy one of the few days of relaxation he had had since his call to the Twelve fifteen months before. Not only had he been preoccupied with his ecclesiastical duties, which entailed regular stake conference assignments on the weekends, miscellaneous speaking assignments, and weekly trips from Ogden to Salt Lake City to attend the council meetings in the temple, but he also had continued to serve as the principal of the Weber Stake Academy, where he shouldered administrative as well as some teaching chores. Interspersed with these heavy and continuing duties were frequent appointments for counseling and temple sealings. And overlying all this were the preeminent responsibilities deriving from his family, which had now grown to five with the birth of Louise Jennette (Lou Jean) on October 13, 1906. So, on July 4, 1907, David O. and Emma Ray; their two young sons, Lawrence and Llewelyn; and baby Lou Jean went to Huntsville for a carefree day with the extended clan. "Drove to Huntsville with Ray and the babies," recorded the apostle. "Enjoyed a family reunion at the old home." And the luxurious feelings gener-

74

ated by a rare day free from the stresses of his customary duties spilled over into his diary: "A day of rest. There is nothing I have to do, there is nowhere I have to go. A day of relaxation."

But the following day, he picked up his burden once more: "School work," he noted laconically. "Arranged to settle with bank on note of $3,000 which I endorsed with David C. Eccles for the knitting co." And entries made during the ensuing two weeks reflect the scope and variety of his activities and concerns, of which these are a sampling: "Uncle Isaac is very sick. At home with school matters. . . . Ordained Gustave Olsen a patriarch. . . . At Saltair, joint excursion of Stake SS and MI Association. . . . In Huntsville—on hills with Papa. Administered to Uncle John Grow who is very sick of appendicitis. His appendix is broken. He is critically ill. . . . Lawrence has the whooping cough. Rather a severe attack. . . . Boarded 8:25 A.M. train for Salt Lake. Attended opening exercises of the 20th Ward S.S. and the class work and closing exercises of the 21st Ward S.S. One of the greatest needs in SS work today is efficient teaching. Oh it is lamentable to think how poorly our children are *herded* not to say *taught* in some of our classes. . . . Drove to Huntsville. Cut hay. Took Llewelyn with me and we stayed over night. Tommy and I visited Uncle John, who is still very weak but recovering. . . . There is no air that seems so pure as good old Huntsville air. . . . While in the field received word that Sister Caroline Peterson Renstrom died this morning at 8:18 o'clock. A noble woman gone to her rest. She was the first woman who welcomed me as a ward teacher. Drove to Ogden, after calling on Bro. Renstrom, and took train at 5:45 P.M. for Salt Lake. . . . Returned home at midnight and met Ray for the first time in two days."

And so went the busy, almost frenetic life of the thirty-three-year-old apostle, husband, father, professor, and part-time farmer. The fragmentation of effort that his numerous duties entailed precluded him from devoting long, uninterrupted segments of time to any one activity.

So, at an early age he was disciplined to the juggler's art—
the skill of keeping many balls in the air at once without al-
lowing any of them to fall to the ground. It required a deft
touch, supreme concentration of effort, and adroit maneu-
vering so that nothing was left unattended despite the
strict economy of time imposed on any one activity.

Often a man confronted with such multiple demands
on his time will sacrifice family needs to other responsibilities. David O. McKay never did so. He endeavored to in-
terweave his church, professional, and business activities
with those of his family. This he did by taking family members with him when he performed other duties, as we have
already seen, and as we shall see him do in his later career
to an even greater degree. And the time he did spend with
his family was always quality time with recreational activities being planned so as to involve the entire family, if
possible. A favorite group diversion at the time about
which we now speak—1907—was buggy riding. At that
day, the automobile was still an oddity, it being only five
years since the first mass-produced automobile had appeared: the topless, fenderless Oldsmobile of 1902. Now
and then one of these strange-looking objects could be seen
chugging around Ogden's streets, to the chagrin of some of
the more pessimistic and conservative members of the
community who were confident that the automobile was
merely a passing fad like plugged hats. And the great pre-
ponderance of the horse-drawn vehicles over the
mechanized automobile seemed to lend credence to this
view at the time. So of a summer's evening, usually on
weekends, many Ogden families could be seen riding
about in their buggies, enjoying the scenery and the cool,
refreshing breezes that wafted down Ogden Canyon from
up Huntsville way. "In the evening took Ray and the Babes
out buggy riding," Elder McKay recorded on Wednesday,
July 17, 1907. A postscript revealed one of the reasons for
this midweek outing: "Later we packed up ready for my
trip."

The trip alluded to was a lengthy one he and Elder John

Henry Smith had been assigned to take into the San Luis and San Juan stakes, remote areas in southwestern Colorado and Northwestern New Mexico. The two apostles left the next morning by train with Denver as their intermediate destination. Winding its way up Weber Canyon and through the draws and vales beyond the Wasatch to the open terrain of Wyoming, the train traveled without incident until it reached the Continental Divide. There the two elders and the other passengers were startled to see the twisted remains of an engine that had blown up a short while before, killing an unidentified man and seriously injuring the fireman and brakeman. Not long afterward, a tragic collision between their train and one traveling west was narrowly averted. "The siding where the west bound train was supposed to switch, was filled with freight trains," Elder McKay explained; and "a signal fire had been lighted in time to warn our onrushing train of the danger. The two engines came to a stop a few rods apart."

The delay caused by this near accident snarled the schedule, requiring a brief layover in Cheyenne, where they arrived at 4:15 A.M. This made it possible for Elder McKay to take an early morning stroll around the frontier town, which had been an eyewitness to the Mormon exodus and to the cavalcade of wagon trains that had rumbled past on their way to the Oregon in search of asylum or El Dorado. Never having had the opportunity to inspect it before, the young apostle was pleasantly surprised at what he found in Cheyenne. "Evidences of intelligence and progression were manifest on every hand," he wrote approvingly, "beautiful homes, well-kept lawns, a cool inviting park . . . and stately business blocks." Arriving in Denver at midmorning, the travelers had the opportunity to inspect this booming young metropolis, lying on the eastern breast of the Rockies, and which the diarist pronounced to be "progressive."

After counseling with missionaries in Denver in the afternoon, Elders Smith and McKay boarded a sleeper bound for the San Luis Valley. Bedding down after a light supper in the gleaming dining car, David O. did not awaken until 5:30 the next morning, when he was aroused by the "old engine," which was "puffing with all its strength, pulling the train over the mountains." Any uneasiness he may have felt at recalling the fate of the engine that had exploded in pulling a train up the much gentler grade leading toward the Continental Divide was calmed by his complete absorption in the beautiful scenery. The description of what he saw deserves to be quoted verbatim, revealing as it does the writer's considerable powers of observation and expression: "The scenery was beautiful; stately pines and quaking asps abounded. The wild locust was in full bloom and growing profusely. The wild columbine decked the hillside; the shrubbery everywhere was green, and the whole landscape—side hills and hollows—seemed adorned in the richest hues." Then followed this graphic description of the tortuous path followed by the train as it wound through the towering Rockies: "The railroad goes through gorges, spans chasms, penetrates tunnels, and winds, and winds and bends from hillside to hillside until it reaches the summit. Then it falls steadily and easily along a little mountain stream, down into the San Luis Valley."

Eating their breakfast at Alamosa, the two apostles took the narrow-guage Denver and Rio Grande to LaJara, where they were met by a member of the stake presidency and driven to Sanford, where the first session of the stake conference was held on Saturday, July 20. The Saints convened in a new chapel which, although it was not quite completed, was pronounced to be "a credit to the Saints in this ward."

Accepting a challenge from some of the young athletes, Elder McKay started to play ball with them after the meeting "but soon got out of breath" and withdrew. After a satisfying supper with his hosts, one of the leading couples in the area, the visitor retired to what he hoped would be a restful sleep following two nights on the train, which, though quite comfortable, produced a vague sense of nausea to a sleeper because of the swaying and pitching caused by the sharp turns and the uneven road bed.

The discomfort of travel and being away from home was forgotten in the spirit of excitement and enthusiasm that characterized the meetings on Sunday. "The conference has been a success in every way. The people are encouraged."

On July 22 the two apostles were driven to Manassa where, on July 24, they participated in celebrating the sixtieth anniversary of the arrival of the Saints in the Salt Lake Valley. Returning to Sanford after lunch, the visitors attended the comic opera "H.M.S. Pinafore" staged by local talent, looked in on a dance afterward in Manassa, and retired to a home where the accommodations were very pleasant. There Elder McKay found a letter from Ray, which carried the unhappy news of the passing of Uncle Isaac, the kindly man whose Scottish origins were always evident in his slight highland accent. It was sad to see another vacant spot created in the close-knit McKay clan. And David O. was concerned about the unspoken things in his wife's letter: "She said she and the babes were pretty well, but I know from interruptions she had while writing that the babes are unwell."

It was with some feelings of dejection, therefore, that Elder McKay left Manassa the next morning. He and Elder Smith were driven in a spring wagon to Romeo, a small railroad station nearby, where they caught the train to Durango. Traveling thence into northwestern New Mexico, the two apostles held a series of meetings in Farmington and Fruitland, where the Latter-day Saints predominated. Here Elder McKay conversed with an old man named George W. Adair, who lived in Washington County, Utah, during the year of the Mountain Meadows tragedy. Being employed in carrying mail between St. George and Cedar City, he was in Cedar City when the events surrounding the Fancher Party were maturing. "He saw the message that was sent to . . . Pres. Young," wrote Elder McKay of the conversation. "He saw the answer from

Pres. Young. He said to me 'I am a living witness that the Church of Jesus Christ of Latter-day Saints had nothing to do with that massacre. Brigham Young, Geo. A. Smith knew no more about that affair than you did!'" The old man went on to relate other circumstances surrounding the incident which the diarist recorded but about which he made no comment.

Elder McKay met others in these remote communities who aroused happier and more personal memories: "Met old Huntsville friends, Mozelle Hall, Luella Hammond Hall, Sister Wm. Hall and Joseph Wheeler; also a grandson of Capt. Hunt, a grand daughter also, children of Marsha Hunt." He had a genuine admiration for people such as these who, living in comparative isolation a long distance from Church headquarters, maintained the high standards of their religion, cherished the heritage of their pioneer ancestry, and devoted their lives to the interests of the Church. He was amazed by the example of the husband of his former neighbor, Mrs. William Hall, who was a member of the stake presidency: "At the Bishop's home we met Pres. William Hall. He is now 74 years old; but since April he has travelled twelve hundred miles by team. He has just made his round of the stake, a distance of six hundred miles."

And for the first time since his call to the Twelve, Elder McKay was directly exposed to the Navajo Indians, a dignified people among whom the Mormon elders had been proselyting for decades. In Fruitland he encountered numerous Navajos who came frequently to trade their jewelry and blankets for necessities. He marveled at the wide assortment of Navajo products at one store, which, he learned, did "one thousand dollars business each week in blankets alone." Across the San Juan River was the north side of the Navajo Reservation, which the apostles were unable to visit on this tour. "The river is too high, at present, to cross without a boat," David O. explained, "or I should have visited the old native huts . . . that we can see standing lonely in the sun, or, which we see marked at night by the old camp fires."

Elder McKay and his traveling companion returned from this lengthy and important trip in time to make their report to the Brethren on August 7. It was especially important to the new apostle because it was the first extended trip he had taken since his call to the Twelve; it had introduced him to a culture and life-style quite foreign to anything he had experienced before; and it served as an introduction to the nomadic kind of existence he would lead during many of the remaining years of his life. Before the end of his career, David O. McKay would become the most widely traveled of any of the apostles up to that time, not excluding the early apostles chosen by the Savior before his ascension. He would travel by every known means of conveyance, in every kind of weather, and in all seasons. He would be exposed to accommodations of every kind, from those suitable for a king to those of the humblest order. And through it all, he would retain his composure, dignity, and sense of humor. David O. McKay was the model of the happy traveler, interested in what he saw, in whom he met, in how the work was progressing, and in acting well his part at all times and in all places.

Aside from this lengthy trip into Colorado and New Mexico, Elder McKay filled other assignments relatively close to home in the early part of his apostolic ministry. In addition to his first stake conference assignment at Blackfoot, he had filled appointments in the Benson, Bannock, and Malad stakes to the north; and in the Ensign, Pioneer, and Liberty stakes in Salt Lake City, stakes that had been created just two years before his call to the Twelve by a division of the original Salt Lake Stake. In visiting the Liberty Stake, Elder McKay first became acquainted with stake president, Hugh J. Cannon, the man who several years later would accompany him on his world tour.

His first trip to the midwest took Elder McKay to Independence, Missouri, in February 1908. There he counseled with members, inspected Church properties, and traced the activities of the early Saints in that area almost eighty years before. While there he also conferred with the president of the Hedrikite Church, which owns part of the land considered to be within the original Independence temple site designated by the Prophet Joseph Smith, land the Hedrikites would not sell notwithstanding the persuasiveness of a David O. McKay.

The visiting General Authority then engaged in another "first" when he toured the Central States Mission with the mission president, Samuel O. Bennion. In counseling and instructing the missionaries with whom he met, Elder McKay was able to speak with conviction and authority born of his relatively recent experiences in Scotland. But he not only *talked* about the philosophy and the procedures of missionary work, he and President Bennion, who twenty-five years later would be called as a member of the First Council of the Seventy, *demonstrated* them by actually engaging in missionary work. So following a street meeting this pair held in Springfield, Missouri, David O. characterized the experience as "glorious."

On the day he reported his trip to Independence and the mission tour, March 11, 1908, Elder McKay also reported his resignation as the principal of the Weber Stake Academy and the appointment of his successor, Professor McKendrick. While he continued as a member of the board for several years, thereby perpetuating his influence on the school, this resignation ended David O. McKay's direct involvement in the administrative and academic affairs of the academy.

Like most things in life, the apostle's employment at the school had had its good and bad aspects. As far as the strictly academic duties and his relationship with the students were concerned, it had been pure joy. As to his administrative responsibilities, however, the job had its dark side, with financing being his chief nemesis. During most of his term as principal, Elder McKay had been his own chief fund-raiser. This was a particularly onerous task during the last two years as he had struggled to obtain the funds to complete the new building. He had looked to two main sources of help—wealthy businessmen and the Church. Among the first group, the two most outstanding were David Eccles of Ogden, a successful businessman, and Samuel Newhouse of Salt Lake City, a powerful and wealthy mining entrepreneur. In the spring of 1907, Mr. Newhouse, a nonmember, generously contributed $5,000, which relieved a serious financial bind. And David Eccles, a lifelong friend, came to Elder McKay's rescue on several occasions. In mid-October he reported that David Eccles had again helped to raise money "to meet obligations of the Academy." A month later, David O. met with the Weber Stake presidency to appeal for help "to clear the Academy of an indebtedness of $10,000."

Amidst the pressures of generating funds, overseeing the construction work, and discharging the administrative chores of the school, Elder McKay was stunned when a workman, Douglas Stone, fell to his death while working on the new building. The funeral was an especially difficult one for the young apostle, who was the principal speaker, given the comparative youth of the deceased and his tragic death while working on a project for which Elder McKay felt responsible.

Three months after Elder McKay stepped down as the principal of the Weber Stake Academy, the new building was dedicated by President Joseph F. Smith. "The building is now out of debt," the retiring principal reported. "It had a cost of forty thousand dollars, including heating apparatus and seating accommodations."

Having had the responsibility for the academy lifted from his shoulders, and having been released from his service in the superintendency of the Weber Stake Sunday School a year before, Elder McKay was free to devote more time to his worldwide responsibilities. He began to play a more active role in the Sunday School general superintendency, where his knowledge and expertise as a professional teacher were used more and more. He became directly involved in the preparation of teaching manuals and courses of study. And his philosophy of teacher training and administrative coordination through union meetings began to permeate the Sunday School organization, both at Church headquarters and in the field. Within a few years these concepts, which soon spread to the other auxiliaries, had become so firmly implanted and were implemented with such vigor and effectiveness that the auxiliaries began to exert a dominant influence within the Church. This trend was reinforced by the organization of the correlation committee, which coordinated the preparation of lesson materials for the auxiliaries. Later a priesthood correlation committee was organized that performed a similar function in preparing lesson materials for the priesthood quorums. David O. McKay played a key role in the formation and the direction of both of these committees.

Within eight years after his call to the Twelve, the influence of Elder McKay in the development and teaching of instructional materials and techniques had spread throughout the Church. By 1914 members of the general boards of the auxiliaries routinely accompanied General Authorities on stake conference assignments. There, among other things, they taught stake and ward auxiliary leaders in lesson preparation and presentation, a procedure that could easily be traced to the teaching revolution touched off in the Weber Stake by young David O. McKay in the first years of the Twentieth Century.

The emphasis on gospel scholarship generated by the initiatives of David O. McKay created excitement and commitment among a whole cadre of young, dedicated Latter-day Saints striving for academic excellence and for an accommodation between the intellectual goals of the universities and the spiritual goals of the Church. Men such as these were attracted by or were recruited by the correlation committees to help prepare instructional materials for the priesthood quorums and the auxiliaries. "Listened to John A. Widtsoe read the manuscript of a work he is preparing for the Melchizedek Priesthood entitled 'A Rational Theology,'" Elder McKay reported on October 22, 1914. He judged the product to be "a very good work." This manuscript was published as an independent volume, received wide distribution, and served as intellectual and spiritual fodder for thousands of Latter-day Saints over many years. Between 1914 and 1921, when he was called to the Twelve, John A. Widtsoe, noted educator and university president, wrote extensively for the correlation committees.

For many years, Stephen L Richards, brilliant young attorney and a member of the faculty of the University of Utah College of Law, worked closely with Elder McKay on Sunday School curriculum matters. An entry made on November 12, 1916, two months before Stephen L Richards was called to the Twelve, reflects a relationship that was formed years before around a common interest in writing and teaching and that would continue for several decades into the future: "Spent Sunday with Stephen L Richards on Sunday School matters," he reported.

A series of talks delivered to classes in theology by James E. Talmage, called to the Twelve in 1911, was compiled in *The Articles of Faith*, which received wide distribution and exerted a profound influence on the thinking of thousands of members of the Church. These and other writings of Elder Talmage were used extensively by the correlation committees in preparing lesson materials over the years.

Other educators later called to the Twelve, Richard R. Lyman in 1918 and Joseph F. Merrill in 1931, also contributed to the burgeoning volume of Church instructional materials needed by the correlation committees to fill the intellectual and spiritual needs of a rapidly expanding and ever more sophisticated Church membership. All of these men were contemporaries of Elder McKay, being a few years older or younger than he. And all of them, in a sense, were his disciples in the movement toward excellence in gospel scholarship, a movement of which he was the catalyst.

The classroom was the forum in which this excellence

was pursued. Unlike the pulpit, the classroom allows for an interchange between the teacher and the pupils and for the resulting cross-fertilization of ideas, which frequently produces results that neither the teacher nor the pupils intend or foresee. This was the forum in which the training and skills of Elder David O. McKay showed to the best advantage. Here he was in his element, interacting with a small handful of students on a personal level in an environment ideally suited to the teaching of concepts and the analysis of facts. David O. McKay felt comfortable and confident in this setting. And he doubtless would have been content to confine his teaching efforts to the classroom. But the calling to which he had been summoned, while enabling him to disseminate his teaching techniques throughout the Church, had placed him in a position where he rarely was able to apply them in the forum for which they were designed—the classroom. His elevation to the apostleship had introduced him to a new forum for teaching and motivation, the Salt Lake Tabernacle, whose cavernous interior with its high, vaulted ceiling; the seemingly endless rows of hard wooden benches; and the mammoth organ hovering over the pulpit and choir seats has brought apprehension and uncertainty to many seasoned speakers. And when the Tabernacle's benches are crowded with people, expectantly waiting to hear words of wisdom and inspiration, the pressure on a speaker can rise to levels of almost unbearable intensity.

Because he and the other two new members of the Twelve were sustained at the very end of the April 1906 general conference, Elder David O. McKay had six months in which to prepare for his maiden effort at the Tabernacle pulpit. Although he had prepared carefully for the occasion, he was anxious about it and not a little nervous: "Along with the enjoyment of the spirit of this conference," he said in his talk, "my soul has had a struggle with a feeling of dread of this moment, and if I am not able to make you hear . . . it is because a great deal of my energy has been expended in suspense." He then made a plea to the audience that would be repeated many times in many places over the years: "I pray for your sympathy, and for your faith and prayers, that the words which I utter may conform to the spirit of this conference." (CR, October 1906, p. 111.)

The young apostle proceeded to develop the theme that all members of the Church jointly share the responsibility for its strength and progress, using D&C 107:99 as his text. Here he emphasized the responsibility of each member to learn his duty and, having learned it, to act in the office to which he is called with all diligence. As to learning, he admonished his listeners that "reason alone is not a sufficient guide in searching for truth" and that "there is another, higher, more sure guide than reason." This superior guide, he said, is the guide of faith, "that principle which draws our spirit into communion with the Higher Spirit which will bring all things to our remembrance, show us things to come, and teach us all things." (Ibid., p. 113.)

As to the duty one has to act in his designated office, he pointed to the anomaly that while everyone is important and needed, no one is indispensable: "There is no man so important who cannot sink without making even a bubble, not a ripple in the great ocean of life; at the same time his importance is so great that his actions go a long way towards establishing the power, the dignity, the advancement of God's kingdom on earth." (Ibid., p. 115.) He cited examples of how individual members, living ordinary lives out of the spotlight, can add strength and solidity to the Church through their honesty, integrity, and loyalty.

Appropriately, the young apostle had commenced his career at the Tabernacle pulpit by emphasizing the first principle of the gospel: faith. And faith, he assured the audience, would lead to the discovery of boundless spiritual wealth, making available to all who possess it a vast store of knowledge, past, present, and future. Although the listeners had heard this theme developed numerous times in the past, in the hands of David O. McKay it took on a new aspect. What differentiated it on this occasion was the extensive use by the speaker of quotations from secular poets and writers, these being used judiciously to buttress a point or to elaborate an idea. While other Tabernacle speakers had used this same device, they had not done so to the same extent as Elder McKay nor with the same discrimination and telling effect. So, he amplified the role of faith in our lives with this quotation from the seventeenth-century English poet John Dryden: "Dim as the borrowed rays of moon and stars to lonely, weary, travelers, is reason to the soul; and as on high those rolling fires discover but the sky, not light us here, so reason's glimmering ray was lent, not to assure our doubtful way, but guide us upward to a better day."

Thereafter, through his long apostolic career, David O. McKay, betraying his professional training and bias, shared with the Saints a rich store of classic literature, quotations chosen with care and perception. It was the rule rather than the exception that he would quote one or more of his favorite authors to drive home a point. And occasionally, as he did at the October 1908 general conference, he treated an audience to a wide variety of literary offerings and allusions. He quoted from or referred to Shakespeare, Burns, Tennyson, Carlyle, and Farrer as he pleaded for the development of true manhood and womanhood and as he admonished the Saints to take a stand against vile literature. (CR, October 1908, pp. 108-13.)

The perceptiveness of the excerpts he quoted reveals a vast knowledge of English literature, a knowledge he fed by the constant reading of good books, stocking his mind with ideas, images, and elegant phraseology. These were the materials he frequently used in crafting the sermons he delivered in the Salt Lake Tabernacle and elsewhere.

However, Elder McKay did not always dwell on broad, theological themes in his Tabernacle offerings. He often spoke out with vigor against evils that beset the Church and community. So at the October 1908 general conference, where he censured vile literature, he also condemned the widespread saloon traffic and those who violated the Sabbath. Alluding to a resolution adopted a week before favoring prohibitory laws against these practices, the speaker called on the members to take action in order to give meaning to their vote: "It was easy to say 'yes' to the resolution," he told the audience. "But what is wanted now are men, true men, who cannot be bought or sold, who scorn to violate truth. . . . That 'yes' the other day merely meant this: We have buckled on the armor; we have unsheathed the swords. . . . Let us be true today; let us act; let us act." (Ibid., p. 110.)

And he was quick to defend the Church against unfair attacks. In a talk delivered at the April 1912 general conference, he referred to widespread criticisms being leveled at the Church: "The power of the pulpit has been arrayed against us. Following that, the power of the press. Has there ever been, in the history of the church, such a widespread attack, from the standpoint of the press, as there has been within the last few months?" (CR, April 1912, p. 53.) He also referred to a scandalous film that had been showing in London, "A Victim of the Mormons," and to scurrilous charges made against the Church at a recent meeting of the Evangelical Alliance of Greater Boston.

In view of the observable strengths and virtues of the Latter-day Saints in terms of education and their social and spiritual qualities, the speaker was at a loss to understand the reason for these vicious assaults: "Why do they think that we are not true Christians, that we are not loyal citizens, that we are not true men and virtuous women? . . . We can exclaim with the Prophet Joseph Smith 'Why persecute us for telling the truth?'"

Elder McKay concluded that the reason for these persecutions could be laid at the door of either ignorance or "malicious vindictive men who try to make capital out of the unpopularity of Mormonism." (Ibid.)

Not content merely to identify the problem and to indicate the sources from which it grew, he suggested a solution or antidote: "God help us to go forth from this conference imbued with the spirit of the Lord . . . determined to live a life of virtue and purity that will command the strength of the world and the admiration of it. In short, let us provide things honest in the sight of men. . . . Then will the church stand as a light to the world. That is her destiny; and though enemies may hurl their shafts to destroy, they will fail just as the beetles and the moths fail to obliterate the electric light in the street." (Ibid., p. 57.)

During the long years that he addressed the Saints from the Tabernacle pulpit, David O. McKay treated every major principle of the gospel, considered practically every aspect of the Church's organization and procedure, and analyzed and commented on the roles of the Church and its individual members in a changing world. He also defined the conditions for spiritual growth and material prosperity, elaborated the earthly and eternal blessings that derive from obedience to gospel principles, and admonished the Saints about marital fidelity and domestic accord. He encouraged the disheartened, chided the arrogant, and instructed the ignorant. And yet, after decades of mounting the stand and addressing the Saints from the Tabernacle pulpit, he never lost the sense of nervousness and apprehension that gripped him when he delivered his first sermon there in October 1906. Not long before he became the president of the Church, after more than forty years of apostolic service, he made this confession before a Tabernacle audience: "It is always more or less an ordeal for me to face an audience, and particularly a congregation in this historic Tabernacle. I've been in hopes for years that I would outgrow that feeling, but I still think, study, and pray in anticipation; I tremble as I stand before you with the sense of inadequacy to give a timely message as it should be given; and after it's over, worrying in self-reproachment for having failed to do justice to the cause. . . . So I ask for your sympathy, your help this morning. I particularly pray for guidance of the Holy Spirit." (CR, September–October 1949, p. 116-17.)

This confession comes as a surprise to those who heard

President McKay speak or who now see filmed replays of his addresses. His appearance and demeanor convey no hint of the agitation and uncertainty that apparently churned beneath the calm and assured image projected to an audience. And it is even more surprising that the inner sense of oratorical inadequacy followed him from the Tabernacle to hundreds of other pulpits he occupied in wards and stakes throughout the Church. There, with smaller audiences, one would have thought he would have been free from the turmoil that gripped him in the Tabernacle. It was not so. At stake or Sunday School conferences held in such diverse places as Alberta, Canada; Woodruff, Utah; Snowflake, Arizona; Paris, Idaho; Big Horn, Wyoming; St. Johns and St. Joseph, Arizona; or Manti and Meadow, Utah; he was afflicted with the same sense of inner anguish. And the task was worsened when local brethren failed to make adequate preparations or where transportation arrangements were slow or housing inadequate. So on January 2, 1908, when Elder McKay arrived at Malad, Idaho, for a stake meeting, he found the door to the chapel locked and no one in attendance. "They came later," he noted philosophically. And on November 12, 1914, he and Elder Joseph McMurrin drove forty-four and a half bumpy miles in a Maxwell to Meadow, Utah, arriving just in time to begin a meeting. And on May 13, 1915, he traveled through deep mud in an open wagon to meet a speaking assignment at Burrville, Utah.

Week after week he traveled to nearby or remote areas, sometimes under stressful conditions, preaching the gospel, setting the affairs of the Church in order, and counseling and motivating both leaders and members. The only things that interrupted the rhythmic flow of this nomadic routine were illness, emergencies, and an occasional vacation. On March 5, 1914, a stake conference in Morgan, Utah, was canceled because of a small-pox epidemic. Two weeks later, his companion assigned to attend the Carbon Stake conference in Price, Utah, Rulon S. Wells of the First Council of Seventy, was quarantined with his family and was therefore unable to accompany him. And on September 24, 1916, he missed the pleasure of having another of the Seventy join him on an assignment to Richfield, Utah, when Elder J. Golden Kimball caught the wrong train and ended up in Bingham Canyon.

Intermixed with his speaking assignments at various Church meetings were appointments to address civic and other groups not connected with the Church. On March 7, 1916, for instance, he spoke at the funeral of Joseph Strang, a prominent Jew in Ogden, Utah. Two months later he was invited to speak at the funeral of another prominent non-member in Ogden, William Glassman. Because of illness, however, Elder McKay was unable to attend; but he dictated an address that was read at the services conducted by a Presbyterian minister. While the apostle ordinarily accepted invitations to speak to nonmember groups, he sometimes declined, as in the case of a noted revivalist, Dr. Mills, who on the day of the Joseph Strang funeral invited Elder McKay and the Saints to participate in a revival meeting scheduled in Ogden. He declined the invitation but wished the doctor well.

When the United States entered World War I on April 6, 1917, Elder McKay's life and routine underwent a radical change. On that same day, the Eighty-Seventh Annual Conference of the Church convened in the Salt Lake Tabernacle. And the following day, April 7, he was the first speaker at the afternoon session. "As I came to the conference this afternoon," he began, "one of the presidents of stakes accosted me saying: 'Well, are your nerves shattered because of the war?' I answered 'no, not because of the war, but they are pretty well unstrung at the thought of having to speak this afternoon,' and that is a fact." (CR, April 1917, p. 46.) After making his customary plea for divine guidance and that the Lord would remove his "feelings of timidity" he launched into a thoughtful sermon that reconciled the supposed inconsistency between a world torn by war and the concept of an omnipotent, loving God. Why would our Heavenly Parent allow the devastation and death wrought by war? Elder McKay's understanding of Mormon theology made the answer easy: "I do not believe that God has caused the misery, the famine, the pestilence, and the death that are now sweeping the war-torn countries of Europe," he told the Tabernacle audience. "He has placed man upon the earth . . . 'that he might be an agent unto himself.' Men may choose the right or they may choose the wrong; they may walk in darkness or they may walk in light . . . but the Lord does not take from them their free agency." (Ibid.) Therefore, he concluded, the chaos in which the world found itself was not God's doing or responsibility but was "an inevitable result of disobedience to God's laws."

Two weeks after delivering this sermon, Elder McKay was one of a delegation appointed by the mayor of Ogden to wait on the governor to help devise ways to mobilize the local food supply in the interest of the war effort. And soon after, he became heavily involved in the campaign to sell Liberty Bonds to help finance the war. When attending a citizens' meeting in Ogden several months later when the sale of bonds was being promoted, he reported that the Church had recently subscribed to an additional $250,000 in bonds, whereupon the chairman of the meeting, a Catholic, said, "Three cheers for the Mormon Church."

And he also was active in counseling and recognizing young men as they planned to depart for the army. On September 7, 1917, the day before his forty-fourth birthday, Elder McKay went to Huntsville to attend a reception honoring twenty-nine young men from the upper valley who were leaving for military service. It was a proud day and a sad day. The apostle was pleased with the alacrity with which these young men had heeded the call of their country and he was sad because of the dangers they faced and the loneliness that would be felt by those left behind, not to mention the gaping hole in the community's work force to be created by their departure.

Elder McKay had special empathy for the families of these volunteers because his younger brother, Morgan, had already entered the service and was training at an aviation camp near San Antonio, Texas. Morgan returned home in mid-November on a short leave, during which David O. spent considerable time "arranging" his brother's affairs. Then in March of the following year, the elder brother made a special trip to Virginia to visit Morgan before his departure for France. While in the East, Elder McKay stopped in Washington when he was given a pessimistic assessment of the conflict by Utah's Senators, Reed Smoot and William King, who believed the war would last from three to five years, a prospect that was depressing to the entire McKay family.

The apparent reason why David O. gave so much special attention to his young brother during this period was the death of their father on November 9, 1917. Elder McKay learned late on the eighth that his father lay gravely ill in the Dee Hospital in Ogden with what his brother-in-law, Dr. Joseph R. Morrell, had diagnosed as a "strangulated bowel." Arriving in Ogden early the next morning, he went directly to the hospital. "Well, my boy," said the family patriarch on seeing his apostle son, "my time has come." Remonstrating with him, David O. told his father he would be much better after an operation and able to finish his temple work. The father, who had earlier told other members of the family he did not want them to "hold" him as he had "held" their mother, responded, "I don't like the idea of an operation." But he finally agreed to it and was operated on soon after. On coming out of the anesthetic, he talked animatedly with his doctors and family members and remained "clear in his mind" up to twenty minutes before his death, which occurred later that day. His oldest son and namesake reported that the family patriarch "died without a struggle."

With the passing of this durable man, upon whom so many had relied for so long, the reins of leadership of the extended McKay family passed to David Oman McKay, who, in addition to being the eldest son was also the eldest living child. Thereafter, all family matters involving the progeny of David and Jennette Evans McKay ultimately came to his attention for scrutiny and, if necessary, for final decision. This was a role to which he naturally succeeded, not only as an incident of his primal birth, but also because of his eminence in the high councils of the Church and his innate qualities of leadership. But he wore the mantle easily and without pretence. Indeed, it is doubtful that any of the members of the family were conscious of any hierarchical ladder in their councils and deliberations, the role of David O. as the existing earthly head of the clan being assumed and accepted as one might acknowledge, without reflection or comment, the gravitational forces that keep the planets in orderly orbit.

The onset of America's involvement in the great war was followed by an outbreak of influenza, which began in the early part of 1918 and which by the end of the year had billowed into an angry and ominous storm. In mid-January, Elder McKay was afflicted with a mild case of the flu, which he identified as the "grippe." However, it was nothing serious, nothing akin to the virulent disease that later became a deadly epidemic, which, among many others, carried President Joseph F. Smith to his grave.

The number of deaths caused by the war and by the rapidly spreading flu epidemic accelerated during 1918. As summer geared down, the reports of casualties of American soldiers in Europe and elsewhere increased in frequency, as did memorial services held in their honor. Elder McKay was frequently asked to participate on these occasions. So on his forty-fifth birthday, September 8, 1918, he reported speaking at a funeral in Layton, Utah, in honor of William H. Layton, who had been killed in France. Sharing the pulpit with Elder McKay was Utah's first non-Mormon governor, Simon Bamberger, who had been drawn to Layton by the prominence of the young man's family. And not long after, Elder McKay spoke in the Ogden Tabernacle at the funeral of Leland Brewer, a young man who had been killed in an army training camp.

By this time, the prevalence and virulence of the flu had

caused health officials to warn against attendance at public gatherings. And by the end of October, this warning had evolved into an outright ban as the incidence of the disease increased alarmingly and as the resulting deaths multiplied. On the last day of October, Elder McKay reported that during the previous week he had repeatedly been called to the bedside of those afflicted with influenza to bless them, and that he had conducted at least one funeral each day, all of them being held in the open air at graveside. He also noted that members of his family had been gravely ill for several weeks but that they had all recovered without complications.

The last day of October also marked the occasion when President Joseph F. Smith's remarkable vision of the redemption of the dead was read to and approved by the First Presidency and the Quorum of the Twelve. In less than a month thereafter, President Smith, the sixth president of this dispensation, died unexpectedly from the influenza. Like so many who shared his fate, he was buried quietly at graveside services, where his family, his brethren in the ministry, and a few close friends bid him farewell. His passing marked the end of the leaders of the Church who had personally known the Prophet Joseph Smith. It was the beginning of a new era that would see the Church emerge as an international organization of vast influence and strength.

Two of those who mourned at President Smith's graveside would play key roles in the internationalization of the Church—Heber J. Grant, who succeeded President Smith, and David O. McKay, who would be elevated to the prophetic office six years after President Grant's death. These two would lead the Church for forty-six years, the former for twenty-seven of them, during which its financial base would be broadened and strengthened, and the latter for the remaining nineteen years, during which its stakes would be firmly planted in New Zealand, Australia, England, Germany, Switzerland, Hawaii, Western Samoa, Argentina, Guatemala, Uruguay, Tonga, Brazil, and

The general superintendency of the Deseret Sunday School Union, 1919. Left to right: *Stephen L Richards, first assistant; David O. McKay, general superintendent; George D. Pyper, second assistant.*

American Samoa. Moreover, they would serve longer in the apostleship than anyone to the date of this writing (1985), President Grant serving for sixty-two years and seven months, and President McKay for sixty-three years and nine months. Against this background, it is interesting that eight days after President Smith's funeral and a week after President Grant was sustained as the president of the Church, the new leader and Elder David O. McKay and their wives went to Santa Monica, California, where they spent three weeks together. While no record exists of the discussions that took place during this interval, one may infer that the leadership of the Sunday Schools was considered, as within a week after their return to Utah and two days after Christmas, President Grant set Elder McKay apart as the general superintendent of the Sunday Schools in all the world. And on April 3, 1919, he was appointed Church commissioner of education. Elder McKay selected Stephen L Richards as his first counselor in both organizations and Richard R. Lyman as his second counselor in the commissioner's office. And three and a half months later, the commissioner and his counselors appointed thirty-three year old Adam S. Bennion as the superintendent of Church schools. This promising young educator would be called to the apostleship thirty-four years later by the president of the Church, David O. McKay.

In these early associations are seen the seeds of distant events that had a powerful impact on the Church and upon the individuals involved. Time and circumstances bring about unexpected, unforeseen, results, some interesting and inspirational, others traumatic and tragic. It is an inestimable blessing that providence shields from our view a too detailed foreknowledge of future events.

With the end of the war in Europe and the exhaustion of the worldwide influenza epidemic, things began to return to normal. As he had done when the United States was preparing for the war, Elder McKay became involved in various ceremonial events as American troops returned to their homes. So on January 17, 1919, he welcomed the 145th Field Artillery as it passed through Ogden en route to Logan, where it was to be demobilized.

In the war's aftermath, an avid interest in national and international political issues revived. An issue of paramount importance was whether the United States Senate should ratify the Treaty of Versailles, which included a provision to create the League of Nations. President Woodrow Wilson, who had led the U.S. delegation in the talks at Versailles, and who was one of the chief exponents of the league, encountered stiff opposition to ratifying the treaty from the Republican-controlled Senate Foreign Relations Committee, chaired by Senator Henry Cabot Lodge. In an effort to stir up broad popular support for the treaty and the league, President Wilson undertook an ambitious speaking campaign, traveling by train across the country. His message seemed to take root more readily in the western United States than in the East. It was in this area, therefore, during the waning days of the summer of 1919, that the president concentrated his efforts, knowing well that a senatorial vote from an arid, sparsely settled western state was as potent as one from the more populous states in the

East. In an attempt to blunt these efforts, those who opposed ratification of the treaty in its original form mounted
a counterattack, using articulate speakers to present the
opposition view. Under these circumstances, J. Reuben
Clark Jr., skilled in international law and a rising luminary
in Washington's diplomatic firmament, gave a lecture in
the Salt Lake Tabernacle on September 2, 1919. The main
target of the lecturer, who had celebrated his forty-eighth
birthday the day before, was the League of Nations. On the
stand at the Tabernacle was the speaker's longtime friend
from their University of Utah days, Elder David O. McKay,
who offered the invocation. Nine days later, Elder McKay
attended another of J. Reuben Clark's lectures on the
league, this one in the Ogden Tabernacle. These talks,
which echoed the counsel of the Founding Fathers to avoid
entangling alliances with European nations, coincided
with the mainstream of Mormon thought at the time. Yet
the political implications and overtones arising from the
use of Church buildings to air these views in the midst of
President Wilson's aggressive campaign for ratification
were troubling to the Church leaders. So on September 20,
1919, on the recommendation of Elder McKay, it was decided that the Tabernacle (and, inferentially, other Church
buildings) could no longer be used for such presentations.

Five days after this action of the Brethren, President
Wilson was overcome with exhaustion in Colorado after
having delivered thirty-four major addresses and many
rear platform talks and after having participated in numerous press interviews and parades during his whistle-stop
crusade. A week later the president's weariness proved to
be the forerunner of a thrombosis that partially paralyzed
the left side of his body. The surprise ending to this drama,
which indirectly affected Elder McKay and, more directly,
his future counselor, J. Reuben Clark, Jr., came when the
ratifying action was defeated through the influence of President Wilson, who ultimately opposed it because of unacceptable changes that had been made in the document by
the Senate.

This episode, involving issues of international scope in the secular world, was the prelude to a global drama affecting the Church that would feature Elder David O. McKay of the Twelve, with Hugh J. Cannon, editor of the *Improvement Era*, in a supporting role. The curtain rose in the autumn of 1920 when President Heber J. Grant assigned Elder McKay to travel around the world in the interests of the Church. His instruction was to observe the operation of the Church in remote areas while strengthening and motivating members and leaders alike; to study the administration of the Church school system in the Pacific; and, if he felt inspired to do so, to dedicate the formidable land of China for the preaching of the gospel. Implicit in the assignment was the duty to enhance the image of the Church in the eyes of government officials and the public generally and to be alert to ways in which the work could be advanced in the countries he would visit. In retrospect, this assignment also appears to have been part of a "hidden agenda" that neither President Grant nor Elder McKay perceived at the time as the tour formed the basis of important initiatives to be taken by David O. McKay when he became the president of the Church more than three decades later.

It is a truism that there is never an ideal time to undertake an important assignment or project, never a day when everything is in harmonious, plumb-perfect order so that a difficult task can be undertaken with calmness, assurance, and certainty that nothing important has been left undone. So in this instance, Elder McKay's call did not come at a time when all aspects of his life had coalesced into a perfectly ordered system. In fact, it came at a time of great stress and considerable confusion. In the first week of September, Sister McKay gave birth to a son, Robert, bringing to six the number of the living children of the McKays. The eldest of these, David Lawrence, soon after received a call to serve in the Swiss Mission. His farewell was held in the Ogden Fourth Ward on Sunday, October 15, 1920. There was an unusual bustle in the McKay household as the final arrangements were made to see Lawrence on his way. And immediately thereafter, the main focus of the family was to help prepare Elder McKay for his world tour. These preparations were interspersed with various family and social activities—the blessing, for example, of the McKay's baby boy, Robert, three weeks after Lawrence's farewell; and a dinner party held in the Hotel Utah on November 3 in honor of the two world travelers.

By the first week in December, all was in readiness for the departure. On the second, the companions met with the First Presidency and the Quorum of the Twelve in the upper room of the temple. There Elder David O. McKay was set apart by President Heber J. Grant, and Hugh J. Cannon was set apart by President Anthon H. Lund, first counselor in the First Presidency. Special blessings of health, protection, and inspiration were conferred upon the apostle; and his companion received an unusual promise from President Lund, fulfilled to the letter, of freedom from seasickness, an ailment with which he had been grievously afflicted in the past. However, he was unable to thank the counselor for this blessing during life as President Lund passed away March 2, 1921, exactly three months after the blessing and setting apart.

Chapter Seven

The World Traveler

The travelers decided to follow the sun. So, they made their way by train from Salt Lake City to Vancouver, B.C., from where they embarked for Yokohama on December 7, 1920, in the *Empress of Japan*. The pair soon discovered not only that their relationship was characterized by mutual admiration and respect, but also that they liked each other. "His selection was a happy one," Elder Cannon wrote of the apostle. "He was admirably suited for the important work, and it may be stated at the outset that he measured up to every expectation." After commenting on Elder McKay's genial disposition and outgoing ways, he added, "It was discovered that his personality is built largely upon the fact that he is so tremendously and righteously human. Anything other than perfect frankness is abhorrent to his honest soul." (Unpublished ms. of world tour, Church Archives, ch. 1, p. 4.)

Given the length and the arduous nature of their trip, it is fortunate that the relationship between the two men was seasoned with an undercurrent of wry and sometimes self-deprecating humor. This aspect of their relationship first surfaced during the voyage to Yokohama. Elder Cannon, almost jubilant over his own freedom from seasickness, wrote of his companion, tongue-in-cheek: "Brother McKay, being the leader of this tour, maintained his supremacy in the matter of sea-sickness as in all other things. He does nothing by halves, but treats every subject exhaustively, going to the very bottom of it, and this occasion was no exception. Sea-sickness is undertaken with the same vigorous energy which he displays in running for a train." (Ibid., ch. 2, p. 13.)

As for David O., he wrote of this voyage in a letter to Stephen L Richards and others. After telling of the heavy gales at sea and of how the contents of his "digestive organs joined in unison with nerve and muscle," he said he knew from his experience in crossing the Atlantic that he "had better dress carefully and get up on deck." At that moment of extremity, it was inopportune if not a little annoying that "Brother Cannon jumped out of bed as bright and pert as a ten-year-old boy. He could steady himself as though he were anchored. With no apparent difficulty, he dressed himself, and even shaved—an operation which, though ordinarily simple enough, seemed to me under the circumstances, almost marvelous." The final indignity came when Hugh J., dressed, shaved, and ready for breakfast, said to his bilious companion, "If you aren't feeling well, I suggest that you don't look in the mirror." (Ibid., p. 4.)

A winter crossing of the northern Pacific is a tempestuous and gloomy affair. So when the *Empress* sailed beyond the sight of friendly Vancouver, it was as if a dark and forbidding blanket had enveloped the ship, shielding it from everything except the gales, which blew incessantly; the mountainous waves, which loomed up in endless ranks; and the continual rolling, creaking, and groaning of the ship. As the voyage progressed, with no change in the weather, a morose and edgy mood settled upon the passengers and crew alike, which did not lift until the morning of December 22 when the ship dropped anchor just outside the breakwater of Yokohama Harbor. The sun, rising in a clear sky, illuminated a placid sea, dotted with the white sails of a fishing fleet gliding seaward for the daily catch. Across the harbor could be seen a pleasant landscape that imparted a sense of spring, not winter; and beyond, a hundred miles inland, loomed majestic Mount Fuji, which the Japanese had invested with certain sacred and mystic qualities.

Ashore, the travelers were met by the Japanese Mission president, Joseph M. Stimpson, another of that vast army who willingly wear out their lives in God's service without notoriety or acclaim. President Stimpson and his wife had served for eleven years in this remote land. With them in their comfortable Tokyo home were three children, the eldest of whom spoke English and Japanese with equal fluency.

At this time, there were only 125 members of the Church in Japan, the meager harvest of almost twenty years of diligent missionary work. Most of these were members of small branches in Tokyo, Osaka, and Kofu, all of which were visited by the delegation from Salt Lake City. There were a few members in Hokkaido whom the apostle also intended to visit but did not because of a strong impression he felt to turn back after being ferried to the interisland steamer on a tug.

Elder McKay also made courtesy calls on Dr. Kamada, the president of the Kaio University in Tokyo, and on Mr. Konoto, the immigration commissioner of Japan. The last call was made at the commissioner's home, where the apostle was first exposed to the charming customs and courtesies of Japanese society. The maid who answered the door dropped to her knees on seeing him and slowly bowed until her head touched the floor. Again, when the maid brought refreshments, she dropped to her knees to serve them. And the demeanor and attitude of the host were characterized by a habitual courtesy and outward deference, marked by gracious bows and nods and engaging smiles. As usually happens when foreigners are first exposed to this oriental courtesy, Elder McKay and his companion soon found themselves reciprocating their host's hospitality with unaccustomed bowings and noddings of their own.

Aside from the usual public meetings held with the members of the Church and meetings or conferences held with local civic leaders, Elder McKay spent much of his time in Japan counseling with and instructing President Stimpson and his small corps of missionaries. A memorable meeting was held in Tokyo with the entire mission staff, which included, in addition to President and Sister Stimpson, Elder Howard Jensen, the mission secretary; Elders Bodily and Whitaker from Hokkaido; Elders Owen McGary and John Hicken from Osaka; and Elders Pyne and Holley from Kofu. One can imagine the exciting if not intimidating effect upon these young missionaries, laboring so far away from home, of meeting in an intimate setting with an apostle of the Lord and his distinguished companion. There can be little doubt that it formed the basis of enraptured journal entries and oft-repeated stories and reminiscences shared with family and friends in years afterward. But whatever may be our speculations about the impact the visitors had on the missionaries, we are left without doubt as to the effect the latter had upon Elders McKay and Cannon: "To think of these young and inexperienced missionaries and their earnest efforts . . . is to praise the Lord," wrote Elder Cannon. "One is reminded of other modest characters, now acknowledged heroes, the ancient prophets and apostles of the Bible and the early leaders of the Church." (Ibid., ch. 4, p. 8.)

Having completed their mission in Japan, the companions traveled from Tokyo via Osaka to Shimonoseki, from where they booked passage to Pusan, Korea. As their ship, the *Koma Maru,* angled northwesterly into the Korea Strait, the Salt Lake travelers were almost equidistant from Hiroshima and Nagasaki, the two Japanese cities that their country would devastate with atomic bombs almost a quarter of a century later.

"Landing in Pusan, Korea, the visitors felt they were in another world," wrote Brother Cannon, "and their hasty journey through that land to Mukden, Manchuria, accentuated the feeling." (Ibid., ch. 5, p. 1.) From Mukden, the missionaries traveled by rail into China proper, stopping first at Shanhaikuan, where they caught their first glimpse of the Great Wall of China and received their first impressions of that country's ancient civilization. Through the perspective of the intervening sixty-five years, with their wars, their political upheavals, and their economic and cultural revolutions, this appraisal of the three major oriental countries the travelers had visited is significant: "The transition from bright and colorful Japan," wrote Elder McKay's companion, "an aggressive and virile world power in the making, to somber and gloomy China . . . is less abrupt because the traveller passes en route through Korea, an intermediate country less cheerful than the one and less funereal than the other." (Ibid.)

During the long and tiring trip from Mukden to Peking, the status of China as a captive giant was dramatically brought home to the Utahns. The train depots along the route of travel were guarded by foreign troops, mostly Japanese. But at one station, they were surprised to find American troops in charge, one of whom was given a bear hug by Elder McKay, which pleased the young soldier "after his astonishment had subsided." (Ibid., p. 4.)

Upon arriving in China's capital city, swarming with rickshas and walkers, intermixed with an occasional automobile or small horsedrawn carriage, but entirely devoid of street cars or buses, the two Americans at last found a suitable hotel after receiving the runaround from a man who deliberately or ignorantly gave wrong instructions to the ricksha runner—whom Elder Cannon facetiously called the pull-man.

Elder McKay's first impression of Peking on the Saturday afternoon of his arrival was unquestionably negative. The swarms of mendicants, the noise, the bustle, and the hassle in finding his hotel seemed to augur against dedicating the land for preaching the gospel of peace. But he awoke Sunday morning, January 9, 1921, with a different feeling. Accompanied by Elder Cannon, the apostle, placing himself in the hands of the Lord, walked through narrow, crooked, and crowded streets "almost directly to the

106

walls of the 'Forbidden City.'" Entering the gate, the missionaries "walked past shrines, pagodas and temples fast falling to decay," encountering numerous people along the way until they reached a peaceful grove of cypress trees. Only two men were seen in the grove, and they soon left. "A hallowed and reverential feeling was upon [us]," wrote Elder Cannon. "It was one of those occasions which at rare intervals come to mortals when they are surrounded by a Presence so sacred that human words would be disturbing. The Brethren were very sure unseen holy beings were directing their footsteps." There in the heart of China's capital city, "unnoticed and undisturbed by the multitudes who were almost within a stone's throw of them, they supplicated the Lord . . . after which Brother McKay offered the dedicatory prayer." (Ibid., ch. 5, pp. 5, 6.)

Expressing gratitude for the many blessings conferred upon them and invoking the Spirit of the Lord to guide their way, the apostle prayed: "In this land there are millions who know not Thee nor Thy work, who are bound by the fetters of superstition and false doctrine, and who have never been given the opportunity even of hearing the true message of their Redeemer. Countless millions have died in ignorance of Thy plan of life and salvation. We feel deeply impressed with the realization that the time has come when the light of the glorious Gospel should begin to shine through the dense darkness that has enshrouded this nation for ages. (Ibid., pp. 7-8.)

After formally dedicating the land for the preaching of the gospel, the apostle offered a prayer and admonition that have served as the standard for those who, during the intervening years, have labored among the Chinese-speaking people in the Orient: "May the Elders and Sisters whom Thou shalt call to this land as missionaries have keen insight into the mental and spiritual state of the Chinese mind. Give them special power and ability to approach this people in such a manner as will make the proper appeal to them. We beseech Thee, O God, to reveal to Thy servants the best methods to adopt and the best plans to follow in establishing Thy work among this ancient, tradition-steeped people." (Ibid., p. 9.)

Today, over sixty years after the event, we have begun to see some of the fruits of proselyting in China that have appeared since Elder McKay turned the key, including the existence of a temple in the Orient erected principally for those of Chinese descent. But what we have seen to date is but a shadow of what has been predicted to emerge in the decades ahead.

With the dedication completed, Elder McKay's main purpose in China had been fulfilled. There remained only the perfunctory task of paying a courtesy call on the United States ambassador, Charles R. Crane, who spoke encouragingly of the positive role the Latter-day Saints could play in China, given their penchant for hard work and their phenomenal success in planting a thriving civilization in America's western desert.

Boarding a train in Peking, the missionaries traveled to Shanghai via Tientsin, the major seaport of North China. The last leg of this journey, which took thirty-two hours on a fast train, extended through part of the Shantung Province. It was here the famine that then raged in China was most severe. From the train windows, the travelers could see the blight and desolation etched on the land and reflected in the cavernous faces that looked at them pleadingly at stops along the way.

Chaos reigned in Shanghai, where they arrived near midnight to find that their hotel reservations had been canceled. Other guests who had suffered the same fate were seen dozing uncomfortably in chairs and on divans in the hotel lobby. It was learned later that a distinguished American doctor considered himself to be one of the more fortunate ones because he was able to stretch out on a billiard table. In these circumstances, Elder McKay and his companion felt even more highly favored to be bedded down on cots hurriedly set up in a drawing room, which they had to vacate early the next morning before the others were astir.

After two restless nights, one on a bumpy train and the other on lumpy cots, the Mormon elders enjoyed the luxury of a cabin aboard the *Tenyo Maru*, which was to take them to Kobe, Japan. After a smooth crossing of the East China Sea, the ship made an intermediate stop at Nagasaki, which was then the chief coal-loading station in the Far East. While a happy, hardworking crew of stevedores—which included men, women and children—hand loaded several tons of coal on the *Tenyo Maru*, the travelers went ashore to see the sights of Nagasaki. "It would be worth a trip across the Pacific to see this beautiful, land-locked harbor," wrote Elder Cannon, "with the green terraced slopes [and] the unique and picturesque houses lining the water and extending to the tops of the surrounding hills." (Ibid., ch. 6, pp. 6-7.)

Had the visitors known of the carnage a single missile from an American plane would inflict upon this peaceful port twenty-four years later—thirty-nine thousand killed and twenty-five thousand wounded—their perceptions of it and of the complexities and inconsistencies of human and international relations would have been radically altered. As it was, they reveled in the peace and beauty of the moment, as they reveled in the pleasant voyage to Kobe, which exposed them to the many mountainous islands of the inland Sea of Japan.

After traveling by train to Tokyo, where several days were spent arranging for the transfer of authority of the Japanese Mission from President Stimpson, who had been honorably released, to President Lloyd O. Ivie, Elder McKay and his companion departed from Yokohama on the *Tenyo Maru*. "It was a perfect bedlam," Elder Cannon wrote of the scene at the Yokohama pier. "The band was playing, porters were hurrying aboard with luggage, [and] mail wagons were forcing their way through crowds, bringing the last mail to the vessel." (Ibid., p. 11.)

David O. McKay

The scene that opened when the *Tenyo Maru* docked at Pearl Harbor, Oahu, Hawaii, provided a shocking contrast with the scenes of misery and want the travelers had witnessed in China. "This was truly a fairyland," exulted Elder Cannon. "Palms, ferns, flowers and luxuriant tropical foliage, all contribute their part toward making this a terrestrial paradise." (Ibid., ch. 7, p. 1.) After being welcomed by mission president E. Wesley Smith and a large group of smiling, singing Latter-day Saints, and after being bedecked with fragrant, ceremonial leis by Sister Kamohalii, the travelers, thankful to have solid ground under their feet after seemingly endless days on the Pacific, were taken immediately to the new and comfortable mission home in Honolulu, a home Elder McKay dedicated before leaving the islands. From there, after a short respite, the visitors set out upon a crowded, somewhat hectic schedule that included trips to several of the islands and numerous meetings held among the eleven thousand members of the Church then living in Hawaii.

The first item on Elder McKay's agenda was to visit the Church school at Laie, across the island of Oahu from Honolulu. Traveling by auto, the party drove over the Pali on a paved, serpentine road from which could be seen the magnificence of Pearl Harbor on one side and on the other a beautiful valley that was then almost completely blanketed with pineapple and sugarcane. Near the school the Church owned and operated a large plantation, which Elder McKay carefully inspected with the practiced eye of a farmer, born to the soil.

The apostle was pleased with what he found at the school. Its student body was comprised of young people, ages seven to fourteen, drawn from the rich mixture of nationalities that made up Hawaii's population—Americans, Chinese, Japanese, Filipinos, Portuguese, and, of course, Hawaiians and other Polynesians. The school was directed by Elder Cannon's cousin, acting principal William T. Cannon, Jr., who supervised a faculty of several sisters who had been called as missionaries: May S. Christen-

110

sen, Evelyn Olsen, Edythe L. Bell, Jane Jankins, Genevieve Hammond, and Elizabeth Hyde.

Near the school and the Church plantation was the Hawaii Temple, which President Heber J. Grant had dedicated in November 1919. The visiting apostle and his companion were shown through the temple and its beautiful grounds by temple president William M. Waddoups, who would later serve as president of the Hawaiian Mission. The visitors were amazed that although it was February 7, the middle of frigid winter in Salt Lake City, the delicious breakfast served by Sister Waddoups featured all the fresh strawberries they could eat. And around the home could be seen a profusion of banana trees heavily laden with their golden fruit.

While the temple president's wife set an extremely good table for the visitors, she was hard put to equal, and could not have hoped to excel, the culinary extravaganzas staged by the Polynesians during the tour of the islands. As if in disbelief of the sumptuous fare placed before them, Elder Cannon took the time to record the menu of a particularly memorable breakfast: It "consisted of beef, eggs, shrimps, several kinds of fish, various vegetables, fruits of all kinds, chicken, the characteristic Hawaiian poi, bread, French toast, green onions and pie." With such a meal to start the day, he expressed an inclination "to balk if asked to conjure up a dinner." (Ibid., ch. 7, pp. 5-6.)

This gracious and abundant hospitality was one way the Polynesian Saints expressed their love and appreciation for Elder McKay and his traveling companion and for the emissaries of the Church who had preceded them. Coincidentally, two of the elders of former times who ranked highest in the estimation of these island Saints were the fathers of Hugh J. Cannon and E. Wesley Smith—President George Q. Cannon and President Joseph F. Smith. The early work of these two prophets had been performed on Maui, and it was to this island that Elder McKay led the party after completing his work at Laie.

Driving to Pulehu after reaching Maui, Elder McKay

conducted a meeting in a small chapel located on a site where, tradition has it, 97 of 100 people who had come to hear George Q. Cannon and Brother Napela speak were converted amidst a refulgent spiritual outpouring. As the brethren joined in prayer at this historic place, they were infused with an extraordinary spiritual fire and fervor. "It was an occasion which none of them will ever forget," wrote Elder Cannon, "for they stood almost in the visible presence of celestial beings." (Ibid., p. 9.)

From Maui, Elder McKay sailed to Hawaii, the largest of the islands, where inspirational meetings were held with the Saints at Hilo. Here, also, the world travelers renewed acquaintances with old friends—and, in the case of Elder Cannon, relatives—Edwin K. Winder and his wife, Alma Cannon Winder, who were serving as missionaries. Brother Winder, the district president of the island, was the grandson of John R. Winder, a former counselor in the First Presidency, and his wife was a granddaughter of George Q. Cannon.

From Hilo, the party sailed to Kauai, considered by many to be "the real garden" of the Hawaiian Islands, and thence back to Oahu, where at Laie the apostle ended the formal tour with a highly spiritual testimony meeting.

The evening before they left the islands, the travelers were honored at a party and reception held at the mission home in Honolulu, where over four hundred people—both members and nonmembers—gathered to wish them bon voyage. The music for the evening was furnished by the internationally famed Royal Hawaiian Band, conducted by Major Kealahai, who came voluntarily with his musicians because of their admiration for the Church and because several of the members of the band were Latter-day Saints.

Many of the musicians were at dockside the next morning to serenade the departing visitors, who were again bedecked with leis, showered with gifts, and sent away with fond alohas by a large gathering of Saints. A fellow passenger, witnessing this unbelievable outpouring of love and affection, asked slyly, "Don't you fellows feel lonesome out in the world like this without any friends?" (Ibid., ch. 8, p. 9.)

The *Maui*, on which Elder McKay and his companion sailed from Oahu, was destined for San Francisco, where they were to remain only two days before embarking on another ship for the South Seas. On arriving in fogbound San Francisco, however, they discovered that their departure would be delayed because of a snafu in obtaining visas. And while they were waiting for this difficulty to be ironed out, word came that President Anthon H. Lund had passed away. So the travelers detoured to Salt Lake City for the funeral, leaving there a second time on March 26, 1921. A few days later found them on the *Marama* bound for Tahiti.

This leg of Elder McKay's planetary tour took twelve days, during which his ship crossed the equator. Hailed before King Neptune's Court for failure to observe the monarch's dress decree for the day—grubbies or a swimsuit—the offending apostle was merely ordered to appear at dinner with his hair parted in the middle instead of being ducked as were other offenders. By this means he was able to maintain some apostolic dignity and independence while entering into the frivolities of the day on his own terms, frivolities that were reminiscent of the pranks and palaver of the university fraternities with which he was familiar.

Tahiti, though similar to Hawaii in some ways, as in its volcanic origins, was very different in others. Here, for instance, French, not English, was the dominant language; the Church had only a scattering of members compared to the significant numbers in Hawaii; and, unlike Hawaii, transportation between the islands was occasional and highly erratic. It was this last item that prevented Elder McKay from even meeting the mission president, L. H. Kennard, during his stay at Papeete, the chief city of the Tahitian group. Three months before the apostle's arrival, President Kennard had traveled to one of the outer islands to check on the work, confident he would return long before the visitor's arrival. Such confidence, born of inexperience with the slow-paced life-style of Tahiti, proved to be grossly misplaced, as he returned long after Elder McKay's departure.

These circumstances made the apostle's visit to Tahiti very unsatisfactory but not entirely fruitless, since one of the charges given to him by the Prophet was to appraise conditions worldwide as a basis for action or for changing policy to improve or expedite the work.

After a brief stop at Raratonga in the Cook Islands, where the outcome was essentially the same as in Tahiti, Elder McKay and his companion sailed to New Zealand, landing at Wellington, on the south end of the north island. They were met by President George S. Taylor and several missionaries.

Here the visitors were introduced to the marvels of the Hui Tau, an annual celebration among members of the Church in New Zealand. The Hui Tau for 1921 was held near Huntly, a small community in the Waikato district where the Maoris predominated. There several large tents, comparable to those used by traveling circuses, had been set up to accommodate the members who came long distances to attend. One of the largest of the tents doubled as a meeting place and as an enormous sleeping room. Beds were made on the ground, each sleeper occupying a space of about four feet. Since the beds remained in place during the day and served as cushions during the services, Elder McKay observed: "For the convenience of those people who like to sleep in church, I recommend this combination scheme most highly." (Ibid., ch. 12, p. 3.)

The visitors also were introduced to the *hongi*, the customary Maori greeting, which resembles a kiss but involves the nose, not the lips; the vocal salutation *haere mai*, accompanied by vigorous gesticulations, jumping, dancing, and grimacing; and the *haka*, or war dance, which in its frenetic and gigantic gyrations makes the *haere mai* appear relatively sedate. Elder Cannon was "fascinated and yet worried" by all this "because surely some acknowledgment must be made of this most demonstrative welcome." (Ibid., p. 5.)

As the Hui Tau unfolded, the visitors were deeply impressed by the depth of the spirituality and commitment of the Maori Saints. "The glory of the 'Hui Tau,'" wrote Elder Cannon, "is seen and felt in the twelve or fourteen worshipping assemblies which culminated in a wonderfully inspirational Priesthood meeting." (Ibid., p. 9.)

After leaving Wellington, the travelers successively visited Suva in the Fiji Islands; Nukualofa, capital of the Tongan Islands; Neiafu of the Vavau group; Apia in the Samoan Islands; and Pago Pago. In each of these exotic and beautiful places, Elder McKay met with the missionaries and members, giving them words of instruction and encouragement. President Mark V. Coombs of the Tongan Mission came aboard at Nukualofa and accompanied the brethren to Samoa, where President Coombs had served a mission years before.

Joined by mission president John C. Adams, Elder McKay and his party held a series of highly spiritual meetings in Samoa. A large gathering of members and non-members, estimated at fifteen hundred, assembled on the spacious grounds of the mission home at Apia, where the visitors were formally welcomed by the mission president and by local civil authorities. In addition to smaller gatherings where the apostle was able to teach and inspire in a more intimate setting, he met with Church-school officials to review the status of the faculty, student body, and curriculum.

The crowning experience of the visit to Samoa was a series of meetings held in Sauniatu, a small village where, according to Elder Cannon, "The Spirit of the Lord was remarkably manifest." (Ibid., ch. 16, p. 4.) At the end of the visit, their departure was delayed for more than an hour while Elder McKay and his companion administered to the afflicted. As they departed amidst many tears and well wishes, Elder McKay felt impressed to return and to offer a prayer with them. "As he prayed for and blessed the multitude," wrote Elder Cannon, "one was unconsciously reminded of that touching farewell which the Savior took of the people, as recorded in the Book of Mormon, Third Nephi chapters 17 and 18." (Ibid., ch. 16, p. 6.) The Saints recorded the apostle's words as well as they could remember them, placing them in the cornerstone box of a monument that was later erected to commemorate the event.

Returning to New Zealand, Elder McKay held meetings at and around Auckland and inspected the Church college at Hastings. From there he and his companion proceeded to Australia, where, with mission president Don C. Rushton, he held meetings with the Saints and missionaries in Sydney, Melbourne, Adelaide, and Brisbane, as well as in Tasmania.

As the travelers prepared to leave Australia, there was concern whether they could obtain their visas from the British to enter India and Egypt and from the Dutch to enter Java in time to embark on their ship, the *Marella*. At Sydney, where the *Marella* was docked, they were "assured" by the British and Dutch officials that "the papers could not possibly be prepared in time." When this disheartening news was received, an inherent quality in Elder McKay's makeup surfaced, which Brother Cannon had observed frequently during the course of the tour, a quality that was a source of amazement to him: "Brother McKay's principle," wrote Hugh J., "is to go as far as he can, trusting in the Almighty to open the way further." Acting on that principle, the apostle left by train for Brisbane with President Rushton, instructing his companion to remain in Sydney until the paperwork was completed and to then come on the *Marella* to Brisbane, from where they would depart together for Java! Elder McKay's positive attitude and faith were rewarded when, in what to some was a miraculous result, the visas were issued on time so as to enable Brother Cannon to board the ship and to meet the apostle at Brisbane. "Herein lies an important lesson," wrote Hugh J., "which Brother McKay never failed to emphasize. Even though a stone wall appears to cross your path, go as far as you can, and you will usually find an opening through which you can pass." (Ibid., ch. 19, p. 8.) This quality in Elder McKay's character surfaced again and again throughout his long career. It accounts in large part for the success of many programs in which he was involved, including the Welfare Program, which, in its earlier years, was developed through the tenacity, the will, and the self-confidence of men like David O. McKay and those associated with him.

Leaving Brisbane, the *Marella* sailed to Java, where the companions met the last Latter-day Saint they were to see until they reached the Middle East. At Surabaja they were met by Frank W. Becraft of Ogden, one of Elder McKay's former students, who was employed in Java by the Krain Sugar Company.

After visiting Batavia in Java, the two Utahns sailed to Calcutta, India, via Singapore, on the tip of the Malayan peninsula, and Rangoon, Burma. Once in India, they embarked on a wearing train trip of over eight hundred miles through the northern provinces to Delhi. En route, they stopped in Agra, where they marveled at the Taj Mahal, "a Dream in Marble." And all along the way, they were struck by the poverty of the people, similar to though not quite as severe as the poverty in China. Men and women were seen plowing with forked sticks and irrigating their fields by hand with water dipped from the river in the manner of their ancestors centuries before. And it seemed strange to these Americans to see camels and some elephants intermixed with the customary domestic animals.

The reason for the long trip to the interior of India was to visit the few known Church members there, all of whom lived in the northern part of the country. On reaching Delhi, however, it was learned from letters awaiting them there that all of these members except John W. Currie of Srinigar had left the Church. And because of the long delay entailed in getting transportation to Srinigar, which was two hundred miles from the end of the railway at Rawal Pindi, any thought of visiting him was abandoned.

That decision having been made, Elder McKay and his companion undertook another lengthy, tiresome train trip, this one to Bombay, from which they sailed for Port Said on the Mediterranean. The only intermediate stop was at barren and forbidding Aden on the southern tip of Arabia.

Journeying by rail from Port Said to Cairo, Elder McKay and Hugh J. passed through Zagazig, reputed to be the place where the children of Israel were headquartered during their Egyptian captivity. This link to their own Israelitish ancestry aroused a keen interest in the travelers, which was greatly intensified when, in Cairo, they were shown the place where, presumably, the baby Moses was placed in the ark of bulrushes amidst the flags by the river's brink. While they might well have doubted that the event occurred at this precise location, as they were later to doubt the modern placement of ancient biblical sites in the Holy Land, visiting the spot brought to vivid reality many things related to their religious convictions that previously had existed only in the realm of speculative thought.

Early one morning before sunrise, the Utahns traveled by automobile the seven miles from Cairo to the pyramids of Gizeh along a road lined with acacia trees, passing on their way hundreds of donkeys and camels laden with fruits and vegetables destined for Cairo's markets. Mounting one of the pyramids, the pair was met with a sight few are favored to see—an Egyptian sunrise viewed from the apex of an ancient tomb: "Looking eastward," wrote Elder Cannon, "one gazes upon the fertile Nile Valley with its fields of corn, its majestic date palms, its vegetable gardens. In the distance the picturesque spires and minarets of Cairo glisten in the morning sun. To the north, west and south is the Libyan desert as barren and devoid of vegetation as the Sahara." (Ibid., ch. 22, pp. 4, 5.)

After viewing the Sphinx and after making a hurried visit to fabled Memphis, Elder McKay and his friend traveled by a fast train from Cairo to Kantara, where they crossed the Suez Canal on a pontoon bridge. They then boarded another modern train, complete with sleeping and dining cars, and within a few hours they were in Jerusalem.

Despite the cumulative, somewhat deadening effect of seeing some new city or thing almost every day over a period of several months, the travelers were genuinely impressed and excited by their visit to old Jerusalem. "No real Christian can approach it without being overwhelmed by feelings of deep reverence," wrote Elder Cannon. "David O. McKay, himself an Apostle and a special witness, and as sincere a believer in the divinity of Jesus Christ as any man who lives, was deeply moved." (Ibid., ch. 22, p. 7.)

What aroused such emotion was the realization that they were actually walking the streets the Savior had walked and seeing many of the things he had seen. It is true that the ornamentations—the altars, the crosses, and the gold and silver adornments—found at Calvary, the

Elder David O. McKay (right) and Elder Hugh J. Cannon riding on camels in front of the Sphinx during their world tour.

Holy Sepulcher, and other places of historic significance were out of keeping with the Jerusalem of Jesus' day, but these could not obscure the basic things the Savior would have seen—the narrow, crooked, and crowded streets; the white buildings; the dazzling sunlight; the sparse vegetation; and the white limestone hills surrounding the city.

Elder McKay and his companion visited most of the places that the scriptures and the accounts of Palestine have invested with an aura of unreality but that became fixed in their minds with precision and certainty: Bethlehem, the River Jordan, the Dead Sea, the Garden of Gethsemane, Mount Temptation, Bethany, Jericho, Elisha's Fountain, and Mount Moriah. Most impressive and memorable, however, was their visit to the Mount of Olives. Finding a quiet and secluded spot, the companions knelt to offer thanks and to implore the Lord for his blessings. "It was an impressive occasion," wrote Elder Cannon. "The veil separating the brethren from the presence of the Lord seemed very thin." (Ibid., ch. 23, p. 2.)

The fervent prayers offered on this occasion included a plea that "the Jews might be returned to the land of their fathers in fulfillment of ancient and modern prophecies." (Ibid.) Ironically, an incident that occurred while they were in Palestine illustrated some of the difficulties to be encountered in such a fulfillment. On November 2, 1921, while the brethren were in the Holy City, rioting broke out. So serious was it that all the shops in Jerusalem were closed and British soldiers, with armored trucks and machine guns, were called on to occupy the city. The difficulty arose from a declaration by Lord Balfour of England that Palestine should be occupied by the Jews. The instantaneous reaction of Moslem residents in the area foreshadowed the decades of conflict that would ensue over this volatile issue, which had its roots in the ancient enmity between Isaac and Ishmael and which is still very much alive.

Before Elder McKay left Salt Lake City the second time on his world tour, President Grant had asked him to meet a Church representative in Syria to help distribute money that had been raised to help destitute Armenian Saints. He had been advised while in Cairo that this representative was Joseph W. Booth, a former Syrian missionary. However, since Elder Booth had left the United States several months after Elder McKay and his companion had departed, and since they had not been in communication in the interim, it was not known exactly where he could be found. Therefore, it came as a surprise when a man approached the apostle at the Haifa train depot and greeted him with "Isn't this Brother McKay?"

The trio then traveled to Beirut by automobile along the shore of the scenic Mediterranean, passing en route the ancient coastal cities of Tyre and Sidon. From Beirut, they crossed the Lebanese mountains to Baalbek, marveling at the denuded hills where once had flourished a verdant forest from which Solomon had obtained some of the famous cedars of Lebanon for his temple. Proceeding thence to Aleppo, the three brethren made arrangements to go to Aintab, their destination, which was in the heart of an area frequently troubled by Turkish marauders. Confidence in their safety had not been bolstered by the statement of a British general who, on the voyage from Bombay to Port Said, had told Elder McKay, "Unless you are prepared to leave your head behind, you should not go to Aintab." (Ibid., ch. 23, p. 8.)

On the afternoon when the eighty-mile trip to Aintab was planned, all the baggage had been placed in the automobile when the apostle, on an impulse, felt impressed not to go. The next morning, however, everything appearing to be in order, the three brethren left Aleppo. The trip was uneventful, although along the way the skeletons of many burned automobiles were seen, stark reminders of the thieves who stalked the land. It was learned later that a company traveling the same road in carriages and wagons that same day was held up and robbed of all its valuables, including sixty horses.

It will never be known what possible dangers these brethren escaped or what other purpose was served by heeding the prompting Elder McKay received in Aleppo. But the apostle had been promised by President Grant in the blessing setting him apart that he would be able "to avoid dangers, seen and unseen." (Ibid., ch. 23, p. 8.) So repeatedly during the world tour, he had received and acted upon such promptings, confident that in doing so he and his companion would be blessed and protected from all spiritual and physical dangers.

At Aintab, the three brethren were received with enthusiasm, gratitude, and reverence. The Saints there had suffered extreme hardships and deprivations since World War I, and they looked upon the arrival of the apostle as a direct answer to their fervent prayers. After distributing the money to them that had been raised by a Church-wide fast, and after arranging for their removal from the danger zone to either Aleppo or Beirut, Elder McKay and Brother Cannon returned to Port Said, stopping en route at Damascus, one of the oldest inhabited cities of the world; at Nazareth, where the Savior lived during his early life; and at the Sea of Galilee, where some of the important events of the Lord's ministry occurred.

Boarding the *Ormando* at Port Said, the two brethren sailed to Naples; visited Rome; and traveled across Europe, the channel, and England, enjoying a reunion with old friends and associates at Liverpool, from where they embarked for the United States.

During a short stay in Lausanne, Switzerland, while traversing Europe, Elder McKay had a joyful reunion with his son Lawrence, who was laboring there as a missionary. "If no other reward were to come to [Lawrence] for his devotion to this work," wrote Elder Cannon, "he would be repaid in the pride and love written on his father's face as they sprung into each others arms." (Ibid., ch. 24, p. 7.)

Chapter Eight

The Mission President

L ittle did David O. McKay realize when he waved good-bye to Orson F. Whitney at the Liverpool dock-side that within a few months he would return there to replace him. The call from President Heber J. Grant to serve as the president of the European Mission came as a surprise to Elder McKay, especially in view of his recent return from the world tour. He was pleased to accept, however. Not the least of his pleasure derived from the fact his family would accompany him.

Elder and Sister McKay and their children Llewelyn (who had received his call to serve in the Swiss German Mission), Lou Jean, Emma Rae, Edward, and Robert left from the Ogden depot on November 8, 1922. Lawrence was still on his mission at the time. Traveling to Montreal, the McKay clan, whose size, according to its patriarch, aroused either envy or sympathy among fellow passengers, boarded their ship, the *Montcalm,* on November 17. The eight-day voyage to Liverpool convinced the entire family (except Llewelyn, who did not miss a meal) that their husband and father had not exaggerated in describing the traumas of seasickness. The worst hit was Emma Rae, who advised her mother after two days on the Atlantic that she had reconsidered and had decided not to go to England after all.

Things looked up for everyone when the *Montcalm*

docked at Liverpool's Mersey River pierhead. And they approached normalcy when the clan settled into their comfortable mission residence, Durham House, 295 Edge Lane. Here two-year-old Bobbie began to rule the roost as he had done in Ogden; and Mama Ray quickly brought order out of chaos as she gave the strange house those little touches that made the family feel at home.

As the new mission president assayed his duties, two things quickly became apparent. First, the task was greater than he had realized. It entailed serving as the president of the British Mission as well as supervising eight other large missions — Swiss-German, French, Swedish, Norwegian, Danish, Netherlands, Armenian, and South African—with the responsibility to train and motivate their leaders, missionaries, and members. Second, the work would have to be carried on in a climate of public ridicule and abuse. As if to steel him for the onslaught ahead, President McKay's predecessor had left a sheath of newspaper clippings in the mission president's desk, bearing such glaring headlines as "Mormon Missionaries Assaulted by Students in Edinburgh, Scotland"; "Latter-day Saints Wild Hyde Park Scene"; "Assassins Who Carry Out Orders of Utah Saints"; and "Women in Chains of Slavery." One of those in the forefront of the effort to demean and embarrass the Saints in England was a militant woman named Winifred Graham, who was wholly unrestrained in her virulent, anti-Mormon rhetoric. "Winifred Graham and her . . . associates have opened the flood gates of hell," Elder McKay wrote in a letter to the First Presidency, "and are deluging England with the vilest slander that impure minds can imagine." He expressed the hope that "the Lord would take her in hand" because he hated to fight a woman. (Letter of February 27, 1924, DOMP.)

The new mission president and his family also felt this opposition at a personal level when the father attempted to register Lou Jean and Emma Rae in the Liverpool College for Girls. There he was icily informed by the registrar that she had been instructed not to enroll any more children of the Latter-day Saints. "The bigotry of the people here," wrote David O. in one of his rare efforts at vituperation, "is quite in keeping with the dense fog that hangs like a pall over Liverpool." (Letter of December 15, 1922, DOMP.)

But the European Mission president had weapons with which to combat this opposition. First and most important was his faith in the mission of the Church and in the Savior whose personal witness he was. The inherent tenacity and forcefulness of his personality and character were useful weapons, as were the missionaries, two thousand strong, who were a constant source of amazement and strength to their president. He had also inherited the editorship of the eighty-year-old *Millennial Star*, the official organ of the Church in Great Britain, which gave him an effective voice with which to reach most of the members of the Church and an important segment of the public.

Using these and other available tools, David O. McKay promptly went to work with his accustomed vigor and dispatch. He attempted to mute the public outcry against the Church by directly challenging newspaper editors who printed false articles about the Mormons. Within three months of his arrival in Liverpool, he was pleased to see some favorable results from this strategy. "Regarding the work here, it is moving along slowly and encouragingly," Elder McKay wrote in a letter dated February 5, 1923, to his quorum president, Rudger Clawson. "Even the *Sunday Illustrated* that has been printing and re-hashing the Frank J. Cannon and Jarman stuff is leaving us alone." (DOMP.)

Elder McKay's media campaign was conducted hand in hand with his more traditional duties as a proselyting administrator and motivator. Soon after arriving in England, he commenced a heavy schedule of meetings that continued throughout his service as mission president. He toured all of the missions under his jurisdiction, except the South African Mission, in the course of which he held numerous conference gatherings that combined instructions to missionaries and preaching services. Occasionally he also held meetings of all the conference presidents within a particular mission where proselyting techniques and special problems or challenges were discussed. Assignments were made in advance to the conference presidents to discuss specific topics. The agenda for a meeting of conference presidents of the British Mission included, for instance, talks on "Time Wasting Tendencies among Elders," "How Best to Use Auxiliary Associations as Missionary Factors," "Difficulties of Conference Presidents and How to Overcome Them," and "The Conference President as an Exemplar." (Report of April 5, 1924, DOMP.) Another subject that the mission president raised repeatedly wherever he went was how to enroll members as missionaries. It was during this period that President McKay coined the phrase "Every member a missionary," which became a keystone of his administration as Church president and which expresses a proselyting philosophy that underlies missionary work even today. That this concept was adopted almost at the inception of his tenure as mission president is evident from the already-mentioned letter to President Clawson dated February 5, 1923: "We are making an effort," Elder McKay advised his quorum president, "to use the local priesthood and the church membership as a means of influencing non-members to investigate the truth. Our aim is to have every member a missionary, not in the sense of leaving their homes or work, but in the sense of opening the way for elders to get in the presence of men and women who honestly desire to know the truth."

And it was to these elders and sister missionaries that President McKay devoted most of his time and energy. He knew that the success of the proselyting effort rested squarely upon these men and women, most of whom were young and relatively inexperienced. In all, there were about two thousand missionaries who served in the European Mission during Elder McKay's tenure, and these were figuratively adopted by him into his family. He seems to have applied the Napoleonic theory of generalship, which holds that a small force is sufficient for the task if the leader "bivouacs" with his troops. So, the president endeavored to become well acquainted with the missionaries, learning and calling them by their first names and showing a genuine interest in each one.

Of the two thousand, there were some who later achieved special distinction. Some of those whose names will be recognized by many readers are Russell H. Blood, who later married President McKay's daughter Lou Jean and became a skilled physician and surgeon; Wilford G. Edling, incumbent chairman of the Church finance committee; McKinley Oswald, well-known athletic figure after whom a Salt Lake gymnasium has been named; Selvoy J. Boyer, who later presided over both the British Mission and the London Temple; and Ezra Taft Benson, who became a member of the U.S. Cabinet and who is now the president of the Church. Elder Benson served as the president of the Newcastle Conference in the British Mission, and at a conference meeting held October 14, 1923, President McKay wrote of his promising young associate: "President Benson bore strong testimony and said the only panacea for the world is the restored gospel."

Because of Elder McKay's long absence from home occasioned by the world tour and his service as mission president, it was decided to release him at the end of 1924. He was replaced by fellow apostle James E. Talmage, his former University of Utah president, who, in going to England, was returning to the land of his birth. The incoming mission president and his wife hosted the McKays at a farewell dinner in Durham House on November 4, 1924. The guests of honor were given a cabinet of silverware as a token of appreciation for their services in the mission field.

In reporting his mission to the Brethren, Elder McKay noted matter-of-factly that prejudice against the Church in Europe was still heavy. The good news, however, was that mobbings of the elders were much less frequent. He also made two substantive recommendations that were later implemented: first, that the operation of the presidency of the British and European missions be separated; and second, that the Swiss-German Mission be divided. He also urged that members of the Twelve make more frequent visits to the area, noting parenthetically that the stakes could get along quite well without visits from the Twelve, but that their strength and inspiration were sorely needed abroad.

Elder McKay mentioned another great need that he would be notably prominent in helping to fill when he became the president of the Church—the need for better buildings in Europe. During his service as a missionary and as mission president, the Saints in Europe were, for the most part, housed in deplorable buildings, usually rented and often wholly unsuitable as places of worship. It was not uncommon for the members to have to sweep away the debris left by thoughtless smokers before they could hold their meetings, amid the stench of stale tobacco smoke. This condition stemmed in part from the proselyting strategy the Church then followed, a strategy that encouraged new converts to migrate to the United States. This in turn led to a neglect of the Church's physical facilities abroad since the strategy necessarily implied that in the Church's blueprint for the future, the chief function of nations outside the United States was to provide converts for the growing church in America. The elevation of David O. McKay to the prophetic office many years later resulted in a reversal of this strategy, with a consequent emphasis upon converts remaining in their home countries. This, in turn, resulted in a major upgrading of Church buildings abroad.

Called on unexpectedly as the first speaker following President Heber J. Grant's keynote address at the April 1925 general conference, Elder McKay gave a brief summary of his mission. He repeated much of what he had reported privately to his brethren: that despite determined and widespread opposition, the work continued to grow and flourish. "The Church of Jesus Christ of Latter-day Saints," he told the Tabernacle audience, "as was the church in the meridian of time, is everywhere spoken against, and its missionaries falsely accused." He pointed out that often the best way to oppose slander is to ignore it, because "the more you oppose it the more it grows." (CR, April 1925, p. 12.) The speaker was "delighted" to report, however, "that in spite of this condition the work of God is growing by leaps and bounds in the European Mission." (Ibid., p. 13.) After reviewing the work generally, Elder McKay bore one of the strongest testimonies of his apostolic career, filled with missionary fervor: "I testify to you that God lives, that he is near to his servants, and will hear and answer them and guide them when they come to him. I know that my Redeemer lives. I know it! I know that he has spoken to man in this age. I know that his church is established among men. God help us all to be true to it and help the world to see it as it is." (Ibid., p. 15.)

On returning home, Elder McKay soon took up his responsibilities with the Sunday School, his first love. And because of his missionary service, his world tour, and his creative ideas about proselyting, he soon began to exert a strong influence on missionary work at Church headquarters, serving on the missionary executive committee and regularly instructing the newly called missionaries prior to their departure for the field. The impact he had on impressionable young men and women can be gauged from a letter Elder McKay received from a fellow member of the Twelve who quoted a missionary who had served in the Swiss-German Mission while David O. was European Mission president: "I know I will be another man when I get back from Berlin," wrote the missionary. "President McKay is always wonderful and can make a man feel like going through fire after he makes a few inspiring remarks." (Letter of April 17, 1923, from Richard R. Lyman, DOMP.) It was as an inspirer of missionaries and of involvement in missionary work by the general membership of the Church that David O. McKay would make one of his most significant contributions as the president of the Church.

Chapter Nine

Family, Church, and Civic Duties

After 1901, Elder McKay was greeted each new year by an anniversary that reminded him of the dominant theme and influence in his life. It was on January 2, 1901, that he and his petite, vivacious bride, Emma Ray Riggs, were sealed in the Salt Lake Temple by John Henry Smith, of the Twelve. Afterward, the dawning of each new year evoked memories of that signal event and of the blessing in his life of this unusual woman, his friend and sweetheart and the mother of his seven children. The demeanor and appearance of Emma Ray Riggs McKay coincide with this appraisal by her husband who reminisced about their marriage in his diary on January 2, 1932: "During that time," he wrote reflectively, "I cannot recall that she has spoken a cross word to me. She has been an ideal sweetheart, a charming companion, and a loving wife."

This extraordinary, almost incredible, behavior during thirty-one years of marriage had been reciprocated by Emma Ray's husband and was to be perpetuated by them throughout the remainder of their lives.

This example of marital harmony should not mislead us into the false belief that life in the McKay household was devoid of all differences of opinion. What it indicates, rather, is that this pair had the necessary maturity and reciprocal feelings of love to enable them to resolve any real or imagined conflicts. They were, therefore, able to disagree without being disagreeable.

The allegiance Elder and Sister McKay had toward each other was also extended to their children, only six of whom lived to maturity. Royal Riggs McKay, the third son and fourth child, had died in 1912 at age three, causing one of the few genuine sorrows in the lives of his parents. The other six grew to honorable adulthood, married well, and rendered significant service in their professions, their businesses, their church, and their homes. At the beginning of 1932, the three older children were already married. Lawrence was married to Mildred Calderwood; Llewelyn's wife was Alice Kimball Smith; and Louise (Lou Jean to her family and friends) was the wife of Russell Blood of Kaysville, the Utah ancestral home of the influential Blood clan. Still at home were pretty, twenty-year-old Emma Rae, her mother's namesake, except for the spelling of the second name; an active teenager, Edward, fondly called Ned, age sixteen; and the youngest child, Robert, or Bobbie, as he was then called, who was an exuberant eleven-year-old.

On New Year's Day, 1932, fifty-eight-year-old David O. McKay decided to take his two young sons on an outing to enjoy the winter snow and to work off some of their nervous energy. Since the idea, doubtless inspired by the two boys, seemed not to appeal to either the mother or sister, Ned and Bobbie piled into the family car for a pleasant outing with their father, an outing that, before it ended, took on more the aspect of an odyssey.

When the McKay's talked of an outing, they ordinarily had in mind only one place: Huntsville. Symbolically, Huntsville, as we have already seen, is also located east of a small Mormon village named Eden. A few miles northwest of Eden lies Liberty; and over the mountain north of Liberty is Paradise, another Mormon village, whose name suggests the perception the early settlers who named it had of their town. But whatever distinction the residents of

Eden, Liberty, and Paradise claimed for their communities, it seems likely that in the minds of the McKays, their chief claim to fame was their satellite relationship to Huntsville. To say this is neither to demean these charming, neighboring communities, nor to attribute to the McKays an inordinate sense of pride or self-importance. It is rather a reflection of the fierce feelings of loyalty these transplanted Scotsmen felt for their ancestral fields and homestead.

Traveling north through Bountiful, Centerville, Farmington, and Kaysville to Ogden, the trio there turned east to make their tortuous way up Ogden Canyon toward their destination. As they emerged from the canyon a familiar yet strangely new sight opened to their view as the beautiful Ogden Valley, blanketed with snow, lay before them. Straight ahead was Huntsville and off to the left lay Eden. The old familiar landmarks were all in their accustomed places, as were the homes, barns, chapel, and small cluster of commercial buildings. What gave the scene an aura of newness was nothing tangible or susceptible of easy definition. It was a sense, an impression, doubtless influenced by the time of day, the slanted rays of the January sun, the crispness of the air, and the winter haze that hung close over the valley floor, fed by the friendly smoke that curled from Huntsville's chimneys.

While Ned and Bobbie were happily occupied with their sledding in the deep snow, whose surface bore an icy glaze, their father was busy inspecting his horses, which were pastured nearby, and visiting with his brother, Thomas E. McKay, who then lived in Huntsville. This gentle man, who idolized his famous, elder brother, and who once characterized him as the kind of man who, if he were learning to swim, would dive in all at once rather than inch into the pool as a more timid soul might do, was later to acquire prominence and reputation of his own when he was called as an assistant to the Twelve.

So far the day had been almost idyllic for the father and his sons. They had been together in a place they loved, near friendly kinsmen and out in the crisp air, which had given them a tingling feeling of alertness. But, the remainder of the day, which was now waning toward sunset, was to convince them of the truism that every silver lining is attached to a cloud, or that every life is exposed to both sunshine and shadow.

The cloud that now overshadowed them was nothing of tragic concern. But it was an annoyance. What happened was that an axle broke on their trusty—or at least their once-trusty—Paige, a car that in its day had rank in the automotive world. The ruts and chuckholes of the canyon had been more than the Paige could withstand and, the axle had cracked, bringing the McKay outing to an abrupt halt.

The Huntsville of that day was not, nor is it now, a metropolis. While it boasted a skilled blacksmith and someone who pumped gas and changed tires on the side, there was no one in town with the mechanical skill to repair the Paige, even had there been a parts shop. The only answer was a tow down-canyon to Ogden. Here accommodating Thomas E. came to the rescue to provide the tow. Meanwhile, David O. called son-in-law Russell Blood in Kaysville to request that he meet them at Ogden. From there, Russell drove the apostle and his two frozen sons to Kaysville, where they were able to borrow a Chevrolet from the son-in-law's father, Henry H. Blood, one of Kaysville's best-known residents who, in addition to his Church roles as a stake president and mission president served as Utah's governor, being elected in November 1932.

Five days after the outing with his sons, Elder McKay returned to Huntsville to use the services of the blacksmith, who was unable to repair his Paige. He rode two of his horses, one at a time, to the blacksmith shop, where he waited while they were being shod. "The valley was beautiful under a blanket of pure white, newly fallen snow," wrote the horseman, who, in return for the loving care he bestowed on his animals, expected prompt obedience from them. Elder McKay had carefully trained these horses to respond to his call. The process of training was laborious, both for the animals and their owner. A nephew of Elder

McKay, Dr. George R. Hill, who witnessed a training session, reported it with awe. The uncle patiently led the horse, again and again, through the routine of answering his whistle or call. Every show of obedience was rewarded with a kind word, a pat, or a morsel of food. Disobedience brought gentle yet firm reproach. By untiring repetition of the process, there was fixed in the animal's mind the correspondence between the master's summons, the horse's response, and the reward at the end. Once a horse had been trained in this way, it would promptly come to its master at a given signal, though standing in the farthest part of the pasture.

Although David O. McKay's regard for men's inherent qualities never allowed him to equate them with horses, there were similarities in the processes he used to train and lead both. He was patient and gentle yet firm in teaching his followers. After one had been trained in his duties, Elder McKay expected loyalty and able performance in return.

The frequent interludes the apostle spent at Huntsville always revived his spirits and broadened his perspectives, enabling him to bring new enthusiasm and insights to his work. At this time he was faced with a heavy agenda of Church and civic responsibilities, in addition to his duties to a still-maturing family. Included in his assignments at Church headquarters was the superintendency of the Sunday Schools of the Church, an assignment he had filled since 1918. At his side as first assistant stood a long-time friend and associate, Stephen L Richards of the Twelve, who was like a Jonathan to this David, loyal and dependable, and who, less than two decades later, would stand with his friend as the first counselor in the First Presidency. Elder McKay was also an advisor to the Primary organization at this time, an assignment that ordinarily was nothing but pure joy, but that at the moment was fraught with tension. The difficulty lay in an unfortunate controversy that had arisen between the president of the Primary, May Anderson, and one of her board members, Emily Stewart. The problem, which ordinarily would have created no stir at all, was made exceedingly complex in that Emily Stewart was the much-loved daughter of George Albert Smith, with whom David O. had been associated in the Council of Twelve since his call to that body in 1906. Elder Smith's love for his daughter was counterbalanced by the sense of duty and loyalty Elder McKay had for the president of the Primary, whom he served as an advisor. During the first two weeks of January, Elder McKay held several meetings with the aggrieved parties in an unsuccessful attempt to reconcile their differences.

It is a tribute both to Elder Smith and Elder McKay, who were caught in the crossfire of a dispute that stretched their conflicting loyalties to the limit, that it did not adversely affect their personal relationship as was shown thirteen years later when George Albert Smith as the president of the Church selected David O. McKay as his second counselor.

Another headquarters assignment that now occupied much of Elder McKay's time was the preparation of a manual for priesthood quorums, an assignment that was congenial to his interests and that made good use of his exceptional writing and teaching skills. And a civic responsibility, closely allied to his apostolic duties, which now claimed much of his attention, was his chairmanship of the Utah Council on Child Health and Protection. David, who had previously been a delegate to a White House convention on child health and protection, and who in December 1931 had participated in a regional conference held in Helena, Montana, consulted with Utah's Governor George Dern on January 8, 1932, about the personnel to serve on the state executive committee of the council. And he was otherwise involved in this assignment in delivering talks, in preparing summaries of conventions, and in presiding at council meetings.

But most of Elder McKay's efforts were directed toward his apostolic duties to preach the gospel and to set the affairs of the Church in order in areas to which he was assigned by the presiding brethren. He regularly attended stake conferences, where he trained local leaders and admonished and inspired the general Church membership. He was frequently called on to speak at sacrament meetings and firesides, where he exerted a powerful influence, especially on the youth, not only by his words but by his regal appearance and demeanor. There was something about this man, about his posture and stance and about the impression he conveyed, that taught and inspired at a level far above his words or beyond anything he had objectively achieved. Ralph Waldo Emerson, whom Elder McKay once characterized as the wisest American, referred to this intangible quality as character, that element in a person's makeup that demonstrates by subtle, spiritual means what he actually is and that causes others to judge him by that standard rather than by what he has said or achieved. Bryant S. Hinckley, the father of President Gordon B. Hinckley of the First Presidency, hinted at this facet of David O. McKay's makeup in an article written for a Church publication: "David O. McKay has done many good things and said many beautiful things," wrote the author, "but somehow he is finer than anything he has ever said or done." (IE, May 1932, p. 446.)

One need only to have seen this man in his prime to understand this statement. He looked like a prophet. Tall, powerfully built, and ruggedly handsome, with white, wavy hair; hazel-brown eyes that were at once piercing and kindly; and even features, David O. McKay commanded attention and respect wherever he went, whether sitting or standing, whether speaking or silent. Once he had spoken, there was the feeling, the impression that he had concealed more than he had revealed, that he had held back things of deep import. And silence on his part served only to enhance his mystique. In the parlance of today, this man had charisma, that intangible something that arouses popular loyalty and enthusiasm and sets the one who possesses it apart from others.

With all that, David O. McKay was not an elitist; he was down to earth and approachable and made all who came into his presence feel at ease, whether of high or low station. And it was this unusual combination—an exclusive character and a friendly, democratic attitude and spirit— that endeared him to the people and increased his effectiveness in instructing and motivating them.

An apostolic assignment Elder McKay received in late January afforded an unusual opportunity to use his special qualities and talents. He was asked by the Brethren to install Alonza Arza Hinckley as the new president of the California Mission, replacing Joseph W. McMurrin, who, according to Elder McKay's appraisal, was a "pretty sick man." As part of this assignment, the apostle was also asked to tour the mission with the new president, holding meetings with the missionaries and the Saints in a vast area that included most of the states of California, Arizona, and Nevada.

David O. was driven to the train depot by "Mama Ray and Emma Rae" early Friday morning, January 22, where he was met by sixty-two-year-old Alonzo Hinckley. The two men boarded their Pullman sleeper at the Union Pacific Station, which anchors the west end of Salt Lake's South Temple Street, and settled down for the overnight trip to Los Angeles, where they arrived at 8:15 the next morning. The long ride enabled the travelers to renew an acquaintance that had its origins years before when Elder McKay visited the stake in Delta, Utah, where his companion had presided for so many years. There, as a young stake president, Alonzo had been promised, in a blessing pronounced by his stake patriarch, that one day he would be called to the Quorum of the Twelve. As he traveled to Los Angeles with an apostle who was three years younger than he, and who had then served in the Twelve for twenty-six years, that blessing may have seemed remote and improbable to Alonzo Hinckley, given his age and his relative obscurity compared with his better known and more literate and articulate elder brother, Bryant S. Hinckley, who presided over the Liberty Stake in Salt Lake City and who was a confidant of Church president Heber J.

Grant. The fact that Alonzo A. Hinckley was called to the Twelve two years after David O. McKay installed him as the president of the California Mission, indicates again the revelatory process by which men are called to the apostleship.

A first act of Elder McKay and the new mission president after arriving in Los Angeles was to visit the ailing Joseph W. McMurrin, who was a member of the First Council of the Seventy, and who, though still a very sick man, seemed to be improving. It is not unlikely that Elder McKay's visit with President McMurrin recalled the incident of long ago in Glasgow, Scotland, when the sick man's kinsman, James L. McMurrin, prophesied that David O. McKay would one day be elevated to "the leading councils of the Church."

After reviewing the proposed itinerary for the tour of the mission with Elder McMurrin, the apostle and President Hinckley turned immediately to their task, making preparations for their first district conference, which was held the next day at nearby Baldwin Park. The agenda of meetings for this conference set the pattern for the tour that would occupy the next eighteen days—instructional and testimony meetings with the missionaries; counseling sessions with the district and branch leaders; and general, motivational meetings with the Saints.

Before boarding the *Golden Sentinel* for Tucson, Arizona, the evening of January 26, Elder McKay, joined by Presiding Bishop Sylvester Q. Cannon, who was in the area on Church business, met with representatives of the Western Electric Company, which was heavily involved in the rapidly burgeoning movie industry at nearby Hollywood. They were shown an hour-long film in sound featuring Church authorities and the Tabernacle Choir and organ. Foreseeing the potential of this novel media tool, the apostle wrote enthusiastically, "Very promising—possibilities unlimited." It was several decades later, during President McKay's administration, that the offspring of the movies—television—came to full flower, increasing manyfold the "possibilities" he foresaw during the infancy of the movie industry for telling the story of the Church. His rugged good looks, his poise, his presence of mind, and the spiritual aura he projected ideally suited David O. McKay for the role he would play in leading the Church into a new era of mass communications.

At Tucson, the small handful of California missionaries laboring there was augmented by a pair of elders from the Mexican Mission who joined in their meetings. The influence of the Mexican and Spanish cultures on the area was impressed on Elder McKay when he visited the centuries-old San Xavier mission outside the city. Standing alone in the Arizona desert, its white walls gleaming in the warm winter sun, San Xavier was to Elder McKay a monument to the diligence and dedication of the nameless corps of Catholic priests who had constructed, maintained, and operated it over the years, bringing a touch of elegance to the wilderness. The apostle did not allow doctrinal and cultural differences to blind him to the qualities of human character and spirit that had produced and preserved such an architectural jewel in a harsh desert setting.

The next day found the travelers in San Bernardino, an old Mormon outpost abandoned at the time of the Johnston Army invasion in 1857. There Elder McKay was impressed with the flourishing citrus groves that blanketed the area and that were threatened by unseasonably low temperatures. The citrus farmers were battling the freeze with smudge pots that burned through the night, raising the temperature in the groves but leaving a residue of acrid smoke during the day.

At a district missionary meeting held at Santa Ana on January 29, the presiding officer, twenty-year-old Jonathan Cannon, caught Elder McKay's eye. "He is an exceptional character," noted the apostle, who, like his associates in the Twelve, was constantly on the alert for promising young leaders who might be looked to in the future to help carry the burden of priesthood responsibility.

In succession, numerous meetings were held in Los

139

Angeles, San Diego, Fresno, Sacramento, and San Francisco, California, and in Reno, Nevada. Commenting in his diary on his trip over the Sierras, Elder McKay noted with surprise that over forty feet of snow had fallen there during the winter.

When his schedule permitted it, Elder McKay visited in the homes of the Saints, which always proved to be a mutually beneficial experience, his hosts savoring the opportunity of entertaining an apostle of the Lord, and the visitor being encouraged by the faith and obedience shown by Mormon families who lived exemplary lives out of the glare of publicity and notoriety. At San Diego, for instance, David "was entertained at dinner by President and Mrs. William Tenny, San Diego Branch President, and at supper by Brother and Sister Carrol Kemp—both choice families— six children in the former, five in the latter."

It was not feasible or wise for the apostle and his companion to remain in constant motion. So intermittently they stole time away from their crowded schedule of travel, meetings, and interviews for recreation. Not having a Huntsville to which he could retreat, David O. ordinarily used these interludes to read, write, or merely reflect. But occasionally he indulged in a movie. So on Monday evening, February 1, en route from San Diego to Fresno during a stopover in Los Angeles, he and Alonzo Hinckley attended the Biltmore Theatre to see the well-known actor William Gillette perform in "Sherlock Holmes." "He did very well," wrote the diarist of the star's performance, "but Old Age has laid his heavy hand on the Veteran Actor."

This was not an off-the-cuff appraisal by one unacquainted with the dramatic arts. Rather, it represented the reasoned judgment of one who, while not an active thespian, was keenly interested in this art form, as he was in other artistic expressions. This interest can be detected in his devotion to the plays of William Shakespeare, in his regular attendance at movies and plays, and in his patronage of serious theater at his alma mater, the University of Utah. The portrait of David O. McKay that hangs in the foyer of the Pioneer Memorial Theatre on the University of Utah campus speaks eloquently of his genuine interest in the theater. And this aspect of his personality casts the apostle in an entirely different light than the one in which we see him training his horses or supervising farming operations at Huntsville, or the one in which we see him preaching a sermon, instructing an associate, or counseling one in distress. Elder McKay was not a narrow specialist. He was, rather, a generalist, a cosmopolitan whose interests were as varied and extensive as were the challenges of the international church he was one day to head.

Returning to Salt Lake City after completing the mission tour, the apostle resumed the customary round of meetings, conferences, and family responsibilities. March 16 found him at Provo, where he addressed the Brigham Young University student body on the subject of "Life's Ideals." Always at his best with young people, Elder McKay felt especially good about this meeting, calling it "an inspiration."

In mid-April, David O. was at Kaysville to speak at funeral services for Grandma Barnes, a relative of son-in-law

David O. McKay, center, as superintendent of the general board of the Deseret Sunday School Union, the members of which are shown here.

Russell Blood and one of the pillars of that community. A few days earlier, he had stopped in Kaysville to administer to this eighty-six-year-old saint en route home from Eden, where he had spoken at funeral services for ninety-three-year-old Janet Farrell. As the years passed, the apostle was called on more and more to speak at funeral services as he gained in prominence and as his contemporaries commenced to answer the call of death. But he ultimately found it necessary to limit his acceptance of such invitations because of time strictures. And he was forced to decline other speaking invitations for the same reason, as this entry of April 29 attests: "Attended to correspondence, declining five more invitations to deliver baccalaureate sermons. Have accepted only two this year. Other appointments are too pressing."

One speaking assignment he never declined, and which he was always honored but somewhat intimidated to fill, was to speak in general conference. At the April conference this year he delivered a thoughtful sermon in which he reaffirmed his commitment to the Savior and to His gospel "as the one perfect way to happiness and peace." Of the Master, the apostle told his audience, "With my whole soul I accept Jesus Christ as the personification of human perfection—as God made manifest in the flesh, as the Savior and Redeemer of mankind." (CR, April 1932, p. 62.) From that premise, he moved to the conclusion that Christ's church partakes of the Savior's perfection: "So it is with the church which Christ has established," he said. "Since it is founded by the Perfect One, it follows that when properly interpreted it too approaches perfection." (Ibid., pp. 62-63.) The speaker then focused on certain principles and programs of the Church, including faith, fasting, and aid to the needy, concluding with this apostolic prayer: "God help us to contribute our might and influence to the perpetuation of the Church of Jesus Christ, of which we can truly say: 'Persecution has not crushed it; power has not beaten it back; time has not abated its force; and what is most wonderful of all, the abuses and treason of its friends have not shaken its stability.' May neither prosperity nor popularity hinder its progress any more than these other forces, and may teachers and parents unite in impressing youth particularly to be loyal to that which we know is good for humanity and contributive to eternal salvation." (Ibid.)

Being a parent as well as a professional teacher, David O. followed his own admonitions by inculcating principles of loyalty to church and family among the McKay clan. With the aid of Emma Ray, this was done by precept at family home evenings, where principles of the gospel were explained and discussed; and by example through frequent instances of family cooperation and participation. As if to demonstrate the exemplary aspect of their parental leadership, David O. and Emma Ray led out in two family enterprises in the spring of 1932. On April 2, just before conference, Elder McKay pitched in to help with the spring house cleaning, which was expertly supervised by Sister McKay. "Assisted in house cleaning," recorded Emma Ray's willing helper, "moving book cases, beds, bureaus, etc." In a postscript that revealed his inner feelings about housework, the diarist added: "Plenty of exercise but not much inspiration."

In May it was Elder McKay's turn to lead out in a family activity when he organized a work party at the Huntsville farm that included himself, "Mama Ray, Emma Rae [and] Bobby." At the end of the day he noted approvingly: "All cooperated in planting three-fourths of an acre of potatoes. Plans worked ideally." Two days later, the father returned to the farm with Ned and Bobby where they "sorted potatoes." Lending further emphasis to the fact that Huntsville was not merely a place for fun and recreation or a resource for the development of family loyalty and good work habits, Elder McKay noted with satisfaction: "First class potatoes, sell for 65 cents per cwt [hundred weight]!" Also, revealing an interest in the development of agriculture in the area and presaging the construction of the Pine View dam, he recorded, after noting that the Ogden River was booming: "Too bad this volume of water isn't stored for use later on in the season."

Another outing of a more somber nature was arranged a few days later when, on Decoration Day, the family visited and placed flowers on the graves of Grandma Riggs, who is buried in the Salt Lake Cemetery; Royle, whose grave was then in the Ogden Cemetery; and Elder McKay's parents, whose graves are in Huntsville. They then joined with other members of the extended McKay clan for lunch in the old home and returned to Salt Lake City in the evening in time to attend a picture show.

So went the flow of life in the family of David O. and Emma Ray McKay, a family constantly on the move, exuberant, friendly, close-knit, and seemingly without cares or difficulties. A closer look, however, reveals that, like all families, the life of the McKay's was now and then in ebb tide. This anxious entry in Elder McKay's journal on August 25 broke a two-month silence during which Emma Ray had battled a nagging throat infection: "Mama Ray underwent a tonsillectomy—a severe shock to her system. Much worried all day." Although an optimistic entry a week later indicated she was "considerably better," Sister McKay was unable to recover from the operation as had been hoped. Her condition continued to worsen until October 2, when she was hospitalized for what, according to her husband, seemed "inevitably necessary to the best interests of her health—a thyroidectomy." At the first session of general conference, held five days later, acting patriarch Nicholas G. Smith, who also was the bishop of the Seventeenth Ward, the ward to which the McKays then belonged, offered the invocation, in which he mentioned Emma Ray by name, asking for a divine blessing in her behalf. Elder McKay appreciated this thoughtful gesture and thanked the bishop for it, although he was concerned about the effect of it on Emma Ray, who was a very private person, and who "did not want anybody but her closest friends to know that she was in the hospital." Four days later, the complicated surgery was performed successfully by Dr. Leslie B. White assisted by Dr. Silas Smith. The concerned husband and his son Llewelyn gave the patient a blessing of healing and comfort, and "later in the day, she rallied, and seemed to gain in normalcy." From that point, Emma Ray began to mend rapidly. By November 14, she felt well enough to accompany her husband on an outing to Huntsville. "My sweetheart stood the trip so well," he recorded happily, "we went to the theatre at night upon our return to Salt Lake City."

With Emma Ray safely on the mend, Elder McKay felt at peace as he boarded the train the next morning for Chicago en route to the East Central States Mission, which he toured in a whirlwind six-day trip, during which he held the customary meetings in New Martinsville, Huntington, and Charleston, West Virginia; and Richmond, Virginia, and Ashland, Kentucky.

Returning home safely, Elder McKay rounded out the year by discharging his customary duties, enjoying the holiday season with his family, and looking forward to an extraordinary change in the presiding quorum of the Church.

Chapter Ten

Call to the First Presidency

T he roots of the anticipated change in the First Presidency that attracted the interest of Elder McKay, indeed, of the whole Church, as 1932 drew to a close reached back to December 11, 1931, when Charles W. Nibley, the second counselor to President Heber J. Grant, passed away. Given the sense of unease that gripped the nation because of the deepening depression and the obvious need for vigorous and creative leadership to guide the Saints through the crisis, it was confidently expected by most "Church watchers" that the vacancy in the First Presidency would be filled at the April conference in 1932. While that may have been the perception out in the Church, it was not so with Elder McKay and the other members of the Twelve. At least, it was not so after February 18, 1932. On that date, this cryptic entry found its way into David O.'s journal: "An important announcement was made this day by President Heber J. Grant. It is not to be made known until some time in the future." Unfolding events revealed that this vague sentence referred to action that had been taken by President Grant not long after the death of Charles Nibley, the Prophet's longtime friend and confidant. After consulting with his first counselor—who was also his first cousin—Anthony W. Ivins, the Church president had written a letter to J. Reuben

Clark, Jr., who was then the U.S. ambassador to Mexico, inviting him to fill the vacancy in the First Presidency. Torn by the attractive professional and economic prospects his high government status held out for the future, and by apparent feelings of uncertainty as to whether he could merge smoothly into a Church hierarchy about which he had no intimate knowledge, Ambassador Clark delayed answering President Grant's letter until after Christmas. While expressing a willingness to accept the call, he explained in detail the obligations he had assumed when he accepted the ambassadorial post in Mexico and the detriment that would inure to the government, to the Church, and to him personally were he to leave immediately. On this account, he raised the question whether, under the circumstances, President Grant might want to pass him by and to select someone else. Determined that this brilliant, tough, outspoken man was the one he wanted at his side, the Church president said he would wait, a wait that extended to April 1933, sixteen months after Brother Clark was invited to become a member of the First Presidency.

As 1932 wound to a close and as the April 1933 general conference approached, David O. and the other members of the Twelve knew that the time for public disclosure of the secret President Grant had shared with them the previous February 18 was near. During the intervening months, they had had the opportunity to assess the meaning of this unusual move, both as it would affect the Church and them individually. That the Prophet had seen fit to go outside the Twelve and the other General Authorities to select a counselor was unusual but not unprecedented. David O. and the other members of the Twelve knew, or were soon to learn, that both Joseph Smith and Brigham Young had reached out beyond the close circle of General Authorities to select counselors, the most recent instance being Brigham Young's selection of his son John Willard Young. But that was in 1873, the year in which David O. McKay was born. In that sixty-year interval there had been no repetition of this unusual procedure. It was, therefore, something Elder McKay had never witnessed or experienced personally. So the impending change placed him and the other members of the Twelve in an unstructured and, in some respects, an awkward position. The awkwardness arose from the disparity between the ecclesiastical experience of the Twelve and the man who was to become one of their presiding officers. The incumbent members of the Twelve had at the time collectively rendered a total of 256 years of apostolic service, traveling the world to preach the gospel, to set the affairs of the Church in order, and to testify of the Savior. Intermixed with the thousands and tens of thousands of sermons they had delivered and the countless counseling sessions they had conducted in their globe-circling travels were the numerous meetings they had directed or participated in at Church headquarters, where matters of policy and procedure had been discussed and decided and where, through the spirit of prophecy and revelation, they had received incomparable spiritual instructions and insights. Against that vast reservoir of experience and service was the record of the new counselor in the First Presidency who had never held a position of significant priesthood leadership. Indeed, he had not been ordained a high priest prior to his call to the First Presidency.

While Ambassador Clark had gained well-deserved academic and professional eminence and had rendered distinguished service to his country, his achievements in these fields were hardly more illustrious than those of several members of the Twelve. Reed Smoot, for instance, had served in the United States Senate for thirty years, achieving a solid reputation for integrity and ability and gaining an insight into a grasp of government at its highest level. The Twelve also included two former university presidents, James E. Talmage and John A. Widtsoe, both of whom had once presided over the University of Utah. They were skilled administrators, were highly literate, and possessed impeccable academic credentials. While Elder McKay had not functioned at the same academic level as these two apostles, he had made his mark in education, serving as the principal of the Weber Academy and for many years as the superintendent of the Church's world-wide Sunday School system and as the Church commissioner of education. The Twelve also counted among its number an able attorney, Stephen L Richards, who had been rated by the dean of the law school at the University of Chicago as the most brilliant student he had ever taught. And the junior member of the Twelve at the time was Joseph F. Merrill, a former distinguished professor and department head at the University of Utah who was heavily laden with academic honors.

Against this background, it is understandable why the call of J. Reuben Clark, Jr., to the First Presidency created an awkward situation for the members of the Twelve and for him. However, President Clark appears to be the only one who gave voice to these feelings. In the first talk he delivered in the Tabernacle after being sustained, the new counselor in the First Presidency said: "If any of you have misgivings, I can only say that your misgivings can hardly be greater than my own. I am keenly aware of my own deficiencies. I come late in life to a new work." (CR, April 1933, p. 102.)

The introduction of a newcomer, and, to most of the Twelve, a stranger, into the presiding quorum of the Church seemed to make no significant impression on the apostles. The diaries of David O. McKay will be searched in vain for any comments about the action or about the man who now became one of his presiding officers. It was almost as if President Clark's call was a matter of indifference to him, an attitude the other members of his quorum seemed to share. This reaction must seem extraordinary to anyone accustomed to the jostling for position and power that occurs in most organizations. Ordinarily the action of ignoring in-house personnel and bringing in a chief executive from the outside creates resentment and discord. That the appointment of President Clark did not produce this result is assignable chiefly to the fact that those called to the apostleship are obligated by covenant and personal disposition to follow the direction of the Prophet without hesitation. When, therefore, he has spoken on any matter of policy, procedure, or organization, the apostles are bound to accept and to follow his direction. To do otherwise would be to set themselves in opposition to the one whom they sustain as God's earthly mouthpiece and, hence, in opposition to God himself.

Indicative of the apparent unconcern of the Twelve that someone from the outside had been called to the First Presidency was the sermon delivered by Elder McKay at the April 1933 general conference when President Clark was sustained. Without dealing in personalities or alluding to the organizational changes, he said at the outset: "I think this conference will take its place among the most impressive conferences ever held in the church, in its timely teaching, in its inspirational uplift, in the awakening of a desire to live better, and in its confirmation of the truth of the Gospel of Jesus Christ." With that preamble, he launched into a detailed discussion of an issue that was then of paramount concern to the leaders of the Church. This was the issue of the proposed repeal of the Eighteenth Amendment, which had made illegal the sale of alcohol. That the Brethren spoke out in opposition to repeal, contrary to their usual policy of silence on political matters, reflected a perception that this issue also carried heavy moral overtones for the Church and its members. So the speaker pulled no punches in denouncing the evils of alcohol and in reasoning with his audience as to why repeal would be a mistake. "Today the liquor question, another earth-born giant, stalks through the land," he began. "And the question of how best to shackle him is now put squarely before the people." (CR, April 1933, p. 90.) His answer, of course, was to leave the Eighteenth Amendment in place. He advanced three reasons in support: First, statistics compiled after Prohibition went into effect showed dramatic decreases in arrests for drunkenness and a consequent decrease of crime of over 40 percent. Second, the sponsors of the Twenty-First Amendment could cite no valid reasons supporting repeal, offering only a return to the social evils that Prohibition had helped to curb. And third, that repeal would greatly inhibit the growth of spirituality. "The world today perhaps as never before needs more spirituality," said the speaker. "Booze and depravity mingle together harmoniously, but booze and spirituality, never." (Ibid., p. 93.) In conclusion, Elder McKay made plain the ultimate reason why he and the Brethren opposed repeal. "Out of the high plane of spirituality comes the message from the President of the church given to the world that intoxicating liquors, strong drink, and tobacco are not good for man. That is God's word given authoritatively and on that truth we stand." (Ibid., p. 94.)

In his talk delivered at the October general conference, Elder McKay again took up the theme of repeal, rejecting the monetary argument advanced by some proponents, who, he said "lay much stress upon the fact that if our prohibition laws are repealed we shall have more revenue. In this latter case," he added derisively, "money seems to take precedence over manhood." (CR, October 1933, pp. 13-14.)

The call of President Clark effected little, if any, change in Elder McKay's duties in the Twelve. He continued to fill his committee and other assignments and to attend to his usual apostolic chores as assigned by the president of the Twelve or the First Presidency. As the weeks and the months passed, he and the other brethren began to notice a decline in the health of President Anthony W. Ivins. This whole-souled, disciplined man, who was called to the Twelve a year after Elder McKay, was now in his eighty-second year. His body, which in his early years had become tough and resilient from work out-of-doors as a livestock operator, had of late begun to weaken as a result of the sedentary life he had lived since being called to the Twelve in 1907. And since 1921, he had served President Grant as a counselor, enjoying the full confidence of the Prophet, not only because of his integrity and ability but because of their shared heritage through the Ivins clan of New Jersey. In the talk delivered at the April 1934 general conference, President Ivins seemed to hint that the end was near for him. In unplanned, extemporaneous remarks he said at the outset: "Before commencing my remarks, my brethren and sisters, I desire to express the gratitude I feel that the Lord has lengthened out my days to be present at this general conference of the church." (CR, April 1934, p. 95.) This excellent man would not live to see another one. He passed away peacefully on September 23, 1934, creating the second vacancy in the First Presidency in less than three years. In the interval between his death and the October general conference, President Grant called sixty-one-year-old David O. McKay to fill the vacancy caused by the death of President Ivins. He was sustained at the third general session of the conference on Saturday morning, October 6, 1934, thus beginning a service in the presiding quorum of the Church that would continue for over thirty-five years, a record exceeded only by Joseph F. Smith.

This milestone aroused memories of President McKay's past, memories of his parents and family and of the experiences and influences of long ago that had helped to shape his life and character. At the priesthood meeting on the evening of October 6, the day he was sustained, the new counselor paid a tribute to his parents. Alluding to his mother, the speaker told of an incident when he was an infant which his uncle later shared with him. As the baby played on the floor, the uncle teasingly make a deprecating remark about him. At that, the mother picked up the child and, nestling him to her cheek, said defensively, and somewhat reproachfully, "You don't know; he may be an apostle some day." President McKay said this statement may only have implied a fond hope the mother had for her baby. But whether it was the expression of a hope or a prophetic utterance, he regretted that his parents had not lived to see the fulfillment.

The speaker also recalled again the extraordinary experience in Glasgow during his first mission when President McMurrin had uttered the prophecy that had had such a profound influence on his life. At that time, however, he was not as much impressed by the prospect of being elevated to the leading councils of the Church as he was by the warning that Satan had desired him, that he might sift him as wheat. This, he explained, recalled to mind the temptations to which he had been subjected in the past and imbued him with a strong desire to keep the faith and to be of service to his fellowmen. He also said the spiritual aura of that meeting imparted to him a knowledge and conviction he had never had before but had fervently sought. "Never before had I experienced such an emotion," he explained. "It was a manifestation for which as a doubting youth I had secretly prayed most earnestly on the hillside and in the meadow. It was an assurance to me that sincere prayer is answered 'sometime, somewhere.'"

At the Sunday morning session, the new counselor expressed love and appreciation for his associates, singling out a few by name for special comment. He characterized President Grant as a "true friend" and surrogate father to whom he had felt free to go for paternal counsel after the death of his own father. "His nature is as open, as pure and clear as a faultless crystal," he said of the Prophet, concluding with the prayer that he would not disappoint him and that he would be true to the trust the Prophet and the Lord had placed in him.

Referring to his early acquaintance with President Clark at the University of Utah, the speaker said "I admired him then. I considered him one of the choicest young men I had ever seen or had ever known." And, anticipating a close association with him in the future, he added, "I love him as a friend, and to be associated with him now in this high quorum, the highest in the church, makes me feel very happy and thankful, but also very humble." (CR, October 1934, p. 90.)

President McKay also paid a collective tribute to the Council of the Twelve. "You cannot find a group of men whose lives are more consecrated," he said of the brethren whose close association he left with reluctance. "You must live with them to know them. You must be in daily contact with the burdens they are carrying, with their concern and anxieties for the youth, their willingness to go to the ends of the world at a moment's call if need be to establish better conditions, to make the world happier, more peaceful, more just." (Ibid., p. 91.)

The speaker used these optimistic words as the springboard for his first major address as a member of the First Presidency. Delivered during the depths of the Great Depression, when the leaders of the Church faced one of their greatest challenges in many decades, this talk reveals one of the salient qualities of President McKay's leadership: his buoyant faith and optimism, even in the face of serious difficulties. "I have thought that I have detected in men and women who have called upon me . . . just a little evidence of discouragement," he told his Tabernacle audience. "And yet, it is our right to be happy. It is the destiny of man to have joy, and I ask, during the few moments that I further stand before you that you direct your attention with me along some lines which may help us to keep that joy, notwithstanding the economic conditions and the failures that have brought about many moments of discouragement and sadness." (CR, October 1934, p. 91.) President McKay then developed the theme that happiness is not an external condition but is a state of the spirit and an attitude of the mind. He saw the key to this in the Savior's statement, "The kingdom of God is within you." (Luke 17:21.) He therefore admonished his listeners to look within and to feast on the spiritual and intellectual riches to be found there: faith in God; love of family; appreciation of the beauties and bounties of the earth; and enjoyment of friends and associates. And as to the physical needs of the people, he gave this assurance: "There is no need of any child being hungry in this church. Let us thank God for the organization and say we will buckle to and make our contributions so that these conditions will be removed."

In summary, he told the assembled Saints: "And so,

brethren and sisters, what if we do have economic distress, universal almost? Let us ever keep in mind that life is largely what we make it, and that the Savior of men has marked clearly and plainly just how joy and peace may be obtained." (Ibid., p. 95.)

In this sermon, we also see President McKay's predominant emphasis on spiritual and intellectual matters over physical or temporal things. It was not that he ignored or neglected the latter. It was rather that he believed the inner man, his thoughts and attitudes, controlled and determined his outward conduct, and, therefore, his physical circumstances. In ordering his priorities, therefore, David O. McKay always gave precedence to the health, status, and proper attunement of the spiritual self.

Yet this focus did not preclude President McKay from being heavily and persistently involved in physical or temporal things as his regular activity at the Huntsville farm attests. And at the level of his First Presidency responsibilities, this appears from his intimate connection with the development of the Church Welfare Program, as will be seen later.

Chapter Eleven

New Responsibilities— Beginnings of the Church Welfare Program

B efore his call to the First Presidency, David O. McKay had planned to travel east with Emma Ray on a lengthy trip to take care of Church, business, and family matters. The call, with its readjustments and pressures, required that the trip be postponed. By February 1935, however, affairs at the office had settled down to the point that David raised with President Grant and President Clark the question of whether it would be appropriate for him to make the trip, one object of which was to pick up a new car at Detroit. President Clark, who was notoriously cautious about traveling, expressed concern about his associate driving that long distance, especially during the winter. When it appeared that this concern might delay the trip until spring, President Grant intervened to say that the second counselor couldn't drive very fast in a new car, so he might as well go immediately rather than to wait.

With that presidential approval, he and Emma Ray left Salt Lake City on February 16. After picking up their new car in Detroit, the pair drove first to Pittsburgh, where they met some of Emma Ray's relatives whom she had never seen before and from whom she obtained helpful genealogical information. Traveling from there to Philadelphia, the McKays spent a few days with Lou Jean and her doctor husband, Russell Blood. Driving on to Washington, D.C., President and Sister McKay were greeted by Lawrence and Mildred, who had been living in the nation's capital for several years. A special attraction for the travelers was the two grandchildren who, regrettably, were growing up away from their watchful eye.

While in the vicinity, President McKay held several meetings with local members and leaders, attended to some Church and personal business, and met with a number of national leaders. His guide in making the rounds of Washington's officialdom was Utah's Senator Elbert D. Thomas. It was satisfying to the visitor to hear Vice-President John Nance Garner refer to the Tabernacle Choir broadcasts "as one of the best things on the air." More important, David was interested to learn firsthand about the steps being taken by the government to alleviate the economic depression that had descended on the nation. These insights would prove to be invaluable as, under the direction of President Heber J. Grant, he would lead out in laying the groundwork for the Church's own welfare program.

Because of bad weather in the midwest, the McKays decided to return home by the southern route. To take advantage of this detour as best he could, President McKay wired ahead to the presidents of the Southern States and the Texas Louisiana missions to arrange for special meetings. At Jacksonville, Florida, he joined with President LeGrand Richards of the Southern States Mission in holding meetings with the missionaries and with the Saints. "President and Sister Richards seem to be filled with the spirit of their mission," he wrote of the visit, providing his personal appraisal of the man who, within a few years would be called as the presiding bishop of the Church and who, still later, would be called to the Twelve by President David O. McKay. Similar meetings were held in New Orleans with President Rowan and the missionaries and Saints of the Texas Louisiana Mission. Attending the meetings held here was David's old friend James H. Moyle, the U.S. commissioner of customs, who was in New Orleans on official business. This superior man was the father of Henry D. Moyle, who years later would be called by President McKay as one of his counselors. He took the Church leader and his wife and the mission president on a motorboat inspection of the harbor facilities at New Orleans and on an enjoyable spin up the Mississippi.

After leaving New Orleans, the travelers went to Kelsey, Texas, where President McKay held another series of meetings. From there, they angled northwesterly to Denver and thence to Salt Lake City, where they arrived as spring was breaking.

This lengthy trip and the contacts he made in Washington, D.C., gave President McKay some important insights into the hardships caused by the depression. These were much on his mind as the April general conference approached, as they were on the minds of the other members of the First Presidency. The question of the role the Church should play in this deepening crisis had been discussed often by the Brethren. It was this question that dominated a special meeting of the First Presidency, the Twelve, and the Presiding Bishopric held just before the last general session of the conference. It was the sense of this council that the Church should go its own way in providing assistance for its members without the help of the federal or state governments. While no specific action was taken then, this idea was discussed in more depth in the intervening months before the general conference in October 1935; and on Friday October 4, 1935, the First Presidency, the Twelve, and the Presiding Bishopric convened to consider it further. At that time it was decided that the bishops be asked again to make a detailed survey to determine the extent to which the members of the Church were in need. As early as 1933 a similar request had been made, but the response had been sporadic and incomplete. President McKay expressed himself strongly on the subject, asserting that the bishops should be "awakened to a realization that this investigation that we propose to make is real, and these cases that are in dire need should be ferreted out."

While the development of a broad, consistent program of welfare for the members of the Church would have to await the marshaling of facts, the definition of goals and procedures, and the confirmation of the Spirit, there were things of a general nature the Brethren could do and say in the meantime to assist and encourage the Saints. So at the general priesthood meeting on Saturday, October 5, 1935, the members of the First Presidency admonished the brethren to get out of debt and stay out of debt and to pay their tithes and offerings, both as a way to provide aid for the poor and to invoke God's blessings through obedience to the commandments. President McKay said: "We have in the Church one of the best systems in the world of aiding one another—the fast offerings. Our young people should be taught it from their youth; our older people should practice it and set a proper example."

As the machinery was put in motion to gear up for a Churchwide welfare program, the key administrative figure at Church headquarters was President David O. McKay. The controlling head, of course, was the Prophet, Heber J. Grant, who initiated the program but who, through delegation, placed the details in the hands of subordinates. President J. Reuben Clark would have been the logical one to play this role—and in later years he did play an important role in the development of Church welfare—as he had been a key figure in discussions about such a program dating back to 1933 when he first became a counselor. But President Clark's outside commitments were too heavy to enable him to give the continuing and consistent direction that such a vast program required. In the first eighteen months of his service as a counselor, before the time President McKay came aboard, he had spent over half of his time in the East or out of the country involved in various government assignments and in handling personal matters. He had, for instance, spent several months in late 1933 and early 1934 serving as chief counsel to secretary of state Cordell Hull at the Seventh Pan American Conference at Montevideo, Uruguay. He was also heavily involved in the Foreign Bondholders Protective Council. And after President McKay's call, he became affiliated with the Mexican Eagle Oil Company in directing complex negotiations in Mexico; was elected to serve on the Commission of Experts on the Codification of International Law of the Pan American Union; and was elected to the board of editors of the American Journal of International Law. He, of course, undertook all of these assignments with the approval, indeed with the encouragement, of President Grant. And, in addition to these distractions, President Clark was actively involved in the political fortunes of Alfred M. Landon, the Republican presidential nominee in 1936.

So, with the first counselor unable to function in a consistent way, President McKay, at the Prophet's request, stepped into the breach to give administrative direction to the rapidly developing welfare program, which, in its early phases, was called the Church Security Plan. Following the action approved at the October 1935 general conference, aggressive steps had been taken to make a survey of the welfare needs and the resources of the Latter-day Saints. To help gather and collate the facts and make initial recommendations, there had been called into service the able young president of the Pioneer Stake, Harold B. Lee, who had shown unusual creativity and discipline in caring for the needs of the members of his stake. Elder Lee, who was later to become the first managing director of the welfare program, as also a member of the Twelve and, ultimately, the president of the Church, was, at the time, a Salt Lake City commissioner. Others had been called to assist him in conducting the welfare spadework, and on March 18, 1936, one of them, Campbell Brown, joined Elder Lee in a meeting with President McKay to make a report and to receive instructions. The second counselor in the First Presidency wrote of that meeting: "In council with President Harold B. Lee and Campbell Brown who reported their findings on the recent survey made regarding the economic conditions of our church members. Their recommendations are excellent and far reaching." Six days later, President McKay met again with Brother Lee to discuss and analyze the report and recommendations in preparation for a special meeting of bishoprics, stake presidencies, and mission presidents to be held in the Assembly Hall following the last session of the general conference on April 6. In the interval between March 24 and the general conference, these basic recommendations were discussed and refined in consultation with President Grant and other General Authorities, including President J. Reuben Clark, who returned to Salt Lake City on April 1 "after an extended absence."

Following the morning session of conference on Monday April 6, a meeting of all General Authorities was held where the security plan was presented and approved. And at the special meeting held that afternoon following the last general session, President Grant, after greeting the assembled stake presidencies, bishoprics, and mission presidents, called on President McKay to make the presentation. He first referred to the survey that was conducted after the last general conference. The survey revealed that 17.9 percent of the entire Church membership, or 88,460 persons, were on relief. To enable the Church to assume this load, which previously had been borne by either federal or state government, a fast-offering goal of one dollar per member per year was set. Tithing faithfulness was encouraged, whether paid in cash or in kind. Each bishop was urged to accumulate by the following October general conference enough food and clothes to provide for every member of his ward during the coming winter. It was emphasized that ordinarily assistance received by the members was to be in exchange for work or services rendered, not as charity. It was assumed that while the direction and coordination of this effort would be in the hands of the Presiding Bishopric, the First Presidency would appoint a Church Relief Committee to assist the bishopric. All members then employed on WPA projects were asked to retain this employment but were admonished to do an honest day's work for a day's pay.

In concluding remarks, President McKay told the brethren that the organization necessary to accomplish the goal—the organization of the priesthood—was already in place. He reminded them that this organization had been established by divine revelation and that all that was necessary for success was "to turn on the power and to start the wheels in motion."

Following the conference, Elder Melvin J. Ballard was appointed chairman of the Church Security Committee with Harold B. Lee and Mark Austin as members; and at the October general conference in 1936, Campbell Brown, Stringham Stevens, and Henry D. Moyle were added as committee members. At that same conference, President McKay, who for months had been immersed in the mechanics and details of the program, sounded a call that typified his approach to any assignment or project. This was a call to spirituality. "It is something to supply clothing to the scantily clad," he told the audience, "to furnish ample food to those whose table is thinly spread, to give to those who are fighting desperately the despair that comes from enforced idleness, but after all is said and done, the greatest blessings that will accrue from the church security plan are spiritual. Outwardly, every act seems to be directed toward the physical: remaking of dresses and suits of clothes, canning fruits and vegetables, storing foodstuffs . . . all seems strictly temporal, but permeating all these acts, inspiring and sanctifying them, is the element of spirituality." (CR, October 1936, p. 103.)

Once the committee was in place, President McKay's direct contact with the operation of the welfare program was minimized, although for several years, he continued to be the principal member of the First Presidency who gave it administrative direction. Meanwhile, it was President Grant who provided the overall impetus for the work through his stirring and dramatic talks given at general conferences and at regional and stake meetings.

Although launching the Church Security Plan con-
sumed more of President McKay's time during 1936 than
any other single activity, there were many others, some
new and some old, that filled his days to overflowing. The
new assignments lay chiefly in the temporal realm, in the
activities of the commercial corporations owned or controlled by the Church. Attendance at the board meetings of
Zions Securities Corporation, Utah Home Fire Insurance
Company, Heber J. Grant Company, Beneficial Life Insurance Company, and the Utah State National Bank began to
occupy blocks of his time, as did dealings pertaining to the
Layton Sugar Company and the Amalgamated Sugar Company. While President McKay did not have a business
background, his orderly habits, practical wisdom, and
spiritual perceptions added an important ingredient to the
deliberations of these businesses. And, with experience,
he gained skills that significantly benefited their operations.

However, these activities, as important and time-
consuming as they were, hardly occupied a tithe of his
working hours. He devoted his efforts largely to the ecclesiastical aspects of his calling, to counseling and instructing
Church leaders and members; to expounding the gospel in
stake, ward, and mission meetings; to administering First
Presidency headquarters responsibilities as delegated by
President Grant; to traveling abroad in the interests of the
Church; and to participating in various ceremonial affairs.

The scope and the intensity of his counseling responsibilities are suggested by this diary entry of March 23, 1936:
"Held continual series of consultations." Also, on May 14
he found it necessary to block out time during the day
for a "consultation with Ray." As the marriage season
approached, he was inundated with requests to perform
temple marriages. A record of sorts was set on May 29
when he yielded to the pleas of six couples, whom he
sealed in the Salt Lake Temple.

An increased interest in temples and temple work was
generated at this time when it was decided to construct a

163

new temple in Idaho. When word of this plan was leaked, Church leaders in several Idaho communities urged the Brethren to construct the new house of the Lord in their areas. Most prominent among these was a promising young counselor in the Boise Stake presidency, Ezra Taft Benson, who pleaded the case of his city in a meeting with President McKay on March 10 and who, four months later, came with his stake president, Scott B. Brown, to renew the appeal. While demographic considerations dictated the selection of Idaho Falls as the temple site at that time, Ezra Taft Benson, as the president of the Twelve, played a key role in 1983 in selecting the site of Idaho's second temple, this one in Boise.

Several major trips distinguished 1936 for President McKay. Earlier in the year, accompanied by Emma Ray, he went to Hawaii on Church and business assignments. They left Salt Lake City on January 15, traveling to San Francisco in a special car furnished by the railroad company. Unwinding in the comfort of his drawing room after a hectic round of meetings and conferences before his departure, he confided to his journal: "I am weary, tired and have a headache and am glad to go to bed, having had to force myself to work today." A good sleep recharged his energies, and the next day the apostle was busy working on a projected book on the teachings and testimonies of New Testament writers.

The travelers had originally planned to spend some time with Llewelyn and his family in Palo Alto, where the son was working on his doctorate at Stanford University. But a snowslide over the Sierras and a minor accident delayed their arrival in San Francisco, making it necessary to go directly from the train depot to their ship, the S.S. *Lurline*. Busy with the details of boarding, and assuming that the delays had robbed them of the family visit he and Ray had longed for, David O. suddenly switched roles from distinguished Church leader to beloved grandfather when he heard the sweet voice of one of Llewelyn's children call over the bustle of the pier, "Hello Papa Dade." The reunited families barely had time for greetings and embraces all around before the benign grandfather and his sweetheart boarded their ship, bound for San Pedro down the California coast and thence for Hawaii.

It being the first time he had passed through the Golden Gate since he and Hugh J. Cannon did so during their round-the-world tour in 1921, President McKay recalled the earlier event with nostalgic pleasure. "What changes since then," he recorded reflectively. But as the *Lurline* breasted the powerful ground swells off the coast, it became apparent there was at least one thing that had not changed. "Squeamish," he recorded biliously. "I am not a good sailor." Ray seemed to fare better until the return trip when, overwhelmed by nausea, she moaned, "And they call this joy." Suggesting the roughness of the return passage, three days after uttering this complaint, Sister McKay and her husband barely escaped serious injury when they were "hurled from one side of the ship to the other," landing on their backs.

But that frightening experience lay in the future as they continued to San Pedro, where they remained for a day while the *Lurline* loaded stores and passengers. The ship departed at 10:00 P.M. January 18 and arrived at Honolulu five days later. The McKays were greeted by a happy group of Saints who serenaded them in Hawaiian fashion and loaded them with colorful, fragrant leis. Among the greeters were Ralph E. Woolley, Oahu Stake president; the Hawaiian Mission president, C. H. Murphy; and William Waddoups, president of the Hawaii Temple.

In the few days President McKay remained in the Islands, he held a series of meetings with leaders and members of the Church, including a large conference in Honolulu for Sunday School workers from throughout Oahu. He visited the temple and checked on affairs at the Church's Laie plantation. He also inspected the Kohala Mill of the Union Sugar Company, conferring with its executives about business matters of mutual interest.

But of all the experiences President McKay had on this

trip, the inspiring meetings with the Saints, the lavish feasts, and the magnificent scenery, the one that affected him most was a visit to Pulehu on Maui. There stood a monument erected in honor of George Q. Cannon, one of the early missionaries in the Hawaiian Islands. The visitor noted in his diary on January 30, 1936: "Fifteen years ago President Hugh J. Cannon, E. Wesley Smith . . . and I had a remarkable spiritual manifestation here." In his account of the incident, Hugh J. Cannon wrote that as they engaged in prayer, "they stood almost in the visible presence of celestial beings." And in reviewing the world tour after the lapse of several years, Hugh J. Cannon said of the Pulehu manifestation, "There are few, if any, experiences which are more impressive than was this." (Hugh J. Cannon unpublished narrative of world tour; copy in possession of author.)

Two other trips President McKay took in 1936 also aroused nostalgic reflections, both of them to the same place. On April 28, he and President Clark traveled to Omaha, Nebraska, where, in company with sculptor Avard Fairbanks and others, they selected the site for Dr. Fairbanks's heroic sculpture *Tragedy at Winter Quarters*. During the next five months, the site was prepared and the monument put in place. In late September, David again traveled to Omaha to participate in the dedication of the monument in the Mormon Pioneer Cemetery in Florence, Nebraska. During these visits, the counselor was powerfully reminded of the struggling trials of his people during their exodus west. He seemed to gain a sense of immediacy about the drama when he visited the old house in which Brigham Young lived during his stay in Winter Quarters and inspected the towering cottonwood tree supposed to have been planted by the Lion of the Lord.

Sandwiched between these two official trips to Omaha was a trip to Boston in mid-June whose purpose was strictly personal. There, on June 18, David and Ray proudly watched as their son Lawrence received a master of law degree from the Harvard School of Law. Aside from the understandable feelings of parental pride the occasion brought, it also foreshadowed the fulfillment of a long-held desire of the parents that their eldest son and his family return to Utah to live. Within months after receiving his degree, Lawrence entered into a partnership with Henry D. Moyle in Salt Lake City. This enabled the parents to enjoy more frequent contact with their young lawyer and the father to receive counsel from one in whom he had implicit confidence. And President McKay was anxious for another hand to help with the work on the Huntsville farm—a feeling that doubtless received a strong endorsement from Robert, who was the only son available to help the father plant potatoes in Dry Hollow in early June. Ned, who graduated from the University of Utah the next day, was too busy to help; and Lawrence and Llewelyn were still out of state. Robert got some relief from his role of sole assistant on the Fourth of July, when thirty-five members of the extended McKay family joined at the old homestead to celebrate. The men and boys commemorated their country's birthday by baling hay in the morning before an afternoon of recreation, food, and visiting.

Incidents affecting two men with whom President McKay had shared the apostleship provided alternate moments of joy and sadness during 1936. The joyful experience involved his friend and neighbor Matthias F. Cowley, who lived on north West Temple just around the corner from the McKay's apartment building. This pair had been bound together, in a sense, by the fact that Elder Cowley resigned from the Twelve on October 28, 1905, because of his refusal to accept the Manisfesto as interpreted by the First Presidency, and David O. McKay was ordained an apostle and sustained as a member of the Twelve on April 9, 1906, to fill a vacancy in the Twelve. On May 11, 1911, Elder Cowley was disfellowshipped because of his persistence in refusing to accept the Manifesto. And during much of the intervening years, President McKay and the former member of the Twelve lived as close neighbors and as members of the Seventeenth Ward. On April 2, 1936, Matthias

Cowley handed to President McKay, for delivery to Heber J. Grant, a letter that acknowledged his error and pleaded that his disfellowshipment be lifted. The alacrity and apparent pleasure with which President Grant acted on this request is shown by the fact that the next day, April 3, 1936, Matthias Foss Cowley was restored to full fellowship in the Church.

The sad incident involving a fellow apostle was the death of Alonzo A. Hinckley in December. President McKay was one of the speakers at the funeral of his friend who served as a member of the Twelve for only twenty-six months. The death of this man at the comparatively young age of sixty-six, after having served in the Twelve for such a short time, was a reminder to all of the tenuous nature of life and of the uncertainty that waited at every turn in the road.

Chapter Twelve

Maturing as a Counselor

Following a customary pattern, President McKay took inventory of his personal and family life at the beginning of 1937. He was pleased to record that Lawrence had received his master of law degree from Harvard and had begun practicing law with Henry D. Moyle, and that Llewelyn had completed the classwork for his Ph.D. from Stanford University and was on the faculty at the University of Utah. He noted that Lou Jean and Russell were living in Cleveland, where the doctor was completing his training at the Cline Clinic; that Emma Rae was teaching at Granite High School; that Ned was in the mission field; and that Robert was doing well academically in high school and was the president of his senior class. As for the father and mother of this active, progressive family, the diarist merely recorded: "Mama Ray and I are happy parents and still sweethearts."

While President McKay made specific note of the maturing of his family, we find the record of his maturing as a counselor only in the maze of entries that chronicled his day-to-day activities. Now he had served in the First Presidency for over two years, time enough to have become fully acquainted with his duties and prerogatives. It was no small step to move to the First Presidency after more than a quarter of a century of service in the Twelve, a deliberative council whose chief role is to supervise the Church's worldwide missionary effort and to regulate and set in order the affairs of the Church throughout the stakes and missions. These activities, however, are carried on with the entire membership of the quorum and under the overall direction of the First Presidency. While the Twelve confer regularly with the First Presidency in their weekly temple meetings, they usually are not privy to the wide range of Church responsibilities discharged by the latter, matters pertaining to finances, physical facilities, personnel, temple work, public relations, and the myriad activities carried on under the umbrella of the Corporation of the President—or, in earlier years, the Trustee in Trust.

So, it took time for President McKay to become thoroughly acquainted with all the sources of power and influence that inhere in the First Presidency and to become accustomed to the correlative load of duty and responsibility that follows in their wake. The indoctrination he had received in the previous two and a half years in the authority and responsibility of the First Presidency was vital in preparing him for the events of 1937. During much of this year, both President Grant and President Clark were away from Church headquarters. The Prophet made long trips to the East, to California, and to Arizona during the year, holding meetings, tending to Church affairs, and, intermittently, enjoying a little recreation. President Clark was still heavily involved in business and professional matters that took him away from Utah often, and for extended periods. And during the summer, both the Prophet and his first counselor spent three months in Europe in the interests of the Church. In these circumstances, the principal responsibility for administering Church affairs at headquarters rested with President McKay. His daily routine was one constant round of meetings and consultations. Even though the organization of the Church Security Committee and the appointment of Harold B. Lee as the managing director had transferred the detail of the program from the First Presidency to others, there were still numerous questions of policy and procedure that only the First Presidency could decide. At this time, that meant David O. McKay.

During the infancy of Church welfare, numerous ideas to advance the work were proposed. Two of these surfaced during 1937. On April 29, President McKay, joined by several members of the security committee, drove to Layton, Utah, where they witnessed a demonstration of the Bonham Brothers tractor. It was proposed that the Church, apparently through a franchise agreement, manufacture and market their machines, either to local welfare projects or on the open market. While President McKay and the others who witnessed the demonstration were impressed with the operation of the machine, the idea of manufacturing and marketing it was abandoned as being infeasible. A few days later, David O. went to Tooele, Utah, with members of the committee to consider a proposal to divert water from Tooele Valley to Salt Lake Valley by means of a tunnel in order to irrigate fertile land on the east side of the Oquirrhs. Again, the idea was rejected. Despite the apparent lack of merit of these and other suggestions, no attempt was made by President McKay to dampen the creativity and enthusiasm of the committee. All ideas to advance the work were given respectful consideration. Many were accepted and implemented; and others, like these two, were abandoned. In this manner, step by step, and sometimes by trial and error, the vast Church welfare program developed. And, like an infant, it had to learn to crawl and then to toddle before it could walk and run as it does today.

Through faith, persistence, and skill, the program began to take root and flourish. Its growth was promoted by frequent training sessions at the general, regional, and stake levels. On July 2, 1937, for instance, President McKay presided at a special meeting in Barratt Hall, where all General Authorities and all members of general boards were instructed in the objectives and procedures of the security plan. And on December 12, he presided at a regional meeting in Barratt Hall where twelve hundred local leaders were in attendance.

Although the Church Welfare Program was still in its formative stages, it had already begun to attract national attention. "The March of Time," a popular newsreel of the day, featured the Church's welfare efforts in a special film that President McKay viewed on January 26: "It is very good," he noted, "and will undoubtedly wield helpful influence throughout the world whenever it is shown." That evening, he addressed another special gathering of Church security plan workers held in the Granite Stake Center. President McKay characterized it as a "very important meeting."

President Grant returned in early March from a lengthy trip, and President Clark returned from the East a month later, so the entire First Presidency was together for a short while before and after the 1937 April general conference. In brief remarks delivered at that time, the second counselor, after developing the theme that divine authority by direct revelation is the most distinguishing feature of the Church, had this to say about his two colleagues in the First Presidency: "I will also testify that divine authority rests in rich abundance upon him whom the Lord has chosen to stand at the head of this work at the present time. I am deeply grateful for the opportunity I have had to sit in council with President Grant and President Clark." And then in one of the finest eulogies he ever gave to his leader, the speaker said of President Grant: "I wish every person in this church might have had the same opportunity to look into President Grant's noble spirit as I have; to know him as I have had the privilege to know him; to glimpse his unbounding generosity, his love for mankind, and particularly for those who are true and loyal to the church; to realize how fearlessly he stands for right. If you realized these virtues more fully, I am sure that when you kneel down to pray there would be a note of thanksgiving in your heart and in your words which perhaps there has not been heretofore." (CR, April 1937, p. 122.)

In an apparent attempt to negate some of the criticism

that had been leveled against President Clark because of his frequent absences from Church headquarters, the speaker had this to say about his friend: "I would like to pay a tribute to President Clark, a man of sterling integrity, who loves this work above everything else in this world. He is loyal and true, sound and clear in judgment, a valiant servant of the Lord." (Ibid.)

Some time after conference, David O. organized a party to go to Huntsville. There, with four hired men assisting, he supervised the planting of over two hundred trees, siberian elms, evergreens, and cottonwoods. Some of the fruit of this work party can still be seen in Huntsville in the pleasant shade and the gracious setting these trees provide. That President McKay's participation was not limited to supervisory duties is suggested by this diary entry: "I am so stiff I can hardly straighten up."

Apparently concerned about his physical condition after this outing, and fully conscious that he was approaching the age when most people retire, David soon enrolled in a calisthenics and body-building program. "Today I took my first lesson at the gymnasium," he recorded with satisfaction on May 21. This began a practice he was to follow intermittently for many years. Often his work schedule was so erratic he could not consistently block out the time required by his gymnastics. But he used the facilities of the nearby Deseret Gymnasium as often as circumstances allowed. It was the combination of his inherited health and vitality, the development of his physique as a youth on the farm, and his regular habit of exercise at Huntsville or at the gym that contributed to President McKay's longevity.

Being as active as he was and as determined to keep abreast of his responsibilities, it is not surprising that now and then his enthusiasm and expectations outran his capacities. Such was the case on the last day of May, when he gathered up sons Lawrence, Llewelyn, and Robert and grandson Dickie for a work party at Dry Hollow Farm. There the workers repaired fences, cleared dead trees from the grove, and dredged clogged ditches. So vigorously did President McKay work that he injured a knee, which made him lame for some time.

It was only a short while before this outing that Dickie and another grandchild, Midean, were baptized in the Tabernacle font by Lawrence. Afterward the party went to the reception room of the Church Administration Building, where "Papa Dade" confirmed the pair, giving them each a special blessing. Amidst his crowded schedule of meetings, conferences, and consultations, it was these occasional interludes with members of his family that brightened President McKay's days and added interest and zest to all that he did. Not only did he enjoy the members of his immediate family, but he derived much joy from the frequent contacts with his brothers and sisters and their families. In late April, three sisters, Jeanette, Ann, and Katherine, paid a surprise call at his office. David O. adjusted his schedule to accommodate them, and the four enjoyed a pleasant interlude, visiting and reminiscing. In recalling the happy occasion as he made his daily entry, the diarist commented on his "sweet, darling sisters." And on his sixty-fourth birthday, Jeanette entertained all the brothers and sisters and their companions at her home in Ogden. These get-togethers were always the occasion for lively conversation, good humor, and happy reflections. And, in a larger sense, they were a sort of celebration honoring their parents, David and Jennette Evans McKay, who lived their lives in quiet obscurity in a remote Utah valley but whose faith and dedication were, in the end, exhibited for all to see in the lives of their children. The home in which these children were reared was, in reality, a workshop of applied Christianity where they learned, through example and precept, the principles that enabled them to live joyously and abundantly. In the sermon President McKay delivered at the October general conference a few weeks after the birthday gathering, he dwelt on this very theme. After quoting the Savior's words "I am come that they might have life, and that they might have it more abundantly," he stated: "We believe, however, that this abundant life is obtained not only from spiritual exaltation but by the application to daily life of the principles that Jesus taught." The speaker then elaborated these four principles that all of the McKay children had learned so well: First, a belief in a supreme being, "an assurance that he can be approached for guidance, and that he will manifest himself to those who seek him." Second, a recognition that life is a gift of God and therefore divine: "The proper use of this gift impels man to become the master, not the slave of nature." Third, the need for personal integrity: "By this I mean, plain, everyday honesty, sobriety, and respect for others' rights." And fourth, the need for social consciousness, or that which "awakens in each individual the realization that it is his duty to make the world better for his having been in it." (CR, October 1937, p. 103.)

In this same sermon, President McKay cited an example of social consciousness as reflected in the developing welfare program. He told of a special fast day that had been held by the Saints in the Salt Lake Region to raise funds for a new storehouse. "The committee asked the people to go without two meals on that day and contribute the equivalent cash for the project. The leaders anticipated raising about $4,000. The people contributed over $15,000—realization exceeding anticipation nearly four times!" (Ibid., p. 102.)

With the return in September of President Grant and President Clark from their three-month tour in Europe, Brother McKay was given a welcome respite from the heavy administrative load he had carried alone in their absence. At the insistence of President Grant, he and Ray went to Yellowstone for a short break just before the October conference; and a few days after the conference they went to California for a one-week holiday. Sharing the fate of his brethren who are held in such esteem by the Saints, it was almost impossible for President McKay to steal away for an uninterrupted vacation in an area where the Church was established in large numbers if any of the local Saints knew he was there. So when his presence in Southern

California became known, he was bombarded with requests to speak or to counsel. While he was able graciously and in good conscience to decline most of these, yet the few he accepted interrupted the calm and seclusion he had sought by traveling to California.

In the first week of 1938, President McKay engaged in an activity that he always relished and looked forward to with anticipation. On January 6, he met in the Assembly Room of the Salt Lake Temple with a large group of missionaries who were receiving special training before going to their fields of labor. Dressed in an immaculate white suit, with his wavy and abundant white hair framing a face whose ruddy cheeks and bright eyes radiated a healthy vigor, the man standing before the missionaries commanded their attention and respect before he had uttered a word. In this setting, David O. McKay had a celestial quality about him, a quality that was enhanced by the subject matter he treated. Here he spoke of sacred things, of the sanctity and eternal nature of the marriage covenant, of the process of perfection through obedience and sacrifice, and of the dependency of men and women on the Father and His Only Begotten Son.

These sensitive themes comprise what some have referred to as the curriculum of the University of the Lord. And, accepting this analogy as implying that in the temple are taught the most advanced concepts of Mormon theology, it would have been difficult to find one more qualified to fill this role than David O. McKay. Trained as a professional teacher, well informed on Church doctrine and procedure, and experienced in the reality and power of spiritual phenomena, he was able to impart understanding and conviction about concepts that only a few are able to teach effectively.

But the intellectual concepts President McKay taught in this setting and elsewhere hardly had more impact than his visual image, which of itself conveyed lessons about the fruits of righteous living and about the embryonic divinity that exists in man. Here was an exemplar worthy of emulation.

This was not the only setting in which President McKay regularly taught and motivated missionaries. Often he participated in the regular training classes held in the "Mission Home," a cluster of renovated two-story houses on State Street north of the Beehive House, where he gave practical instruction about proselyting and about the agony and ecstasy of actual missionary work.

In addition to his role of teaching and inspiring missionaries, the counselor also had the responsibility to give administrative direction to the missionary work. He was involved in the overall supervision of the work and in the calling, assigning, and setting apart of mission presidents. One of these gave him special satisfaction when on January 18 he joined in setting apart Matthew Cowley—the son of his friend Matthias—as the president of the mission in New Zealand. President McKay would later have a closer association with this eloquent man, who, while David O. served as a counselor to President George Albert Smith, was called as a member of the Twelve.

Later in the year, President McKay was troubled by the decision to remove the missionaries from Germany because of the saber rattling going on there. On March 11, 1938, German troops had marched into Austria on the pretense of helping "to restore order." And in the summer, the Nazi Fuehrer had begun his propaganda campaign against neighboring Czechoslovakia, which ultimately resulted in its downfall. These actions and the intermittent rages of the German leader had caused the Brethren to withdraw the missionaries from Germany and to reassign them temporarily to other Western European countries. On September 20, however, President McKay received a telephone call from Alfred C. Rees in Copenhagen. He had presided in Germany and advised that because of the negotiations in progress at Munich, "the danger of war was over," and that subject to contrary direction from the Brethren, he intended to take his missionaries back into Germany. Ten days later, the famous Munich agreement was entered into. Britain's prime minister, Neville Chamberlain, declared it would guarantee "peace in our time." It was against this background that authorization was given for the Mormon missionaries to return to Germany to proselyte. Their presence there was short-lived, however, and ended a few months later when Elder Joseph Fielding Smith of the Twelve, who supervised the evacuation of all foreign missionaries from Europe, was set apart by President Grant and President McKay on April 19, 1939, just five months before Hitler's panzer divisions poured into Poland.

While the pressures of war were building up in Europe during 1938 and the first part of 1939, life with its customary twists and turns went on as usual at Church headquarters. As President McKay approached the April general conference in 1938, he felt a sense of weariness that could have been traced to a bout with the flu he had had in mid-February and to the rigorous schedule he had kept during the three and a half years since being called to the First Presidency. Later events were to point to another cause.

He was the first speaker at the second general session held on Sunday afternoon, April 3. Alluding to the "present day difficulties and perplexities"—depression at home and war clouds abroad—the speaker used as his text this paraphrased statement of Lord Nelson: "Now is the time for every man to accept responsibility and to do his duty." He proposed both a spiritual and a temporal application of this principle. Spiritually, he admonished "each individual to work out his own salvation." This, he cautioned, was to be done "with fear and trembling," in the course of which "we should seek the strength and grace of God for inspiration to obtain the final victory." Temporally he prescribed hard, consistent work. "Too many men are claiming that the world owes them a living," he charged, "and are sitting effortlessly by expecting the world to throw its luxuries into their passive laps." But whether one seeks a spiritual or a temporal goal, the process of attainment is the same: "He must rise by his own efforts," President McKay told the audience, "and he must walk by faith. . . . He who would ascend the stairway leading upward . . . must tread it step by step from the base stone to the summit of its flight. Not a single stair can be missed, not one duty neglected if the climber would avoid danger and delay, and arrive with all safety and expedition at the topmost landing." (CR, April 1938, pp. 16, 18.)

With his major conference address behind, the following day should have been one of relaxed enjoyment for the second counselor. Instead, it turned out to be one of the most agonizing days of his life. As he sat on the stand Monday, President McKay was stricken with a pain so intense it was difficult to breathe. Emma Ray, who sat nearby in the section reserved for the wives of General Authorities, noted her husband shifting in his chair in an apparently fruitless attempt to find a comfortable position. The distracted look on his face convinced her that he was in pain. Knowing of her husband's stoicism, which would have precluded him from seeking aid under the circumstances, Sister McKay quietly left her seat and, using a telephone beneath the choir loft, summoned the family doctor. At the hospital, where the patient was taken during a break in the meeting, the doctor diagnosed the ailment as a kidney infection and prescribed medication and hospital rest. After a few days, the president was allowed to leave the hospital. But he did not feel well. At the temple meeting on Thursday, April 14, after helping set apart the new Presiding Bishopric, LeGrand Richards, Marvin O. Ashton, and Joseph L. Wirthlin, he sat in the same chair the new General Authorities had occupied and received a blessing from his brethren. Two days later, he checked back into the hospital. This time it was the Dee Hospital in Ogden—later renamed the McKay-Dee Hospital in his honor—where, during an illness, he seemed to feel more at home, being nearer to his beloved Huntsville. After four days at the Dee, where he underwent a battery of tests, David returned home. Slowly he began to mend, working intermittently at home or in his office. When by mid-May he had not fully recovered, President Grant "ordered" his ailing counselor to go to California, where, free from the daily office routine, it was hoped he could completely recover. On May 17, the day before leaving Salt Lake City, David O. McKay, doting grandfather, participated in one of those family functions that meant so much to him when he baptized grandson Russell Blood.

Twelve days of restful seclusion in California did wonders for the patient. He returned home on May 30, tanned and rested and ready to resume his arduous duties. But this lengthy illness, coming in President McKay's sixty-fifth year, was a warning to be more heedful of his health. It also was the harbinger of other illnesses he was to endure in the years to come and perhaps the first clear signal of his mortality.

But David O. McKay was not given to morbid introspections. He plunged into his duties on returning home as if he had not been ill. The following day he participated in a special radio broadcast to the Saints in Samoa, using a media tool that he learned to master. It had been seventeen years since he and Hugh J. Cannon spent a month among these loving people, and it was the first time since then that these people had heard the voice of the apostle whom they would have worshipped had he not forbade it.

A variety of activities dominated President McKay's schedule during the last half of 1938. In late June he traveled to the Northwest, where he dedicated a new chapel in Portland, Oregon, and organized there the 123rd stake. That the Church was then on the threshold of astounding growth, bidding to expand into a populous worldwide organization, is shown by the fact that in the thirteen years from the organization of the Portland Stake to the time David O. McKay became the president of the Church, sixty-eight new stakes were organized, while during the nineteen years of his tenure as president, three hundred and fifty-six new stakes came into being.

During late July and early August, President McKay spent over two weeks in New York, attending the Hill Cumorah pageant, "America's Witness for Christ," directed by H. Wayne Driggs, and reviewing the operations and management of Church farms in the area. He also conducted and spoke at two services held in the Sacred Grove, where the boy prophet Joseph Smith was visited by the Father and the Son. Reflecting on the extraordinary spiritual origins of the Church, the apostle devoted one talk to an analysis of the reasons for accepting the testimony of Joseph Smith. An immediate and unsettling result of Joseph's announcement of his vision had been ostracism by religious leaders who were incensed by the boy's declaration that the existing creeds were an "abomination" and their leaders "corrupt." One thing that convinced the speaker of Joseph's veracity was his response to this ostracism. Earlier President McKay had written about this facet of Joseph Smith's life: "In a very short time he found himself standing alone. Alone—and unacquainted with the learning and philosophy of his day. Alone—and unschooled in the arts and sciences. Alone—and no philosopher to instruct him, no minister to guide him. . . . Thus he was left alone to embark upon the ocean of religious thought, having rejected every known vessel with which to sail and never having built one or even having seen one built himself. Surely if an imposter, the bark he would build would be indeed a crude one." (MS 85:88.)

At home following the New York trip, President McKay was heavily involved with the missionary activities already mentioned and with preparations for the October general conference. When the second counselor presented the General Authorities for a sustaining vote on October 7, he read out the name of thirty-two-year-old Richard L. Evans as the newest member of the First Council of the Seventy. This talented young man, who a few years before had become the voice of the Salt Lake Tabernacle Choir national broadcasts, would work closely with President McKay in the years ahead, especially in the area of Church publications and media communications. Fifteen years later as the President of the Church, David O. called Elder Evans as the newest member of the Twelve, the fourth apostle he selected after entering the prophetic office.

It was during the last half of the year that President McKay's involvement with preparations for the 1947 centennial celebration began to accelerate. Earlier on April 1, the Utah legislature had adopted a resolution recommending the appointment of a committee to study the feasibility of holding a "World's Fair" in Utah in 1947 and to report its findings to the next legislature. Governor Henry H. Blood appointed President McKay as the chairman of a seventy-five-man committee to fill this mandate. Displaying a talent for organization, the chairman, in turn, appointed nine subcommittees and an executive committee to correlate their work. Through the following months, President McKay met regularly with the executive committee and others as the details of the findings to be presented to the legislature were hammered out. During this period, and later, President McKay was greatly aided by the work of A. Hamer Reiser, who handled numerous details for the chairman and who in years ahead was to assist him in many ways.

By December the issue of financing the centennial celebration came to the fore, and in an effort to ascertain what financial aid might be available from state and local governments, President McKay met with Governor Blood and Salt Lake City Mayor John Wallace to explore the matter. Satisfied from this meeting on the twelfth that there would not be adequate financing to sponsor a world's fair as had been proposed originally, the chairman, with the approval of his committee, proposed to the legislature that the celebration be localized to the state. On that basis, the next Utah legislature created the 1947 Utah Centennial Commission, authorizing the chief executive to appoint the commission members. Under that authorization, Governor Blood appointed President McKay chairman of the commission, providing him with an able staff headed by Gus P. Backman, executive secretary, and fourteen commission members drawn from among both Mormon and non-Mormon leaders in the state. In addition to providing cultural, educational, and entertainment events for the enjoyment of the public, the commission aimed at using the centennial to stimulate the beautification of the entire state by encouraging local communities to promote the remodeling and painting of old buildings and the landscaping of both public and private properties. And, in order to make the natural attractions of the state more readily available to both residents and visitors, the commission sought to promote road building or improvement and the construction or remodeling of lodging accommodations, having in mind the increased use and enjoyment of the canyons along the Wasatch and of Zion, Bryce, Cedar Breaks, and the Wayne Wonderland recreation areas.

Here was work enough to keep the commission and leaders and citizens throughout the state fully occupied during the eight years preceding the centennial. But the terrible war that would erupt soon intervened to take the center stage of thought and action and to relegate the plans for the centennial to the wings.

Chapter Thirteen

The Dislocations of War—and Illness

The Nazi attack on Poland on September 1, 1939, vastly altered the perceptions, practices, and policies of the Church with respect to its international activities. As already indicated, Elder Joseph Fielding Smith was set apart on April 19 of this year by President Grant and President McKay to oversee the missionary work in Europe. When it became apparent that war in Europe was inevitable, the First Presidency sent word to Elder Smith on August 24 that all missionaries in Germany should be transferred to neutral countries. Acting under this direction, the East German missionaries were assigned to Denmark and the West German missionaries to Holland. However, when Holland promptly closed its borders, it became necessary to send the West German missionaries to Denmark also. These moves proved to be fruitless, however, as the action of England and France in declaring war on Germany on September 3 made it necessary to evacuate all foreign missionaries from Europe. In his role as the member of the First Presidency principally responsible for missionary work, President McKay carefully monitored and supervised this complicated operation. Because of the precipitate manner in which the evacuation became necessary, passage was booked for the 697 evacuees (including 611 elders, 63 young women missionaries, and 23 others comprising mission presidents and their families) on any craft that was available. They returned to the United States on twenty-three different ships, most of them freighters. The first group arrived in New York City on September 7, 1939, and the last on March 4, 1940. This last group included President McKay's brother, Thomas E. (who had presided in Europe), his wife and daughter, and four missionaries.

Despite having left his field of labor as directed by the First Presidency, Elder Thomas E. McKay maintained close contact with the members and leaders of the Church in Europe. On July 26 he approached his brother about arranging to bring some Latter-day Saint children from Europe to the United States for their safety. These discussions continued intermittently as the social, political, and diplomatic implications were weighed. And, on the diplomatic front, the pressures exerted by the war in Europe erupted in South America when Argentina suddenly balked at issuing visas to Mormon missionaries. On the same day President McKay conferred with his brother about the refugee children in Europe, he was also involved in discussions about the Argentine visa problem. It was decided to enlist the aid of a U.S. senator from Utah, William H. King, in an effort to unsnarl it.

This, of course, was merely a prelude to the decision the Brethren ultimately made to withdraw the missionaries from other foreign lands where war raged or was threatened. And where it was feasible to do so, President McKay, in his role as steward of the Church's vast missionary network, personally welcomed and reassigned the missionaries as they returned to American shores. So, in early November 1940, he traveled to San Francisco, where on the sixth he met the S.S. *Mariposa*, which carried fifty-seven missionaries who had been summoned home from New Zealand, Australia, Tonga, and Samoa. After arrangements were made to handle the baggage of the sea travelers, President McKay met with them in the San Francisco Ward chapel where, after a session of testimony bearing and instructions, they were given new assignments, some to the California Mission and others to the Northwest, to Texas, and to Hawaii.

On the twenty-seventh of the month, President McKay left for New York City, where on December 1 he met thirty-two missionaries from South Africa who arrived on the S.S. *President Polk* and who were similarly instructed and reassigned. On the day of his departure from Salt Lake City, the second counselor received a poignant reminder of the dislocations of war. Representing the First Presidency, he met with Archduke Felix of Austria, who was on a lecture tour of the United States, endeavoring to earn a livelihood by this means. This once wealthy and influential member of the Austrian nobility had been forced to this extremity when the Nazis invaded his country in 1938.

Meanwhile, as the international tensions intensified and as the Church acted to make the adjustments they dictated, the flow of President McKay's other administrative responsibilities and his personal life continued unabated. On January 4, 1939, the second counselor represented the First Presidency at cornerstone-laying ceremonies of the Church welfare storehouse at Seventh West and Seventh South in Salt Lake City. And four and a half months later this facility, whose white storage bins now comprise a familiar part of the city's skyline, was completed and opened for public inspection. On May 25, all of the General Authorities were given a tour of the facility and afterward enjoyed a dinner prepared from welfare commodities and served in the warehouse.

In the interval between these events, David O. participated in two other significant welfare functions. First, during the April general conference in 1939, he addressed a "glorious meeting of the church welfare plan held in the Assembly Hall." And second, a multistake welfare meeting was held in Sacramento, California, where he and Elder Harold B. Lee instructed stake and ward leaders in welfare principles. Reflecting the increasing confidence he had in this able young associate, he recorded, "Brother Lee handled the matters very thoroughly and clearly and gave valuable instructions." This genuine praise, given in secret, was reflected publicly two years later when President McKay enthusiastically joined in approving President Grant's decision that Harold B. Lee be called to the Twelve.

From Sacramento, President and Sister McKay traveled on to San Francisco, where they toured the World's Fair. Of special interest to the visitors was the Church exhibit, with which the apostle was "very favorably impressed." He commented with pride on the "young men in charge of the work," clean cut and bright elders to whom he could relate so well, having come out of those same ranks many years before. A few months later President McKay received another reminder of the competence and effectiveness of youthful missionaries when on June 26 he interviewed Elder Marvin J. Ashton on his return from the British Mission. The son and namesake of the first counselor in the Presiding Bishopric, Elder Ashton had labored for a while with Elder Mathias Cowley, who was called to Great Britain after his reinstatement. The apostolic relationship between this tall young elder and President McKay's old friend from the Seventeenth Ward was, of course, unknown at the time. But it is interesting to reflect on the unusual companionship of these two men. The elder was called to the apostleship by President Wilford Woodruff in 1897, and the younger would be called to that exclusive brotherhood seventy-four years later by Joseph Fielding Smith, almost two years after President McKay's death.

Other trips taken by President McKay during 1939 included two to New York, the first in early June, when he attended to affairs involving the Church properties near Palmyra. While in the East on this occasion, he and Sister McKay met Emma Rae and Ned. On June 9, the four of them took in the fair that was in progress there.

It was during 1939 that the McKays' life-style underwent a radical change. For many years the family had occupied a large apartment in a building directly across the street north of Temple Square. With an increase in the number of grandchildren, and with the prospect that this trend would accelerate, David and Emma Ray decided to purchase a large home in a residential neighborhood. The one selected was a two-story red brick home with a basement and an attic, located at 1037 East South Temple Street. Behind was a detached garage built of the same red brick and a yard where exuberant grandchildren could exhaust their pent-up energies and yet be near enough for grandparental supervision—and enjoyment. This fine family home had been owned by the prominent Dayton family. On May 23, the McKays met with Newell Dayton, chairman of the board of Tracy Collins Bank & Trust Company, and signed the papers for the acquisition of their new home. It would remain their city residence for over twenty years until after President McKay's call to the prophetic office, when he and Ray moved into a Hotel Utah apartment in the interest of convenience and efficiency. A week after signing the papers, the McKays were busy preparing for the move.

While this move was a source of excitement and happiness to President and Sister McKay, it was not made without tinges of nostalgic sadness. The new home with all its advantages lacked the special view the apartment afforded—the view of the spired temple, which loomed above their North Temple dwelling. This massive gray granite structure was a constant reminder of the happy origin of their married life whose foundation had been laid within its sacred walls. And a few steps across the street took the apartment dwellers within the quiet seclusion of Temple Square for a moment of meditation or a restful organ recital. The new home was a mile and a half away from all this as it was away from the convenience of downtown shopping and entertainments and from David O.'s office.

Another facet of the new acquisition that caused some twinges of regret was the trade of their Ogden home as part of the consideration. While this home had been rented since the McKays' move to Salt Lake, yet it was a sentimental reminder of their early married life and of the community in which all their children had been born. Now, the sale of

*Home of David O. and Emma Ray McKay on 1037 East South Temple Street.
The McKays lived here from June 1939 to July 1960.*

this home severed the tangible ties they had to it and to
Ogden, although the emotional attachments to them would
remain forever.

Not long after President McKay welcomed home Elder
Marvin J. Ashton, a future apostle, he bid farewell to
another apostolic associate, Elder Melvin J. Ballard, who
died in July. Elder McKay and Elder Ballard, who were
both born in 1873 in remote, adjacent Utah Valleys, had
much more in common than the contiguity of the time and
place of their birth and a shared apostolic calling. They
were alike in their handsome appearance and in the
spiritual aura they projected. Both exerted strong, positive
influence on young people, many of whom sought to emulate them. And in their youth, both received spiritual insight into their future leadership roles, Elder McKay on his
mission and Elder Ballard as a boy when the patriarch
Zebedee Coltrin foretold his call to the apostleship.

President McKay had visited his friend in the hospital
on the twenty-fifth, when he pronounced him to be "seriously ill." The patient was reported to be "better" the fol-

lowing day. But four days later, Elder Ballard passed away at the comparatively young age of sixty-six. The second counselor in the First Presidency, who eulogized him at the funeral held on August 3, would outlive the deceased by thirty years—years of trial, trauma, and triumph.

David O. returned in mid-November from a tiring trip to the East, where he had gone to inspect Church farms and other properties in New York City and its vicinity. He was weary and was troubled by nagging abdominal pains. A few days later he checked into the Ogden Dee Hospital, where on the first of December he underwent surgery for a double hernia. As he fought off the supefying effects of the ether, the patient was heard to mumble, "I don't think it's worth it." The difficult months that followed would convert that tentative appraisal into one of absolute certainty.

Before President McKay could mount a recovery from the operation, he was stricken with a pulmonary embolism resulting in severe congestion of the lungs. What was expected to be a few days' stay at the hospital stretched into six weeks. Here the patient spent an uncomfortable Christmas and New Year's, brightened only by the visits of family and associates and by the flood of cards, letters, and flowers that poured in from all quarters. His secretary, Clare Middlemiss, made periodic visits from Salt Lake City, bringing the mail and taking back general instructions. But David O. did not feel up to any work of substance. Although the pain connected with the surgery had subsided, the onset of the pulmonary problems had made it impossible to exercise as he otherwise would have done, thus impeding the speed of his recovery and creating a debilitating effect on his whole system.

By January 14, 1940, President McKay's condition had improved to the point where he was allowed to return home. "Suffered no ill effects from the 36 mile drive," he confided to his journal after being comfortably settled in his own bed. When after two weeks it became apparent that the biting cold and the smoke-clogged atmosphere in Salt Lake City was impeding his recovery, President McKay went to balmy Southern California, where he remained for a month. Returning home on March 1, he went to his office five days later, the first time he had been there in over three months. After only a week, however, it was clear that the damaged lung had not healed completely. So David O. headed again for warm country, going first to Phoenix, Arizona, and then to Los Angeles, from where he returned to Salt Lake City on March 28.

By now the ailing counselor was rapidly making progress toward full recovery. It was fortunate this was so, because on February 5, during his convalescence, President Heber J. Grant was afflicted with a severe stroke while on a combined business and vacation trip to Southern California. That morning the Prophet fell as he got out of bed. Discovering that his left side was paralyzed and his speech impaired, President Grant was admitted to St. Vincents Hospital in Los Angeles. Joseph Anderson, President Grant's secretary, who had accompanied the Church leader to California, promptly contacted President McKay, who went to the mission home where the Prophet was staying and then to the hospital with him. From then until his return to Salt Lake City, the second counselor was a frequent and concerned visitor to his leader's bedside. On February 7, two days after being admitted to the hospital, President Grant made what turned out to be his last journal entry during six weeks of intensive treatment and therapy at St. Vincents. "Spent the day at the hospital," noted the patient. "Brother Anderson called at noon, and at my suggestion he wrote six letters to those who had sent flowers to me at the hospital, thanking them for their remembrances. He brought them up this evening, and I signed them, and he took the train for home. He leaves at my suggestion and that of President McKay."

On April 7, during the general conference, the Prophet's second counselor delivered the first public address he had given since November 1939. After expressing thanks for the opportunity to attend the conference and for the faith and prayers that had speeded his recovery, the speaker provided the assembled Saints with this insight into the illness and condition of their leader: "I am deeply gratified this morning for President Grant's remarkable improvement in health," David O. began. "I was with him when he went from the California Mission home to the St. Vincents Hospital February 5, and thereafter for ten days or more visited him almost daily." Then, referring to a special trip the counselors had made to Los Angeles, the speaker said: "I met in council with him and President Clark March 23 and noted how greatly he had improved. Truly the Lord has answered the prayers offered in his behalf. He is a great and inspired leader; and most earnestly we pray for the prolongation of his life, and his enjoyment of health and happiness." (CR, April 1940, pp. 112-13.)

It is likely that this prayer, and thousands of other similar prayers, helped to prolong President Grant's life for another five years. And a result of that, and of the Prophet's weakened condition, was to place heavier responsibilities on the counselors. It was at this point that President Clark began to reduce the number and extent of his outside commitments. President McKay's restored vigor, after a long convalescence following major surgery and its aftermath, enabled him to help carry the extra burden.

A few weeks after the April conference, the two counselors met with Church attorney Robert L. Judd and Elder Albert E. Bowen of the Twelve, himself a distinguished lawyer, to consider a major change in the legal structure to govern the Church's temporal interests. Out of this and later conferences came the decision to organize a corporation sole under Utah law, a legal entity tailored especially for ecclesiastical organizations. Its purpose is to simplify and formalize the procedures of a church in the acquisition, holding, and disposition of real and personal property. When it was perfected, this legal structure replaced the more cumbersome Trustee-in-Trust form that had been used by the Church since the days of the Prophet Joseph Smith. In legal contemplation, the president of the Church is the corporation sole, acting alone without a board of directors. This vast authority, which is quite apart from the Prophet's power in directing the strictly ecclesiastical affairs of the Church—preaching the gospel, perfecting the Saints, and directing temple work, including work for the dead—is shared only with those whom the Prophet, as the corporation sole, designates as authorized agents. It was in their capacity as authorized agents of the corporation sole that President Clark and President McKay were able to control and to give direction to the temporal affairs of the Church during times when President Grant's disabilities prevented him from doing so; and their status as members of the First Presidency enabled them to act similarly as to all ecclesiastical matters in accordance with the revelations. (See D&C 81:2; D&C 107: 9, 22.)

The insights David O. McKay acquired in the following eleven years about the role and authority of counselors in the First Presidency during times of a president's disability were of vital importance in influencing his policies about the substance and form of First Presidency administration when he became the head of the Church. And the added authority and responsibility that rested with the counselors during such periods further prepared him for shouldering the full load when the prophetic mantle fell on him.

As spring advanced in 1940, bringing warmer weather and longer, more pleasant days, President McKay felt a surge of new energy as he grasped the reins of his responsibilities, which for months had lain slack in his hands. During the first week of May, two important welfare matters claimed his attention. On the third he conferred with Elder Albert E. Bowen, Brother Harold B. Lee, and Church legal counsel Robert L. Judd to formalize a cooperative plan to provide housing for needy members in the Salt Lake region. And four days later he visited Welfare Square and inspected the work going forward on the large grain-storage bins. The pouring of cement went on almost continuously for over three months. By late August, the facility was completed and on the twenty seventh President McKay presided at ceremonies at the site, where he offered the dedicatory prayer. "The first car load of wheat was poured into the bins this morning just after the services," he wrote of the event.

The tempo of other work quickened at the same time— the endless round of council and board meetings, interviews, dictation, speaking engagements; the activities and travel incident to the reassignment of missionaries already noted; and ceremonial appearances. Of the latter, the most significant during the last part of the year was a ceremony at Idaho Falls. There on October 19, President McKay formally dedicated the temple site and laid the cornerstone. Delivering the major address and offering the dedicatory prayer, he dwelt mostly on spiritual themes. He affirmed the reality and power of forces through the veil and admonished his listeners to be obedient to their promptings and diligent in using the facilities of the holy temple.

Amidst the busy whirl of his official duties, David O. continued to carve out islands of quality time for family and personal affairs. On May 23 he laid everything aside to visit and reminisce with "an old missionary companion," John S. Smith. These occasions were not marked by an attitude of condescension on David O.'s part nor did he patronize old friends who came in this way. His interest in and love for them was genuine. He gave them the same undivided attention he bestowed on visitors of more distinguished rank. Indeed, this was one of President McKay's most notable qualities—the quality of focusing his full concentration on the person with whom he was conversing at the moment, walling out all external distractions. One talking with David O. McKay never felt he was intruding or that the apostle would rather be somewhere else or talking with another person, or, perhaps even worse, that he was a mere blip in the great man's consciousness, flitting there among matters and personalities of more monumental importance. So President McKay would never interrupt his conversation with someone to nod or wave to another, or to shake hands with a passerby, or to pardon himself while he spoke just a word to someone else who had approached. Instead he focused only on the person with whom he was speaking.

A week after his visit with Elder Smith, David O. joined forty members of his extended family at the Huntsville homestead for Memorial Day. As part of the celebration, the family "dedicated an appropriate monument to mother and father." And this family affair, occurring near the beginning of summer, bore a symbolic relationship to another one that occurred near summer's end. On September 8, the McKay clan gathered again at Huntsville, this time to commemorate David O.'s sixty-seventh birthday. On both occasions, there were striking evidences of the mutability of life. President McKay gave voice to this perception after attending Sunday School in the old ward chapel on his birthday. "I was impressed with the fact that the years have made almost a complete change in the personnel of the town," he wrote. And reflecting the poetic-philosophic qualities that ran deep in his nature, the diarist added these observations about advancing age: "Old time is a relentless pursuer and crowds birthdays upon us all too fast. Although we are powerless to stem the overflowing stream, yet we can pause at each annual milestone and consider and perhaps enjoy what the past year has brought."

But beneath the swiftly changing events that swirled and cascaded on the surface of David O. McKay's life lay a foundation that was deeply planted and immutable. It was this that imparted the sense of substance and solidity so evident in his being; and the frequent pilgrimages President McKay and his clan made to the old homestead revived and renewed their remembrances of the things that did not change—their love of God and their appreciation of their family heritage.

Chapter Fourteen

Into the Storm

The dawn of 1941 found the United States still at peace but slowly drifting toward war. The outbreak of hostilities in Europe had fueled the enlistment of many young men, including Latter-day Saints, and the obvious dangers of war had caused the activation of many military units in the United States. There were, of course, sizable numbers of Latter-day Saints among those who were called into service. And this presented new challenges, not only to those directly involved but also to their families and to the leaders of the Church. So as early as February of 1941, the Brethren were faced with many questions, including whether LDS servicemen should wear the temple garment while on active duty. On the fourth of the month, President McKay discussed this sensitive issue with Clifford E. Young, one of President Grant's sons-in-law, who in two months would be called as one of the first Assistants to the Twelve.

Recognizing early that all the needs of Latter-day Saint servicemen could not be met by local priesthood leaders, the Brethren decided to call someone to fill this role. The man selected was fifty-eight-year-old Hugh B. Brown, a seasoned Church leader and a major in the Canadian Army in World War I. President McKay met with Brother Brown on April 28, at which time he was called to "take care of" the LDS servicemen in the army camps in California. He was set apart three days later. As the movement of Mormon men into the armed services accelerated with the approach and the ultimate advent of United States involvement in the war, he was appointed the coordinator for all LDS servicemen. This assignment, in which he worked closely with President McKay, was a prelude to more distinguished service he would render when his mentor, as head of the Church, called him as an Assistant to the Twelve in 1953, as a member of the Twelve in 1958, and as a counselor in the First Presidency in 1961.

Along with the preliminary mobilization that was underway, the United States had taken other steps by 1941 that portended its involvement in the war. One of the most significant was the Lend-Lease Act passed in March. American ships, planes, tanks, and other war materials were made available to the Allies under an arrangement that was a direct intrusion into the war against the Axis powers. The innocuous cloak of "lend-lease" could not disguise the fact, and no one was misled. It was expected in many quarters, therefore, that this and other touchy issues would soon draw the United States into the European conflict.

While there were tense relationships between the United States and Japan, it was not the general perception that the terrors of war would descend upon America from that quarter. Moreover, few, if any, observers had even a vague idea that the United States would receive its baptism of fire into World War II because of a Japanese attack on Hawaii when, on August 2, President McKay left Salt Lake City bound for Honolulu. With him were Sister McKay and twenty-five other Utahns, including Joseph L. Wirthlin, second counselor in the Presiding Bishopric, and his wife, Madeline. A main object of the trip for President McKay was to dedicate the recently completed tabernacle and stake center in Honolulu. Equally important were plans for meetings with the missionaries of the Hawaiian and Japanese missions, both of which were headquartered in

David O. McKay

Hawaii, and for the dedication of other buildings in the Islands.

President McKay and his party sailed out of the Golden Gate on August 6 on the S.S. *Mariposa*, the same ship that nine months before had brought the fifty-seven missionaries to San Francisco from New Zealand, Australia, Tonga, and Samoa. As their luxury liner eased into Pearl Harbor five days later, the passengers were captivated by the large array of naval vessels sheltered there, especially the huge men-of-war berthed along battleship row. Of particular interest to President McKay and the other Utah passengers was the S.S. *West Virginia*, flagship of the Pacific Fleet, which was commanded by Captain Mervyn Bennion, a Latter-day Saint and the son-in-law of President J. Reuben Clark.

The welcoming party that boarded the *Mariposa* from a tug before the ship had berthed included Ralph E. Woolley, president of the Oahu Stake; his daughter Virginia; his first counselor, Edward L. Clissold; and Jay C. Jensen, president of the Japanese Mission. Shortly after, laden with fragrant leis, the visitors received a second welcome with alohas and more leis from a large group on the wharf, which included the Hawaiian Mission president, Roscoe Cox, who was then headquartered in Hawaii. President and Sister McKay were taken directly to President Woolley's comfortable home, where they were greeted by Sister Woolley, "the queen of hostesses," according to David O.'s appraisal.

Four days after arriving in Honolulu, President McKay held an all-day session with the Hawaiian missionaries. In addition to providing spiritual uplift and motivation, the president showed a great interest in the details of the work, making extensive notes or giving instructions about such diverse matters as the average daily routine of a missionary, cottage meetings, harmony between companions, and the relationship between lady missionaries and the elders. His succinct advice about the remedy for indifferent members was, "Give them something to do."

198

The following day, the leaders, missionaries, and members of the Japanese Mission had the honor of "holding the first session of the conference" in the new tabernacle. The Japanese Mission president, Jay C. Jensen, conducted. Except for his remarks, the addresses of President McKay and Bishop Wirthlin, and a prayer by one of the elders from the mainland, all of the program was presented by Japanese Saints. An all-Japanese choir rendered the well-known Latter-day Saint hymns "For the Strength of the Hills," "Ye Who Are Called to Labor," and "We Thank Thee, O God, for a Prophet," the latter being sung in Japanese. The names and the topics of the speakers of Japanese origin tell a story in themselves. The first speaker, Tomizo Katsumuma, who bore his testimony, was reported by President Jensen to have been the first Japanese convert, having been baptized in Logan, Utah, on August 8, 1895, while he was a student at Utah State University. He was followed by Elder Kay Ikegami, who delivered his talk on the Restoration in Japanese. Kazuto Koroki, who spoke next, talked about the Articles of Faith. Then Chester Ishimoto addressed the subject of the priesthood; Sister Setsuko Okimoto shared her feelings about what the Church means to a Japanese mother; Yoshio Komatsu talked about opportunities for youth in the Church; and Walter Teruya developed the theme of Latter-day Saint ideals. In his concluding remarks, President McKay drew an analogy between the harmony of colors in the new tabernacle and "the harmony of feeling that makes social intercourse delightful" among the people of different nationalities and races who made up the congregation. These barriers, real or imagined, that exist in the minds of some, had been surmounted by the love of Christ and the acceptance of his gospel. In the words of Paul, "There is neither Jew nor Greek, there is neither bond nor free, there is neither male nor female: for ye are all one in Christ Jesus" (Galatians 3:28.)

It is sobering to realize that within less than four months after this occasion, the fabric of harmony the speaker had lauded was ripped by the assault on Pearl

Harbor. The truly converted members did not allow the incident to alter their feelings toward the Japanese Saints, who had no control over it. Yet the shadow of suspicion that was attached to everyone of Japanese ancestry, fed by innuendo, sloganeering, and a frenzy of hatred, tended to ostracize them. This alone created deep misunderstandings that badly injured the accord President McKay had observed.

But it is encouraging, too, to realize that young Yoshio Komatsu, who spoke on this occasion, stands today as one of the General Authorities of the Church. He is known to us as Adney Y. Komatsu of the First Quorum of Seventy. Elder Komatsu discontinued using *Yoshio* because of confusion with another person who bore the same name.

The second day of the conference, President McKay dedicated the new Oahu Tabernacle; and two days later he had an experience that, in retrospect, seems to have had symbolic significance. On August 19, he and Sister McKay and several others were the guests of Captain Bennion aboard the *West Virginia*. They found the huge flagship, bristling with guns, berthed between the cruisers *Honolulu* and *Indianapolis*. The captain conducted the visitors on a personal inspection tour of the seemingly impregnable ship with its thick steel-plate hull and every known armament and device of naval technology. A descent into the depths of this floating fortress created a false sense of security. Once the mind became convinced that so much steel, iron, copper, and brass could actually float, it was easy to impute invincibility to the ship. And a leisurely dinner in the Captain's cabin, at a table set with gleaming silver, conveyed a false sense of repose, especially because of the courtly manner in which the captain presided at the meal. After reflecting on the occasion, the thing that impressed President McKay most was not the awesome might of the battleship, but the character of the man who commanded it. "Captain Bennion is a modest, capable man," wrote David O., "a trusted officer, a true gentleman."

Three and a half months after this pleasant interlude,

the *West Virginia,* rocked by torpedoes, bombs, and internal explosions, and gutted by fire, lay helpless at the bottom of Pearl Harbor, its aura of invincibility and repose shattered. And the gracious Captain Bennion, along with scores of his officers and men, lay dead, many entombed in the ship's shattered remains, consigned to a watery grave until the time when the ship was later raised, refitted, and recommissioned.

Out of this tragedy was to emerge a basic divergence of opinion toward the war between President McKay and his fellow counselor, J. Reuben Clark. The latter, devastated by the death of his son-in-law, whom he loved as his own, was reinforced in latent views on pacifism and United States isolationism. He therefore opposed the involvement of the United States in the European conflict and was reluctant for the United States to respond to the overt attack at Pearl Harbor. David O., on the other hand, although more pacific in personality than his friend, spoke out positively in support of the U.S. government's action. His views did not represent an advocacy of the killing and misery that the war entailed, but a pragmatic assessment of the realities facing the United States and the tragic result of an Axis victory. He sketched these views in a general conference address delivered several months after the attack on Pearl Harbor: "The upsetting of the world has forced us into war, and we should be recreant not to go forward," he told his Tabernacle audience. "Peace cannot come until the mad gangsters having in their hands science-produced explosives, mechanized equipment, and giant tanks, are defeated and branded as murderers, and their false aims repudiated, let us hope forever." (CR, October 1942, p. 68.) While the speaker expressed these militant views without equivocation, he respected those who held contrary views, recognizing the complexity of the issue. And he was also alert to the equally complex problem of forging a just peace once hostilities had ended: "Yes, the conflict must continue," he told his audience, "though its aims and purposes to many seem terribly complicated, and the establishment of a just peace [must be sought], a task as herculean as the terminating of the war itself." (Ibid.)

But these awful events and thorny issues lay in the future as David O. made the reflective diary entry about his visit with Captain Bennion aboard the *West Virginia*. What faced him immediately during the few days before the return voyage to the mainland was a series of ceremonial events, some pleasing and one heart wrenching. The pleasing activities included an inspection of the Church plantation at Laie, especially the Oahu Stake welfare project of ten acres planted in taro; a visit to the Hawaii Temple; the dedication of a recreation hall at Hoolehau; and a general reception at the new tabernacle, where hundreds of visitors toured the building and enjoyed refreshments and the music of the Royal Hawaiian Band.

The event that caused David O.'s heart to ache was the dedication of a recreation hall at the Kalaupapa Leper Settlement on August 21. Isolated from family and friends in a depressing environment that offered no challenge and little hope other than that found in gospel teaching, the inmates of this dreary place were the same as dead, yet painfully alive. President McKay held a meeting with the members of the little branch there and dedicated their new recreation hall. Among the speakers was a leper named Samuel K. Ka-ne, who, according to the president, "gave one of the most appealing sermons I have ever heard."

President McKay and his party left the Islands aboard the S.S. *Mariposa* on August 25, negotiating the return voyage in six days. The month of September was devoted mainly to preparations for the October general conference, although President McKay took time to speak to Ray's Literary Club, where he shared his perceptions of Burns, Pope, and Wordsworth, three of his favorite poets. He also accepted an invitation to speak at the missionary farewell of Robert Anderson, the son of his associate Joseph Anderson, the secretary to the First Presidency. The only other missionary farewell he participated in during 1941 was that of his youngest son, Robert, who was honored in June in the Twenty-Seventh Ward prior to his departure for Argentina. The previous month the father had joined Robert, the outgoing president of the Pi Kaps, in a reception line in the fraternity house, where the University of Utah faculty and their wives were honored.

President McKay's preparations for the general conference were extensive. He not only delivered major addresses but at the request of President Grant and President Clark conducted all the sessions. The highlight of the conference was the participation of President Grant, who had made a significant recovery from his stroke of the previous year. He delivered the keynote address to begin the conference and offered words of blessing at the end.

This conference also saw the installation of sixty-one-year-old Oscar A. Kirkham as the newest member of the First Council of the Seventy. He joined six other new General Authorities who were sustained at the previous April conference, representing one of the largest increments of new General Authorities in a single year in over a century. Those added to the ranks in April included young Harold B. Lee, only forty-two, who was later to become the president of the Twelve, a counselor in the First Presidency, and ultimately the president of the Church. His youth, his extraordinary achievements in Church welfare, and his deep spirituality marked this man from the beginning of his apostolic ministry as one who likely would gravitate to the prophetic office. The other five new General Authorities sustained at the same time as Elder Lee were called to the new office of Assistant to the Twelve—Marion G. Romney, a future counselor to Harold B. Lee and Spencer W. Kimball; Thomas E. McKay; Clifford E. Young; Alma Sonne; and Nicholas G. Smith. In presenting these five new brethren it was explained that they would be "set apart to act under the direction of the Twelve in the performance of such work as the First Presidency and the Twelve may place upon them." (CR, April 1941, p. 95.)

President McKay was to enjoy a pleasant association

with all seven of these men, first as a counselor in the First Presidency and later as the president of the Church. And although he was older than all of them, he would outlive four: his brother Thomas and Elders Clifford E. Young, Nicholas G. Smith, and Oscar A. Kirkham; and the first of the group sustained as an Assistant to the Twelve, Marion G. Romney, would be the first man called to the Twelve by President David O. McKay.

While welcoming these brethren into the ranks of the General Authorities during 1941, President McKay also bade farewell to two brethren who were serving as General Authorities when he was called to the service in 1906: Elder Reed Smoot, a member of the Twelve who died on February 9 in St. Petersburg, Florida, and Elder Rulon S. Wells, who passed away May 7 in Salt Lake City. Death also touched one of David O.'s friends outside the ranks of the General Authorities this year when Alonzo E. Hyde died. This man was the star of the first football team fielded by the University of Utah. And the one who offered the main eulogy at the funeral was his former teammate, David O. McKay. The reminiscences of those days on the gridiron the speaker shared with the audience were not spoken merely to salve the grief of the family but reflected a continuing interest in this rugged sport. Nor could he ever quite mask a bias for the teams of his alma mater, as this diary entry implies, made after he and Llewelyn had attended the 1941 Thanksgiving Day game at the University of Utah stadium: "The University of Utah was victorious again. The Utah State boys did some excellent passing. But their team is not equal to the University of Utah boys."

Only seventeen days after this outing with his son, the event occurred that suddenly catapulted the United States into war, which no one wanted but which most Americans expected. The news President McKay received on December 7 was incredible. The placid image of the scene he carried in memory of the *Mariposa* gliding out of Pearl Harbor less than four months before was now marred by reports of the destruction the Japanese bombers had inflicted on the U.S.

fleet. More disturbing were the reports that filtered in later of the American servicemen who were killed or maimed by the surprise attack. Like all other groups, the Mormons bore their share of grief as the casualty lists were published. Most prominent among the Latter-day Saints who lost their lives or were wounded at Pearl Harbor—and perhaps symbolic of all the others—was Captain Mervyn Bennion. Taken before his talents and achievements had reached full flower, and cut off prematurely from family and friends, his death seemed so senseless and without logical justification. As already noted, President Clark was devastated by the death of this much loved son-in-law. And his natural revulsion toward the militarism that had brought about the captain's death was heightened by pacifist views President Clark seems to have imbibed from his Quaker ancestry, views that hardened as he opposed the policies of the incumbent Democratic administration. Symbolic of this hardening attitude was President Clark's acceptance of membership in the National Advisory Council of the American Peace Society in June 1939. And in November 1944 he reaffirmed that commitment by accepting an assignment as a member of the board of directors of this group, reputed to be the oldest pacifist organization in the United States. Notwithstanding this, and despite repeated statements made in public and in private deprecating America's involvement in the war, J. Reuben Clark joined with President Grant and President McKay in messages directed to the leaders and members of the Church that acknowledged the duty of Latter-day Saint servicemen to honor the call of their government and that defined how they should conduct themselves while in the service. So a First Presidency message issued six days after Pearl Harbor exhorted those in military service "ever to have in mind the life and teachings of the Master; hour by hour to keep out from their hearts, in the camp and on the battlefield itself, all cruelty, hate, and murder; always to have in their thoughts the few short years of time as against the unnumbered cycles of eternity." (MFP 6:140-41.)

David O. McKay

Ten days later the First Presidency sent another letter to bishops and stake presidents. It focused on an issue raised frequently after Pearl Harbor as to whether missionary calls should be discontinued. The letter advised: "We have given the matter very careful consideration, and we see no reason why, for the present at least, we should not continue to call missionaries in sufficient numbers to maintain the missions as now manned." To spike any efforts to use a mission call to dodge military service, it warned: "However, no young man should be recommended for a mission for the purpose of evading military service." (Ibid., p. 142.)

During 1942, the First Presidency sent at least thirty-six messages to the field, about half of which dealt with the war and related matters. One of these read at the April general conference expressed the need to send missionaries into the field, defined the relationship between Church and state, and affirmed the duty of Latter-day Saints to respond to a call to arms: "The members of the church have always felt under obligation to come to the defense of their country when a call to arms was made," the statement read, "[and] on occasion the church has prepared to defend its own members." Yet, this did not mean the Church condoned war and killings but that its members "are citizens or subjects of sovereignties over which the church has no control. . . . When, therefore, constitutional law, obedient to these principles, calls the manhood of the church into the armed services of any country to which they owe allegiance, their highest civic duty requires that they meet that call." And in these circumstances, the statement went on to say, the responsibility for the killings that resulted rested upon those who sit in places of power, "those rulers in the world who in a frenzy of hate and lust for unrighteous power and dominion over their fellow men, have put into motion eternal forces they do not comprehend and cannot control." (Ibid., pp. 157-61.) Finally, it addressed this admonition to the young Latter-day Saints in the service: "We say live clean, keep the commandments of the Lord, pray to Him constantly to preserve you in truth and righteousness, live as you pray, and then whatever betides you the Lord will be with you and nothing will happen to you that will not be to the honor and glory of God and to your salvation and exaltation." (Ibid., p. 161.)

A second message read at the same conference by President McKay reported on the thwarted attempt to bring refugee children to the United States: "We were arranging to bear the expense of bringing here refugee children from Europe, and of caring for them after their arrival," he told the conference audience, "but the hazards of war stopped the movement of children to this country." (Ibid., p. 163.)

A lengthy message read at the October general conference elaborated the same themes touched on in April and added this condemnation of Communism and Nazism: "Each of these systems destroys liberty, wipes out free institutions, blots out free agency, stifles free press and free speech, crushes out freedom of religion and conscience." The conclusion that followed provided justification for United States involvement in the war: "Free peoples cannot and do not survive under these systems." (Ibid., p. 183.)

While the main focus of President McKay and the First Presidency on the war involved questions of personal and political morality and the safety and well-being of LDS servicemen, there were nagging war-related problems on the home front that also claimed their attention. Among these were dislocations caused by the influx of large numbers of military personnel into the area, the establishment of military and war production facilities, and the migration of Latter-day Saints from rural communities to the urban centers. To smooth these transitions, frequent contacts were made between Church leaders and government and military representatives from Washington, D.C. Typical of these was a meeting the First Presidency held with William J. Hickey, plant specialist of the Defense Plant Corporation on February 9. Consideration was then being given to the establishment of a naval supply depot in an area north of Salt Lake City. The government had settled on a thousand-acre tract near Clearfield that at the time was used chiefly to raise sugar beets. President McKay and others were concerned that such prime agricultural land would be taken out of production and had proposed alternate sites near Farmington and Clinton. By May, when the issue was moving toward a final resolution, and when it appeared that Clearfield was the government's first choice, David O. made a determined effort to bring about a different result. On the eighth of the month, two days after he had spoken at the funeral of the wife of Elbert D. Thomas, President McKay took the senator to inspect the proposed Clearfield site. There, after showing him around, David O. made an urgent plea to the senator to use his political influence to save those acres. So involved was he in the issue, it seemed almost that the president looked upon the area as part of the Fields of McKay. And perhaps there is more truth in this than one might imagine. Ogden was David O. McKay's adopted home, and this choice acreage lay just to the south.

Not content to leave the matter in the hands of the Utah senator alone, David O. enlisted the aid of his old friend James H. Moyle. Brother Moyle, who was well known in the nation's capital, placed calls to Secretary of State Cordell Hull and Marvin H. McIntyre of President Roosevelt's administrative staff. He painted for these officials a word picture of a thriving agricultural complex with over 450 acres of sugar beets, 230 acres of tomatoes, 200 acres of hay, 31 acres of potatoes, and 5 acres of onions. All this was to no avail, however, as this diary entry of May 20 suggests: "The Clearfield thing has blown wide open," wrote David O. "The President has said if we can't put it where we want it, we will take the facility outside Utah."

It was not that President McKay didn't want the facility in Utah. He only wanted it in a location that would serve the needs of the military and at the same time would have as little adverse effect as possible on Utah's agriculture. When it became apparent that it was either Clearfield or another site outside Utah, the opposition of President McKay evaporated.

It is difficult at this relatively remote time to understand the fear of a Japanese attack that then gripped the West Coast of the United States—and even the intermountain area. There were frequent blackouts—or brownouts—in large cities, including Salt Lake. As trains traveling at night approached the West Coast, they were blacked out; and whenever possible, large public gatherings were avoided. It was this circumstance that caused the First Presidency to decide against holding the April general conference in the Tabernacle. President McKay noted that this decision was dictated by "the exigency of the time." Instead, the various sessions of the conference were held in the Assembly Room of the Salt Lake Temple, where only "the General Authorities and stake presidencies" and some other leaders were in attendance. However, the proceedings of some of the sessions were carried by radio into the homes of the Saints.

As the tempo of military mobilization accelerated, the trickle of Latter-day Saints into the service swelled into a flood. President McKay was reminded of this a few weeks after conference when he spoke at a meeting at Fort Douglas, located on the bench east of Salt Lake City, where "185 Mormon boys" had gathered for sacrament service. Of these, the speaker noted with interest, 84 were returned missionaries. As he scanned the faces of these clean-cut young men, the apostle was haunted by the thought of the dangers or even of the violent death that faced some of them, and his heart went out to them in a surge of compassion and love. The unusual circumstances of the meeting produced a spiritual aura that doubtless was felt by all and about which President McKay commented in this diary entry of May 10: "It has been my privilege to partake of the sacrament with people in many parts of the world, but this was one of the most impressive services of the kind I have ever attended in my life."

Although the war and its attendant problems dominated the thoughts and activities of President McKay during this period, the flow of his other responsibilities continued without letup. Intermittent entries like "The letters as usual are sky high on my desk" (February 12) or "A constant stream of people from the moment I arrived at the office" (March 18) suggest the volume of the administrative tasks he handled on a continuing basis.

During this period, President McKay continued to play the key role in Church welfare, although with the decline of President Clark's outside commitments, which dropped significantly after President Grant's stroke, the first counselor had begun to be more involved in the program. On January 16, President McKay met with Henry D. Moyle, the chairman of the welfare committee, to discuss the policy governing welfare canneries. It was decided that Church canneries would be divided into three groups, those producing for Church-wide, for regional, or for intrastake distribution. Also, it was decided that certain canneries be required to upgrade their operations by installing additional equipment. These matters were later presented to President Clark, who ratified them.

A few weeks later, President McKay learned firsthand about one of the most effective demonstrations of the welfare plan in action when on March 1 he attended the conference of the Mt. Graham Stake in southeast Arizona. The communities of Duncan, Arizona, and Virden, New Mexico, in that stake had suffered serious damage because of flooding on the Gila River. Without direction or help from Church headquarters, the local leaders had promptly taken action according to welfare principles to assist those who had suffered damage. As he inspected the ruination caused by the floods and heard reports of what had been done to mitigate it, two things stood out in David's mind: He was surprised by the extent of "the devastation caused by the floods"; and he was impressed by "the energy and brotherhood" that had been shown by the local leaders who were "rehabilitating themselves." At the center of this effort at self-rehabilitation stood a forty-seven-year-old human dynamo, Spencer W. Kimball, the president of the Mt. Graham Stake, who seemed to be about the nearest thing to perpetual motion President McKay could have imagined. This diminutive, affable man had almost single-handedly aroused his brethren to an extraordinary pitch of effort and dedication. And the visitor could hardly have failed to detect the steel in the spine and the implacable will that lay beneath the facade of Brother Kimball's self-deprecating affability. To hear the stake president's account of what had taken place, one would have been led to believe that he had shirked his duty and that if someone with but a trace of initiative and industry had been in charge, the results would have been acceptable. It is not likely, however, that David O. McKay was misled by any effort of the stake president to divert attention away from what his leadership had produced. Nor is it improbable that these two master spirits communicated on a plane above their intellectual perceptions where they would have recognized each other as kindred spirits, foreordained to occupy the prophetic office.

It is interesting to reflect that at the time of this meeting, David O. McKay had worn the apostolic mantle for thirty-six years, while it would not be placed upon Spencer W. Kimball for over a year from then. Yet in less than four years after the death of the elder of the two, the younger man would become the president of the Church.

It is also interesting to note the contrasting appearance and style of these two men while marking the similarity in their basic objectives and achievements. Tall and rugged with a deliberate, measured style in the pulpit, where he reflected a literary bent, President McKay projected the classic image of the prophet-teacher-thinker. On the other hand, President Kimball, more spare and slight, with his fiery delivery and vigorous, challenging rhetoric, projected the image of the prophet-man of action. Yet both aimed for the same goal: preparing a people ready to receive the Savior at his second coming.

As expected, President McKay continued to enjoy special family events and celebrations during 1942. On February 1, he was honored to bless his eighth grandchild, Margaret Joyce McKay, at services in the Yale Ward; on May 7 he welcomed his ninth grandchild, Emma Rae's son and first child, whose arrival Papa Dade learned about as he sat in council with his Brethren in the temple; and on June 10, he performed the marriage of Ned and his bride, Lottie Lund. The reception for this handsome couple was held in the Delta Gamma sorority house that evening. And to no one's surprise, Papa Dade loaded all the available grandchildren into his car during the Christmas holidays for a "glorious afternoon" of sledding at Huntsville. Unfortunately, this delightful outing ended in near tragedy when upon going down Ogden Canyon on the trip home, the president's car slid on the icy road. In order to avoid a collision with an oncoming car, he crashed into a retaining wall. Dickie was knocked unconscious temporarily and Midean suffered a rather severe blow on the head. Fortunately, however, no one was seriously injured.

It was sixteen months after President McKay attended the conference in the Mt. Graham Stake that he greeted Spencer W. Kimball in his Salt Lake City office as a fellow apostle. The date was July 15, 1943. However, his ordination was to be delayed until October of that year at the time of the semiannual general conference. And it was eleven days after his visit with Elder Kimball that President McKay noted in his diary: "I brought the news to Brother [Ezra Taft] Benson that he had been chosen an apostle in the church. It came as a great shock and surprise to him."

These two able young men, both of whom were serving as stake presidents at the time of their calls to the apostleship, were ordained within minutes of each other by President Heber J. Grant. Spencer, the elder of the two, was ordained first, a circumstance that resulted in his succeeding to the prophetic office at the death of President Harold B. Lee. Because of the infirmities brought on by his stroke, President Grant lacked the strength to stand during the ordination of these two new members of the Twelve. So each in turn knelt before the aging prophet's chair as he laid his hands on their heads to ordain them and to confer the apostolic authority upon them according to the ancient pattern.

The vacancies in the Twelve that these two brethren filled were caused by the deaths earlier in the year of two brethren with whom President McKay had been closely associated for many years: Sylvester Q. Cannon, a former presiding bishop of the Church who passed away on May 29; and Rudger Clawson, the president of the Twelve, who died on June 21. As to the latter, President McKay noted in his diary on June 25, the date of the funeral, that all of the General Authorities met at the mortuary "at the bier of our friend and associate . . . to say our last farewells." Later in the day he spoke at the funeral services in the Assembly Hall as he had spoken there earlier at services for Elder Cannon.

Because of his advancing age, his elevation to the presiding quorum of the Church, his eloquence, and his graciousness, President McKay was called on increasingly to speak at funerals for his friends and associates. When it was feasible to do so, he always accepted these invitations because he wanted to honor the deceased as he wanted to bring comfort and understanding to the bereaved families. Sometimes previous commitments made it impossible to accept an invitation. And sometimes an acceptance despite a crowded schedule created tense moments of split-second timing as on June 21 when he spoke at Elder Sylvester Q. Cannon's funeral. Immediately afterward, he drove to Ogden, where at 3:00 P.M. he spoke at funeral services for an old friend, James H. Douglas.

It was during this same month—a seeming month of death—when, on the twelfth, he eulogized another player from the University of Utah's first football team, Fred M. Pohlson. Earlier in the year, he had bid farewell in the same way to his longtime associate in the Sunday School, George D. Pyper, whose funeral was held in mid-January; and a

213

few days later he spoke over the remains of Jay C. Jensen, the president of the Japanese Mission, who had taken ill in the field.

During this year, David reached the classic milestone of three score and ten, the traditional standard for mortal longevity, and although he was frequently reminded of and frequently talked about death as he buried his friends, his activities and attitudes reflected nothing but life and vigor. Ample corroboration of this is found in three diary entries made in April: "Left early this morning for Huntsville," he recorded on the fourteenth. "Arrived there at 7:30 A.M. Worked all morning preparing the ground for planting. It is impossible to find a man to help; so it looks as though I shall have to do most of it myself." A week later, this: "Left early for Huntsville to work on the farm." On an impulse he returned in five days: "It was fortunate for me and for the horses that I decided to go," he wrote of the incident, "for all the horses were out of the pasture. A strong wind had blown the gates open. I found the horses two or three miles away. I hitched them on the back of my car and drove to the farm."

President McKay managed to get through this difficult season despite the shortage of hired farm workers by increasing his own hours at Huntsville and by occasional assistance from family members. After a strenuous summer during which the seventy-year-old apostle worked harder on the farm than he had for years, he felt the need for a "respite." Under the circumstances, a change of scene would have seemed to be a logical way to seek it. But logic played little or no part in the McKays' feelings about Huntsville. To them it was a place for all seasons. And so, there was nothing extraordinary or inconsistent about the fact that while David O. had spent most of his spare hours during the summer toiling on the farm like a hired hand, at summer's end that is where he spent his vacation! "In order to take a short respite from the strenuous duties of the past several months," he recorded on August 30, "I have decided to go to Huntsville for a few days where I hope to build up a little reserve strength."

He spent eight pleasant days there where the first signs of autumn, which comes early to this high mountain valley, were the harbingers of the coming harvest. The prospects of reaping the fruit of his labors from fields that his father also had tilled seem to have evoked feelings of permanence and continuity. At least, that may be inferred from the title he assigned to a talk he delivered at the Huntsville Ward during his vacation. He called it simply "Anchored." His text was the first chapter of 2 Peter. While the earth yields its fruit to those who plow, plant, fertilize, water, and cultivate, the fruit of the Spirit springs from intangible sources—from faith, virtue, knowledge, temperance, patience, godliness, brotherly kindness, and charity. The speaker admonished his hearers to make their "calling and election sure," even as Peter had admonished the ancient Saints to do by the cultivation of their spiritual and intellectual qualities, qualities that should be kept "always in remembrance." (See 2 Peter 1:5-7, 15.)

A few days after delivering this perceptive sermon and after returning to his duties in Salt Lake City, the speaker went home for lunch to find all of his grandchildren waiting to wish him a happy seventieth birthday. After the usual singing and well-wishing, they presented him with a global map, symbolic of his worldwide responsibilities and authority. And that evening, thirty-six family members sat down to an elaborate meal, the preparation of which Mama Ray had carefully supervised.

The respite President McKay had gained from the few days of relaxation at Huntsville and the quiet celebration with his family helped to fuel his energies for the semi-annual general conference, and for a grueling tour of Mexico that followed soon thereafter. The conference was especially taxing as he was called on by President Grant and President Clark to conduct all the sessions in addition to delivering major addresses at the Saturday morning general session and at the general priesthood meeting. Still suffering from the effects of his stroke, President Grant was able to attend only half of the general sessions. Following the pattern set at previous conferences held after the United States' entry into the war, members of the general public were not invited to attend the sessions of the conference, which were held in the Tabernacle.

In his major address Saturday morning, October 2 (CR, October 1943, pp. 28-33), President McKay defined four bulwarks he considered essential "to defeat cruel, ambitious war lords in Europe and in the far east"—the bulwarks of the battle front, the essential industries front, the agricultural front, and the home front. Viewing the battle front, he mourned the loss of "the very flower of young manhood" whom he saw being "crushed under the wheels of the juggernaut of war." But he saw no alternative but "to push relentlessly forward until the murderous dictators" had been defeated. He expressed intermingled surprise and pride at the "unparalleled" productivity of United States industry. He was impressed with the performance of agriculture that had continued to fill the nation's larder despite shortages of new equipment caused by the preemptive demands of the war machine, and despite a dwindling work force caused by the accelerated conscription of farm youth. But he was frankly worried and dismayed by the deterioration the war had produced in family life. Aside from the social ruptures caused by the rapid induction of so many into the armed services, he was appalled by the delinquency and the sexual license of young people who were still at home. Statistics of juvenile courts he quoted showed a 200 percent increase in sexual offenses since Pearl Harbor. He traced this in large part to a "waning influence of parenthood." He also pointed the finger at "false teachings, and ideals inculcated by pseudo-philosophers." He deplored the decreasing birth rate, condemning couples who sought "the pleasures of conjugality without a willingness to assume the responsibilities of rearing a family." And he denounced divorce, especially among Latter-day Saints who had been sealed in the temple, branding as a traitor to his sacred covenants a man who would abandon his wife and family because he had permitted himself "to become infatuated with a pretty face and comely form of some young girl who flattered him with a smile."

Not content merely to define and denounce the evil, the speaker prescribed a remedy. He urged more thorough and thoughtful training of youth at home. He called for an increased emphasis on the spiritual foundations and the eternal nature of temple marriage. And he challenged those entering marriage to do so with honest intentions "of building a home that will contribute to the bulwarks of a noble society."

Viewed overall, this stands as one of the most pointed and hard-hitting sermons of President McKay's apostolic career. The explanation is found in the trying circumstances in which it was delivered and the resilient character of the speaker. In those dark days, there was no certainty that the Allied forces would prevail. The possibility of an Axis victory cast a veil of uncertainty over all, and plans for the future were tentative and short term. With moral decay nibbling at the body of the Church at home while war raged abroad with increasing ferocity, a voice like that of David O. McKay stiffened the faith and resolve of the Latter-day Saints. He was like the ancient watchman on the wall whose vantage point and perspective enabled him to warn his fellows within the enclosure below of the threatened point of attack from the enemy and of the defensive measures necessary to ward it off. And this watchman, looking beyond the immediate conflict to the future, shared with his followers a vision of tomorrow that was at once a spur and a rein to the Latter-day Saints: "It is the duty of everyone," David O. told his audience, "to strive to make it possible that no soldier now dreaming of a happy homecoming may return to find a broken home or its ideals shattered by the sinful indulgence of a member of the family." And in conclusion he uttered a sentence that became one of the principal themes of his prophetic presidency:

"One of the highest ideals of life is to keep secure and free from sorrow the homes of the church and of the nation."

Ten days after the conference, President McKay left for one of the few tours he was to make of Mexico. Crossing the border at El Paso, Texas, on October 14, 1943, he met at Cuidad Juarez with W. P. Blocker, U.S. consul general, and Mexican officials of the State of Chihuahua. Thus began a month-long tour of this vast and beautiful country where, all along the route of his travel, the visitor conferred with Mexican officials and worshipped and counseled with local leaders and members of the Church. After traveling for many days and visiting with and observing people of every class and station, he recorded these observations: "Mexico is a wonderful land, inhabited, generally speaking, by a gracious people. Their history since Cortez landed in 1519 where Vera Cruz now stands is a story of a bitter and tragic struggle for freedom."

One of the purposes of President McKay in making this trip was to inspect potential building sites. In Mexico City he looked at several but did not find one to his liking. However, he was encouraged by the prospects for Church growth in the nation's capital, observing that there was "an opportunity to have four branches in Mexico City." At this time the Church population was sparse in all of Mexico except in the northern colonies that had been established in the late nineteenth century. And the prospects for any significant growth in the near future seemed remote, the expectation being that the conversions would continue at the same slow rate experienced during the preceding decades. However, a significant change in Church administration in the coming years, which, as we shall see, was in large part the result of initiatives taken by President McKay as the head of the Church, would produce an almost inundating flow of conversions.

When President McKay considered the prospects of four branches in Mexico City, he doubtless foresaw considerable growth in the years ahead. It is doubtful, however, that he saw the extent and the rapidity of such growth. He likely would have been surprised, if not amazed, to have known then that within forty years the Church population in Mexico would climb to well over a hundred thousand and that a beautiful temple would stand in metropolitan Mexico City. And from the perspective of visualizing four branches in the nation's capital, it is difficult even to surmise his reaction to the knowledge that in a two-day period in 1975, thirteen new stakes were created in Mexico City and its environs from the division of several older stakes.

Chapter Fifteen

Perspective—A New Leader

Abackward glance often casts in rosy hues events that at their happening seemed dark and depressing. Such is the case with the family of David O. McKay during 1944. The war, with its hungry demands for more men, had reached out and touched the apostle's clan, bringing the loneliness of separation and the threat of injury or death to loved ones. As the year dawned, son Edward and son-in-law Russell Blood were already in the service. And on March 14, Robert, who had been home from his Argentine mission for only a month, was inducted into the army. David O. accompanied his youngest son to Fort Douglas for the induction and returned home to find Mama Ray "weeping bitterly over the departure of her baby boy into the army." And it was a source of regret to the parents that Edward had to leave Salt Lake City under military orders shortly before Robert returned from South America, thereby missing a hoped-for reunion of the brothers.

A few days after Bob's induction, the family was excited and pleased with Russell's return "from somewhere in the South Seas." But his stay was brief and he was soon off, again creating gnawing uncertainties about the personal dangers that might lie ahead, the length of the separation, and the outcome of the conflict. Meanwhile, Ned had been assigned to a destroyer escort flagship on convoy duty between the United States and Europe. He had been granted a short leave and left Salt Lake at 3:00 A.M. on July 27 on a military plane bound for the East Coast. Returning home alone after seeing the son fly away, the father confided to his diary feelings that he likely kept from Emma Ray, who he knew already carried a heavy burden of worry and sorrow. "I was grieved to see him go," wrote the father, "especially since he has again missed seeing Bob whom he has not seen for four years." Not long after, Bob arrived for a short furlough and then left for further training at Camp Barkley, Texas.

And so it went for the McKay family during the uncertain days of World War II, with different members coming and going as their military orders directed. Always lying just below the surface of their outward relationships was the uncertainty, even the fear, of what tomorrow would bring, perhaps the unwanted telegram or call announcing the injury or death of a loved one. That this was one of the leading families of the Church brought no assurance of immunity from the sorrows and tragedy inherent in a conflict of such magnitude and ferocity. Thus, President McKay's clan fell under the shadow of war, a shadow that gave a subdued and somewhat melancholy tinge to every activity. Yet a few months would see an end to the conflict, and the experiences that at the moment seemed hard to bear, softened by the healing balm of time, would occupy a place of honored remembrance in the picture book of the mind.

Meanwhile, war did not suspend life, which had to continue regardless of the depressing outward circumstances. So while President and Sister McKay were worried about the safety and welfare of their family, the flow of their domestic life and of the president's apostolic ministry continued unabated.

A favorite social activity for David O. and Emma Ray was to mingle with family or friends at dinner. Early in January, 1944, they hosted such a gathering in their home where the guest list included, in addition to members of their family, Elders John A. Widtsoe and Albert E. Bowen of the Twelve and President LeRoy Cowles of the University of Utah and their wives. Following the meal, entertainment was provided from among the guests when Lawrence and Lou Jean played a duet and Emma Lucy Gates Bowen, Elder Bowen's wife, who had gained international fame as a concert soloist, sang for the group. In less than a week, the McKays were guests at the home of Elder and Sister Stephen L Richards at a similar gathering. And in the spring they attended a dinner at the Hotel Utah in honor of the sixtieth wedding anniversary of President and Sister Heber J. Grant. These gatherings, which were always marked by good conversation, good food, good humor, and good entertainment, provided an important social outlet for President McKay, who, like Emma Ray, enjoyed the company of family and friends.

As already noted, war did, however, suspend normalcy at Huntsville insofar as the operation of the farm was concerned. Through 1944, farm workers continued to be extremely hard to find. So, beginning in early spring, David O. spent long hours there "attending to farm duties," which included every phase of the laborious process of husbandry, including "pitching hay," which occupied an entire morning two days before the July 24th celebration. And these physical activities were in addition to the customary chores he continued to perform around the home as when during Emma Ray's May cleanup he spent an afternoon painting the front porch. Attesting to President McKay's dedication to the work ethic is this amazing entry, made, appropriately, on Labor Day, four days before he turned seventy-one: "Worked sixteen hours today. Cleared out an irrigation ditch up on the farm; hitched up a colt to a mower and dug out a lot of weeds that were irritating me. Later at home I mowed the lawn and after that, washed the car." And, as if to allay any concern that sixteen hours of hard labor was too strenuous for someone his age, he wrote on his birthday: "I am feeling exceptionally well."

Parenthetically, it is noted that of the dozens of greetings he received this birthday by card, letter, or in person, the only one he felt to record was one from Joseph Fielding Smith, the man who would succeed him as the president of the Church. Elder Smith wrote to David O., "I appreciate you and am happy to work with you." That President McKay made the effort to record this expression of confidence suggests the importance he attached to the qualities of friendship and loyalty, qualities that ranked high in his index of human character. It may also reflect the veneration he had for Elder Smith's father and namesake, Joseph F. Smith, who had called President McKay to the apostleship.

At the April general conference, a new apostle was sustained. President McKay's diary entry of April 6 notes: "I presented the general authorities of the Church for sustaining vote. Brother Mark E. Petersen, 43, was sustained as the new apostle to fill the existing vacancy." The impeccable character and the whole-souled dedication of the new appointee were such as to inspire the faith and confidence of the Saints. And Elder Petersen's distinguished journalistic career, capped by his elevation to the presidency of the Deseret News Publishing Company, added an important new element to the deliberations of the Twelve.

The elevation of Mark E. Petersen to the Twelve brought him into even closer association with President McKay, under whose leadership he would serve for almost three decades. Although quite different in temperament and style, there was a special bond between the Scotsman and the Dane that was never more evident than in August 1963, when they met in Wales for ceremonies that symbolized the growth of the Church in that land and cemented President McKay's ties to his maternal ancestors. Then presiding over the West European Mission, Elder Petersen hosted President McKay and his party at a dinner in Cardiff and then accompanied them to Merthyr Tydfil, where on August 25, a Latter-day Saint chapel was dedicated by the president in the little Welch town where his mother was born. Elder Petersen honored his leader in the way he knew best by publishing and distributing to those in attendance a special edition of the *Millennial Star*, which not only focused on the special events to take place in Merthyr Tydfil but commemorated President McKay's ninetieth birthday, which came a few days later. And in a sense, this incident symbolized the apostolic relationship that always existed between this pair as they watched and participated in the growth of the Church throughout the world, and it underscored the diversity of national background of those caught in the gospel net.

It was only a few weeks before Elder Petersen was sustained as a member of the Twelve that President McKay participated in setting apart his friend Hugh B. Brown as the president of the British Mission. Elder Brown left Salt Lake City on March 4 for New York City, where he embarked for England on a convoyed vessel. In ten months, almost to the day, he was back in Salt Lake City with a serious illness that required major surgery. And after a four-month convalescence, he returned to England to take up his duties again. Indicative of the shifting tides of Church leadership, which thrusts first one and then another to the fore, is the fact that while Elder Brown was not called to the Twelve until 1958, fourteen years after Elder Petersen, in 1961 he was called to the First Presidency, where he served for nine years as one of Elder Petersen's presiding officers. Then, at the death of President McKay, he returned to the Quorum of the Twelve, where he was subordinate to Elder Petersen until his own death. Perhaps there is no aspect of the Twelve more revealing of their maturity and dedication than the submissive, uncomplaining way in which they accept such changes in leadership status.

It was shortly after the April general conference when Elder Petersen was sustained that President McKay's administrative load became much heavier. This was occasioned by the serious illness of President Clark's wife, Luacine. For the ensuing four months, the first counselor was greatly distracted from his customary duties because of the confinement of his companion on whom he had relied so heavily. So with the Prophet, Heber J. Grant, still being incapacitated, President McKay stepped into the breach to shoulder most of the load of the ongoing affairs of the Church. President Clark's vigil ended on August 2 when his wife slipped away quietly. In a show of loyalty and love for his associate in the First Presidency, and in tribute to the deceased, President McKay promptly gave direction that the Church's flag fly at half-mast and that a wreath of flowers be placed on the door of the Church Administration Building. Following the funeral services, which were held two day later in the Twentieth Ward chapel, President McKay dedicated Sister Clark's grave.

The burden of sorrow President Clark carried following his wife's death, in which President McKay and his other associates shared vicariously, was made heavier by the rapidly declining health of their leader, Heber J. Grant. As 1944 drew to a close, the Prophet's active participation in the administrative affairs of the Church declined markedly. And by spring the following year, it had practically ceased, except as to matters only the Prophet could decide. The counselors went periodically to President Grant's home to present the matters requiring his attention, as it had become increasingly difficult for him to move about. On April 5 they conferred with him at home about filling the two vacancies in the First Council of Seventy created by the passing of Samuel O. Bennion and Rufus K. Hardy, who had died on successive days in early March. It was decided to call S. Dilworth Young and Milton R. Hunter as replacements; they were sustained the following day.

On the ninth, David O. noted that "President Grant called at the office a few minutes. Met with both counselors." Apparently this was the last time the aged Prophet was in his office in the Church Administration Building. However, President McKay and President Clark continued to keep in touch with him by telephone and by visits to his home. On May 13, the day before he passed away, David O. and Emma Ray called at the Prophet's home. He was quoted as telling them, "I feel terrible but I have no pain." The second counselor noted in conclusion: "He is terribly weak." And the following day, President McKay noted the passing of his leader with whom he had shared the apostleship for almost forty years: "Called up to President Grant's home. Failing rapidly. Arrived there just a few minutes before he passed from this life at 6:30 P.M. Later got in touch with George Albert Smith who is in Boston, Massachusetts, and notified him of President Grant's death."

This telephone call was David O. McKay's first act of subordination to his new leader, who succeeded to that role instantly at the death of President Grant. With the dissolution of the First Presidency, Elder McKay took his place in the Twelve junior to George Albert Smith, president of the Quorum, and George F. Richards. It was in this capacity that he participated in the funeral arrangements and services for the deceased Prophet, whose body lay in state for two days in the Church Administration Building. He was buried May 18 following a service in the Tabernacle, where President McKay was one of the speakers. Two days later, David O. eulogized his departed friend and leader at memorial services held in the Twenty-Seventh Ward. The speaker's views about the dominant characteristic of the man whom he had served as a counselor for eleven years are best summarized in these words: "I have never known a man who exemplified so completely the mastery of mind over matter—whose will could so masterfully bring under subjection physical whims and desires. Perseverance and self-mastery are qualities that will always be connoted with the name Heber J. Grant." (IE 48:334.)

The day following the memorial service, Elder McKay met with his brethren of the Twelve in the upper room of the Salt Lake Temple. There the apostles prayed and counseled about weighty matters pertaining to the work of the Church. David O. made this terse diary entry about the principal action taken during this five-hour meeting: "A reorganization of the First Presidency was effected. President George Albert Smith, who was sustained as president of the church, chose J. Reuben Clark as his first counselor and David O. McKay as his second counselor." During the

The First Presidency, April 1946. Left to right: J. Reuben Clark, Jr., first counselor; David O. McKay, second counselor; George Albert Smith, president.

same meeting, George F. Richards was sustained as the president of the Quorum of the Twelve. This council of apostles decided it would be unwise to delay reorganizing the First Presidency, because of the accelerated growth of the Church and the need for prompt action in handling administrative matters, a need that cannot be served well when decisions rest with a group of twelve men.

This change in leadership had little impact on President McKay's duties in the First Presidency. The only difference came from President George Albert Smith's ability to assume some administrative and ceremonial functions that President Grant's disabilities had prevented him from handling. However, this advantage was limited by the new leader's frequent bouts with a variety of illnesses that could be traced to a fragile physique (which had plagued him from youth) and a tendency toward nervousness. So apart from the sorrow attending the death of his friend and mentor, Heber J. Grant, David O.'s official life and duties continued as before. The familiarity he and President Clark

had with the complexities of Church administration relieved the new leader of a heavy burden of detail, leaving
him free to chart the course and to devote himself more
completely to spiritual matters.

While this period saw little change in the governance of
the Church or in David O.'s official duties, it saw a revolution in international secular affairs. A week before President Grant's death, General Alfred Jodl of the German
Army, representing Admiral Karl Donitz, who had taken
over the direction of the German state, signed the pact of
his country's unconditional surrender at Reims. This action
was ratified at Berlin two days later on May 9, and suddenly the European conflict was over. President McKay's
comment on this historic event reflects the mixed sense of
relief and sadness it evoked: "VE day! At long last . . . Hitler and his henchmen have unconditionally surrendered to
the Allies. There have been forty million casualties during
this almost six year conflict."

The emergence of new leadership in defeated Germany
had been preceded by the installation of a new president in
the victorious United States when on April 12 Franklin D.
Roosevelt passed away. And within a few months after succeeding to the presidency, Harry S. Truman made the fate-
ful decision to use the atomic bomb against Japan, which
suddenly ended hostilities in the Pacific. President McKay's
reaction to this news indicates the triumph and vindication
many felt at the defeat of a nation that had precipitated a
terrible war by surprise attack: "News flashed to Salt Lake,"
he wrote on August 14, "that Japan had surrendered after
three years eight months and a week to the day that their
infamy at Pearl Harbor plunged the United States into a
two front war that cost countless lives and billions of dollars. Salt Lakers are jubilant!" The sense of relief and
thanksgiving the First Presidency felt at this welcome news
is shown by their decision to close the Church offices the
following day to afford a time of prayerful contemplation
about the chaotic events of the preceding years and the
war's end.

President McKay's reflections about the end of hostilities evoked both sorrow and joy. He mourned with the thousands of Latter-day Saints and others whose loved ones had been killed or maimed or had fallen prey to the temptations of the flesh. Some of these had suffered what seemed to be irreparable injuries of broken bodies or homes or a terrible void from the death of loved ones who would never return. For these, and especially for those who were members of the Church, the apostle felt a shared sorrow as if he had suffered their tragedies personally. Yet a comparison between his own circumstances and those who had lost so much gave him an overwhelming feeling of gratitude. All of his loved ones had survived the conflict unscathed and could look forward to normal lives.

It was coincidental that during the morning of the day Japan surrendered, President McKay greeted a son who had just returned from Europe. Llewelyn had been in Germany on a government assignment, and his father "got excused from the expenditures committee meeting in order to drive to the airport" to meet him. His son Edward was in Salt Lake City on leave, and toward the end of the month the father and this son celebrated in a way peculiar to the McKays, as this entry of August 25 attests: "Ned and I worked on the farm most of the day." And while it would be several months before all the members of the clan would fulfill their military obligations, it was a great relief to David O. and Ray that they were all safe and whole.

In these circumstances, it was with elation that President McKay, his brother Thomas, and their wives left Salt Lake City in early September to attend meetings of the stake in Lovell, Wyoming. With the war just ended and David O.'s seventy-second birthday approaching, it was decided to make the trip one of combined business and pleasure. The happy foursome traveled to Yellowstone National Park, one of the McKays' favorite vacation spots. There on his birthday Ray gave her husband a handsome leather sport jacket, which he pronounced to be "just the thing for Yellowstone." After fishing awhile in the morning, the brothers drove the 127 miles to Lovell, where that evening and the next day they spoke at four meetings of the Big Horn Stake conference. Back at Yellowstone, they fished at the junction of the Madison and Fire Hole rivers, returning to Salt Lake City on the eleventh.

The stay at Yellowstone was cut short because of the pressures that were building at home. The most urgent item on the agenda was the dedication of the Idaho Falls Temple. The completion of this sacred building had been delayed because of the preference given to war-related construction. But it had been completed at last, and now with the war ended, the Brethren and the Saints looked forward to a time of peace and rejoicing as another House of the Lord was dedicated. Within a few days after returning from Yellowstone, President and Sister McKay retraced their steps as far as Idaho Falls, where from September 23 to 25 they participated in the first temple dedication in almost twenty years. The inspiring solemnity of the occasion was reminiscent of other similar experiences the McKays had enjoyed in the dedication of temples in Hawaii, Canada, and Arizona and presaged the accelerated pace of temple building that would take place during President McKay's administration.

As the Salt Lakers returned home, they came upon a scene south of Blackfoot that sickened them and drove from their minds the peaceful thoughts and images the temple dedication had aroused. A head-on collision had demolished two cars and had crushed the bodies of the passengers. David O. was waved past the wreckage by officers who had arrived to take charge. But after driving beyond the crash site, he stopped and walked back to offer assistance. "The scene was a slaughter," he noted later. The blood, the cut and mangled bodies and the moans and the agonizing cries of pain from those who had survived were terrifying. The trauma was increased when President McKay discovered that the five occupants of the south-bound car were Latter-day Saints returning home from the temple dedication—Clarence Neslen and Newell Josephson and their wives and Sister Norma Romney. Unfortunately, Sister Neslen and Brother Josephson were killed and the others seriously injured. President McKay remained at the site until the bodies and the injured had been moved and then spent all night at the hospital giving comfort and assistance.

At home the counselor found a mountain of paperwork. And there were the usual pressures connected with preparations for the October general conference, which commenced Friday October 5. President McKay delivered the keynote address at the Sunday morning session. Hopeful that the end of the war signaled the dawn of an era of peace, the speaker took his text from Micah 4:3-4. He reasoned that the solution to external problems lay within the human heart and mind: "The future safety of the world depends not so much upon the changing of defenses," he told the audience, "as upon the changing of men's way of thinking and acting. . . . Hate and envy, suspicion and greed must be supplanted by sympathy, forbearance, tolerance, and justice." But the speaker's fervent hope for peace did not beguile him into the false belief that it would be easy of attainment: "Yes, World War II is ended, but old battles are yet to be fought; new victories yet to be won before the peace for which we pray can be realized." As he ticked off the old enemies and assayed the weapons and resources available to combat them, he focused chiefly on one: "Only in the complete surrender of our inner life may we rise about the selfish, sordid pull of nature. We should seek first the kingdom of God." (CR, October 1945, pp. 131, 132.)

As usual, President McKay was surrounded by a crowd of well-wishers as he slowly made his way from the Tabernacle to his automobile following the morning session. In that day there was no underground tunnel connecting the Tabernacle and the Administration Building as there is now. Nor was there a security force then—or the need for a security force—as there is today. And so it was a laborious process to move through the crowd that thronged Temple Square. As he inched along, a young couple approached him eagerly with three children in tow, two boys and a girl. The parents reminded President McKay that he had performed their temple marriage several years before and that to commemorate that event, they had named all their children after him. They then introduced David and Oren, the boys; and Kay, the little girl, explaining apologetically that when Oren was named "we didn't know what the 'O' in your name stands for." Given his sense of humor, it is likely David was unable to suppress a smile when he met Oren and learned the origin of his name.

It is an anomaly in a way that one as dignified as President McKay, who in the pulpit projected a somewhat grave and austere image, should have had a keen appreciation for things humorous. This aspect of his character is suggested by the frequency with which we see a genuine smile on his face in pictures taken during leisure moments. There shines forth from these pictures the image of a man who enjoyed life to the full and who understood and related to the foibles and shortcomings of humankind. An incident of which the author was a witness confirms this. It occurred when President McKay was about ninety at a banquet for Temple Square guides held in the LaFayette Ballroom of the Hotel Utah. The President's son, Robert, who was a counselor to Elder Richard L. Evans in the Temple Square presidency, had persuaded his parents to attend the affair. As they entered the room, everyone stood and quietly watched as the McKays made their way ever so slowly across the room. They required help to mount the several stairs; then they moved deliberately toward their chairs. After the president had helped Sister McKay into her seat and had carefully sat down, he looked out over the audience, which had maintained absolute silence during this ritual, and with a smile said cheerfully, "This really isn't so bad when one considers the alternative."

Another incident that occurred about this same time is one he retold with great relish. He entered the elevator in the Hotel Utah one day to find a boy who shook the president's hand with admiring awe. The young man got off the

232

elevator a floor below Brother McKay's apartment. But when the Prophet, who moved very slowly with the help of a companion, finally exited on his floor, he was surprised to see the same boy standing in the hall panting from his race up the stairway, and with his hand extended for another shake. "I just wanted to shake hands with you once more before you die," the boy explained.

By the end of October, the harvest was practically over at Huntsville, which enabled David O. to turn more attention during his "spare time" to chores around the house. Considering the season of the year when the sun sets early, and the length of time he was at the task, this entry of seventy-two-year-old David O. McKay on October 27 should give pause to retirees who excuse themselves from physical labor on account of age: "Worked on the lawns and yards at 1037 East South Temple from 5:00 to 9:30 P.M."

This rather unusual work schedule was dictated by a welcome break in the weather and the desire of the householder to have everything shipshape for the approaching winter before leaving on a lengthy trip to Arizona and California. He and Sister McKay left for Mesa, Arizona, on November 2, three days after he had preached at the funeral of his fellow General Authority and former bishop, Nicholas G. Smith. This genial, gracious, and gentle man, who was loved by all, was the first of the Assistants to the Twelve to pass away, and was only sixty-four at the time of his death.

At Mesa, the counselor presided over a historic five-day conference of Spanish-speaking members of the Church. General sessions were held in ward buildings, where these descendants of Lehi received special instruction from the visiting apostle. What gave the conference historic significance, however, was that it featured five temple endowment sessions conducted in the Spanish language. Never before had this sacred ordinance been administered in a language other than English. President McKay noted that the participants had "gathered from Mexico City to Salt Lake and from coast to coast" to join in an event that foreshadowed the translation of the temple ordinances into many languages and the proliferation of temples around the world.

That he presided at these special meetings underscored the key role David O. McKay played in the international-ization of the Church, a role that commenced with his world tour in 1921 and culminated with his initiatives in constructing temples abroad and in emphasizing that Zion is not merely a place but also a condition of heart and mind. Not long after his elevation to the First Presidency, President McKay gave voice to this concept: "The foundation of Zion then will be laid in the hearts of men; broad acres, mines, forests, factories, beautiful buildings, modern con-veniences will be but means and accessories to the building of the human soul and the securing of happiness." And again: "To change men and the world we must change their thinking, for the thing which a man really believes is the thing which he has really thought; that which he actu-ally thinks is the thing which he lives. Men do not go beyond their ideals; they often fall short of them, but they never go beyond them." (IE, 38:245.)

During the Church's first century, a key message to its converts was to gather to America, the land of Zion. A physical gathering was essential in order to develop a sub-stantial body of Saints who would form the nucleus for ul-timate global expansion. And the enduring success of a plan for global expansion entailed a modification of the in-sular views that Mormon isolation in the western United States had tended to foster. The Prophet who bridged the gap and ushered The Church of Jesus Christ of Latter-day Saints from a status of powerful provincialism to one of in-ternational influence was David O. McKay. At every stage of his development, there were hints and signs of the place he was to occupy in the mosaic of Mormon history. In es-sence his message was that the restored gospel of Jesus Christ is a philosophy and way of life for all people, in all places and in all seasons. Therefore, the principles, ideals, and disciplines that had propelled the Church to a place of power and prominence in Western America would in like manner elevate it to a place of power and prominence on the stage of the world. It was to such a goal this stubborn yet gentle Scotsman had dedicated his life. And repeatedly throughout his career appeared incidents and circumstances that reflected this goal, as in the case of the special conference he held in Mesa, Arizona, in November 1945.

Leaving Mesa, David O. and Emma Ray traveled to California to visit members of their family. Edward and Lottie were in San Diego, where the son was completing his naval commitments. And Lou Jean and Russell were living temporarily in Upland. Sandwiched between these reunions was a district conference President McKay held in Bakersfield, where he instructed and motivated the local Saints and the missionaries who were laboring in the area.

Repeating the patterns of sunshine and shadow that characterized the lives of the McKays, they experienced another trauma in mid-December when Emma Ray underwent an appendectomy. "She is doing pretty well but of course is not out of danger," the concerned husband recorded on December 16. Two days later, she had "a restless night." But by the twenty-first, she was reported to be "convalescing very nicely." And she was permitted to go home the day before Christmas.

Because of her incapacity, David O. personally took care of most of the arrangements usually handled by Emma Ray at Christmastime—purchasing gifts, signing cards, and decorating the tree. And once she was home, his solicitude for her was constant and complete. It went far beyond the deferential courtesy he always showed to her—standing up, for instance, when she entered a room—and extended to the prompt fulfillment of every requested or suspected want.

As the McKays reminisced and reflected during this holiday season, their joy was full. The war was over. Their health was basically sound. Their family was developing in a pleasing way. They had interesting and loyal friends.

They were comfortably situated in a lovely city residence—
and Huntsville was only an hour's drive away. Moreover,
the challenges and opportunities of President McKay's
apostolic ministry held out the prospect of a future filled
with excitement and variety.

Chapter Sixteen

The Centennial Celebration

As the tensions of war abated and as the flow of life settled into a more peaceful routine, President McKay was able to pick up the threads of matters that had received only cursory attention during the conflict. High on the list of things that had been relegated to the wings was the Centennial. While some essential matters had been handled quietly behind the scenes while the war raged, now, with the great celebration less than two years away, it was time to spotlight the Centennial front stage center. The time and place selected for the opening salvo of what proved to be an impressive barrage of oratory about the coming event was the Sunday morning session of the April 1946 general conference, held in the Tabernacle. President McKay was the first speaker at this session, which traditionally has been looked on as the most significant session of a general conference because of the larger audience it reaches through radio (and now television) transmission. Knowing that his words would be heard by most of the Latter-day Saints in Utah and surrounding areas, the speaker took the opportunity not only to sketch the plans for the celebration but to give his listeners a historical perspective of the drama the Centennial commemorated. He traced the outlines of the Mormon exodus, beginning with Joseph Smith's prophecy that the Saints would

David O. McKay

be driven to the Rocky Mountains. He followed them across the prairies, plains, and mountains to their valley retreat, noting in transit the epic march of the Mormon Battalion. Explaining that he cited these events "as illustrative of the spirit and achievements of the Utah pioneers," he capsulized the reasons and justification for a celebration such as the Centennial by quoting these words from the pen of one of his favorite authors, Thomas Carlyle: "In this world there is one Godlike virtue, the essence of all that ever was or ever will be Godlike in this world—the veneration done to human worth by the hearts of men." (CR, April 1946, pp. 135-41.)

Then came a catalog of the cultural and entertainment events to be featured, an explanation of why and how the plans had been scaled down due to budgetary limitations and delays caused by the war, an acknowledgment of the dedicated labors of his associates, and an official announcement about the length of the celebration.

At this point the speaker launched into a discussion of how the Saints and the community could assist by sprucing up: "Improve the appearance of churches, seminaries and other church buildings," he admonished, "by suitable landscape plantings, by painting and by needed repairs. Let all public edifices reflect the pride of the people to which they belong by making them respectable in appearance. Make Utah a rose garden by planting . . . extra bushes in every yard. Remove all dead trees from the landscape that stand as disgraceful monuments to our negligence. Clear vacant lots, particularly here in Salt Lake City, of weeds which are unsightly and which become later in the summer a fire hazard. Utilize these vacant lots this year for the growing of needed foodstuffs." (CR, April 1946, p. 139.)

To this point of the talk, there was nothing of an unusual or controversial nature that could have excited debate or opposition to what was suggested. The aim to clean up and beautify the state was a laudable one in which all segments of the population could join without dissent. It would increase property values, improve appearances, arouse civic pride, and stimulate business activity. And, what made it palatable to all was that it had a universal appeal that did not run counter to the views of any religious society or, indeed, of anyone else, including those who professed no religious beliefs.

The speaker then asked a rhetorical question that promptly altered the mood of some of those who heard or read his words: "These are physical features," he said. "What about our uniting for a moral cleanup?" President McKay then defined what he had in mind. "There is evidence of the presence of 'bunco' men in the city who are preying upon unsuspecting travelers. . . . Is it possible that Salt Lake is looked upon by these crooks as a 'fixed' city?" The statement that followed doubtless increased the pulse rate of some Salt Lake City officials: "Some of you know what that 'fixed' signifies. What about gambling, the slot machine racket, and race horse betting? What about beer and whiskey joints, and the flaunting of immorality on the public streets?" As to a remedy for all this, President McKay added: "I am sure that the mayor and other municipal officers of Salt Lake City and of other cities will appreciate our uniting with them in efforts to reduce lawlessness and immorality to a minimum." (Ibid., p. 140.)

The public reaction to this aspect of President McKay's talk was prompt—and expected. Devoted members of the Church and nonmembers who shared their views about civic morality enthusiastically endorsed his challenge. "We want to congratulate you on your stand on the moral cleanup in the city," reported one group whose representative called the office on April 10. The criminal element was soon heard from. On the twenty-ninth it was reported to President McKay that an underworld spokesman had said; "That Mormon preacher ain't going to tell us what we can do. We will shut down for a while. But we are smarter than he is." And the attitude of some of Salt Lake's officialdom was revealed in a defensive statement of the city's police chief that was published in the local press. However, on April 17 one of the inspectors from the police force met with President McKay and reported the chief as having said, "I am sorry that I wrote what I did in the article about the sermon and I shall be glad to cooperate in cleaning up the city." A week later one of President McKay's associates called the office to leave this report: "Tell President McKay that I have given the information in the proper quarters that he [President McKay] is satisfied and has gone to sleep."

While the campaign that followed the "Mormon preacher's" sermon did not eradicate vice from Utah's capital, it certainly reduced it, and the vestiges that remained slowly disappeared into the underworld before the celebration reached its zenith in the summer of 1947. The glacial speed with which this occurred, however, is suggested by a report that came to President McKay a few days before Christmas that roughly five thousand slot machines were operating in Salt Lake City and county and that the owners were paying twenty dollars a month on each machine for "protection."

This vigorous antivice campaign David O. McKay waged was one of the few times in his long career when he crossed over the line to influence civil officials in the discharge of their duties. Ordinarily he and other Church leaders were loath to intrude into Caesar's domain out of respect for the principle of separation of church and state. The counselor was especially sensitive about this as he had lived through the trying days of the underground, the fight for statehood, and the controversy that had engulfed Reed Smoot and B. H. Roberts when they attempted to take their seats in Congress. But in this instance he had no hesitancy in doing what he did, because he saw the issue to be essentially moral, justifying his direct involvement. Moreover, civil laws were being violated with the knowledge and the apparent consent of those charged with their enforcement. But beyond that, as the chairman of the Utah Centennial Commission, David O. McKay occupied an official position created by state statute, which invested him with the authority and the duty to speak out about matters that affected his office. That he elected to mount his campaign from the pulpit of the Tabernacle was in fact irrelevant, although some critics, as was true of the police chief, took umbrage at the preacher's outspoken criticism of things that technically were beyond the scope of his apostolic mandate. There would be other times, as we shall see, when David O. McKay stepped over this line. But it was a rarity when he did so, and, as was true here, he acted decisively and without equivocation or apology when the time came.

With the antivice campaign moving satisfactorily (which received a strong impetus in late summer when Monsignor Duane Hunt lent his support) and with the committees functioning smoothly, the major remaining obstacle was financing. This was essentially resolved on August 9 when, in a meeting with Governor Herbert B. Maw, President McKay was assured of the full support of his administration in obtaining a five-hundred-thousand-dollar appropriation to finance the Centennial activities. In delivering his State of the State message to the Utah legislature on January 14, 1947, Governor Maw referred to the "magnificent job of planning" the Centennial Commission had performed under the chairmanship of President McKay. He commented on the committees, "made up of hundreds of leading citizens in every part of the state" that had been preparing for the numerous cultural, educational, and entertainment events the celebration would feature.

This vast army of workers was made manageable through an efficient headquarters organization the chairman had put in place. Already mentioned were Gus Backman and A. Hamer Reiser, on whom David relied most heavily. Later, David Trevithick would come aboard as an assistant to Gus Backman. In addition, President McKay had appointed five state chairmen of subcommittees: Gordon Weggeland, public relations; John D. Rice, clean-up and paint-up; A. B. Paulsen, state parks; George H. Smeath, landscaping; and Raymond J. Ashton, planning and zoning.

While a majority of the workers on the state and local

committees were members of the Church, many prominent nonmembers also participated, as in the case of John
D. Rice, a devoted Catholic, who was a well-known Salt
Lake attorney. The main focus of the celebration, of course,
was to commemorate the centennial anniversary of the
arrival of the Mormon pioneers in the Salt Lake Valley.
And a less sensitive or less wise chairman could have made
that the sole focus, thereby excluding all nonmembers from
participation. This chairman, however, reflecting again his
penchant for broadened views, insisted that the celebration focus on all aspects of Utah's early history. The monument erected at the mouth of Emigration Canyon to commemorate the Centennial best illustrates the perspective of
the chairman. The monument represents and honors not
only the Mormon pioneers but also the Indians, trappers,
mountain men, and Catholic padres, all of whom had preceded the Latter-day Saints into the area.

Although President McKay had an excellent staff,
skilled professionals to direct the entertainment events,
and a host of willing leaders and workers at the local level
to assist, there was no one with whom he could share the
burdens of ultimate responsibility for the success or failure
of the enterprise. That he felt the weight of this responsibility would be revealed in many ways during the months
ahead, especially as the pressures mounted with the approach of the actual celebration. Without question, this
was one of the most challenging assignments David O.
McKay had ever faced. Except during 1922 to 1924, when
he presided over the European and British missions, his
entire ministry since 1906 had been performed in the con-
text of a collective leadership. Both as a member of the
Twelve and of the First Presidency, the responsibility for
the planning, execution, and success or failure of any undertaking rested on the entire quorum. And even as a mission president, he functioned within well-established
guidelines under the supervision of the Twelve, which
comprises the General Missionary Committee of the

Church. But as the chairman of the Centennial Commission, he stood alone. And the sense of loneliness such a position necessarily entailed was magnified by the glare of national publicity to be focused on the event.

As David O. McKay faced this crucial test of his generalship, there were numerous other demands made on his energies so that now and then he must have felt like a harrassed juggler trying to keep all the balls in the air at once. His ecclesiastical and ceremonial duties continued to occupy the largest segment of his time. At the office there was a dizzying daily round of meetings with the First Presidency and other General Authorities and with various committees and organizations for which he had administrative responsibility. Missionary work was one of his heavy assignments, entailing daily activity and follow-up as he directed the missionary assignment committee or counseled by telephone or post with mission presidents about a myriad of problems. And at general conference, he ordinarily met personally with as many mission presidents as possible to receive their reports and to give counsel and instruction. So following the formal sessions of the April general conference, he conducted lengthy personal interviews over a period of several days with many of the mission presidents, including Heber Meeks of the Southern States; Roy W. Doxey, Eastern States; Creed Haymond, Northern States; Francis Child, Western States; Lorin Jones, Spanish American; Glen G. Smith, Texas; and Samuel Bringhurst and David I. Stoddard, the outgoing and incoming presidents of the Northwestern States. And interspersed with these interviews were meetings with stake presidents and other leaders who wanted counsel or who merely wanted to shake hands and say hello.

A few weeks before the April general conference, President McKay sent another mission president on his way when, on January 28, 1946, he set apart Elder Ezra Taft Benson of the Twelve to preside over the European Mission. The choice of this able young apostle to fill a crucial role was dictated in large part by his expert knowledge of agricultural matters, knowledge needed to rebuild and revitalize a shattered and dispirited Europe.

And a few weeks after the conference, David O. greeted a returning mission president in the person of Hugh B. Brown, home from presiding in Great Britain.

Always intermixed with the president's strictly ecclesiastical duties was a continuing stream of ceremonial functions, visits, and interviews. One such event that drew his attendance on the first day of 1946—a reception honoring Dr. Leroy Cowles, the outgoing president of the University of Utah—signaled a busy year of involvement in academic circles or activities. He later counseled with Dr. Cowles's successor, Dr. A. Ray Olpin, and in mid-October participated in the new president's inauguration. In the first week of January, he was the guest speaker at the Weber State College's founders' day celebration; in late May he delivered the baccalaureate address at Ogden High School, and a week later he performed the same service at Brigham Young University's baccalaureate. On July 23, he was on the campus of the University of Utah, where he delivered an address on the Mormon pioneers to the student body. And, of course, throughout the year he attended various meetings of the Church Board of Education and the BYU Board of Trustees.

An annual ceremony David O. could not avoid, even had he been of a mind to do so, was the Pioneer Parade on July 24. This year, 1946, he saw it with his brethren from the special reviewing stand, and as soon as it was over he headed for Huntsville. Two days before that, the First Presidency had received Israel Smith, the president of the Reorganized Church, whose genial personality and special rapport with his cousin, President George Albert Smith, had helped to thaw some of the frigid attitudes that unfortunately had iced over in previous decades.

Visiting government officials and even aspiring politicians who sought audience with members of the First Presidency were usually accommodated without regard to the personal views and predilections of the Brethren. It was a matter of courtesy and good public relations. In this spirit, President McKay received young Harold E. Stassen on October 7. In his diary, David O. referred to the former governor of Minnesota, who had resigned his high office to join the navy, as a "potential presidential candidate." Had the diarist known then of Mr. Stassen's quadrennial impulse to reach the White House, which has seized him regularly in all the intervening years, he doubtless would have referred to him as the "perennial presidential candidate."

It was not long before President McKay entertained Mr. Stassen that he and the other members of the First Presidency had received the British consul general and, later, the British ambassador to the United States.

Amidst the constant hum of his official activities, President McKay never lost sight of the source of his greatest joy and the mainspring of his life: his home and family. He expressed his feelings about them often. "To the Latter-day Saint the home is truly the cell-unit of society; and parenthood is next to Godhood," he told the Saints gathered in a general conference. (CR, April 1919, p. 77.) And in addressing the members of the Church worldwide, he said: "Next to eternal life, the most precious gift that our Father in Heaven can bestow upon man is his children." (JI 84:620.) The year 1946 brought him a welcome harvest of happy family associations. Shortly after April conference, Bob returned home from Korea and was later discharged from the service. And in less than three months this, the youngest child, was married when on June 28 President McKay performed a temple sealing for him and his lovely bride, Frances Ellen Anderson. The ranks of the McKay grandchildren were increased this year when Lottie gave birth to a baby girl the last day of April; and on August 27, Emma Rae balanced the gender scales when she gave birth to a fine son. And when Ned and Lottie brought the new granddaughter from San Diego for a visit, a special family reunion took place, which the proud and happy patriarch recorded on June 4: "[We went] to the airport to meet Edward and Lottie and daughter. Robert met Edward for the first time in five years. Missionary work, college and military assignments having prevented their meeting together before."

With his youngest son back in the fold at last, the doting father seemed to feel impelled to introduce Bob again to the "pleasures" of Huntsville. So four days after the released serviceman came home, David O. escorted him to the farm "to take care of matters needing attention." The sons had long since learned that the so-called "matters" requiring attention at Huntsville were of infinite variety and endless duration. And the yearly recurrence of the chores surely must have reminded them of their father's teachings about eternity being one eternal round. Now and then, however, something out of the ordinary appeared on Huntsville's work agenda, as occurred two weeks before Robert returned home: "Went to Huntsville," President McKay recorded on March 25, "to direct the changing of the channel site. I found that it had not been done properly. I asked the men to meet me up there rain or shine." And throughout the summer of 1946, rain or shine, seventy-three-year-old David O. McKay worked on his farm at every opportunity. The day after Bob's marriage the last of June, he worked "all day." Two weeks later he was there working "from sun up to sun down." And throughout the balance of the summer he made similar intermittent diary entries, belying any idea that he was merely a gentleman farmer. Without doubt the most extraordinary of these is this one appearing under date of August 20: "3:00 A.M. Left for Huntsville. Worked until dark, returning home at 9:00 at which time Sister McKay and I left for a wedding [reception]. After the wedding we entertained guests."

Shortly after the October general conference, President McKay returned to Salt Lake City following a quick trip to California, where he had gone to unwind from the pressures that had built up during the preceding months. On October 15, he spoke in the afternoon at funeral services for

Grace Callis, the wife of fellow apostle Charles A. Callis, and in the evening attended the inaugural banquet for the new University of Utah president, A. Ray Olpin. David O. felt tired and dispirited as he went to bed, and he awakened the next morning with much the same feeling—and with pain. On doctor's orders he checked in at the LDS Hospital for observation and a battery of tests. Two days later he was operated on for an embolism. "I approached this operation with apprehension," David O. recorded afterward, "because of a former experience I had when an embolism occurred. Knowing of that attack several doctors consulted together and took every precaution to avoid a recurrence. As a result I am in excellent condition." He then added this postscript, which proved to be overly optimistic and premature: "The operation was highly successful and I am now on the high road to recovery."

But the patient had to wait ten days after that entry before he was allowed to go home. And after he had been home for ten days, this: "With a view of going to the office tomorrow I called my doctor. Imagine my disappointment when instead of approving my going to work, he ordered me to bed for two or three days." In consoling himself, the patient betrayed the irritation and urgency his confinement had produced: "However, I am sure this is only a temporary set back for I am already 'chafing at the bit' to get out of the house."

However, it was not until after the first of the year that President McKay was able to resume his customary duties. Intermittently he went to his office for a while to take care of routine matters. And now and then he attended a meeting. But he wasn't strong enough to take up his full burden, however much he wanted to. By the first of December, when it became apparent that his convalescence would be longer than he had expected, David O. decided to seek a warmer climate, which, it was hoped, would speed his recovery. So on December 2, he and Emma Ray left for the coast in a new 1946 Buick he had purchased just three days before. They traveled via Phoenix and on reaching the Valley of the Sun decided against going on to California. "Glorious sunshine here today [in Phoenix] in a cloudless sky," he recorded on December 7. It was here the travelers remained for a pleasant interlude in the warm Arizona sun.

The McKays returned to Salt Lake City in time to prepare for Christmas and to enable David to check on matters at Huntsville and to look in at his office before leaving by train for California on December 27 with Bishop and Sister Joseph L. Wirthlin. This trip was in the line of President McKay's duties as the chairman of the Utah Centennial Commission. In that capacity, he had been invited to be seated on the reviewing stand at the annual Rose Parade in Pasadena. And afterward he and Ray and the Wirthlins attended the Rose Bowl game. There the University of Utah football alumnus critically watched the "modern" gridiron warriors, whose tempered play could scarcely compare with the rough-and-tumble, no-holds-barred brand of football he and his teammates had played around the turn of the century.

By the time he returned from Pasadena, President McKay was fully recovered from the aftereffects of his surgery and ready to undertake the grueling activities of the Centennial year. The first official event of the celebration was the inauguration of the Centennial queen, Calleen Robinson, which took place at the State Capitol on January 16. Several thousand people crowded the rotunda of the capitol as the chairman crowned the lovely young woman who would reign over many ceremonial events during the year. A few days later, President McKay and members of his committee conferred with noted New York choreographer and dancer Helen Tamaris, who was in the city holding auditions to select the dancing cast for "Promised Valley," which would be the showcase of the entertainment events. This production concerned the chairman more than any other single thing about the Centennial. It was scheduled to run throughout the heart of the celebration and was expected to play to a larger audience than any other event. He knew, therefore, that in the public mind the success or failure of the entire Centennial would ride on this play. So, although the staging of such a performance was foreign to President McKay's experience and inclinations, and although he relied on the professionals to provide the technical expertise, he watched over every aspect of the production with the same care with which he tended his fields and trained his horses.

On March 1, the chairman and Emma Ray attended the first of the several Centennial athletic events when they went to Snow Basin to witness a national ski competition. "We nearly froze up there," the seventy-three-year-old diarist noted, "but it was a glorious day and the scenery was superb." This was not the first or the last time David O. McKay's innate optimism overshadowed adversities. Indeed, this was one of the salient qualities of his character, this propensity to emphasize the positive aspects of a situation. He was not unlike the terrified hiker who, when treed by a bear, congratulated himself on the magnificent view.

Toward the end of the month, the chairman again became involved in the technicalities of the "Promised Valley" production when on the twenty-seventh he conferred with C. Lowell Lees and Lorin Wheelwright about the script. And later that threesome was joined by Crawford Gates, the composer of the score for the production, of whom President McKay wrote: "Mr. Gates is a genius. The music he has written is superb." These meetings gave David O. a tremendous lift, providing an assurance that the play would be successful. The elation and sense of relief this produced are reflected in this joyful entry: "Things are beginning to shape out," he recorded on March 28. "I told President Smith and President Clark this morning I feel as though I am walking on air . . . that a big load seems to have lifted."

The lightsome mood this reflected carried over to a banquet held five days later, sponsored by the sports division of the Centennial, where the chairman honored eighty

Utah athletes who had won national championships, including the University of Utah basketball team, which had recently captured the NIT title in New York.

On Saturday, April 5, between sessions of the general conference that was then in progress, President McKay attended and spoke at cornerstone-laying ceremonies of the This Is the Place Monument at the mouth of Emigration Canyon. And the following day, at the Sunday morning session of conference, he delivered a major sermon eulogizing the Mormon pioneers. In it he again traced their historic trek and admonished the community to clean up, paint up, and shape up. He also announced the official opening of the Centennial on May 1 and described some of the major events that would take place during the celebration.

In a sense, this served as an outline of the exhausting itinerary of seventy-three-year-old David O. McKay during the next few months as he participated personally in most of the events he described. Even to follow him at a distance through this schedule is wearying.

The opening of the celebration on May 1 started with a picture-taking session, which included photos of the chairman with the Centennial queen, Calleen Robinson, and with ninety-two-year-old Alma Felt, one of the pioneers who had walked across the plains. Following flag-raising ceremonies at the State Capitol, a reception was held at the Hotel Utah honoring 236 immigrant pioneers. The dignitaries and guests then walked to the nearby Tabernacle between two rows of ROTC cadets, and President McKay conducted the inaugural program, which featured a talk by President George Albert Smith. "After a long hard day," the counselor recorded, "I retired happy in the thought that the legal opening of the Centennial celebration had been successfully launched."

From that launch President McKay cruised through a staggering variety of entertainment and ceremonial events of which these are a sampling: On May 28, accompanied by Emma Ray and Lou Jean and her son Russell, David O.

attended the Centennial performance of *Macbeth*, which starred Orson Welles. Five days later he visited the State Fair grounds for a round of picture-taking with Governor Herbert Maw for the official opening of the Utah State Centennial Exposition. On July 3, the chairman traveled to Richfield, where he was feted at the Sevier County Centennial Pageant. Kept up until 1:15 A.M. by numerous visitors and well-wishers, the president arose at 3:00 A.M. to drive to Logan for a parade. He never arrived there, however, because a drunk driver ran him off the road between Nephi and Mona. Fortunately, he was not hurt. But by the time Ned and Bob came to the rescue, it was too late to make the Logan parade. The next day, at Pine View Reservoir, David O. witnessed the Western Divisional Pacific Coast Outboard Motor Championships sponsored by the Weber County Centennial Committee. On the eleventh he acceded to the request of the Heber City chairman for picture-taking with the local queen in connection with Heber's celebration. President McKay drove to Huntsville after the picture-taking and cut two fields of hay and the lawns surrounding the Old Home. "It was after dark before I arrived home," the Centennial chairman-farmer recorded, noting with satisfaction: "I decided that I must still be 'pretty young' to be able to put in such a day and feel as well as I do."

The day after this stint on the farm, David O. attended a Centennial concert in the Tabernacle featuring Helen Traubel of the Metropolitan Opera. Special guests included most of the governors of the United States, who were then holding a conference in Salt Lake City. Afterward, the governors and President McKay and their parties attended an informal reception at the Utah governor's mansion. Events of the two following days also featured the governors when on the fourteenth a state banquet was held where General George C. Marshall was the guest speaker, and on the fifteenth a parade of governors was held in downtown Salt Lake. The parade was followed by a reception at the home of President George Albert Smith. President McKay was hard put to participate in all these events, as earlier on the fifteenth he attended the Centennial celebration in Heber City.

Two days later, the harried chairman enjoyed a brief respite when he and Edward went to Huntsville, where they "worked most of the day on the farm pitching hay and mowing the lawns." At home that evening, the president seemed surprised and pleased to find that his social calendar was clear: "For the first time in weeks," he noted appreciatively, "I remained home this evening."

It was good that he had this interlude free of commitments, as the next few days brought him into the very heart of the Centennial celebration. On the eighteenth, with the assistance of Elder Richard L. Evans, he went through a "dry run" of a "Church of the Air" centennial message, which, after editing, he delivered on the twentieth. The following day found him at Fort Bridger, Wyoming, where he spoke at the last encampment of the 1947 Pioneer Trek, which was comprised of descendants of those who had made up the original Brigham Young company a century before. And the day after that, the twenty-second, he and the other members of the First Presidency met the 1947 trekkers at the This Is the Place Monument, where, according to the diarist, "it seemed that all Salt Lake City turned out to give the returning Sons of the Utah Pioneers a rousing welcome home."

On the twenty-third, President McKay, along with the other members of the First Presidency, rode at the head of a mammoth parade through the heart of Salt Lake City, this pageantry being repeated on the following day. And in the afternoon he rode in Ogden's Centennial parade.

The big day, the twenty-fourth, began with a ceremony dedicating the This Is the Place Monument. A crowd estimated at fifty thousand assembled to witness the unveiling, an event made more dramatic by the presence of hundreds of seagulls that swarmed the area seeking the food the planners had assiduously scattered about each morning weeks in advance of the event. At noon, the Daughters of the Utah Pioneers hosted a commemorative luncheon in the Hotel Utah; in the afternoon a plaque was unveiled at the State Capitol containing the names of the original pioneers; in the evening a banquet was held on the Roof Garden of the Hotel Utah, where Postmaster General James A. Farley announced the imprinting of a Utah Centennial commemorative stamp; and at 7:00 P.M. the second Centennial parade wound its way through the streets lined with an audience estimated at two hundred thousand.

On the day after, knowing that the most hectic part of the celebration was behind him, the chairman figuratively heaved a sigh of relief as this entry implies: "Still rejoicing over the success of the great events that have transpired in the past two days. Now that the peak of the celebration [has been] reached, our worries will not be so great."

But a lessening of his worries did not bring with it a letup in his frenetic involvement in Centennial events around the state. During August, he participated in celebrations in Santaquin, Loa, Murray, and Manti. September 1 found the chairman at Hooper for "Tomato Days," which was part of the Weber County Centennial celebration. David O. was amused by the baby contest, in which "the prettiest baby, the baby with the most hair, the baby with the least hair, the fattest baby, the leanest baby—and every other baby was given a prize." Five days later President McKay was at Brigham City for their Centennial Peach Day celebration; and on the ninth he went south to Cedar City for the Iron County festivities. Near the end of the month, the chairman was again in southern Utah for one of the last events of the year when he attended a Centennial play in Beaver, "Brigham Young and the Pioneers."

President McKay in effect rang down the curtain on the celebration when, in his October general conference address, he expressed "heartfelt commendation" to the people of Utah "for their cooperation and united effort during this Centennial year." He then named several persons

and groups specially, giving to them "all credit for whatever success has been achieved during the 1947 celebration." (CR, October 1947, p. 115.)

There remained only the necessary housekeeping
chores of closing the books and making a final accounting
to the legislature, which extended over several months.
And, of course, the memories of the Centennial remained
bright and were often triggered or rekindled by subsequent
events as on October 20 when President McKay read in his
newspaper that Samuel K. Eck and a passenger had been
killed at Loa when their plane crashed on takeoff after a
motor failure. The article immediately brought to the president's mind a scene of two months before when he was in
Loa for their Centennial celebration. Mr. Eck had publicly
invited the visitor to take a ride with him over the scenic
Wayne Wonderland the next morning in his one-passenger
plane. David O. was happy to decline because he had a
conflicting appointment with a Brother Oldroyd. To his
consternation, "Brother Oldroyd immediately got up and
said that we need not let the appointment stop us from taking the airplane trip." So, left without excuse, but not without trepidation, President McKay had taken the exciting
ride—and now his pilot was gone, along with a passenger,
who could have been the Centennial chairman.

But providence had decreed another scenario for David
O. McKay, who was now moving rapidly toward the most
signal event and period of his life.

Chapter Seventeen

Prophetic Prelude

With the pressures of the celebration behind, President McKay happily turned his full attention to the tasks of his apostolic ministry. Having been preoccupied with Centennial commitments during most of 1947, he had been unable to get into the field as much as he would have liked to do. So, with the dawning of 1948, he began to remedy that deficiency. On January 22, he and Ray traveled to San Bernardino. There he presided over a stake conference in the city where, almost a century before, two of his predecessors in the apostleship, Charles C. Rich and Amasa Lyman, had established a Latter-day Saint colony. Although the Mormon colonizing presence in San Bernardino was short lived because of the withdrawal of the Saints in 1857 at the time of the Utah invasion by Johnston's army, the aura of that pioneering effort still clung to the community, exerting a subtle spiritual influence on the members of the Church who lived or visited there. That influence was not lost on the distinguished Utahn, whose life overlapped the lives of his two apostolic predecessors and whose message was the same as the one they had delivered a century before: God the Father lives; Jesus Christ is his Only Begotten Son; the Savior's church has been restored; and he was a special witness of Jesus' divinity and was the Lord's authorized agent, empowered to speak and act in his name.

Few things pleased and satisfied David O. McKay more than to bear such a testimony. And while he enjoyed and excelled at other aspects of the work—administering, directing, and counseling—it was in teaching the gospel and in testifying of the Savior that he received his greatest sense of fulfillment.

Buoyed up by the inspiration of the San Bernardino conference, the visitors drove on to Los Angeles, where David O. had a more mundane task to perform. There he met with Elder Mark E. Petersen of the Twelve; Preston D. Richards, a prominent Mormon lawyer who lived in southern California; and members of the board of the Los Angeles Times, a publishing company in which the Church owned a stock interest. The purpose of the meeting was to discuss the acquisition of the Hawley Pulp and Paper Company, whose inventories would be useful to the Times, as well as to the Deseret News, whose voracious presses constantly kept the management alert for new sources of pulp.

Back in Salt Lake City, President McKay barely had time to unpack and then to pack again for a lengthy trip through Old Mexico. With him as he departed by automobile on February 4 was Emma Ray, who not only was his domestic companion but who, in a real sense, was a companion in his ministry. Once the children had been reared, it was only rarely that David O. McKay left Salt Lake City without Ray at his side. He not only loved her, but he liked her, too. He liked to be with her. He enjoyed conversing with her. He was intrigued by her poise and style. And he appreciated the qualities of her mind and spirit and the depth of her understanding. While the strictures of his apostolic calling prevented him from divulging confidences to her, beyond that limitation he was open and uninhibited in sharing his thoughts and problems and in seeking her counsel.

Whenever it was feasible to do so, the McKays traveled by automobile. They enjoyed the freedom of setting their own schedule and of traveling at their own pace—which, incidentally, was a fast pace when David O. was behind the wheel. They also enjoyed the privacy and intimacy of being alone and of engaging in lengthy, unstructured conversation as they watched the beautiful and varied scenery as it flashed by.

So it was with anticipation that the happy couple left Salt Lake City on February 4 headed for Mexico. They were met at the border by the mission president, Arwell L. Pierce, and his wife, with whom they spent almost a month touring the vast and beautiful country of Mexico. After holding meetings with the Mexican Saints in El Paso and across the border at La Caseta, the party headed south, sometimes traveling by train and sometimes by automobile. Meetings were held at Cuautla, where a chapel was dedicated, and at Monterrey, San Pablo, Chalco, Puebla, San Marcos, Piedras Negras, and Mexico City. Everywhere the visitors were received with reverential respect, an attitude that was reciprocated by the apostle and his wife. "People whom we met were gracious, kind and hospitable," President McKay recorded as he summarized the tour. "I would say that their national virtue is kindness to children; and their children in turn seem to be respectful and obedient to parents."

Although the apostle was approaching seventy-five at the time of this tour, he and Emma Ray entered into the spirit of the occasion as if they were decades younger. They were good travelers and good sports. That they seldom slept in the same bed two nights in a row, that their schedules were erratic, and that their diet was inconsistent seemed not to bother them. They remained buoyant and forward looking in the face of any inconvenience or annoyance. And their sense of humor did not desert them. The acid test came at San Pablo where, after a bumpy and dusty ride, their car stalled on a lonely side street. The diarist noted that "a group of kiddies gathered around and I saw some men and women who smiled at our predicament." At that moment of embarrassment occurred a ludicrous incident that David O. later recorded with an apparent chuckle: "But the most humiliating experience of all was the hee-haw of a donkey. I took as a personal insult the long drawn out hee-haw of his horrible bray."

In the course of this tour, in addition to admonishing and inspiring the Saints and counseling the missionaries and local leaders, President McKay went out of his way to meet and to cement relationships with Mexican officials. He also inspected potential building sites along the route. And he expanded his knowledge and comprehension of the people and their culture by visiting with those of high and low station and by inspecting the ruins and artifacts of ancient Mexican civilizations.

The counselor returned from his exhausting tour of Mexico in time to recharge his energies and to prepare for the April general conference. The major address he delivered at the morning session on April 5 contained a global overview that caused him to conclude that "the world faces a crisis—a terrible crisis." He saw that crisis as presenting a "choice . . . between dictatorship with the atheistic teachings of Communism and the doctrines of the restored gospel of Jesus Christ, obedience to which alone can make us free." (CR, April 1948, p. 70.) In conclusion, he invoked blessings on the Church and particularly on "our young people who are going to maintain its standards." (Ibid.)

President McKay was convinced that the future strength and vitality of the Church, indeed, of the nation and the world, depended on the proper indoctrination and motivation of the youth. On this account, he never missed an opportunity to speak to youth groups whether in a formal or informal setting. And it was not uncommon for him to speak to small, intimate groups of young people in his own home, to which they had been invited by members of his family. Such a group convened in the McKay home shortly after the 1948 April general conference as this diary entry of April 25 attests: "In the evening met at my home a group of returned missionaries. . . . I talked to the group. Among other things we discussed the Negro question which seems to be coming up frequently these days." And this topic would surface with even greater frequency in the years ahead as President McKay and his brethren struggled with an issue that would be resolved ultimately by a revelation to one of his successors, Spencer W. Kimball.

The benefits derived from President McKay's frequent contacts with young people did not flow merely in one direction. He was always the beneficiary of their enthusiasm, faith, and optimism. And occasionally he derived inspiration and prophetic insight from them, as on January 11, 1947, when, at his son's request, the president spoke to a group of Robert's Argentine missionary companions gathered in the family home at 1037 East South Temple. The speaker treated one of his favorite subjects, the poet Robert Burns, whose 188th birthday was to be celebrated fourteen days later. After the talk, during which the speaker read or recited excerpts from the poet's verses in a delightful Scottish brogue, the conversation turned to some of the missionary experiences members of the group had enjoyed while serving in South America. "The missionaries were emphatic in recommending that missionary work be undertaken in Uruguay," President McKay noted in his diary, adding: "They have convinced me that their recommendations should be adopted." The other members of the First Presidency agreed with the second counselor, who was then the chairman of the Missionary Executive Committee, and within a few months after the meeting in the McKay home, the Uruguay Mission was organized with Frederick S. Williams (a former president in Argentina) as its first president.

It is curious that two months after President McKay met with the group in his home when the discussion about the blacks took place, he visited Spencer W. Kimball, the man through whom the revelation on priesthood would come. At the time Elder Kimball was confined at home with a heart ailment, one of the seemingly endless afflictions he would suffer during the coming years. There was concern then that Brother Kimball's days were numbered, and

President McKay apparently sought to comfort and bless him while there was yet time.

Six days later, President McKay, who was then only three months shy of seventy-five, seemed to be a candidate to join Elder Kimball on the sick list when he worked hard on the farm from six in the morning until four in the afternoon. "At that time, feeling a little tired, I decided to leave for home." When the weariness persisted and when he later began to feel dizzy, the president consulted Doctor Leslie White, who said to him chidingly, "I might have known you wouldn't have called me unless it was something critical." He was hospitalized immediately, and a heart specialist, V. L. Viko, found an "unequalization between my pulse and heart rate—pulse 70 heart beat 110." With an apparent sense of relief, the patient noted a few days later: "Dr. Viko reports there is no organic heart trouble—that I have been over-exerting my heart and that I shall just have to rest." This diary entry made exactly a week after he was released from the hospital provides insight into David O. McKay's conception of what it meant to take it easy: "Accompanied by Llewelyn and his son Dick I went to Huntsville. All three of us worked around the farm all day, Llewelyn and Dick doing most of the strenuous work as I am still under doctor's orders to curtail physical activity." On the third of July he accompanied Llewelyn and Ned to Huntsville, where they spent the day cutting the lawn and preparing the Old Home for the traditional July 4 celebration when "53 members of the family enjoyed the day."

It was not that President McKay set out deliberately to disobey doctor's orders. The difficulty lay in their differing interpretation of what it meant to rest. That he recognized the need to slow down appears from a philosophic entry he made July 6 when he concluded that "a man past three score and ten cannot run so fast as he could when he was in his forties." That touched off six weeks of a comparatively relaxed schedule during which the most strenuous thing he did was to drive to Yellowstone for a few days of vacationing. But when he returned, he felt so invigorated that he went to the farm to tend to a few important matters. As he was training one of his horses, he stumbled over some roots and "fell like a bag of sand," hitting his right shoulder and arm on a tree stump or rock. He managed to get back to the Old Home, change his clothes, and drive alone to Salt Lake City. An examination revealed that there were no broken bones, although he was badly bruised and very sore. By the time his birthday arrived, however, the pain and misery had been forgotten temporarily, and we find him in a contented, expansive mood: "Old age at 75 is not nearly so decrepit as years ago I had anticipated it would be," he wrote reflectively. "This birthday has convinced me that life at 75 is just as bright and joyous as ever when surrounded by loved ones and loyal friends."

But an injury of the kind he had suffered was not easily shaken off at age seventy-five, even if he was David O. McKay. So for several months he had intermittent pain and difficulties causing him to try various remedies and doctors recommended by family and friends. In the meantime, he suffered a severe attack of gastritis, which sent him to the hospital for various tests. On October 14, while David O. was undergoing one of these, the doctor "scolded" him for his failure to follow orders and gave the patient some "good sound advice," which, he promised his diary, "I intend to follow."

Meanwhile, the bustle of his daily activities continued without letup. Official, family, and farm duties claimed most of his attention. But, as always, these were interspersed with numerous personal contacts from members of the Church pleading for his attention and assistance. President McKay never failed to respond to these pleas for help if it was within his ability to do so. So on August 6, 1948, he administered to five-year-old James Nephi Manning, whose anguished parents had pleaded that he bless their son, who had been stricken with a brain tumor. A fortnight after his birthday, the apostle found time in the midst of a busy schedule to counsel with a man and his wife, barely known to him, who were having marital difficulties. And a week after that, an unknown woman "on the verge of a nervous breakdown" appeared at the family home one night seeking help and comfort. After learning her identity, Sister McKay put the stranger to bed in the guest room while the president called the woman's husband, who lived in a neighboring city. When the husband arrived at 2:00 A.M., Brother McKay urged him to stay the rest of the night, "but he thought it best to leave." And during the Christmas holidays, the apostle gave counsel to a distraught woman about her "family troubles."

Aside from these instances, cited by way of illustration, in which President McKay responded to urgent pleas for help, there were innumerable times when, without request, he went out of his way to give comfort to his family and friends. So on Christmas day, after opening gifts with the family, David O. and Ray went to the hospital to visit David O.'s sister Anne and her husband, Tom Farr. And an entry of June 8, 1949, tells a touching tale about this rugged man's love of friends and flowers: "Early this morning I drove up to Farmington to the floral shop and purchased three bouquets of flowers and then drove back to Salt Lake City and up to the LDS Hospital where I called on Orval Adams, John James and Elijah B. Gregory . . . and presented each with a bouquet." A few weeks later, while he was loading hay on the farm, David O. remembered that Huntsville neighbors, Brother and Sister Jesse M. Wilbur, were celebrating their golden wedding anniversary. He promptly drove to Salt Lake City to change and to pick up Ray. On the way back, the McKays stopped at their favorite florist in Farmington, where they purchased two dozen gladiolas for their friends. Noting that he felt well repaid for making the effort to attend because of the apparent happiness it brought the Wilburs, he added with obvious amusement: "They kept us there for an hour or so and then asked us to speak to their friends." By the time he reached home after the reception, President McKay had driven two hundred miles that day.

The encroachment on his private life that celebrity status imposed, as illustrated by this incident, was something President McKay adjusted to with apparent difficulty. He was essentially a modest, private person, reared in a rural atmosphere, who at an early age was thrust into the limelight of the Mormon community. And as he gained in experience, as his personal contacts expanded inside and outside the Church, and as wide media exposure made his name and face known in most households, he became, in a sense, a public asset whose time and efforts were assumed to be available to all. This radical change in status was a bittersweet experience. To be recognized, lauded, and lionized is something that seemingly appeals to the ego and self-esteem of the most modest among us, even to David O. McKay. But the inevitable shrinkage in the circle of privacy that this necessarily entails provides a counterbalance that at times outweighs the positive aspects of public adulation. This is easily inferred from a diary entry of July 19, 1950, made following David O.'s effort to purchase a gift for Emma Ray at a store only a block from his office. "I was forty-five minutes getting back to the office from First South and Main Street so many people stopped me on the street to ask questions, to extend greetings etc." The diarist hinted that it had become so difficult to venture forth on the streets of Salt Lake City that he had about decided to abandon the practice. For such a free spirit as he, for one who was so accustomed to going and coming as he pleased, any decision to restrict his movements about the city was an imprisonment of sorts. But the only alternatives, neither of which was acceptable, were to go in disguise or to ignore or to cut short those who approached him. The latter would have been especially repugnant to one such as David O. McKay, who had cultivated to the highest degree the qualities of courtesy and attentive listening.

It was ironic, therefore, that as the apostle's fame and influence widened, the scope of his private life was proportionately restricted. More and more, especially after he became the president of the Church, Elder McKay's activities in Salt Lake City consisted of his work at Church headquarters, his private life at home, his public appearances, and his social contacts with family and a close circle of friends and associates. Occasionally he would break out of this confining circle. But whenever he did so, there would be a repetition of the mob scene he encountered during his shopping spree in July 1950.

All this made the privacy and seclusion of the Huntsville farm more attractive—and more necessary. And later, after he became the president of the Church, the cottage at Laguna Beach on Emerald Bay took its place as a second hideaway. However, because of its proximity to Salt Lake City and its tendency to remind him of his ancestral heritage, Huntsville remained David O.'s favorite place of refuge. There he could work in the fields, or spruce up around the Old Home, or take a ride on Bess or Sonny Boy, or train some of the young colts that came along with equine regularity.

A typical Huntsville interlude is reflected in this entry for May 9, 1949: "After the meeting I drove up to Huntsville where I attended to the horses, taking burrs out of their manes etc. and also doing other chores around the farm." Sixteen days later, he was there again for another similar session. After working all day, he felt to congratulate himself for the restraint he had shown: "I tried to follow the doctor's orders—orders not to over-do," he wrote self consciously, "and I even held myself in check when one of the horses disobeyed and ran away from me. I wanted to run after her, but I used other methods. I finally had her coming to me of her own accord."

There was a certain satisfaction, a feeling of achievement, in controlling the actions of a horse, in disciplining it to the will of its master. In this sense, President McKay's satisfaction in training horses must have simulated the feelings he had in being able to channel the efforts and energies of his associates.

But much of the work David O. performed at Huntsville produced little if any intellectual satisfaction. It did, however, provide needed exercise to tone and invigorate his body. After working all day on July 16 cutting hay, he observed: "It was a good days work and I enjoyed it very much. Every muscle in my body had been used and as a result I [throb] with aching muscles."

And Huntsville was also a place for play and recreation. The patriarch enjoyed taking his grandchildren there for sleigh rides during the winter months. On January 2, 1950, he celebrated his forty-ninth wedding anniversary by introducing several of them to the joy of riding in an open sleigh in the crisp winter air. "Sleigh riding in Huntsville to me is a joyous past time," he wrote nostalgically. "It takes me back to my youth which now seems only a few years ago. On this occasion some of the children [learned] for the first time the real significance of 'Jingle Bells, Jingle Bells.' "

But Huntsville had its hazards as well as its hours of happiness. President McKay encountered one of these as he and Llewelyn worked together cleaning up around the farm on April 22. As they sought to move a huge stump with the use of a team, the father's foot became entangled in a chain as he maneuvered the horses into position. "I was knocked to the ground," he reported "and the stump which weighed nine hundred to a thousand pounds was pulled on to my legs." Calling to Llewelyn to help "get this thing off me," David O. was able to work his way free. In the process, he suffered torn muscles and ligaments, although an X ray later revealed there were no broken bones. Notwithstanding this, the president was hospitalized on April 28 to guard against blood clots. After a week of what he considered to be a useless confinement, the patient decided it was time to leave: "Although the doctors and nurses and even the superintendent of the hospital were against me, I decided to leave the hospital and I feel that I can do at home everything that is being done here. Consequently at 4:00 P.M. this afternoon I left the hospital." At home he carried on his work from bed for several days, dictating to the secretary who came from his office and counseling with various committees that gathered around the apostle's bed to transact Church business.

It was there in the privacy of his home that President McKay's associates saw him in his favorite and most natural setting. It was from this source, the seclusion and sanctity of his home, that David O. McKay drew the earthly inspiration that propelled him along the sometimes steep and tortuous path of his apostolic ministry. Emma Ray, with her ever calm and placid presence, set the tone of the home. She drew an interesting and perceptive word sketch of it in a talk delivered on April 12, 1952, to the Brigham Young University women, which she titled "The Art of Rearing Children Peacefully." While her remarks were aimed chiefly at parenting, she also focused on the relationship between husband and wife. If we have marveled at the constant attentiveness and consideration President McKay showed toward Emma Ray, these excerpts from her talk may provide a partial explanation: "If she is home, [her husband] wants peace," she told her audience, "no weeping, hysterical wife to pour troubles and complaints into

President and Sister McKay on their golden wedding anniversary, January 2, 1951, with their children and grandchildren.

President and Sister McKay at their home at 1037 East South Temple Street.

his ears. He wants to see a wife who has made herself as beautiful as she can, a woman who has poise and charm, who greets him lovingly and cheerfully, who studies his every mood, and can tell when he wants to talk and when he would like a complete rest. . . . I should say that women should go two-thirds or all of the way to keep peace. . . . Peace in the home is really woman's responsibility, and if she wants happiness, she must work for it. . . . And she always must remember that wisdom is made up of two parts: nine-tenths silence and one-tenth brevity. . . . A husband wants a wife who studies to be intelligent, who can talk when topics of the day are discussed, a wife who tries to be frugal, but who makes home attractive, keeps it clean and in good order, and who studies his interests in every way."

So the public image the McKays projected of a happy

David O. McKay

contented couple, full of love and concern for each other, was no mere facade. It was fortified by a constant recommitment to each other and by daily acts of kindness and consideration. And they joined in showing similar feelings toward their children. A touching manifestation of this occurred during this period when in March 1949, President and Sister McKay arranged to have the body of their son, Royal, moved from Ogden to the Salt Lake City Cemetery. "I dedicated the grave at 4:30 this afternoon," the father recorded on March 16, "and felt very well satisfied that his body had been brought nearer home."

But while the couple grieved over the loss of this son, they rejoiced over the periodic additions to their progeny as when on June 5 of the same year President McKay was privileged to bless his fourteenth grandchild, David Anderson McKay, Robert and Frances Ellen's second child. Moreover, on August 11, 1950, the proud grandparents were pleased to welcome into the family circle Emma Rae and Conway's fourth child, a girl, whom Papa Dade called "a darling baby." And as the size of their progeny increased, the grandparents were grateful to see their older grandchildren mark the way for the others to follow, as when on June 4, 1950, President McKay spoke at grandson Dick's farewell in the Capitol Hill Ward prior to his departure for the Swiss Austrian Mission.

A few months before, on January 15, 1950, President McKay had spoken at another missionary farewell, this one in honor of Stayner Richards, Stephen L's younger brother, who had been called to preside over the British Mission. In his remarks, the president referred to the loyalty the missionary's ancestor, Willard Richards, had shown toward the Prophet Joseph Smith in the Carthage Jail. In recording the event later, the speaker made this observation, which strongly suggests a principal reason why, in the following year, David O. McKay selected Stephen L Richards as his first counselor. Wrote he, "Stayner Richards and Stephen L Richards his brother have inherited those qualities of loyalty." And later in the same year, the death of a cousin of

268

these brothers, George F. Richards, elevated Elder McKay to the pinnacle of missionary work as the president of the Twelve, which is the General Missionary Committee of the Church, and brought him to the very threshhold of the prophetic office.

The death of George F. Richards on August 8, 1950, ended an apostolic association with David O. McKay which the pair had enjoyed for over forty years. As already noted they, along with Orson F. Whitney, had been ordained to the apostleship on the same day, April 9, 1906, by President Joseph F. Smith. Although their service in the Twelve began on the same day, Elder Richards always had been recognized as the senior because he was ordained first. And that status was confirmed by an age differential of twelve years, George F. having been born in 1861. Aside from their ties in the apostleship, this pair was also bound together by a common interest in agriculture, the elder man having owned and operated farms in Box Elder and Tooele counties before his call to the Twelve.

At the semiannual conference in 1950, David O. McKay was sustained both as the second counselor in the First Presidency and as the president of the Quorum of the Twelve Apostles. This was the first time in the history of the Church that someone had served simultaneously in both positions. To an extent, David O.'s service as the president of the Twelve was merely honorary, as at the same conference where he was sustained in that position, Elder Joseph Fielding Smith was sustained as the acting president. Elder Smith, therefore, handled all the administrative details of the quorum, although he counseled periodically with President McKay about them.

In the major talk he delivered at the October general conference, President McKay commented about his departed associate: "With President Smith and others of the Brethren and with all of you, I miss President George F. Richards." And then by way of qualification, he suggested that his friend might be "nearer to us than we think." (CR, October 1950, p. 108.) This statement implies the quality of

President McKay that was predominant among all the other fine qualities he possessed. He was a man of extraordinary spiritual sensitivity. Spiritual phenomena were a reality to him, not merely a topic of conversation or debate. Often he had received spiritual promptings that had illuminated his way, warned him of dangers, and shown him what he ought or ought not to do. He was convinced, therefore, that the earthly death and burial of George F. Richards had not terminated his existence but had merely ushered him into another realm where his spiritual identity and intelligence continued.

Chapter Eighteen

President of the Church

The passing of Elder George F. Richards made it clear that should David O. McKay survive President George Albert Smith, he would become the head of the Church. Having sat in the governing councils of the Church for more than forty-four years and having watched the formal transfer of prophetic authority on two occasions from the circle in which the new president was ordained, Elder McKay was acutely aware of the sensitive and awesome position in which he had been placed by the death of George F. Richards. At any moment the full weight of ultimate responsibility in the Church might be thrust upon him. Although at the time of his apostolic ordination he had been given all the authority necessary to lead the Church, an authority he held in suspension pending the maturing of events, he probably never comprehended the full significance of that until Elder Richards passed away. Then, if George Albert Smith were to die, David O. McKay would be elevated to the pinnacle of Church leadership.

But President McKay was not anxious for the passing of his friend and brother, President George Albert Smith. He had loved him through the years and had supported him loyally as a counselor through the entire period of his presidency. And he had seen enough of the responsibilities borne by the president of the Church that he did not aspire to be subjected to the same pressures.

Throughout the October general conference, President Smith was in apparent good health. "He seemed to be vigorous and well during all the sessions of the conference," David O. had recorded. But the term vigor as applied to President Smith had a different meaning than it did in reference to someone with robust health. He had always been frail and had never been able to participate in the kinds of physical exertions in which President McKay had routinely engaged. Nevertheless, at the time of the October 1950 general conference, he seemed to be in as good health as he had been for some time. In the months that followed, however, there was a marked and unexplained deterioration in his physical condition, so much so that by the first week in February, those close to him were genuinely concerned: "I accompanied President Smith to the hospital for a check up," Elder McKay recorded on the fourth. "He has been running a temperature and the doctors want to make several tests to see if they can get at the source of the trouble." Three days later the patient's personal secretary, D. Arthur Haycock, reported to President McKay that the Prophet was "better." And after visiting him on February 15, David O. noted that his leader was "holding his own," although he showed signs of discouragement. It was later decided to release him to go home, even though the source of his problem was still unknown.

In the days that followed, the reports of his condition were generally negative until the second week in March, when he seemed to take a turn for the better. "President Smith is still improving," President McKay recorded on the eleventh. This optimistic report prompted the McKays to decide to leave for California on a trip they had postponed because of President Smith's condition. They left by automobile the next day, driving as far as St. George, where they stopped for the night. "Spent a very restless night," David O. recorded the next day, "and awoke with the distinct impression that it would be unwise to continue our journey to

Los Angeles." Having learned through the years to heed these spiritual promptings, the travelers immediately retraced their steps and after a six-hour drive arrived in Salt Lake City to spend their "vacation and rest at 1037 East South Temple."

The apparent reason for President McKay's restless concern, and for the impression he received in St. George, surfaced a few days later. On March 21, President Smith's doctor, J. Leroy Kimball, reported that the patient had suffered a "thrombosis," which, as his counselor reported it, "affected the whole right side" and had made his speech "pretty thick." When the diarist first visited his leader after the stroke, he found the Prophet asleep and did not disturb him. The next day he called again, this time with Emma Ray. "He seemed to brighten up during our visit," noted the counselor. "His mind seemed as clear as a bell." But when he visited the home on April 2, the ailing Prophet did not recognize him. President McKay was "shocked" at the patient's appearance. Now, the full implications of President Smith's grave condition seem to have been brought home to the visitor. "I realized that possibly the end was not far off," he noted. "It came as quite a shock to my nervous system for I fully sensed then what his passing means." The next day President Smith recognized David O. when he came, smiled at him, and, as he left, spoke the last word to him in mortality. "Good-bye," he said gently.

Shortly before noon on April 4, President McKay administered to his friend for the last time. "In doing so I broke down with emotion," he recorded. And that evening as he stood at the Prophet's bedside with members of the family and others, George Albert Smith passed away quietly at 7:27 P.M.

At that moment the burden of Church leadership shifted to the capable shoulders of David Oman McKay, age seventy-seven years, seven months. Never before had a leader of the Latter-day Saints served such a long period of apostolic apprenticeship—forty-five years, less five days. And it is doubtful that anyone before him had come to this significant day better prepared than he to fulfill the special mission marked out for him. In his service in the Twelve and in the First Presidency, the new leader had gained extensive experience in every aspect of the work, in the welfare program, in the worldwide missionary effort, in temple work, in directing and motivating subordinate leaders, and in the overall governance of the Church. Moreover, the unprecedented world tour he had taken thirty years before had given him special insights into the international potentials of the Church, a vision that was to form the foundation on which he would build his administration.

In the meantime, there was important and in some respects melancholy work to perform before President McKay could turn his attention to the task of organizing his presidential ministry. President Smith had passed away on his eighty-first birthday just two days before the scheduled commencement of the April general conference. Because of the time strictures, it was not possible to hold the funeral before the opening of the conference on April 6. So at the first session Friday morning, President McKay noted the passing of his leader with regret and explained that shortly before the meeting, the Twelve had met and had requested that President Smith's counselors conduct the exercises of the general conference. In referring to the deceased Prophet, President McKay said of him, "Though his chair is vacant this morning, let us hope that the influence of his Christ-like character will pervade every heart and his high ideals be an inspiration to us all. Truly he was a noble soul, happiest when he was making others happy." (CR, April 1951, p. 3.)

And at the funeral services, which were held the next morning in the Tabernacle, President McKay, in his preliminary remarks, focused on the characteristic that had distinguished the departed leader and his ministry: his love for the people. After noting that the Tabernacle, the Assembly Hall, and Barrett Hall were filled to overflowing, and that the services were being carried by radio to those who could

Official photograph of President David O. McKay, taken in April 1951.

not attend personally, he said "The love you [President Smith] have shown to your fellowmen is reciprocated fourfold. It is hard for us to express our love, but this is one manifestation of it, for truly the love you have given throughout your life is reciprocated in our hearts for you, and we pray for power to emulate your example throughout our lives." (Ibid., p. 161.)

During the remainder of the conference, other speakers extolled the virtues of President Smith, expressed sorrow at his passing, and commented on the influence for good he had exerted during his ministry. Yet with this understandable tendency to look backward and to dwell on a chapter of Church history that had been irrevocably closed, there was an undercurrent of excited anticipation about the next scene of the drama that would soon be opened to view. It had been announced that the concluding session of the conference, scheduled for Monday, April 9 at 10:00

David O. McKay

A.M., would be a Solemn Assembly where a new First Presidency would be presented for sustaining vote. While there was no doubt or uncertainty among those conversant with Church policy and procedure about who the new president would be, there was the customary speculation and second-guessing as to the identity of the counselors. It is apparent that most observers believed that the only real question related to the second counselor, it being widely assumed that J. Reuben Clark would be named first counselor. He was able and dedicated and had served as first counselor to both President Heber J. Grant and President George Albert Smith. Therefore, it was logical that he would be selected to serve President McKay in the same capacity. Indeed, in the minds of some, his appointment seemed to be a foregone conclusion. Those who reckoned this way, however, had lost sight of certain guiding principles: that a presiding officer has the prerogative to select his counselors according to the spirit of prophecy and revelation and that such selections are not made by lockstep precedent. Moreover, not even precedent dictated that President Clark be appointed first counselor, as witness the fact that following the death of Brigham Young, his first counselor, John W. Young, was not even called as a member of the First Presidency that was formed afterward.

But the public perceptions were such that when Stephen L Richards was presented as the first counselor and J. Reuben Clark as the second counselor at the Solemn Assembly, a ripple of surprise, if not disbelief, ran through the Tabernacle audience. Anticipating such a reaction, President McKay had prepared a statement that he read immediately following the sustaining of officers. After explaining how he had "thoughtfully and prayerfully" considered who should be called as counselors, he said: "The impression came, I am sure, directly from Him whose church this is, and who presides over it, that the two counselors whom you have this day approved should be the other members of the quorum of the First Presidency." (Ibid., p. 150.) He then explained that the decision to designate

276

Stephen L Richards as the first counselor was made because of his "seniority in the Council" and because "it seemed advisable in view of my close relationship to these two choice leaders." (Ibid., p. 151.) The Prophet went on to emphasize that while seniority in the council had dictated the precedence of the counselors in this case, such a result did not represent "an established policy," implying that in other circumstances, a different result might follow. Years later this was illustrated when Joseph Fielding Smith was called to the First Presidency but was made subordinate to Hugh B. Brown and N. Eldon Tanner, even though he far outranked both of them in apostolic seniority.

The various factors that made it seem "advisable" to President McKay to give precedence to Stephen L Richards were never elaborated. One need not search long, however, to find an explanation that accords with reason and that neither calls the Prophet's motives into question nor casts a reflection on the competence or qualifications of President Clark. The fact seems to be that David O. McKay and Stephen L Richards were "knit" together as were David and Jonathon of old. (See 1 Samuel 18:1.) There was a special bond between this pair that had strengthened over the years following Elder Richards's call to the Twelve in 1917. And from 1918 to 1934, while David O. served as the general superintendent of the Sunday Schools of the Church, Stephen L Richards was at his side as first counselor. Therefore, President McKay had come to respect and to rely upon the quiet brilliance and competence of this man who was a cum laude graduate of the University of Chicago School of Law, who later served on the faculty of the law school at the University of Utah, and who had gained prominence in legal and business circles before being called to the Twelve at age thirty-eight. Against this background, the new head of the Church was well aware of Stephen L Richards's response to his leadership and was assured that their philosophy of Church administration coincided. Moreover, President McKay was fully aware of his own feelings toward Elder Richards as a subordinate, while there would necessarily have been some uncertainty about the chemistry of the relationship with President Clark once their roles of dominance and subordination had been reversed. Wisdom, therefore, would have seemed to dictate the selection of Elder Richards as first counselor so that in the event the chemistry was wrong after the change, the administration of the Church would not suffer because of any differences between the Prophet and the one second in authority.

Looking at this decision in retrospect, therefore, it seems to have been logical and predictable. Yet it was one that created considerable trauma and misunderstanding. His biographer has detailed the reaction of President Clark and some of his confidants to his change in status. (See D. Michael Quinn, *J. Reuben Clark, the Church Years* [Provo, Utah: Brigham Young University Press, 1983] pp. 120-27.) There can be no doubt that he was surprised if not shocked and perhaps embarrassed by it. This was assignable largely to the erroneous public perception that it represented a de-motion, or that there was a conflict in the First Presidency or that President Clark had in some way failed as a first counselor. And it may be that he wondered whether it sig-naled some lack of confidence in him on the part of his new leader. Such was not the case, as President McKay em-phasized in the remarks he made following the sustaining of officers: "We do not want any member in this church" he said "nor any man or woman listening in to harbor the thought for a moment that there has been any rift between the two counselors who sustained President Smith in the Quorum of the First Presidency, and President Grant for the years that we were together with that inspired leader. Neither should you feel that there is any demotion." Then speaking of President Richards and President Clark to-gether, he said of them: "They are two great men. I love them both, and say God bless them, and give you the as-surance that there will be harmony and love and con-fidence in the Quorum of the First Presidency as you have sustained them today." (CR, April 1951, p. 151.)

The brief remarks made afterward by the counselors underscored these sentiments of the Prophet. President Clark, who spoke first, thanked President McKay "for his kindly words," affirmed his support of him as the Prophet, pledged his loyalty to both President McKay and President Richards, and made the statement that ever since has been associated with him and for which he doubtless will be best remembered throughout the years: "In the service of the Lord, it is not where you serve but how." (Ibid., p. 154.)

President Richards expressed amazement at his own call, attributing it to the kindness of his friend, David O. McKay, and to the friendship between his grandfather, Willard Richards, and the Prophet Joseph Smith. "For more than forty-five years I have had a great man as a friend," he said of President McKay. "His friendship has been one of the main factors of encouragement in my life. . . . This great man has stimulated me in times of discouragement to go forward and give the best I could to this work. I shall never live long enough to pay the debt of gratitude I owe my friend."

As to the effect on his call of the relationship between Joseph Smith and Willard Richards, Stephen L made this significant statement: "I have often felt that the only reason for my being in the presiding councils of the church is in the devotion of Willard Richards to the Prophet Joseph Smith. I believe there are councils on the other side. We have had testimonies of them, and while I cannot understand I can believe that the Prophet, out of consideration for his friend, has had a voice in bringing me into the Council of the Twelve through President Joseph F. Smith, and also in that which has brought me to this position." (Ibid., p. 155.) The speaker went on to express the hope that he could be as true a friend to President McKay as his grandfather was to the Prophet Joseph Smith.

So there were brought together three of the most able and powerful men who had ever comprised the council of the First Presidency, the highest and the governing body of the Church. Each brought special skills and personal qualities to the task. President McKay, a teacher by profession, was the strong, charismatic leader who possessed an unusual ability to communicate ideas and attitudes, as much by his demeanor as by his words. He was a generalist and not a technician. He was iron-willed, positive, and self-confident. There did not appear to be even a trace of procrastination or inertia in his character. He acted with vigor and promptness in all that he did, yet he never conveyed the impression of being hurried or harried. He was calm and deliberate in his speech and movements. And he was the undeniable leader when he became the president of the Church. No one trifled with David O. McKay. No one crossed or contradicted him with impunity. Yet overlaying these qualities of vigor, strength, and toughness, and to an extent muting if not obscuring them, was a kindly, courtly, and loving characteristic that seemed innate. This manifested itself in many ways: in the respectful way in which he treated Sister McKay and other women, rising when they entered or left a room; in his love for flowers and beautiful decor; in his personal grooming; and in the concentrated attention he gave to anyone who addressed him.

The qualities of his counselors complemented those of President McKay perfectly. Both were brilliant, articulate men whose legal training had habituated them to accuracy and precision in thought, word, and deed. One could be assured that anything these men did would be done with meticulous care, and with all the i's dotted and all the t's crossed. Moreover, they were men of stature who inspired loyalty and confidence both inside and outside the hierarchy of the Church. Therefore, they reflected favorably upon the Church, upon its president, and upon the quorum of the First Presidency. And most important, they were men of spiritual conviction who looked upon their leader as a Prophet of God, possessed of divine authority and therefore empowered to direct the church of Jesus Christ upon the earth.

With men of this caliber, trusted and true, David O. McKay could feel comfortable in leaving the reins of head-

The First Presidency, April 1951. Left to right: Stephen L Richards, first counselor; David O. McKay, president; J. Reuben Clark, Jr., second counselor.

quarters administration in their capable hands while he was abroad, solidifying and, in some instances, laying the international foundations of the Church.

There can be little doubt that the extraordinary series of foreign trips President David O. McKay made in the 1950s, commencing a year following his ordination as the Prophet, had their genesis in his 1921 world tour with Hugh J. Cannon. During that global excursion the apostle gained a perspective of the world in its relation to the Church that none of his predecessors had possessed. And it is undoubtedly true that in the intervening years, prior to his ascension to the Prophetic office, this perspective was broadened and sharpened as he matured in the ministry and as his knowledge of the inner workings of the Church increased. So when the mantle descended on him, it is apparent that David O. McKay knew precisely what his presidential role would be and how he would go about playing it. An essential condition to his success was to have the assurance that home base was covered. That condition was satisfied with Stephen L Richards and J. Reuben Clark on the job.

It would take a year before President McKay was ready to launch his series of overseas trips. Meanwhile, there was much stirring at home to claim his attention. For the first several weeks after being sustained, he was inundated with contacts from those wanting to congratulate him or to seek favors. It was foreign to his inclination to put off anyone who approached him, so he usually made himself available to the many who clamored for his attention. "The telephone has rung almost constantly since my appointment," he recorded on April 19. "Many people asking for appointments—businessmen in the city asking for audiences; bishops, stake presidents . . . and members of the church" endeavoring to arrange special meetings. The pressures this generated, added to the stress under which he had been placed by President Smith's passing, prompted this observation: "The past three weeks have been the most strenuous and trying that I have ever spent in my life—and I have been through many trying periods in the past."

In search of a little respite, David O. and Ray left by train for California on April 27, returning in less than a week in time for the president to enter the hospital on May 3 for a prostatectomy. That evening he received a visit and a blessing from his first counselor, and the next day, following the surgery, Llewelyn and President Clark administered to him. "The hospital is a blessing to sick people," he noted gratefully. "My physician, nurses and attendants have been very considerate and helpful."

The skill of the professionals and the patient's robust health shortened his confinement so that he was released in four days, and within a week from entering the hospital he was holding First Presidency meetings at home. But the operation had sapped the Prophet's strength, and he was wise enough to recognize the need to slow down temporarily in order to conserve his energies for the grueling duties that lay ahead. So for almost a month he ran at half speed, holding regular First Presidency meetings either at home or at the office and handling the usual grist of correspondence, interviews, and other meetings at 47 East South Temple.

By June, the president felt strong enough to accept speaking assignments. It being the graduation season, he participated in ceremonies at Brigham Young and Temple universities. At the 'Y' he delivered the baccalaureate address on June 3; and eleven days later he was the commencement speaker at Temple. There he also received an honorary doctorate degree along with Pennsylvania Governor John S. Fine; U.S. Senator Robert C. Hendricksen; the secretary of the army, Frank Pace, Jr.; and the famous comedian Eddie Cantor.

Since the Council of the First Presidency and Quorum of the Twelve was in its customary recess during July, President McKay took the opportunity to spend time with his family and to take care of personal matters. The break even afforded David O. and Ray time for a little babysitting. While their daughter, Emma Rae, and her husband, Conway, were vacationing in Yellowstone with their three sons, the grandparents tended the couple's "darling baby." When the vacationers returned to claim the little girl, there occurred a ceremony familiar to all who have tended grandchildren over a period of several days—collecting, packing, and moving the child's assorted gear. "It took two cars to move the paraphernalia associated with the baby's care," the grandfather noted wryly. And a few days later he and Ray decided they needed another vacation and headed for the California coast in their automobile. En route, as they entered a restaurant in Bishop, California, a man asked the president whether he was David O. McKay. Receiving a yes answer, the questioner disappeared immediately and soon returned with four others in tow who also wanted to meet the Prophet. "So we spent a few minutes chatting with them," noted President McKay. Such incidents, which were not uncommon, add emphasis to the fact that his elevation to the apostleship had shorn David O. of his freedom and privacy.

After stopping in Westwood to visit Lou Jean and Russell, who were then living there, the travelers went to Laguna Beach, where the Church owned a modest beach cottage on Emerald Bay. This was to become a favorite hideaway for David O. and Ray, a place to which they could go intermittently for a few days of freedom from the constant pressures and harassments at Church headquarters. These interludes could hardly be called vacations, however, as the president was in regular telephone communication with Salt Lake to discuss or to decide matters that could not await his return. However, in the seclusion he found there, he was able to reflect and to pray, without interruption or hurry, about the overall progress of the Church or about specific assignments or projects that loomed ahead.

One such assignment that claimed the president's attention during this stay in Laguna Beach was his attendance at the Hill Cumorah Pageant scheduled in New York in mid-August. The McKays left Salt Lake City for Palmyra on August 8, a week after returning from southern California. While the travelers enjoyed the pageant, the aspect of the visit that seemed to affect President McKay most profoundly was the two testimony meetings he held with missionaries in the Sacred Grove. One of these was an all-day session on August 10, when the missionaries were privileged to bear their testimonies and to hear the Prophet share his knowledge and convictions about the Church, whose origin could be traced to that place. One can imagine the powerful impact made upon impressionable missionaries by their white-haired leader whose talk suggested the efficacy of prayer as reflected in the experience of fifteen-year-old Joseph Smith, a mere lad when compared to the missionaries, most of whom were themselves very young. And the more perceptive among the group, in comparing the single act of Joseph's prayer with the consequences that flowed from it—an international church that then counted well over a million members—would have seen a startling illustration of the maxim "Out of small things proceedeth that which is great." (See D&C 64:33.)

But not all of the missionaries present on that occasion were young. Especially was this true of the Eastern States Mission president, George Q. Morris, who was then seventy-seven and who within two months would be sustained as an Assistant to the Twelve, the oldest man up to that point of Church history to attain General Authority rank.

Four days after returning home from Palmyra, President McKay was stricken with an attack of vertigo so severe that it was almost impossible for him to stand without support. He was hospitalized immediately, and his ailment was diagnosed as an inner-ear disorder. The Prophet remained in the hospital for a week, and his condition improved but was not cured. Over a month after leaving the hospital, David O. was still experiencing some difficulty and discomfort: "I am feeling pretty well," he wrote on September 27. "However my nervous system is still impaired and I am fully conscious of the fact that I must not over-do until I am stronger."

Within a few days after this entry, he was in the midst of a busy general conference. As it was the first one following his sustaining as the Prophet, there was an understandable nervousness as he approached it. "It is with mingled feelings of joy and satisfaction, encouragement, anxiety, and apprehension, that I stand before you this morning," he said at the beginning of the first session. (CR, October 1951, p. 4.) As he surveyed the condition of the Church and the challenges it faced, the speaker was pleased with its growth and with the faithfulness of its members. He noted that there were 420 buildings then under construction, an all-time high up to then; that missionary and temple activities were accelerating; and that tithes and offerings were consistently increasing. These and other indicators, he said, gave cause "for satisfaction and gratitude." Yet he was concerned about certain trends, especially "the recklessness and lawlessness of youth." This he ascribed to "the prevalence of pernicious ideas and subversive teachings which pervert the minds of the unstable and uninformed." His prescription for these ills transcended the mere outward observance of the law. "Thoughts are the seeds of action, and precede them," he told his audience. "Mere compliance with the word of the Lord, without a corresponding inward desire, will avail but little. Indeed, such outward actions and pretending phrases may disclose hypocrisy, a sin that Jesus most vehemently condemned." (Ibid., p. 6.) Thus, the message of this leader to the Saints, uttered frequently throughout his prophetic ministry, enjoined the cultivation of integrity and character so that there would be a perfect coincidence between the creed of the Latter-day Saints and their thoughts and actions.

As President McKay surveyed the international responsibilities and potentialities of the Church, he recognized a need to strengthen the headquarters organizations so as to provide adequate and consistent supervision of its burgeoning growth. To help carry this load, the vacancy in the Twelve caused by the elevation of Stephen L Richards to the First Presidency was filled by the call of Marion G. Romney. This fifty-four-year-old attorney, who had been disciplined through long years of service as a missionary, a bishop, a stake president, and an Assistant to the Twelve, brought to the apostolic calling an unusual fervor of testimony and loyalty to his leaders. In his conference talk after being sustained as a member of the Twelve, he said of the Prophet: "I have loved President McKay for a long, long time." He told of his earliest recollection of the president when, in Los Angeles in 1912, Elmer Romney, then a fifteen-year-old refugee from Mexico, learned a lesson he had never forgotten. He said Elder McKay placed a drop of ink in a glass of clear water and, as the ink clouded the entire glass, told the audience that sin would do the same thing to a life. "I have ever since then," Elder Romney said, "been trying to keep that sin out of my life." Another incident related by the speaker that illustrated President McKay's aptitude as a teacher occurred during his world tour in 1921. In Australia, where Elder Romney was serving as a missionary, the touring apostle told how the stalactites and stalagmites in the famous Genolean Caves were formed over the centuries by infinitesimally small deposits from drops of water. "Then he told us that was how a life was built. Every thought we thought, every word we spoke, every deed we did, registered on our character. I never have forgotten that, either," said the speaker. (CR, October, 1952, p. 62.)

Also sustained at the same time were four new Assistants to the Twelve, George Q. Morris, Stayner Richards, ElRay L. Christiansen, and John Longden, men who also brought to the service a wealth of skill, experience, and loyalty.

With these valorous men aboard, and with his health steadily improving, President McKay was almost, but not quite, ready to launch his vigorous international campaign.

While he made arrangements at Church headquarters to enable him to break away, and as he worked with leaders abroad in planning the details of his first overseas tour, President McKay was busy trying to stimulate activity and commitment among the local Saints. He found that the best way to do this was to accept as many invitations as possible to participate in special events in outlying wards and stakes. This enabled him to meet members of the Church on a more intimate basis and to exert the influence of his personal magnetism in motivating people toward a better life. And invariably following such meetings, he would remain as long as necessary to shake hands with and to greet those in attendance.

It is difficult to assess the impact of a personal contact with such a man. Perhaps the experience of Walter Reuther, a powerful United States labor leader, in meeting President McKay personally for the first time, will provide hints. As he left an interview with the Prophet, the visitor told Elder Marion D. Hanks, who was walking with him, that he had met many men of prominence in the United States and elsewhere but that he had "never met a man like that." Later Mr. Reuther said to a large audience as he commented on his interview with President McKay: "I never met a man

like that. I do not think our generation will produce a man
like that." (IE, September 1963, p. 762.) If we multiply by
the thousands the experience of Mr. Reuther in meeting
David O. McKay in person, we may gain a vague idea of
the impact the Prophet had as he mingled with the Saints in
the numerous small, intimate meetings he attended.

On December 2, 1951, for instance, he joined with the
members of the Church in Hooper, Utah, a small village in
Weber County, to dedicate their new chapel. The nineteenth
of that month found him in Woodruff, a remote town in the
northeast corner of the state, where he attended and spoke
at a banquet for stake leaders. There he reverted to a familiar theme when he stressed individual responsibility and the
incremental process of growth and perfection: "Sculptors
of life are we," he told the audience, "with our uncarved
souls before us. Everyone of us is carving a soul. Is it going
to be a deformed one or is it going to be a thing of beauty?"

On March 2, 1952, the president dedicated the new Primary Children's Hospital, high on the avenues in Salt Lake
City. He was welcomed by his daughter-in-law Mildred
McKay and Frances Grant Bennett representing other members of the Primary General Board who had played a key
role in the development of this charitable institution. Here
the Prophet, in addition to surveying the quality and the
humanitarian uses of the facility, lauded the numerous volunteers and contributors without whose help the hospital
would never have been completed.

Two weeks later President McKay traveled to the tiny
community of Overton, Nevada, where he dedicated still
another new building and visited with the Saints, many of
whom had never before seen a prophet, let alone shaken
hands with one!

Following the April general conference (where Bishop
LeGrand Richards was sustained as a member of the Twelve
to fill the vacancy caused by the February 3, 1952, death of
Elder Joseph F. Merrill; and Joseph L. Wirthlin, Thorpe B.
Isaacson, and Carl W. Buehner were sustained as the new
Presiding Bishopric), President McKay hit the trail again

when he traveled into the Deep South for a series of meetings. The principal one was a ceremony at Dalton, Georgia, where he dedicated a monument to the memory of Joseph Standing, a young missionary who was killed by a mob on July 21, 1879. Elder Standing's companion was Rudger Clawson, David O.'s longtime associate in the apostleship, whose bravery on the occasion first brought him to the favorable attention of the leaders of the Church. The ceremony was conducted on May 3, 1952, in an atmosphere of peace and public acceptance of the Church, which prompted the Mormon leader to reflect on the changes in public attitude wrought by time: "The contrast between the problem of mobocracy that cost brother Standing his life and that of today stood out in marked contrast."

The following day in Atlanta, the Church president and Sister McKay were greeted by "one of the most beautifully conducted welcoming ceremonies" they had ever seen. Five young ladies, representing the five southern states of Georgia, Florida, Alabama, Mississippi, and South Carolina, each in turn placed a red rose on Emma Ray's lap as a soprano sang an original composition to the tune of "Only a Rose." The vocalist was a beautiful young woman named Paula Hawkins who was later to attain national fame as a United States senator from Florida.

Leaving Atlanta, the travelers went to South Carolina, where they were greeted in a different, though entirely appropriate, way by Chief Blue, head of the Catawba Tribe of Indians, who was a dedicated Latter-day Saint. Here the president, long accustomed to the dignified ways of the Catawba's western cousins, dedicated their new chapel on the reservation. Touched by the outpouring of love and respect shown in the countenances and demeanor of these reticent but regal people, the visiting leader confided to his diary: "I consider the visit to the Catawba Indians and the dedication of their chapel one of the most important visits I have made."

Arriving in Salt Lake City two days after mingling with the Catawbas, the Prophet and his wife remained home for only a week and then left by automobile for central California. At the wheel was Henry A. Smith, editor of the *Church News*, who was to become a frequent companion of President McKay in his travels, doubling as chauffeur and reporter. On this hurried trip, sandwiched between the swing through the south and his first overseas tour as the head of the Church, President McKay dedicated two buildings, a branch chapel at Avenal and a ward building at Merced. Parting from Brother Smith at Merced, the McKays traveled to the coast and then south to Laguna Beach, where they spent a day and a night before returning home.

During the California trip, a powerful wind, called a tornado by some, struck Ogden Valley, wreaking havoc on Huntsville. Even though the time for departure for Europe was near, David O. felt impelled to assess the damage and to make any necessary repairs before leaving. So on May 24, he took Llewelyn and Edward with him to the farm, where they spent the day clearing the fields of trees that

President McKay astride his favorite horse, Sonny Boy. Photo taken October 12, 1957.

had been blown down. Fortunately, the Old Home and the outbuildings were undamaged.

During the day, the father was fascinated by a new-born colt, Sonny Boy, which "followed the mother [Lady] as though he had been trained so to do [although] it was really the first time he had been with his mother since birth." In the months and years ahead, David O. McKay would derive enormous satisfaction in training and riding Sonny Boy, a vast favorite of his.

Chapter Nineteen

To Europe—
the International
Tours Begin

By May 29 everything was ready for the tour abroad, which in scope and duration far exceeded anything previously undertaken by a president of the Church of Jesus Christ of Latter-day Saints. The destination was Europe. The planned itinerary included visits to nine countries and ten missions with no less than forty-five meetings in fifty-one days. Such a schedule—with grueling hours in planes, trains, taxis, airports, and depots; irregular sleep in a variety of beds; uncertain scheduling of meals and changes of diet from country to country; and the pressures of inspiring and instructing those attending the numerous meetings, coupled with the wearing practice of shaking hands with the audiences afterward—all this would have been considered an overload even for a young man. But for a man who was within three months of his seventy-ninth birthday, the tour seemed implausible on its face. And when one looked more closely and realized that within a year the president had undergone major surgery and had suffered a distressing neural disorder, the whole idea would have seemed unwise and impractical to an observer. Such an appraisal, however, would have failed to consider the enormous inner resources possessed by this rugged man. Nor would it have reckoned with the spiritual uplift he received from the earnest prayers offered in his behalf by the tens of thousands who called him prophet, seer, and revelator.

It was, therefore, a man young in spirit—and young in appearance, despite his age—who departed from the Salt Lake City airport on May 29 with his sweetheart and customary traveling companion, Emma Ray. According to the plans, son Lawrence and his wife, Mildred, would join their parents later. The visual impact the prophet had on those who bade him farewell and whom he met on this tour is suggested by a report filed by a Finnish correspondent: "While sitting in the lounge of the Hotel Vaahuna last night," he reported in late July, "Mr. McKay, in spite of his grey hair, looked forty years old although he will soon be seventy-nine." (DN July 30, 1952.) This newsman, who asked the traveler the secret of his youthfulness, received an unexpected answer: "I have always lived my religion," said the American prophet.

After a one-day stopover in New York, the president and his party enplaned for Great Britain on Scandinavian Airlines, stopping briefly in London and then flying immediately to Glasgow, where the first official act of the tour had been planned—the dedication of a small branch chapel. There the party was joined by Elder Stayner Richards, Assistant to the Twelve and president of the British Mission.

The Prophet's dedication of the charming Glasgow chapel on June 2 had important historic and symbolic implications. Although Mormon missionaries had labored in Scotland for over a century, preaching their doctrines and regularly reaping a rich harvest of sturdy converts, never before had a Latter-day Saint chapel been built and dedicated on Scottish soil. And here to perform the act of dedication was a choice specimen of the fruit of Mormon evangelism in Scotland, David Oman McKay, the grandson of William McKay and Ellen Oman McKay, who were converted and baptized in Thurso in 1850. Throughout the century since the baptism of David O.'s grandparents, the principal focus of Mormon proselyting had been to fuel the growth and development of the Church in the United States, chiefly in the valleys of the Rocky Mountains. Thousands and tens of thousands of converts like the McKays had heeded the call of their leaders to gather to the land of Zion, or America, there to help build up the center stakes of the Church. The converts who lacked the means or the opportunity to migrate remained behind, a scattered and, to a large extent, dispirited minority, relegated to worshipping in small, cramped homes or in unsavory and sometimes unsanitary public buildings.

The dedication of the clean and airy chapel by President McKay as a place of worship for the Glasgow Saints conveyed an important message to them and to the Saints throughout the world. It implied that The Church of Jesus Christ of Latter-day Saints is an international church, not one that thrives only in the western deserts of the United States; that the focus of Mormon proselyting in the future would be to build the Church in any country where the conversions justified it; and that in the future the call of the missionaries would not be to gather to the land of Zion, but rather to come to the spiritual Zion or, in other words, to any place in the world where the pure in heart dwell. (See D&C 97:21.)

Aside from the historic significance and symbolism in dedicating the chapel, this visit to Glasgow held special personal meaning for President McKay. It was here, fifty-five years before, that he had served as the president of the Glasgow Conference of the British Mission. Reflections about those days brought up images of the missionaries and members he had known, of the crowded streets teeming with horses and carriages, and of the beautiful countryside to the north, where were found the picturesque lakes made famous by Sir Walter Scott. The lakes drew him the day after the Glasgow Chapel was dedicated, when his party drove to the largest and most beautiful of them, Loch Lomond, remembered in song and poem. During the day a visit was also made to Scott's nearby home, where he wrote "The Lady of the Lake," whose lines memorialize Inchscailloch and Balmaha, wooded islands in the southern part of the lake.

The nostalgia evoked by President McKay's return to Glasgow and his visit to Loch Lomond carried over to June 4, when he dedicated a chapel at Edinburgh. In remarks delivered on this occasion, the Prophet reminisced about the conversion of his grandparents in Thurso, about the missionary service rendered in Scotland by three generations of McKays—William, David, and David O.—and about the swift passage of time: "Years rush by us like the wind," he quoted from Sir Walter Scott, "We see not whence the eddy comes, nor whitherward it is tending, and we seem, ourselves, to witness their flight, without a sense that we are changed." Then the seventy-nine-year-old speaker, conscious of his advancing years, quoted the poet's last line: "Yet time is beguiling man of his strength as the winds rob the trees of their foliage." But he added a concluding thought of his own that amplified the philosophy that kept him perennially young: "Though time dims our youthfulness and affects the physical body, it cannot touch the spirit." (CN, June 18, 1952, p. 2.)

Having dedicated two chapels in Scotland in three days, President McKay's grand tour of Europe was off to a good start. In these two acts he had made an important statement about the underlying purpose of his tour: to anchor the European Saints to their home countries and to reduce the flow of converts to the United States. And as he flew from Edinburgh to London on June 5, there were already in motion plans, the culmination of which he would announce from Scottish soil at the end of his tour, that would further dramatize his prophetic initiative toward the internationalization of the Church.

During the next week, President McKay held a series of meetings in London with the Saints, with missionaries, and with local leaders. In addition, he inspected various properties as potential building sites and made a hurried, unplanned trip to Switzerland, where he looked at a choice tract the Church hoped to purchase for development. It was this land that would be the object of a special announcement the Prophet would make from Scotland shortly before returning to the United States at the end of the tour.

Departing from Bern, Switzerland, on June 11, the Church president and his party flew to the Schiphol Airport in Holland, where they were met by mission president Donovan H. VanDam and his wife. As arrangements had been made for the visitors to meet Queen Juliana the next day, they were taken directly to Scheverningen, where reservations had been made for them in the Palace Hotel, to enable them to rest and to prepare for the interview.

The next morning the Americans were driven to the palace in nearby Soestdyk, where they were received by Queen Juliana, a gracious hostess, whose regal appointments belied her open, democratic manner. In an informal, half-hour visit, during which she graciously agreed to accept a copy of the Book of Mormon from the Prophet, the Queen was briefed about the proselyting activities of the Church in her country and about the large number of Dutch converts who comprised an important segment of the Church in America.

During the interview, reference was made to the legendary story of "The Hero of Haarlem," to which her majesty commented half-jokingly, half-seriously, "Oh that story. I think that is more common in America than it is here in Holland. I think the Americans invented it." Adroitly rescuing the conversation from what could have been an embarrassing impasse, President McKay told the Queen that whether the story was fact or fiction, it nevertheless illustrated the "outstanding qualities of the Dutch people" as he had observed them. The monarch's appraisal of the Prophet is unknown, but she scarcely could have failed to admire the diplomacy and poise this spontaneous response revealed.

The next day, June 13, was filled with good fortune and joy. And it was a day of solemn reflection about the way in which the Lord prompts his servants through spiritual impulses. The day began with a visit to a site in Rotterdam where once stood an auditorium in which President McKay addressed a congregation in 1922 while he presided over the European Mission. The building had been destroyed during World War II, and only its ruins remained. As the Prophet stood on the barren site, the remembrance of that incident came back with clarity, and at a meeting held that evening he shared it with an audience of over a thousand assembled in a rented hall. "Today," he began, "Sister McKay and I stood on the ruins of the place where thirty years ago a very remarkable experience occurred to me." He explained that while addressing the congregation on that occasion, his interpreter, mission president Zappey, made a statement that President McKay instinctively knew was in error, though he did not speak the language. "I knew that he had given the wrong interpretation, and I told him so, and corrected him," said President McKay. "He turned to me and said that I really had no need for an interpreter, since I understood the language so well." In conclusion, the Prophet emphasized that this experience illustrated the means by which the Spirit often directs the minds of men and women—by the quiet promptings of the still, small voice within.

The arousal of nostalgic memories that occurred when President McKay inspected the bombed-out site in Rotterdam was repeated on June 14, when he and his party arrived in Copenhagen, Denmark. On that same day in 1850, one hundred and two years before, Erastus Snow had stepped onto the pier in Copenhagen, the first apostle of this dispensation to set foot on Danish soil. Greeting Elder Snow and his two companions, George P. Dykes and John E. Forsgren, was Peter O. Hansen, who had preceded them to Denmark. One of the first acts of these four missionary pioneers was to kneel together to offer up thanksgiving to God and to dedicate themselves to his service. The fruits of the labors of these diligent men and their successors were evident to President McKay and his party as they alighted from a plane at the Copenhagen airport. Unlike the arrival of Elder Snow and his lonely group, who were unheralded and unnoticed, President McKay's arrival was greeted with enthusiastic cheers and song by a large group of Latter-day Saints who had gathered at the airport to greet their touring leader. And the local officials acknowledged his arrival too by flying the Stars and Stripes alongside the Danish flag, a touching tribute that brought a tear to the Prophet's eye.

After shaking hands with the greeters, President McKay and his party, guided by mission president Edward H. Sorensen and his wife, left the airport to the accompaniment of cheers and the strains of "We Thank Thee, O God, for a Prophet." At the mission home, to which he was promptly taken, President McKay, after freshening up and enjoying a brief rest, reviewed the packed agenda with President Sorensen. It followed a pattern that, with some variations, was copied in other European cities on the itinerary. That evening, Saturday, a social was held that featured a concert. The next day there were four principal meetings, interspersed with counseling and visiting. An early morning priesthood meeting was followed by a Sunday School session, a gathering that was always a favorite of President McKay's because of his long association with that organization. After lunch, the Prophet met with the full-time missionaries, and at the general meeting that evening the Church leader touched on some of the themes that were interwoven throughout most of the sermons he delivered on the tour: obedience to the gospel, individual responsibility, and the need to bolster the Church in all lands.

From Denmark the president launched a nine-day tour through Scandinavia, visiting and holding meetings in Oslo, Norway; Stockholm, Sweden; and Helsinki, Finland. When he alighted at the Malmi Airport in Helsinki, David O. McKay became the first president of the Church to touch Finnish soil. A delightful variation in the usual meetings occurred there, in part because the day of arrival, June 23, coincided with Sister McKay's seventy-fifth birthday. Following a party at the mission home, replete with cake, candles, and a serenade, the visitors were driven to nearby

Lake Vichtijarvi, where Latter-day Saint youths from around the mission were gathered at an encampment. Following the procedure set in Atlanta a few weeks before, but without the music, several attractive girls each brought a rose to Sister McKay in token of her birthday and her honored role as the wife of the Prophet. So that the others in the party would not feel neglected, they were given corsages or boutonnieres of wild lilies of the valley; and the formalities ended when several missionaries presented Sister McKay with an elaborate floral offering. Then came the music, first the native songs sung with vigor by the full-throated young people, joined in by the missionaries, and last the universally popular "Come, Come Ye Saints" and "We Thank Thee, O God, for a Prophet." While the Finnish lyrics were foreign to him, the familiar tunes and the fervency with which they were sung conveyed an unmistakable message of love and reverence, which brought another tear to the eye of the Prophet.

All this was a fitting prelude to the general session held the next day in Helsinki, where several hundred members and friends gathered to hear the great man speak. They came carrying their own food, knowing that the conflicting John's Day celebration would close all Helsinki restaurants, while expecting spiritual nourishment from the visitor. They were not disappointed. The powerful, white-haired American, whose words doubtless lost some of their impact in translation, conveyed a meaning quite apart from his discourse, through his striking appearance and dignified manners, and through the certainty of his speech.

On his last full day in Finland, the Prophet flew with President Henry A. Matis to Turku, where they were received by Finnish President Juko K. Paasikivi at his summer retreat. One can only speculate about any unspoken thoughts concerning the myths of youth and age that came to the alert eighty-year-old political leader as he shook hands with the young and vigorous churchman, who was only a few weeks shy of seventy-nine.

Germany was next. The first stop in the Deutschland

was at Hamburg, where the plane carrying the travelers was met by Edwin Q. Cannon, president of the West German Mission, and his wife. Also at the airport was the usual complement of Saints, missionaries, and press representatives.

In this ancient city, the largest seaport on the continent of Europe, which boasts the title "Gateway to the World," President McKay observed for the first time the energy and enterprise that had reclaimed Germany from the rubble and chaos of World War II. During seven massive air raids on Hamburg during July and August 1943, more then fifty thousand persons had been killed. More than half of the city's dwellings had been destroyed, and many of its numerous port installations and industrial and business premises had been left in a shambles. In the nine intervening years, most of the physical scars had been eradicated through the industry and thrift of the people. But many unseen emotional scars remained, and the frenetic physical activity that had produced the miracle of reclamation had preoccupied the minds of many, thereby diverting their attention from spiritual themes. In apparent recognition of the special challenges this presented, President McKay focused on the concepts of agency, character, and spirituality in a talk he delivered that night. Addressing nine hundred members and friends gathered in Hamburg's Gewerbehaus, he challenged them: "Let us make our ideals in life the Kingdom of God." Emphasizing the freedom of choice we enjoy as an inherent right, he admonished the audience, and especially the young, to achieve self-mastery over sexual indulgence and physical appetites. "Young men and women," he said, "yes, old men and women also, who resist temptation, grow in strength of character, and place themselves in a position to respond to the influence of the Holy Spirit." Then emphasizing the enduring nature of spiritual attainments as compared to the transitory nature of physical possessions, he concluded: "Strength of character and service to mankind are attributes of nobility we can take back to God."

In Berlin, the Prophet's next stop, he encountered an aspect of the late war that was not evident in Hamburg. Here was seen the confrontation between two competing ways of life, the struggle between dictatorship and democracy, dramatized by the artificial line separating East and West Berlin. Only two months before the Prophet's arrival, the government of the Soviet Zone had sealed its frontier with West Germany in an attempt to halt the flow of refugees to the west. Notwithstanding this, many in Berlin continued to cross the line, not merely for social or business purposes, but as a means of permanent escape. And a technical defect in the order had allowed those in the Soviet Zone to travel to West Berlin by train. This loophole made it possible for fifteen hundred Church members living in East Germany to attend the meetings President McKay held in Berlin from June 27 to June 29. On July 1, however, the day after the Church leader left, that loophole was plugged, thereby slamming the door between the two countries as far as authorized mass travel was concerned. There followed, of course, nine years of large-scale surreptitious movement across the border that, for the most part, was stopped by the construction of a six-foot concrete wall, capped by a barbed-wire barrier, in August 1961.

The tensions that agitated Berlin at the time of his visit there in June 1952 had a profound effect upon President David O. McKay. This is evident from the report he made of his European tour to the October 1952 general conference. "I am sorry that I must now sound a note of discouragement," he told the opening session of the conference, after he had given an optimistic overview of the entire trip. He said he could not refrain from referring to the attitude of "distrust and hatred" shown toward the United States by the governments of Eastern Europe. "How they hate America, and everything American," he told the audience. "They are not only anti-American—they are anti-Christian. By every means possible—newspapers, billboards, documents, radio—they try to inculcate hatred in the hearts of the youth." (CR, October 1952, p. 11.)

Even amidst the tension he felt in Berlin, President McKay went about his apostolic tasks there with the same aplomb and assurance as he did elsewhere. There was the usual meeting with the missionaries devoted to testimony bearing and instruction. The general meeting held Sunday morning in the 1,850-seat Mercedes Palast attracted twenty-six hundred members and friends, the overflow spilling into the aisles with the indulgence of the Berlin police. And here the president repeated the feat he performed in Scotland by dedicating two new chapels, one located in Charlottenburg, in northwest Berlin, and the other in Dahlem, in southwest Berlin.

Accompanied by the East German Mission president, Arthur A. Glaus, and his wife, the Prophet's party flew on June 30 to Hanover where they were joined by President Edwin Q. Cannon. There, in Germany's "Garden City," a third new German chapel was dedicated. And there President and Sister McKay received welcome news from home—a cable from Emma Rae and Conway announcing the arrival of an eight-pound six-ounce grandson!

At the next stop in Frankfurt, the last in Germany, the Prophet was besieged by reporters who grilled him about the Church and its purposes. In elaborating his strategy of strengthening the Church in all lands, he told a reporter, who had asked the question, that "the biggest problem for the Latter-day Saints in Europe is the need for more places of worship." And he also expressed the hope that the Church would be permitted to construct new chapels behind the iron curtain.

As the Prophet delivered his final address in Germany to a thousand Saints and friends assembled in Frankfurt (almost a third of whom were servicemen), he alluded to his last visit there, twenty-nine years before, during his tenure as European Mission president. Then, he said, he had "great respect" for the German people. "Now," he added, "I have even a greater regard for them." And, in his report of the tour to the general conference, he had equally good things to say about the American servicemen whom he met. These, he reported "compared favorably" with the missionaries in their attitudes and actions. "And how proud we are of these choice young men and women," he told the audience, "a credit to their parents, to the church, and to our nation." (CR, October 1952, p. 11.)

Turning south from Germany's heartland in Frankfurt, the Prophet toured the cavernous valleys of Switzerland. Here, in a period of six days, with his traveling party and the mission president, Samuel E. Bringhurst, he visited Zurich, Basel, Lucerne, Wengen Scheidegg, Lausanne, Geneva, Bern, and Interlaken. All along the route, he held meetings with the Saints and their leaders and, when feasible, conferred with local civil officials. Of particular importance was his critical inspection of tracts of land in Bern, one of which would be the object of a dramatic announcement he would make in Glasgow at the end of the tour.

While in Switzerland, the land of towering peaks, the Prophet seemed to think it only fitting that he ascend the famous Jungfrau, which overlooks the Lauterbrunnen Valley above Interlaken. So, on July 8, with members of his party and others, he traveled on Europe's highest railway by a four-and-a-half-mile tunnel through the Eiger and Mönch to the Jungfraujock. There he enjoyed the panoramic view below from an observatory that perched precariously within two thousand feet of the mountain's 13,642 foot summit. And as a memento of the spectacular scenery of the Swiss Alps, President Bringhurst and his missionaries presented President McKay with an oil painting of the Matterhorn, the most famous of all Switzerland's magnificent peaks.

Two days after ascending the Jungfrau, the Prophet was in Paris, where he remained for four days. There he followed the customary routine of meetings and conferences. The highlight of these was one held in the Pleyal Concert Hall on Sunday afternoon; it attracted over half the membership of the entire mission. The members streamed in to the French capital from as far away as Nice on the south, Brussels on the north, and Geneva on the east. Anxious to hear a living prophet and to be part of what had been heralded as a historic event, the Saints came by automobile, train, bus, or on foot, regardless of the inconvenience or expense. The mission president, Golden L. Woolf, and his staff had gone all out to make certain that everything was in order for the comfort and convenience of the Prophet and his party.

The message heard at the meeting was encouraging and stimulating. Yet in a sense it was frightening to the local Saints. It was stimulating to know, as President McKay explained, that the Church intended to accelerate a program of building chapels throughout Europe; and that a chief objective of his tour was to study potential sites and the attitudes of the local members and their leaders. But it was unsettling to some to learn that the counsel of the Prophet now encouraged members to remain in their native lands and discouraged emigration to the United States. A hundred years of proselyting in France, with imported missionaries playing the leading roles, and with many choice converts emigrating to the United States, had created a local attitude of subservience and dependency. The prospect held out by the Prophet's counsel, of a lifelong effort to build the Church in their native lands, required a major readjustment in the thinking of the European Saints. And as any major change, whether in an individual or institution, creates uncertainty, or even apprehension, so this revolution in Church procedure and emphasis announced by the speaker had its unsettling repercussions among the ranks of those who listened.

Before leaving Paris on Tuesday the fifteenth, President McKay made a courtesy call on the United States ambassador to France, the honorable James Dunn. The Mormon leader apprised this American envoy of the purpose and progress of his European tour and explained the activities of the Church in France.

As President McKay had paid respect to his paternal ancestry while dedicating the two chapels in Scotland, he was now determined to pay similar respect to his mother's family, whose roots lay in Wales. Having an extra day before attending a garden reception at Buckingham Palace, the Prophet and his party flew to Cardiff, the Welsh capital. The facilities of this maritime giant on the Bristol Channel had for decades bustled with activity as the hills to the north had disgorged their treasures of coal, iron, and copper across Cardiff's docks, thence to be transported to ports all over the world. And the massive castle that dominated its downtown district, and the remnants of ancient fortifications thrown up by the Roman and Norman conquerors, stood as memorials of the city's imperial and turbulent past.

Traveling northwesterly by automobile, parallel to the Glamorgan Canal, which connects Merthyr Tydfil with Cardiff, the son of Jennette Evans McKay would have been called to reflect on his sturdy ancestry and on the struggling existence of the Welsh miners whose brawn had unearthed the precious ores, the revenues from which had financed the construction of the canal.

President McKay's immediate ancestors were more fortunate than those who worked the mines, having had landholdings and several houses in the Merthyr Tydfil area, whose rents provided a comfortable living for Jennette's parents, Thomas and Margaret Powell Evans. It was in one of these that Jennette was born on August 23, 1850. And it was this building that her son, David Oman McKay, sought out during his brief visit in mid-July 1952. He found the home, Plasagon House, located near the town at a place named Cleydyfagwyr Cefn Coed (Eved) Cwmer.

When President McKay entered the bedroom where his mother had been born over a hundred years before—a room described by him as being "so small that the six-foot bed covers the entire width, and its length . . . barely two feet longer than it is wide"—he was caught up in a reverie: "I thought, as Sister McKay and I stood in that small bedroom, how different life would be now if two humble elders had not knocked at that door a hundred years ago." (CN, September 6, 1952, p. 4.) He was also struck by the vast difference between the descendants of his maternal

305

grandparents and the living descendants of those who had "ridiculed [his] grandfather and grandmother for having accepted the truth . . . [who] made light of their religion, scoffed at them and ostracized them for having accepted Mormonism." (Ibid.) And this comparison made him realize "how unenlightened those neighbors were" when they condemned his grandparents.

But the feelings evoked in visiting his mother's birthplace were not all so weighty and solemn. President McKay had always been amused by the extraordinary spelling of the Welsh place names and by the fierce pride and loyalty of the Welsh people. To illustrate this, he often related an experience he had shortly after being called to the Twelve when attending a stake conference in Malad, Idaho, a town comprised chiefly of Welsh people. As he sat on the stand with the stake president, who was a pureblood Welshman, David O. whispered that he had Welsh blood in his veins. By his reaction, the stake president implied that the visitor said that merely because he was in Malad. So when he arose to speak, Elder McKay told of the exchange that had taken place with the stake president and added: "But I wish to say to Stake President Richards and to you that my mother was born in Plasagon House, Cleydyfagwyr Cefn Eved Cwmer, near Merthyr Tydfil, South Wales, and her name was Evans." At that an old woman sitting in a front row seat arose and said: "That's it, that's it, you are, you are." (L. R. McKay, *Home Memories*, pp. 24-25.)

The day after visiting the humble Welsh home where his mother had been born, the Prophet was a guest at an elaborate garden party given by Queen Elizabeth II at Buckingham Palace. There was no formal reception as had been anticipated but, as David O. reported, "Her majesty Queen Elizabeth, the Princess Margaret, Prince Consort Phillip and other members of the royal family were in attendance during the entire two hours."

To be a guest of British royalty in the elaborate setting of the Buckingham Palace gardens would be a heady experience for most of us. But for one like David O. McKay, who had served in Great Britain as a young missionary when the Latter-day Saints were often the objects of public scorn, the experience had special significance. Aside from any personal satisfaction the Prophet derived from attending this glittering affair, the recognition it gave to the Church was far more important to him.

The task to which President McKay was dedicated by apostolic commitment was to build The Church of Jesus Christ of Latter-day Saints, whose objectives are to proclaim the gospel to the world, to perfect the Saints, and to redeem the dead. To this point of the tour, overt emphasis had been given only to the first two of these objectives as he had counseled the Saints, instructed the missionaries, and preached to nonmember friends. Behind the scenes, however, the Prophet had been trying to acquire temple sites in England and on the continent, a necessary preliminary to fulfilling the Church's third major responsibility.

By this time, negotiations to acquire a temple site in Bern, Switzerland, had been completed, although formal announcement of the acquisition was to be delayed until the Church leader returned to Scotland. Meanwhile in London, before traveling back to Glasgow, the Prophet talked about the aggressive efforts of the Church to compile genealogical data, another important facet of the work to redeem the dead. He explained that several dozen researchers were at work microfilming records throughout Europe and Great Britain at great cost to the Church. This data would be used in performing vicarious baptismal and other ordinance work for deceased ancestors in the temples. This concept, unknown to other Christian denominations, required careful explanation by the Prophet, especially for the benefit of the British press. The idea was credible even to doubters when considered in light of the statement of Christ about the necessity of baptism (See John 3:5), the inability of most people to hear the gospel in mortality, the justice of God, and the precedent of vicarious baptisms performed in biblical times (see 1 Corinthians 15:29).

While the explanations made in London by the Prophet

David O. McKay

about genealogical research and vicarious temple work did
not convert the unbelievers, his words nevertheless cast
the work of the Church for the redemption of the dead in a
logical and appealing way, devoid of the mysticism with
which some had previously regarded it. It is inferred that
President McKay considered these explanations necessary
to help prepare the minds of the public in Great Britain and
Europe for the announcement he made in Glasgow on July
22. At that time he announced that the Church had acquired in Bern, Switzerland, a three-and-a-half-acre site on
which would be constructed the first temple of the Church
in Europe. This announcement underscored the principal
message the Prophet had declared throughout his lengthy
tour, the message to the Saints in Great Britain and
Europe—and elsewhere—to remain in the lands of their
birth, there to strengthen the foundations of the Church.
This mandate became more reasonable and easy of fulfillment with a temple nearby where the members, at relatively small expense, could receive their own endowments
and sealings and perform similar work in behalf of their
kindred dead. And what President McKay knew at the
time of his announcement in Glasgow, but could not reveal
to the world, was that negotiations were in progress to acquire a temple site in London so the British Saints would
not even have to cross the channel, let alone the Atlantic
and the American Continent, to receive the blessings of the
temple.

President McKay and his party left Glasgow's Prestwich Airport the day after his dramatic announcement
about the Bern temple site. After a one-day layover en
route to minimize the effects of flight lag, he arrived in Salt
Lake City on July 26 to a spectacular and wholly unexpected welcome. Massed at the Salt Lake City airport was a
crowd estimated at fifteen hundred, many of whom were
attired in the native dress of the nine countries he had visited. This visual representation of the unity of the Church,
suggested by the overflowing love shown toward the
Prophet, and of its diversity, shown in the striking and var-

308

ied dress of those present, said more about the unique mission of the Church than pen or tongue could have done. And it served to add a bold exclamation mark to the end of David O. McKay's first presidential trip abroad, symbolizing his most significant contribution as the Prophet: the internationalization of The Church of Jesus Christ of Latter-day Saints.

Chapter Twenty

Politics and Pioneers—
the Second Trip Abroad

P resident McKay returned home at the dawn of a heated political campaign. Not only was it a presidential year, but there were many important local contests that aroused great interest and not a little controversy. Among these was the race for the United States senate, in which Marriner Eccles, one of the chief architects of the New Deal in the 1930s, had offered himself as a candidate. Being a Democrat, and having assumed through the years that the hierarchy of the LDS Church had a strong Republican bias, the wealthy Ogden banker sought out his longtime acquaintance and Weber County native, David O. McKay, to ask whether the Church intended to oppose his candidacy. "I answered," the Prophet noted in his entry of August 7, "that the church takes no stand whatever in politics, that there are members of the church who are democrats and members who are republicans and that I personally am going to treat each group fairly." Fifteen days later, David O. made an almost identical entry, following an anxious visit from Secretary of State Heber Bennion, who said the talk on the street was that the Church intended to support the Republican gubernatorial candidate.

As if to steel himself against the onslaught of political visits his expressions of neutrality seemed to invite, he retired to Huntsville the first part of September to reflect on the past, to chart a future course, and to recharge his energies. This pensive entry, written amidst the splendor of an early Huntsville autumn, breathes the love he had for that special place and reveals the feelings of longevity his seventy-ninth birthday had aroused: "On this glorious autumn day," he wrote, "I am feeling so well after the strenuous activity of the past summer months that it is hard to realize that I am seventy-nine years of age!" He then reflected on the fleetness of time and on the different perceptions he had of the span of life viewed as a youth and in retrospect as an aging grandfather: "When I was in my teens," he continued, "and looked forward to three score years and ten, it seemed an *age* away. Now that I have approached four score years, the intervening time seems but a year or so. The experiences of my youth are still fresh in my mind and school days are as only yesterday."

The respite President McKay gained from this Huntsville outing, and from a trip to Laguna he took a week later, helped to prepare him for the October general conference and for the parade of national politicians who would soon beat a path to his door. The first to appear was the Republican vice-presidential candidate, Richard M. Nixon, an incumbent United States senator from California, who came on September 26. The thirty-nine-year-old senator was known chiefly for his role in conducting the congressional investigation of Alger Hiss, former State Department official, who was convicted of perjury in connection with Communist espionage. And more recently he had gained considerable notoriety, and the undying enmity of the left wing of the Democratic Party, for the slashing attacks he had made upon Helen Gahagan Douglas— unchivalrously called the "Pink Lady" by Mr. Nixon—in the 1950 senatorial campaign in California. The rather radical reputation of the visitor was muted somewhat by the presence of the conservative U.S. senators from Utah, Arthur V. Watkins and Wallace F. Bennett, who accompanied him to the interview with President McKay.

David O. McKay

Next came the most colorful of the national politicians to visit the head of the Church this election year, President Harry S. Truman, who was campaigning vigorously for the Democratic candidate, Governor Adlai Stevenson. Mr. Truman was scheduled to arrive on Monday, October 6, the day after the conclusion of the general conference. This fact, coupled with the persistent rumors that the General Authorities favored the Republican Party, prompted President McKay to repeat the Church's policy of political neutrality at the last session of the conference on October 5. "This report is not true," he assured the audience, "and I take this opportunity here, publicly to denounce such a report as without foundation in fact." (CR, October 1952, p. 129.) He then repeated the statement that advocates of both major political parties would be found within the Church and urged its members to register and to vote for the candidates who advocated their views.

As if to stress that the Church leaders did not favor Republican candidates, David O. made a concession to President Truman the next day that was contrary to the usual policy in meeting with political dignitaries. Instead of receiving the country's chief executive in the Church Administration Building, as was customary, President McKay met Mr. Truman in his private car at the train depot. The pair breakfasted together there, and the Mormon leader then accompanied the campaigner to Provo, where he was scheduled to speak at a rally in the Brigham Young University stadium.

As the first of a number of local Democratic leaders boarded the train to accompany Mr. Truman to Provo, they headed for the Prophet to greet him first. To avoid embarrassment to the visitor, David O. took to ducking his head, or looking the other way, when the others came aboard so they would be compelled to greet President Truman first.

Before leaving the Salt Lake City depot, President McKay allowed himself to be photographed with Mr. Truman on the rear platform of the train; and at the BYU stadium rally, he sat beside him for all to see.

Dr. Ernest L. Wilkinson, president of Brigham Young University; Harry S Truman, president of the United States; and President David O. McKay, following President Truman's campaign speech at BYU.

While the speaker's rhetoric was muted to an extent in apparent deference to President McKay, he was hardly a lamb or a Milquetoast in denouncing his opponents. He charged that the Republican Party was "ruled by a little group of men who have calculating machines where their hearts ought to be." And Republican rule, he added, would be a return to the philosophy "each man for himself and the devil take the hindmost." (*Salt Lake Tribune*, October 7, 1952.) When he had delivered these and other equally pithy broadsides against the hapless Republicans, Mr. Truman took his seat beside President McKay and asked innocently, "I wasn't so hard on them was I?" The candor, friendliness, and energetic optimism of this homespun man won a dubious accolade from David O. McKay who recorded in his diary: "I had a higher opinion of him today."

Close on the heels of President Truman was the Republican presidential nominee, General Dwight D. Eisenhower,

313

David O. McKay

President McKay with General Dwight D. Eisenhower, left, and Senator Arthur V. Watkins of Utah.

who arrived October 10 and who was given the same cordial treatment. President McKay sat beaming on the stand of the Tabernacle that night as the general made his plea for support. And four days later the same procedure was repeated for the Democratic standard bearer, Adlai Stevenson, the suave and articulate governor from Illinois.

The parade of major political luminaries through Salt Lake City ended the day after Governor Stevenson left when Senator Robert A. Taft came calling. He was accompanied to the ritualistic meeting with the president of the Church by Utah's conservative Republican governor, J. Bracken Lee, and several local functionaries who basked in the reflected glory of the famous senator who was regarded by many in the party as "Mr. Republican."

And a few weeks after his departure and after General Eisenhower had won a sweeping victory at the polls, Senator Taft's distant cousin, Ezra Taft Benson, was lauded by President McKay on his appointment to serve as the secretary of agriculture in the Eisenhower cabinet. "I am very much pleased to learn of Ezra Taft Benson having been

314

chosen as a member of the cabinet of the United States," the Prophet told a *Salt Lake Tribune* reporter on November 24. After noting that in making this appointment the president-elect had recognized true merit, he concluded: "The appointee's high character, his unimpeachable integrity and his experience in dealing with agricultural organizations and problems make him eminently prepared to render efficient service to our country."

Actually, President McKay knew of this appointment long before it was announced publicly. Indeed, he had given advance approval for Elder Benson to accept it, a protocol followed routinely in the Church after the last decade of the nineteenth century when the Brethren adopted the so-called "Political Manifesto." That mandate prohibits General Authorities from undertaking duties beyond the scope of their ecclesiastical callings without Prophetic approval. Obedient to the restrictions of this policy, Elder Benson had contacted President McKay as soon as overtures were made to him about accepting a cabinet post. The Prophet's response was prompt and positive, notwithstanding the fact that the appointment would practically suspend the new secretary's apostolic duties while he served the government.

A talk President McKay delivered to a joint meeting of the Rotary and Kiwanis clubs of Ogden two days after his statement to the *Tribune* reporter suggests one reason, at least, why he so willingly approved Elder Benson's acceptance of this appointment. There he spoke of "the threatening clouds of Communism and Anti-Christ." Said he to the professional and business leaders of Ogden: "This is the time for us to open our eyes to a realization of the power and threat of the diabolical influences that are opposed to all the blessings and privileges of this land for which we should this day show gratitude." (CN, November 29, 1952.) And two days after the Ogden speech, President McKay gave Elder Benson a special blessing as he prepared to take his place as a member of the cabinet. There the new secretary of agriculture would exert a strong spiritual influence, not only upon the government of which he would be a part, but upon private sector groups with which he would deal and upon foreign agencies. That the Prophet would allow this able man to suspend his formal apostolic duties for several years implies a conviction that this loss would be more than balanced by the influence he would exert in the secular world to help push back the "threatening clouds" about which the Prophet was concerned. And the persistent pronouncements of Elder Benson on this subject, both during and after his period of government service, indicate his concurrence in President McKay's appraisal and his single-minded intention to do something about it.

All this, of course, was symptomatic of the international pressures exerted by the power struggle that arose after 1945 between the communistic and the Western democratic nations, with all its ideological, economic, and political conflicts. Named the Cold War, this struggle was to continue throughout the administration of David O. McKay and was to have a profound effect upon his attitudes and decisions as the head of the Church. It is anomalous, in a way, that this period of worldwide turmoil and uncertainty coincided with the extraordinary efforts of President McKay to extend the international influence of The Church of Jesus Christ of Latter-day Saints, an influence that sought to soften and meliorate the clamor and confusion the cold war brought.

Because of his relationship to Elder Benson, President McKay received a special invitation to attend the inauguration of General Eisenhower. The Prophet arrived in Washington on January 19 in the midst of a heavy fog. Said he to those in his party, "This fog is typical of the fog that has been hanging over Washington politics for twenty years." He noted wryly that "some in the group didn't smile."

The Prophet and his party were met at the airport by Sister Benson and her son, Reed, Elder Benson being preoccupied with last-minute meetings and arrangements for the inauguration that was held the following day. Never before had President McKay witnessed in person the pomp and ceremony connected with the formal transfer of power of the government of the United States. Seated in the open air behind the Capitol, his breath adding to the fog that brooded over the scene, the distinguished spectator from the West watched the impressive ceremony with great interest and awe. While the martial music, the colorful display of flags, and the formal oath-taking by the new national leader were all exciting and moving, he was impressed most by Mr. Eisenhower's preliminary remarks and prayer, in which he asked "for the guidance of a divine providence that he might be able to serve the people of this country." Appraising the impact of this appeal, the diarist felt that "there was truly one heart beat in harmony with the appeal offered by the new president of the United States."

Another six months again found President McKay in the nation's capital, where, at the invitation of Mr. Eisenhower, he attended a national conference on U.S. foreign policy, sponsored by the State Department. There he heard high officials discuss various aspects of the government's foreign policy, chief among whom were the secretary of state, John Foster Dulles, and the United States representative to the United Nations, Henry Cabot Lodge. These presentations, which focused mainly on the complex issues of the cold war, had the effect of confirming President McKay's concern about the Communist threat.

This visit to the nation's capital was actually the final stop of a trip whose main purpose was to honor the Mormon pioneers and to commemorate their westward trek. It was prompted by an invitation from the North Omaha Bridge Commission to attend the dedication of the Mormon Pioneer Memorial Bridge, which spans the Missouri River, linking Council Bluffs, Iowa, and Omaha, Nebraska. Because of the significance of this place in Church history and the name to be given to the $3,500,000 structure, the Prophet and his counselors decided to focus publicity on

David O. McKay

the event. Their apparent purpose was to awaken the members to their pioneer heritage, to remind others of the travails suffered by the Mormons during their exodus, and to express appreciation to the states of Iowa and Nebraska for the hospitality to Brigham Young and the Saints during their time of trial and trauma.

There was assembled an entourage that to some might have appeared to be a Mormon exodus in reverse, streaming from Salt Lake City eastward to Omaha. It consisted of special trains and numerous chartered buses carrying hundreds of Utahns. Leading the way were David O. McKay and J. Reuben Clark of the First Presidency, President Joseph Fielding Smith of the Twelve, and sixteen other General Authorities. Conspicuous by his absence was President Stephen L Richards, who remained home to preside at the funeral of his brother, Elder Stayner Richards, who had died two days before the group's departure. President McKay regretted missing the funeral of his friend, but he had no control over the schedule. But he left a personal message of condolence that was read at the memorial services.

Arriving in Omaha the morning of May 31, the Prophet went immediately to a meeting of all the missionaries of the Northern States Mission. There the white-haired leader, whose hazel-brown eyes eagerly searched the faces of the audience during the preliminary exercises, instructed and motivated the missionaries in their duties. The vigor and verve of the speaker, who was only three months away from his eightieth birthday, robbed all present of any excuse for indolence or half-hearted performance.

In the afternoon, the official party went to the Florence Cemetery in the suburbs of Omaha, where a commemorative service was held honoring the more than six hundred Latter-day Saints buried there. These pioneers met death from exposure, disease, and malnutrition in the shantytown community of Winter Quarters, the Mormons' last staging area for the westward exodus. Here President McKay and others spoke on the tragedies concealed by the

318

silent grave markers, tragedies of deprivation and want, of fear and anguish, caused by the bigotry of erstwhile neighbors to the east. And they lauded the qualities of character and fortitude that typified the survivors who faced an uncertain future in the wilderness to the west.

That evening a special program was held in the Ak-Sar-Ben Coliseum in Omaha, with seven thousand in attendance, where the extraordinary development of Winter Quarters was traced in song and word. What this pioneer community lacked in convenience, charm, and comfort it made up in order and organization. It was laid out with its streets at right angles and was divided into wards, with bishops appointed to guard the spiritual and temporal welfare of their members. Its residents were willing to share their scanty fare with neighbors and, when possible, to help care for the sick, bury the dead, and comfort the bereaved. But amidst such adversity and travail, a striking spirit of optimism and enterprise actuated those who lived in Winter Quarters. And it was this spirit that formed the basis of the program and engaged the attention of those who spoke and sang.

The following day came the formal dedication and the accompanying pageantry. It began with a serpentine motorcade across the bridge to Council Bluffs and back. Then followed a parade featuring the Sons of the Utah Pioneers dressed as members of the Mormon Battalion, their wives being attired in appropriate pioneer gear. Adding a touch of equine class was the Weber County sheriff's posse, whose jurisdiction included famed Huntsville, and whose members and mounts traveled to Omaha in a special train. Spirited band music enveloped the entire line of the parade, which, with the presence of the Mormon Battalion stand-ins, lent a martial air to the occasion. The parade and its spectators dissolved into a huge crowd at its terminus near the Omaha entrance to the bridge, where a stand had been erected. There the local and visiting dignitaries took their places for the dedication ceremony. Among the civic officials present were Governor Robert B.

Crosby of Nebraska and Governor William S. Beardsley of Iowa, both of whom spoke briefly, paying tribute to the tenacity of the Mormon pioneers. Other tributes, the ceremonial unveiling of certain commemorative plaques, and a sketch of the facts and fictions about Winter Quarters and the Mormon exodus by the Church historian, Joseph Fielding Smith, led up to President McKay's remarks and dedicatory prayer. After commending and thanking the local leaders, the two governors, the bridge commission, and the mayor for their initiative in honoring the pioneers and the Church, the Prophet focused on the key to the unusual achievements of the Mormon pioneers: "It was their faith in God," he said, "who could guide them as a living Father, through inspiration and revelation, if they sought him in sincerity, which supported them in this trying time." And the concluding statement of his dedicatory prayer returned to this theme as a beacon for the future as it had been a "pillar by night" for the pioneers: "We praise thy holy name and pray for desires and strength to emulate the faith and high ideals of the pioneers to whose memories we now dedicate it as a fitting memorial."

The final event on the agenda of the dedication committee was a luncheon hosted by the Omaha Chamber of Commerce. Both President McKay and President Clark were called on to speak. These remarks were rescued from the triteness and banality that too often characterize talks given under such circumstances by the stature of the speakers and by the special occasion that had brought them to Omaha. Both were aware of the practical and symbolic significance of the bridge, which not only spanned a river, but which served as an important personal link between the Saints and their nonmember friends who had promoted the name of the bridge and the commemorative celebration. So the president of the Church and his second counselor were warm and sincere in their praise of the government leaders present; of the civic groups, typified by the Chamber of Commerce, which had done much of the planning and execution of the dedicatory program; and of the local residents who had enthusiastically supported the public events.

The trip east for the bridge dedication and the U.S. foreign policy briefing also served as a showcase for an important news item: the announcement of the acquisition of a temple site in London, the publication of which President McKay authorized on June 3, 1953, the day of his arrival in Washington, D.C. It had taken a year to complete the complex negotiations for the purchase of the site and the protracted procedures for authorization to build the temple, grudgingly given by the government agencies involved. With these roadblocks cleared away, President McKay was prepared to take the next important step—the dedication of the sites—toward the construction of temples in London and Bern and toward anchoring the British and European Saints to their homelands.

The Prophet arrived home from Washington just in time for the annual MIA conference, at which he delivered the keynote address on June 12. During the conference he was honored in receiving the Master M-Man Award; and Sister McKay was similarly honored in receiving the Golden Gleaner Award. And immediately afterward President McKay began to lay final plans for another trip to Great Britain and Europe. Concerned that his father was running too fast for his age, Edward went to him and urged that he slow down. The son's success can be measured by this diary entry: "I promised Edward that I would try and do better." Witnessing the flurry of activity that followed Edward's counsel, the son may well have wondered just how hard his father was trying or whether what he witnessed was in fact an easing of the Prophet's schedule. Four days later found David O. at the annual Old Folk's Day celebration, where he spoke and also granted the wish of 104-year-old Anne C. Milner, who confided that her lifelong ambition had been "to dance with the President of the Church." Sunday, two days after that, President McKay dedicated the South Bountiful Ward chapel. And the following Saturday found him at Huntsville, where he,

Llewelyn, and Robert "worked until dark." On July 3, six days after his outing at Huntsville, he heeded Robert's plea for help in getting horses into a trailer at the son's rented farm: "One of the horses stubbornly refused to go up the plank and into the trailer," wrote the soon-to-be octogenerian, "and it took me until 6:30 P.M. to finally convince her that I don't give up easily." The next day he performed a customary ceremonial function by serving as the grand marshal of the July 4 parade. And the day after, as if in expiation for his failure to follow the son's counsel more faithfully, the Prophet blessed the third child of Edward and his wife, Lottie, Mark Lund McKay, grandchild number eighteen.

And so went the schedule of President David O. McKay, who, between commitments, was completing plans for a three-week trip abroad. He did decide to spend four days resting in Laguna Beach in mid-July. But this brief respite was interrupted when word came on the fifteenth that Elder Albert E. Bowen of the Twelve had passed away. The Prophet flew home for the funeral, during which he summarized the outstanding qualities of his deceased associate: "He was intelligent, he was thorough, he had sound judgment, he was sincere, and he was reverent," extolled the speaker.

David O. returned to California by train and remained at Laguna Beach several days, resting and planning for the coming trip abroad. He took the long way home, traveling by way of Snowflake, Arizona, where he participated in the town's diamond jubilee celebration, speaking at the public meeting and enjoying the traditional rodeo.

Arriving in Salt Lake City on July 27, President McKay recorded with satisfaction that the Korean armistice had been signed, "bringing an abrupt halt to thirty seven months of death and destruction." Aside from his joy at the cessation of these bloody hostilities, the Prophet was pleased at the prospects of an increase in missionary activity as the restriction on calls to serve occasioned by the war would be lifted.

By July 30 everything was ready for the second presidential trip abroad. David O. and Ray boarded a train for New York. From there, on August 2, they departed by plane for Great Britain. With them were their son Llewelyn, who met them in New York, and Church architect Edward O. Anderson, who wanted to study the terrain, vegetation, and surroundings of the temple sites as background for the drawings he would prepare.

Arriving in London the next day, the president visited the temple site "to confirm my original impression it is the right place." Receiving the desired spiritual confirmation, he gave direction to proceed with the arrangements for the dedication before boarding a plane for Switzerland, where everything was prepared for the ceremony in Bern. On August 5, 1953, in the presence of several hundred members and friends, President McKay dedicated the site for the first temple in continental Europe. "I want to bring the temple to the people," he noted in a revealing diary entry made after the ceremony. Five days later found him back in London, where he dedicated another temple site, located in a charming rural area outside London.

With these official acts completed, the thoughts of the Prophet turned again to his Scottish ancestry. With Emma Ray and Llewelyn, he traveled to Aberdeen, "The Silver City by the Sea," a name derived from the granite stone of which its principal buildings are constructed. There the travelers met mission president A. Hamer Reiser, members of his family, and two elders. Loading into two cars, the party started for Thurso, located on Pentland Firth, the northernmost tip of Scotland, the birthplace of David O.'s father. Driving first along the coast of the North Sea in a torrential rain, the party motored inland, crossing the barren hills, which were devoid of all vegetation except the Scottish heather. Attesting to the principal occupation in this part of Scotland, the cars were stopped intermittently by herds of sheep that ambled slowly across the road. Arriving at Thurso, the Prophet contacted Mr. Abrock Mac-Kay, a local antiquarian, who was reported to be an expert on the McKay clan. From him, David O. obtained published material about the family and the area and also was given a letter about his grandfather William McKay written by the postmaster of Janetstown, where the grandfather lived.

President McKay had visited this area fifty-four years before, when he served as a young missionary. At that time, he had found the old house his grandfather had built and where his father had been born. Relying on memory, he directed the party to Janetstown, a short distance from Thurso. There he identified what he thought was the "Auld Hous," a small, two-chimney rock dwelling that stood empty and abandoned. Wanting confirmation of its identity, he stopped at a neighboring house, where the owner, Charles McIver, confirmed that the old building pointed out by President McKay was indeed his grandfather's dwelling. Reminiscing about his visit there over a half century before, David O. recalled that the man from whom he sought directions then was also named Mr. McIver. This turned out to be the grandfather of Charles McIver, who referred to the "Auld Hous" as the place where the "Black Minister" used to live. This was the name given to William McKay by his neighbors, derived from his Mormon priesthood and his black hair.

Obtaining permission from Charles McIver (who then owned the house and who used it for storing potatoes) to inspect the "Auld Hous", the Prophet led the party there. Peering inside, he was reminded of his earlier visit and of the profound consequences that had flowed from the conversion of his grandparents in that humble dwelling. With tears filling his eyes, he turned to the group, saying, "If it had not been for two missionaries knocking on this door about 1850, I shouldn't be here today. In this little 'but' and 'ben' [living room and kitchen] house were born my father, Uncle Isaac, Aunt Ena, Aunt Kate, and Aunt Isabel." (IE, October 1953, p. 748.) He then recalled the sweet old lady who lived in the home at the time of his first visit who had cheerily greeted him: "You'll come richt in an' you'll sit richt doon. An' are ye Willie's grandson? Ach 'a nee, ach 'a nee—I'm gettin auld! They used to dip 'em i' the burn—do ye do that noo?" (Ibid.)

It was with reluctance that the Prophet left this lonely, isolated place, so fraught with importance and significance to him and his family. And perhaps fearing that within not too many years all physical evidence of it would be obliterated, he called hopefully to Mr. McIver as his party left, "Please take care of the auld hous." (Ibid.) And later, in reflecting on the visit and the mood it had aroused in him, he quoted this from Robert Burns, expressing the hope that its sentiment would become a universal reality: "When man to man the world o'er shall brothers be, for a' that."

Traveling south from Thurso, the party made its way to Inverness, astride the River Ness and the Caledonian Canal, where, by prearrangement, President McKay met James McKay, a clansman who had a detailed knowledge of the area and its history. Serving as their guide, James took the visitors on a tour of the ancient city. The features of particular interest to President McKay included the castle overlooking the river, built on the site of a fortress blown up by the Jacobites in 1746; the town steeple, a former prison, which holds the town clock and bells; and the Old High Church, which has in its towers one of the bells removed by Oliver Cromwell from Fortrose Cathedral.

While almost everything about Scotland claimed more or less of the attention, admiration, and comments of David O. McKay, there is one significant aspect of the country's tradition to which the Prophet seemed oblivious: the game of golf. Here in the very cradle of golfdom, this noble son of Scotland acted as if the game did not exist. Even when he was in the vicinity of historic St. Andrews, the mecca of golf where the Royal and Ancient Golf Club of St. Andrews was established in 1754, David O. maintained a stony silence about the sport that many around the world regard with almost religious fervor.

The explanation seems to be that the residents of remote Thurso and Janetstown were too much occupied with their flocks and fields to succumb to the frivolity of golf. And when President McKay's sturdy ancestors put down their roots in America, the industrious habits developed in tending their sheep on the heather of Pentland Firth were perpetuated here and transmitted to their descendants. So, work on his farm, not golf, was the chief recreation of Scotsman David Oman McKay.

Chapter Twenty-One

The Prophet Goes South

T he Prophet returned from his second presidential tour on August 19, 1953, pleased with the dedication of two temple sites abroad and renewed in spirit from his sojourn in the land of his fathers. There was much to claim his attention at home, including the plans for still another trip abroad that would be announced the day after Christmas. Meanwhile, there were other important steps to be taken at Church headquarters in pursuit of President McKay's objectives. On September 21, he led a group of General Authorities to the Logan, Utah, temple, where a solemn assembly was held with leaders in that area. There he emphasized the theme that was interwoven throughout his first European tour—that the Church is a worldwide organization and that its stakes should be driven deep into the soil of all nations. And during this meeting, he also developed a new theme that coincided with his emphasis on the internationalization of the Church and that was probably prompted in part by the end of the Korean War, with its consequent relaxation of restrictions on calling missionaries. This new theme, which became one of the catch-phrases of President McKay's administration, was that every member should be a missionary. This call of the Prophet, which was later elaborated and greatly intensified throughout the world, was a key factor in almost tripling the membership of the Church during his administration and increasing the number of stakes from 191 to 537.

The Prophet's initiative to encourage Church members to remain in their home countries was promoted consistently in his private contacts and actions as well as in his public pronouncements. Thus, a few weeks before the solemn assembly in the Logan Temple, Senator Wallace F. Bennett advised President McKay that Senator Arthur V. Watkins was going to Europe in the interest of a U.S. government immigration program and inquired whether he could help in bringing members of the Church to the United States. While thanking him for the offer, the Prophet advised the senator, "We should like our people to remain in Europe and build up strong branches, particularly now that we are taking temples to them."

And on October 29, an important administrative step was taken in preparation for these new temples, as this

President McKay delivering an address to the Brigham Young University faculty on September 18, 1953.

entry in President McKay's diary indicates: "It was felt that a committee should be appointed to begin preparations for the sound and pictures of the temple ceremony to be presented in the temples. I suggested the following for membership on the committee, Joseph Fielding Smith, Richard L. Evans, Gordon B. Hinckley and Edward O. Anderson." A few days later, this committee was approved by the Brethren; and afterward it launched a project that was to simplify, accelerate, and, in a sense, revolutionize temple work.

And a few weeks before this significant event, a media break-through occurred that would revolutionize the general conferences of the Church. On October 4, a general conference session was telecast for the first time beyond the Salt Lake area when it was carried into parts of California, Washington, and Oregon. This new mass communications medium, which seemed tailor-made for the appearance, personality, and dominating presence of President David O. McKay, was not an unalloyed blessing to the Church. It did greatly expand the audience to be reached by the words of the Church leaders. At the same time, it shackled them with time and format strictures that robbed their talks of much of the spontaneity that had characterized the conference fare of earlier days.

This general conference also saw three major changes in the ranks of the General Authorities when Richard L. Evans was called to fill the vacancy in the Twelve caused by the death of Albert E. Bowen; Hugh B. Brown was called as an Assistant to the Twelve, replacing Stayner Richards; and Marion D. Hanks was sustained in the First Council of the Seventy, following in the footsteps of Elder Evans, his friend and mentor, whom he had served as a counselor in the Temple Square Mission presidency, along with President McKay's son, Robert.

Only two months after these vacancies were filled, another one occurred when Elder Matthew Cowley of the Twelve died unexpectedly on December 13, 1953, in Los Angeles. This eloquent apostle had accompanied President

David O. McKay

McKay and most of the other General Authorities and their wives to Southern California to lay the cornerstone of the Los Angeles Temple. The ceremony had taken place on the eleventh, with President Stephen L Richards offering the prayer. At the depot it had been necessary for some of the brethren to carry their own luggage through the cavernous building. Elder Cowley, who had suffered from heart problems previously, but who had concealed them from others, struggled with his bags, exerting severe strain on his weak heart. He passed away in the morning of the thirteenth while President McKay was en route home by train. The Prophet was "shocked," to learn of Elder Cowley's death on his arrival at the Salt Lake City depot; but he was gratified to know "that he passed away without agony or pain." The funeral service was held three days later when eighty-year-old David O. McKay eulogized and mourned the passing of his fifty-seven-year-old friend.

Though most of his mortal years lay behind him, President McKay looked to the future and not to the past as 1953 drew to a close. As already noted, the day after Christmas, the Prophet announced he would leave soon for a lengthy trip through South Africa, South America, and Central America. Never before had a president of the Church visited these countries. Within three days after the announcement, the Prophet boarded a train for New York, via Chicago, the first leg of a thirty-two-thousand-mile trip that would further expand his vision of the international character of the Church. With him was Emma Ray, his favorite traveling companion.

The McKays celebrated their fifty-third wedding anniversary on January 2, 1954, by boarding a plane for London, where they were met the following day by A. Hamer Reiser, president of the British Mission. Brother Reiser would serve as President McKay's secretary during the trip to South Africa, an area then attached to the British Mission.

A five day layover in London enabled the Prophet to confer with the leaders of the British and Swiss Austrian missions about the plans for the construction of the temples in London and Bern. He also held several meetings, including one in the South London Branch, where he shared the pulpit with Elder Henry D. Moyle of the Twelve, who was in England on assignment.

The president's party flew out of London on January 7 in the midst of a fog and a heavy overcast that had blanketed Great Britain and the Continent for several weeks. It would take three days to make the trip to Johannesburg with stops in Lisbon, Dakar, Accra, and Leopoldville. These exotic-sounding places had been only names to the travelers, but now they were identified in their minds with sensory perceptions of sight, sound, touch, or smell. The bright sunshine that bathed the North Africa coast provided a sharp contrast with the dank and gloomy weather that clung to the land northward. And heavy turbulence over Mauritania required the party to make a detour seaward before landing at Dakar, where they were refreshed by the ocean breezes that make this capital of Senegal one of the most comfortable sites on the West Africa coast.

The flight from Dakar to Johannesburg, with intermittent stops at Accra and Leopoldville, was marked by occasional storms. But it afforded the passengers a literal bird's-eye view of the vast African continent and was relatively smooth when compared with the return trip, when a violent storm threw President McKay from his seat.

The Prophet was hardly prepared for the excited and somewhat turbulent reception he received at Johannesburg. Before his arrival, no General Authority had ever set foot on the soil of South Africa. And the fact that the visitor who led the way was none other than the president of the Church aroused the enthusiasm of the South African Saints to almost fever pitch. "People swarmed over the platform and on the roof above," President McKay noted with amazement. Amidst this bedlam could be heard the intermittent strains of the two hymns that typically greeted him on his arrival at a new destination: "Come, Come Ye Saints" and "We Thank Thee, O God, for a Prophet."

The enthusiasm shown by these Saints at the Prophet's

arrival was also present at the meetings held there, although exhibited in a different way because of the more decorous surroundings. There it was evident in the rapt attention given to everything the great man said or did and in the infinite patience shown by the Saints as they waited for the chance to grasp his hand and to speak a word of thanks or commendation of merely to gaze into his face and to bask in the warmth of his love and friendship.

At a meeting held in Duncan Hall at Johannesburg on the eleventh, the Prophet requested that the children sit down front, where he could make eye contact. He then spoke to them specially and directly, illustrating his remarks about moral purity and chastity and the effects of sin by placing a small drop of ink in a glass of clean water. There can be little doubt that these young listeners were as impressed by this demonstration as Elder Marion G. Romney had been many years before and that the object lesson taught would be as influential and lasting in their lives as it had been in his.

The day following the Duncan Hall meeting found the president in the gold-field town of Springs, where he inspected a partially completed chapel. Again he was "overwhelmed by the welcome of church members in the South African Mission." Then followed a three-day visit to Cape Town, where the Church leader held extensive meetings with President Leroy Duncan and his missionaries.

Back in Johannesburg, the Prophet traveled to nearby Pretoria, where he made a courtesy call on the U.S. ambassador, W. J. Gallman.

Following his arrival in South Africa, President McKay abandoned plans to visit the Krueger National Park. Therefore, his yen to see African wildlife, an attraction of the dark continent that stands above most others, was unfulfilled, except that he saw a few zebras and one venturesome baboon family on the drive from Cape Town to Johannesburg. The baboons had congregated around a parked automobile, and the largest of them, a powerful male, and presumably the patriarch of the clan, had hopped to the hood of the car, where he sat in regal dominance.

If the full story were known, the Prophet probably did not regret his inability to go to the park. Indeed, it is most likely that he planned it that way. While he enjoyed sight-seeing and was not averse to indulging in it now and then, the weight of his office laid a gentle rein on such activities in favor of the duties for which he had been called to the apostleship. President McKay was keenly aware that whenever he stepped out of his prophetic office for any reason, it remained vacant, there being no one else who could occupy it while he lived. Thus, wherever he went, he was on duty—was on stage, as it were. And in the glare of publicity that was always focused upon him, his every word and action were reported faithfully to an international audience, hungry for every detail about him.

The return trip from Johannesburg to Dakar was un-eventful, except for the one instance of violent turbulence already mentioned when the Prophet was thrown out of his seat into the aisle. Fortunately he was not hurt—only embarrassed. At Dakar, where President Reiser left the McKays to return to London, it was learned an earlier flight had been arranged to Rio de Janeiro, which avoided an expected two-day wait in the Senegalese capital.

David O. and Emma Ray looked forward to a reunion in Rio with Robert, who was to serve as the president's secretary during the remainder of the tour. However, word did not reach the son of the accelerated schedule, so he was not with the Brazilian Mission president, Asael T. Sorenson, when he met the McKays' plane in Rio at 1:00 A.M. Friday, January 22. The family reunion took place later in the day after the travelers had had an opportunity to rest and refresh themselves.

The two-day break in the schedule had been planned deliberately to give the eighty-year-old prophet and his wife a breather during their exhausting trip. As an indication this interlude was well-timed, Ray confided to her husband on arriving in Rio, "I think I have seen all the water I want to see." They did manage to relax the remainder of the twenty-second, storing energy for the balance of the tour. But the next day it was decided to inspect Rio's most famous landmark, the gigantic statue of Christ at Corcovado. To see this spectacular statuary at close range requires mounting eighteen flights of stairs, a total of 220 steps. Despite warnings and protestations, the adventurous pair made their way slowly and deliberately up the stairs to the vantage point from which they had a good view of the statue. The torturous descent was more tiring than the climb because of the strain on seldom-used muscles.

If President Sorenson and Robert feared that the intrepid hikers had squandered their reserve energies in the climb and descent at Corcovado, they were reassured that evening, when, learning that the flight to São Paulo had been delayed until the next morning, the president insisted on traveling to nearby Tijuca to hold a meeting with a handful of Saints.

When the Prophet and his party arrived at the Rio airport the next morning for the short seventy-five-mile hop to São Paulo, they were apprehensive to see the plane on which they were scheduled to fly. It was a decrepit-looking craft with faded, scaling paint and signs of rust here and there. The confidence level of the passengers plummeted when the steward announced in broken English that they were riding on the plane's last scheduled flight. Their apprehension subsided somewhat, but not entirely, with the explanation that it was being converted to a cargo ship.

The scenario at the São Paulo airport when the Prophet arrived was essentially the same as in Britain, Europe, and South Africa—cheering, tears of joy, a spontaneous rendering of the favorite hymns already mentioned, intermingled looks of love and awe on the faces of the Saints, and a bouquet for Sister McKay. These Saints, however, added a new dimension to the hospitality extended in other lands in the warmth and enthusiasm of their greetings, accompanied by handshakes, pats on the back, and not a few hugs and kisses. Moreover, their singing was bilingual, as those who spoke German and those who spoke Portuguese mingled their voices in the same melody.

Aside from the enthusiasm generated by the Brazilian Saints' greeting to the Prophet and his party, there was a general feeling of excitement among the entire populace, as São Paulo was then celebrating the country's fourth centennial. So, there was an overtone of revelry and gaiety that pervaded the entire city all the while President McKay was there, whether night or day.

The Prophet held the customary meetings of instruction and inspiration in São Paulo as elsewhere, including a separate meeting with the German-speaking Saints. He also attended to an important organizational matter, setting apart Urban W. Haws and William V. Larsen as counselors to the mission president. A highlight of the several gatherings held there was the missionary testimony meeting. Among the young men who spoke was Elder Berlin from Huntsville, Utah, the crippled victim of childhood polio. He related how, when the doctors had given up on him, his parents called in a longtime friend to confer a priesthood blessing. The boy was not only promised recovery but that he would live to fulfill his responsibilities in the Church. The family friend who blessed him was David O. McKay, then second counselor in the First Presidency.

Over the years, President McKay gave numerous healing blessings that, as in this instance, influenced the lives of numerous people. All those whom Elder Berlin taught or ministered to during or after his mission were the indirect beneficiaries of Brother McKay's prophetic blessing, conferred years before in a remote mountain valley in Utah. Adding to this incident the countless other blessings, admonitions, or prophecies uttered by David O. McKay during a ministry of over sixty years and multiplying these by the innumerable persons who were, or will be, the indirect beneficiaries of his ministrations, suggests the vast, unseen influence of the man that can never be portrayed or measured by his public acts or pronouncements.

From São Paulo, the presidential party traveled to Montevideo, Uruguay, where, in addition to the customary greetings and meetings, the Prophet, assisted by the mission president, Lyman Shreeve, laid the cornerstone of a chapel then under construction that was to serve the 850 Uruguayan Saints. In this ceremony, the Prophet and his son Robert would have found cause to reflect on the extraordinary results from the meeting of Argentine missionaries held in the McKay home six years before and on the incalculable power of ideas and spiritual impressions.

A short flight across the sprawling La Plata River carried the travelers from Montevideo to Buenos Aires, Argentina's beautiful capital. Here, in addition to the prearranged meetings with the Saints, with President Lee Valentine and his missionaries, and with civic and business leaders, President McKay was granted an interview with the Argentine general and president, Juan Peron. This suave, handsome man, who had dominated Argentine politics since 1946, received the Prophet with great friendliness, eliciting this comment from the visitor: "I don't know when I have been as graciously received by a head of state."

Mr. Peron had not always received American visitors with such cordiality. Indeed, the first five years of his regime were characterized by a bitter anti-American sentiment. This attitude began to moderate at the time of his reelection in 1951, and by the time President McKay arrived three years later, the general had nothing but praise and goodwill for such distinguished American visitors. That Mr. Peron went out of his way to assist the Prophet and the Argentine Saints, as will be seen, may also trace in part to the anti-Catholic policies that he inaugurated about this time and that, incidentally, were responsible in large part for his sudden downfall only nineteen months after he entertained President McKay.

Evidence that the general's staff had done its homework well is seen in his apology for not offering tea or coffee to his visitors (which, in addition to President McKay, included Robert, President Valentine, and Gilbert Chase of the U.S. embassy). The general was also aware of the public meeting scheduled the following Sunday and said the building that had been engaged for it was unsuitable. He insisted that the Cervantes Theatre, one of the finest buildings in Buenos Aires, be used instead; and when it was learned later that the Cervantes was being renovated, an additional crew of sixty men was employed to complete the work so the theatre would be available for the Latter-day Saints as Mr. Peron had promised. President McKay reciprocated these kindnesses by giving his host beautiful leather-bound copies of the Book of Mormon, the Doctrine and Covenants, and the Pearl of Great Price, which were gratefully accepted. All this augured well for the success of the Prophet's visit and the future of the work in the most highly developed country of South America.

Since there were four days before the meeting in the Cervantes, the Prophet decided to visit small branches away from Buenos Aires. The largest of these was at Rosario, 250 miles to the northwest. There he held a meeting with 250 Saints who had gathered from all the surrounding area. In other communities during a three-day tour of the Argentine countryside, he found only small gatherings of Saints. But whether the congregation was large or small, President McKay spoke with the same warmth and the same sensitivity to the needs of his audience. So on these occasions, he never gave prepared talks but spoke extemporaneously from the heart, addressing the special concerns and challenges of the people.

Almost eight hundred members and friends crowded into the Teatro Cervantes on Sunday, February 7, to hear the Mormon Prophet from North America. And later in the day, he held a special meeting with Welch members of the Church residing in Buenos Aires. There the son of Jennette Evans enjoyed sharing reminiscences about a common ancestry and about the unifying effect of the gospel, which obliterates the distinctions between national or racial origins and which, at the same time, enhances an appreciation for one's ancestral heritage.

The following day, the Prophet and his party made the breathtaking flight over the mighty Andes from Buenos Aires to Santiago, Chile. Here President McKay, accustomed by now to the lively if not tumultous airport greetings of dozens and sometimes hundreds of Saints, was greeted by the two lone members of the Church then known to be living in Chile—Elder and Sister Billie Fotheringham. As the McKays dined with the Fotheringhams that evening in Santiago, would it have been thought fanciful had the diners been told that within thirty years there would be a hundred and thirty thousand members of the Church in Chile, and that a beautiful temple would grace its capital city? Yet that is what happened in the three decades after David O. McKay set foot on Chilean soil.

The next day while in Lima, Peru, en route to Panama City, President McKay penned these prophetic words, summarizing his impressions of the just-completed tour of South America: "I came to South America with the feeling that there would be plenty of opposition to the Church. I go away feeling that all the people need is a better understanding of the Church and its teachings. These are great countries."

At Panama City in Central America, President McKay witnessed the baptism of two Lamanite converts. And, traveling to Guatemala City with mission president Gordon M. Romney, he held meetings with the small, struggling colony of Saints living there.

Motor trouble in Guatemala City made it necessary to cancel a planned flight to Mexico. To make amends for his inability to visit the Mexican Saints during this tour, the Prophet flew to Mexico City in late March, when he counseled and instructed the leaders, members, and missionaries there as he had done previously in South Africa, South America, and Central America.

As President McKay reflected on his visits to these countries to the south, he became convinced there was a flawed attitude among many North Americans that soured relations between the two areas and that, inferentially, impeded the growth of the Church: "There is one definite observation I should like to make," he told a reporter after his return, "and that is the need of more cordial relations between the United States and South American Republics. The North American attitude of superiority engenders ill will throughout these southern republics and should be changed if we are to bring about a better and more cordial spirit of cooperation." (CN, February 20, 1954.)

While there are conflicting opinions about whether the civil authorities have fully recognized and sought to remedy this flaw, the Church, with President McKay's initial leadership, seems to have taken major strides to do so. Most knowledgeable observers agree that a chief factor in the phenomenal growth of the Church in the countries to the south has been the rapidity with which local converts have risen to positions of principal leadership. Stake presidents, bishops, and other local leaders come from the ranks of these national congregations, some of them having been members of the Church for only a short time. These leaders, when called, take their place in the priesthood hierarchy of the Church with full authority to act within their callings, and without any sense of inferiority or subservience. While, as is true in any organization, they are answerable to the presiding authorities of the Church—who happen to reside in North America—the perception is that this is merely the focal point of an international organization of which they are an important and integral part. And this perception, which was fostered by President McKay's initiatives, has, in recent years, been brought into sharper focus as the ranks of the General Authorities have been strengthened by the call of able men from South America, Great Britain, Europe, the Pacific Islands, and the Orient.

In his keynote address at the April general conference in 1954, President McKay traced the growth of the restored

Church from its beginnings, focusing on the accelerated building program and on his recent tour to the south. He concluded by emphasizing an expansion of missionary work and the construction of new temples. And he admonished the Saints everywhere "to exert every effort, and all means within our reach to make evil-thinking men good, good men better, and all people happier." (CR, April 1954, p. 26.)

The impact of David O. McKay's initiatives as the president of the Church and of his participation in the April general conference can be measured in part by this editorial: "Seldom, if ever before, has the church been given a keener awareness of its universality, and of the great missionary work that is being done and that remains to be done. The impact of President McKay's 35,000 mile missionary journey, of the great construction underway or being planned in widely separated areas and of the great increase in stake missionary effort and accomplishment was felt throughout the conference." (DN, April 6, 1954.)

Chapter Twenty-Two

The Prophet Goes West

E ven as the effects of the tour south began to wear off, President McKay was projecting another and even more exhausting tour. This one would entail a forty-five-thousand-mile jaunt into the Pacific and to the lands down under. But it took time to plan the elaborate details of such a tour and to arrange the itinerary so as to accommodate the desires of members and leaders along the way while protecting the health of the eighty-one-year-old leader and his wife. On this account, it was decided that this next tour would not start until January 1955.

Meanwhile, the ebb and flow of duties at Church headquarters continued unabated. May 26 found the Prophet in Provo, Utah, where he was the principal speaker and offered the prayer at ceremonies dedicating twenty-two buildings and thirteen dormitories on the campus of Brigham Young University. He continued to accept invitations to dedicate chapels or to participate in other special events. Typical of these was a trip to Vancouver, B.C., when he dedicated a new chapel on August 1; and a week later he was in Los Angeles, where he addressed sixteen-thousand young people in the Hollywood Bowl, where they had assembled for a special MIA conference. He returned to the BYU campus on December 14 when he dedicated the David O. McKay building, named after him in recognition of his "distinctive contributions to the teaching profession." Earlier in the year, on September 10, he had received another personal recognition when he was awarded honorary membership in the International College of Surgeons "in recognition of his contributions to the welfare of mankind and of his devotion and encouragement of education and humanities endeavors."

Only a few days before receiving this last award in Chicago, Illinois on August 30, David O. spent three stressful hours in a discussion about an educational matter that would attract widespread public notice and comment. This related to a referendum that had been proposed to transfer back to the Church three junior colleges it had conveyed to the state in the 1930s. Out of this meeting came a decision that the Church would remain aloof from this issue, neither favoring nor disapproving it. The implication was clear, however, that should the transfer be approved, the Church would accept it and would operate the colleges. On November 2, however, the voters overwhelmingly rejected the referendum. In retrospect, this episode appears to have been merely the opening salvo of a lengthy conflict over the role of the Church in education.

In the midst of these and numerous other activities, the Prophet devoted much prayerful attention to matters pertaining to the temples and the temple ceremonies. He watched with fatherly concern the progress of the work on the Los Angeles, Bern, and London temples. And knowing that the film presentation of the endowment would be used in the new temples, he spent many hours alone praying and meditating about this sacred matter and counseling with the committee appointed to work on the project. "Spent most of the day in the Salt Lake Temple considering and studying the temple ceremony," President McKay noted on August 15. And a week later he wrote: "Spent morning and afternoon hours at the office giving special study to the temple ceremony." Two months afterward, David O. made a special trip to Los Angeles to witness the placing of a statue of the Angel Moroni atop the temple there. And on December 5, he led the General Authorities to St. George for another solemn assembly where temple work, proselyting, and the challenges incident to the rapid expansion of the Church were emphasized.

Seeing his eighty-one-year-old father work at such a pace, and knowing about the strenuous trip to the Pacific he had planned for the first of 1955, it is understandable that Edward exerted pressure on the president to submit to a thorough physical examination following the October general conference. "Notwithstanding your disobedience these past months," Dr. Viko told the Prophet on October 5, "and notwithstanding the strenuous efforts you have put forth during these days of general conference, I am happy to report that I think you are in pretty good condition. Your blood pressure is normal and your heart is good."

This endorsement by his doctor and his own feelings of health and vigor were sufficient to confirm President McKay's decision to travel to the Pacific. So on January 2, 1955, their fifty-fourth wedding anniversary, he and Ray flew from the Salt Lake City airport. With them was Franklin Murdock, president of the Highland Stake and longtime Church employee, who would serve as President McKay's private secretary during the tour.

At San Francisco, where the travelers remained two days making final arrangements for their leap westward, word was received of a hurricane warning in the mid-Pacific. Confident in his feelings that there would be no danger, the Prophet rejected the suggestion that his flight to Hawaii be postponed. So disciplined was David O. McKay in his reliance on spiritual impressions that his actions were consistently directed by this means rather than by objective evidences. Therefore, the inner prompting that he could make the flight without danger to himself or his traveling companions was sufficient to outweigh the reports of hazardous flying conditions and the warnings and counsel of those expert in weather surveillance.

At Honolulu, Wendell B. Mendenhall, president of the San Joaquin Stake, and Sister Mendenhall joined the presidential party. Brother Mendenhall had rendered significant service in the Church's building program and had been especially active in the development of the Church in New Zealand. The Prophet had invited him along in connection with a planned inspection of these facilities.

At a night stop on Canton Island, a mere speck in the vast Pacific, word was received of a hurricane astride the route of the planned flight to Nandi on the island of Fiji. Inexplicably, this storm veered off its projected course, clearing a comparatively smooth path for the flight of the plane carrying the Prophet and his party. The erratic behavior of this storm, so inconsistent with the customary weather pattern, prompted the experienced meteorologists at Nandi and Suva to christen it "the Screwball." Brother Murdock, who kept a detailed account of this tour, which has been incorporated in President McKay's record, noted other similar instances when the weather deviated radically from the predictions. To the secretary's mind, these anomalies represented physical responses to the spiritual powers exercised by President David O. McKay, whose buoyant, self-confident attitude rejected any hint of fear or concern about the safety of his traveling party. He was on the Lord's errand and therefore had the abiding faith that the Lord would smooth a path through the turbulence and the storms of the Pacific as He had quelled the tempest on the Sea of Galilee.

After motoring across Fiji from Nandi to Suva, the Prophet spent a quiet Sunday, worshipping with a small group of Saints and with the two missionaries who were laboring there. Among the congregation were a man and woman who were children when President McKay first visited Fiji in 1921 and who were witnesses of the extraordinary calming effect of a prayer the apostle had offered during a storm at sea.

While at Suva, a reporter asked the Prophet the reason for his unusual tour of these remote Pacific Islands. "Here their destiny lies," he said of the Latter-day Saints living on these islands, explaining that the Church wanted to improve the educational facilities for these native Saints so they would be able to improve their productivity and build thriving, permanent LDS colonies. So, the message of the Prophet was the same to those on the isles of the sea as it was to those on the great continents of the earth: remain in your native environments and build the Church where God has planted you.

From Suva, the Prophet traveled southeast by ship to Nukualoafa, the capital of Tonga, located on Tongatapu Island. Here the Church leader was met by mission president D'Monte W. Coombs and his wife and by four Tongan members who had come 140 miles in an open sailboat to greet President McKay. This leg of the trip was more reminiscent of David's 1921 world tour than anything else he had experienced to then. The sensation of riding on, not over, the water, breathing the ocean air, and seeing the abundant marine life that abounds in that area brought back vivid memories of the seemingly endless days he and Hugh J. Cannon had spent at sea many years before.

But the experiences that awaited him ashore bore little resemblance to the visit of long ago. Then there were but a few members to bid him welcome. Now he found the newly completed Liahona College, where LDS youth could be trained. And in a bowery on the campus, he found a thousand members of the Church gathered for a native ceremonial ritual, followed by a religious meeting where the Prophet blessed and instructed the Saints.

The novelty of President McKay's visit attracted two thousand well-wishers, members and friends, native leaders, and the British consul to bid the party farewell on January 12. The next day found them in Vavau, another of the 150 Tongan Islands. Here President McKay held a meeting with fifty members of the Church assembled in a small branch chapel in which he and Elder Cannon had held a similar meeting thirty-four years before.

Traveling northwesterly from Tonga, the party of Presi-

David O. McKay

dent McKay's spent four days in Samoa, where, in addition
to the usual meetings and receptions, he inspected the
Pesaga school at Apia, dedicated a school site at Maupasago,
and dedicated a new chapel at Sauniatu. At the latter place,
the Prophet visited the monument the Samoan Saints erected
following his 1921 tour to commemorate an extraordinary
meeting he held there when the veil was very thin and
when all present were moved upon by powerful spiritual
forces. And this visit evoked memories of the song of
farewell sung by the Samoan Saints as he and Elder Cannon departed, memories that had lifted and warmed him
intermittently through the years: "Oh! I never will forget
you," went the refrain. "And sadly repeat my fond adieu,/
Oh! I never will forget you, to Samoa I bid adieu;/Good-
bye, Feleni, my barque now sails away,/away from fair
islands where all is bright and gay."

On this occasion, however, unlike his first visit to
Samoa, Elder McKay flew away instead of sailing. The next
destination was Tahiti. Here, in the islands memorialized
by the authors of "Mutiny on the Bounty," the Prophet
mingled with the Polynesian Saints, whom he loved for
their friendliness and their unqualified faith and loyalty.

Making intermittent stops in the Cook, Samoan, and
Fiji Islands, President McKay returned to Suva and Nandi
on January 21; and two days later he departed for New
Zealand. Arriving at Auckland on the twenty-third, the
traveler inspected a new chapel there and then motored
seventy miles to Hamilton, where the Church had a multi-
million dollar college under construction, located on a 215-
acre site. Near the college campus was a 729-acre farm
owned by the Church where cattle, horses, and sheep were
being raised and where small garden plots had been laid
out for the use of the Saints helping to construct the buildings on campus. Here were facilities and opportunities calculated to encourage the New Zealand Saints to remain at
home, rather than to consider migrating to the United
States. And at the end of his Pacific tour, President McKay

would make an announcement that would further tie these Saints to their native land.

While in Hamilton, the Prophet made a sentimental visit to nearby Tauranga, which had been the headquarters of his departed friend Matthew Cowley during the many years he had served as a missionary in New Zealand. With no disrespect to President McKay, or to others who bore the title, the name Tumaki used in that area usually referred to Elder Cowley, the articulate one, whose fiery eloquence inspired faith and confidence whether uttered in the intimate setting of a Maori hut or in the intimidating environs of the Salt Lake Tabernacle.

From New Zealand the Prophet traveled to Australia, where in nine days, he visited and held meetings in Sydney, Brisbane, Adelaide, and Melbourne. In the outskirts of Brisbane, at Ipswitch, the Prophet dedicated a fine new chapel, which symbolized the message of local stability and continuity he preached all along the route of his tour. And in press conferences he held and as he counseled with local political leaders, he emphasized this important concept while, at the same time, he stressed the loyalty of the Latter-day Saints to the particular governments under which they lived. This was important, not only as a means of impressing the Saints with the international character of the Church, but of allaying any concern of local leaders that membership in the Church carried the seeds of sedition or disloyalty.

Everywhere he traveled in Australia, or elsewhere on his international tours, President McKay received celebrity treatment. Enthusiastic, cheering, singing crowds usually greeted him at every stop, sometimes to the surprise or chagrin of local residents. A group of well-known Australian athletes, aboard a flight to Adelaide with President McKay's party, learned an embarrassing lesson in humility. Seeing a large, noisy crowd at the airport, and assuming they were the object of its adulation, the handsome young men stepped forward to acknowledge the greeting only to find that the cheers and excitement were generated by the tall, white-haired man who came down the ramp after them.

Leaving Sydney on February 8, the Prophet flew to Honolulu, where his party was met by local leader Edward L. Clissold and by his friend and longtime associate, D. Arthur Haycock, who then presided over the Hawaiian Mission. While in Hawaii, President McKay made another symbolic gesture toward his aim of internationalizing the Church by breaking ground for a new college at Laie. Lying across the island of Oahu from Honolulu, this beautiful site near the Hawaii Temple was part of a large tract acquired many years before by the Church. It was here that David O.'s mentor, President Joseph F. Smith, had spent his years

President and Sister McKay upon their arrival at the Mascot Aerodrome in Sydney, Australia, February 5, 1955.

of exile during the dark days of the underground. And it was here a beautiful campus would arise to serve Latter-day Saint students in the Pacific and to become part of its larger, parent facility on the mainland, Brigham Young University in Provo, Utah.

While in Hawaii, President McKay made a nostalgic visit to the small village of Puleli on Maui, where the first LDS baptisms in Hawaii were performed by George Q. Cannon and where the first Hawaiian branch was organized in 1851. Here was found the monument that commemorates this historic place and here the Prophet was carried back in memory to the visit he and Hugh J. Cannon had made thirty-four years before.

The travelers left Hawaii on February 14 and arrived in Salt Lake City the following day after an overnight stop in San Francisco. The Prophet lost no time in briefing the Council of the First Presidency and the Twelve about the tour and about his impression that a temple should be constructed at Hamilton. The council approved, and on February 17, two days after President McKay's return, the *Deseret News* carried an announcement of the plans to construct a temple in New Zealand.

In statements made to the press after his return, the Prophet expressed amazement at the growth of the Church in the Pacific since his 1921 tour, growth he "could hardly accept . . . as fact." And in commenting on the Church schools there, he said: "As great as are their accomplishments, they must continue on a program of expansion." (IE, April 1955, p. 224.)

Chapter Twenty-Three

The Maturing of Prophetic Initiatives

With the completion of his tour of the Pacific, President McKay had finished laying the foundation of the prophetic initiatives that would stand as the bulwark of his administration. Twice he had traveled extensively in Great Britain and continental Europe, preaching his stay-at-home doctrine and acquiring and dedicating temple sites there as a means of making that doctrine attractive and workable. He had broken the ice in Africa and South and Central America, where the seeds of future development had been sown through the enthusiasm and commitment engendered in the local Saints, through friendly contacts with political and civic leaders, and through a refinement in his thinking and attitudes toward these countries and their people. He had completed the most extensive single tour ever made by a president of the Church, surveying the conditions among Latter-day Saint colonies throughout the Pacific and down under, and encouraging education and the development of mechanical and agricultural skills to improve the economic condition of the Saints there and to bind them to their homes. And after returning, he had announced still another new temple, this one in faraway New Zealand.

Amidst these strenuous and time-consuming activities, he had kept the administrative ship afloat at home, had continued his dizzying round of ceremonial functions, and had given powerful impetus to the missionary work through his concept of every member being a missionary. As to the latter, he convened a special missionary meeting in conjunction with the April 1955 general conference whose theme was "The Field Is White and Ready to Harvest." There the Prophet alluded to the marvelous tools of modern transportation and communication the Lord had made available to help reap that harvest. But, as his diary reflects, the most significant elements of success for a bounteous harvest lay with the Saints and the inspiration of the Lord: "Upon you and a million others who are members of the church," he told the leaders at this meeting, "rests the responsibility of declaring unto the world the divine sonship of the Lord."

Against this background, the Prophet began to prepare for still another trip to Great Britain and Europe, where he would reap a harvest from seeds he had planted there several years before. Specifically, he was planning to dedicate at Bern the temple that was scheduled for completion in late summer. It had been decided to arrange a tour of the Tabernacle Choir in conjunction with the temple dedication as a means of exposing the choir to critics and audiences in Great Britain and on the Continent and of riveting the attention of Saints around the world on the drama at Bern. So, on April 1, prior to the general conference, the president met with a select committee to discuss the complicated arrangements for the choir tour. And intermittently, during the months that followed, he reviewed the work of this committee as he also conferred with the special committee assigned to prepare the film version of the temple ceremony.

Meanwhile, there was the usual grist of headquarters work to handle and a number of signal events that occupied President McKay in the interim. In early May he traveled to the nation's capital, where he attended a dinner hosted by President Dwight D. Eisenhower. Twenty-one guests were present, including the Prophet and Elder Ezra

Taft Benson. Significantly, President McKay was given the seat of honor directly across from President Eisenhower, who called on him to say "grace." During the meal, the guest on the Prophet's left, the distinguished business leader John H. Whitney, devoted most of his conversation inquiring about a phrase in the blessing on the food to the effect that individual effort is necessary to eternal happiness. At President McKay's right sat Mr. Dave Beck, the president of the International Brotherhood of Teamsters. He was as much taken up with the wit and charm of the eighty-one-year-old Mormon prophet as was President Eisenhower, who later confided to Elder Benson that he considered David O. McKay to be "the greatest spiritual leader in the world." (Ezra Taft Benson memo of May 28, 1966.)

Ten days after breaking bread with the president of the United States, David O. underwent surgery performed by Dr. Leland B. Cowan, who removed what proved to be a benign tumor from the left side of the Prophet's face. Because there was "more cutting than they had anticipated," the patient's whole head was swathed in bandages. On account of this, President McKay curtailed his public activities for some time during the early summer. A pilgrimage to Huntsville in mid-June completely revived any lagging spirits the surgery or an earlier family sorrow may have produced as this entry on June 20 attests: "The meadow larks, canaries and various other birds were singing. The horses followed me wherever I went. All in all it was a glorious experience."

The sorrow was the death of President McKay's youngest brother, Morgan, which occurred on March 18 in Kellogg, Idaho. Being about twenty years younger than David O., Morgan grew up in the shadow of his famous brother, whom he idolized. But the aura of special distinction that surrounded the oldest of the McKay brothers could not obscure the stature and achievements of the youngest one, who was an outstanding athlete at the University of Utah as well as a distinguished scientist. At the time of his death, Morgan was the plant pathologist for the Bunker Hill and Sullivan Mining Company at Kellogg. President and Sister McKay and son Lawrence traveled to Kellogg via Spokane, Washington, for the funeral, which was held on the twenty-first. Three days later, the entire McKay clan gathered at a memorial service for the deceased in Salt Lake City, where the brother was properly eulogized and honored. Morgan's unexpected death was a particular shock to the entire family, he being so comparatively young and robust.

With his body and spirit healed following surgery and the death of a beloved brother, the Prophet was ready for another leap across the continent and the Atlantic. He left Salt Lake City on August 16, six days after he bid farewell to the Tabernacle Choir, whom he would greet abroad later. In his party were Ray, Edward, and Lottie, and his secretary, Clare Middlemiss, who was thus rewarded for her many years of devoted service to the president.

Soon after their plane touched down at Prestwich Airport on the eighteenth, the travelers knew they were in Scotland, as the young elders accompanying President A. Hamer Reiser pinned sprigs of Scotch heather on them. En route to their Glasgow hotel, and later as the party traveled to Stirling Castle and the Trossacks, President McKay reached deep into his memorized store of the poetry of Scott and Burns, quoting excerpts at length in his almost flawless Scottish brogue. The Prophet expressed surprise that his companions seemed not to appreciate the story, which had given rise to Scott's famed poem "The Lady of the Lake": "None of the group," he wrote with a tinge of disappointment "seemed interested in the story that to me makes the trip to the Trossacks fascinating."

On the nineteenth, the president greeted the choir members on the docks at Greenock, where they had arrived by ship, the S.S. *Saxonia*. Among the greeters was the honorable Andrew Hood, lord provost of Glasgow, who later, in a formal welcome, decried the past prejudice and injustice toward the Latter-day Saints and assured the visitors that the days of persecution in Scotland were ended.

As one would expect, the choir burst into song on stepping ashore, intermingling "Come, Come Ye Saints" with "On the Bonny, Bonny Banks of Loch Lomond." And the next day its overseas concert tour began with a well-received performance in Glasgow's Kelvin Hall. This was followed by performances in Edinburgh on the twenty-first and in London at the Royal Albert Hall on the thirtieth. In addition, members of the choir sang at the groundbreaking ceremony for the London Temple held on the twenty-seventh at which President McKay addressed over a thousand Latter-day Saints who had gathered to witness the commencement of work on their beloved temple. Here the Prophet gave emphasis to the sacred and eternal nature of the temple ceremonies, comprising the University of the Lord, and the responsibility of the Saints to avail themselves of the temple, both for their own exaltation and for the blessing of their kindred dead.

Crossing the channel to the continent, President McKay dedicated a new chapel and mission home in Paris before going to Bern for the temple dedication. It was here, three days before the ceremony, that President McKay celebrated his eighty-second birthday. He was honored at a small gathering in the hotel dining room, where he was toasted by his son Edward and by Elder Gordon B. Hinckley, who was not then a General Authority but who had been intimately involved in preparing the film presentation of the temple ceremony. In commenting on the span of President McKay's life from the obscurity of his birth in a remote mountain valley to that point in time, Elder Hinckley said: "It is a marvelous evolution from a boyhood in Huntsville to a citizen at home in every great city in the world. It is a most remarkable step from ignorance of Mormonism as it was recorded in the nineteenth century to an honored place among great men everywhere you go." Then followed an accolade and toast, joined in by all present: "Tonight we pay tribute and honor to you—a man loved by his people, a man respected by the world, a man honored by the Lord. To you we drink a toast, and say God bless and keep you with us." (IE, November 1955, p. 845.) In his brief response, the Prophet said that any occasion of tribute or commendation such as this one increased his feeling of dependency on the Lord and on the confidence and love of his associates. "If we have these two," he said, "nothing can daunt us. Difficulties can be overcome." (Ibid., p. 846.)

There was a sense of awe and expectancy in the air as President McKay entered the celestial room on Sunday, September 11, for the first dedicatory session of the Swiss Temple. Dressed in a white suit, with wavy white hair framing his ruddy and ruggedly handsome face, the tall, dignified American presented an image that could scarcely have failed to remind those present of the ancient Israelitish prophets. And his words coincided precisely with the visual impression he conveyed, words that sketched God's plan of salvation for men, revealed through His divinely appointed messengers, culminating with the sacred ordinances to be performed in the holy temple.

Blessed with a historic sense, the Prophet had selected "The Morning Breaks, the Shadows Flee" as the opening rendition, sung by members of the Tabernacle Choir. The lyrics of this moving hymn, which were composed by Parley P. Pratt, one of the original apostles of this dispensation, appeared on the cover of the first issue of the *Millennial Star* published in England. Originally conveying the message of a refulgence of light shed on the world by the illuminating rays of the restored gospel, the hymn now implied a new brilliance originating from a major realignment of Church aims and priorities.

The dedication of the new temple actually represented the first completed project of President McKay's move toward the internationalization of the Church. And the use of the film presentation in this temple, opening the way for a single presentation to accommodate the diverse languages of members from different countries comprising a single audience, added emphasis to this signal concept.

As a means of accommodating all the members who desired to participate in this historic event, nine additional dedicatory ceremonies were held following the initial one. On the thirteenth, President McKay held a special meeting in the temple with the missionaries, instructing them in "what it means to be a missionary." And three days later, after all the dedicatory sessions had been completed, he attended the first endowment session in the temple, although he did not actively participate in the ceremony. "I decided to watch and study the ceremony as it was presented," he confided to his diary, "this being the first session ever held in this temple and the procedure being new to all workers."

The Prophet arrived home a week after witnessing the first endowment session in Bern. In the interim, he spent several days in London and Glasgow tending to Church affairs, including the inspection of a charming four-story building in London that would soon be purchased for a mission home.

In Salt Lake City, he immediately launched into the preparations for the October general conference. On the twenty-ninth he conducted a meeting of all the General Authorities in the temple; and the day after, following the opening session of the conference, he met in the Church Administration Building with all the stake presidents from Southern California to plan for the dedication of the Los Angeles Temple, which was scheduled to take place the following spring. The open house, however, was only a few weeks away. Plans for both these events were discussed in detail, and assignments were made to a committee of stake presidents, including a forty-eight-year-old attorney, Howard W. Hunter, whose name would soon become familiar to Saints around the world when, four years later, he would be sustained as a member of the Twelve. It was the quiet but highly effective work Elder Hunter performed in connection with the Los Angeles Temple dedication that brought him to the favorable attention of the Prophet.

From December 1955 through February 18, 1956, over

682 thousand persons inspected the interior of the beautiful Los Angeles Temple, whose architecture was described by one professional as "everlasting." Standing on an eminence that once comprised part of the estate of movie actor Harold Lloyd, this gleaming white structure rising magnificently to a height of 257 feet and capped by a spire supporting a fifteen-foot statue of the Angel Moroni, is visible on a clear day to ships twenty-five miles at sea.

In seeing this beautiful building come to completion, President McKay helped bring to fruition a dream shared by two of his predecessors, Heber J. Grant, under whose presidency the site was acquired in 1937, and George Albert Smith, who had authorized the preparation of the architectural plans in 1949. Throughout the entire period of its construction, President McKay made numerous visits to the site, observing with avid interest each phase of the

President McKay reviewing his notes before addressing the students and faculty at a Brigham Young University devotional assembly on October 30, 1956.

work. Nor was his involvement merely passive, as he frequently made suggestions and consistently gave encouragement and support to the contractor, his longtime friend
Soren Jacobsen.

So when the time for the dedication of the Los Angeles
Temple arrived on March 11, 1956, David O. McKay enjoyed a special personal relationship to the building quite
apart from his role as the president of the Church. This was
reflected in the eloquent and comprehensive dedicatory
prayer he offered that day: "We come before Thee with joy
and thanksgiving," he said, "with spirits jubilant and
hearts filled with praise that we are permitted to participate
in the dedicatory service of this, the twelfth temple to be
dedicated to Thee since the organization of Thy Church."
Alluding to the dramatic appearance of the building and
the unusual interest that had been shown in it by both
members and nonmembers, he observed: "Millions have
had their attention drawn to it—many through curiosity,
some because of its beauty in structure, others because of
its lofty purposes." But, regardless of the aspect of the
building that had kindled an interest in it, the Prophet was
anxious that everyone recognize the ultimate purpose of
the building: "Help us, O Father," he implored, "to realize
more keenly and sincerely than ever before that only by
obedience to the eternal principles and ordinances of the
Gospel of Jesus Christ may Loved Ones who died without
baptism be permitted the glorious privilege of entrance into
the Kingdom of God. Increase our desire, therefore, to put
forth even greater effort towards the consummation of Thy
purposes to bring to pass the immortality and eternal life of
all Thy children."

Two years after dedicating this temple, another one on
the other side of the world awaited dedication. So, in mid-
April 1958, the Prophet left for New Zealand with a large
party that included, in addition to Sister McKay, Elders
Delbert L. Stapley and Marion G. Romney of the Twelve;
Rulon Tingey, who would serve as the president's personal
secretary; newspaperman Theodore L. Cannon; and the

wives of these brethren. Elder Gordon B. Hinckley, Assistant to the Twelve, accompanied by Sister Hinckley, had gone ahead to complete the arrangements for the dedication.

Following a familiar route, the travelers made intermediate stops in San Francisco, Honolulu, Canton Island, and Nandi before touching down at Auckland on April 16. Waiting to greet the Prophet and his party were mission president Ariel S. Ballif and the usual complement of enthusiastic members, whose customary ardor had been greatly increased by the impending event that most of them thought would never take place in their part of the world. With the New Zealanders were members of the Church from Australia, Tasmania, Samoa, Tonga, Raratonga, Fiji, and Tahiti. To express their pleasure and excitement, the members had arranged a special social, with songs, dances, and ceremonials, during which members from the various lands and islands of the Pacific displayed their talents and their distinctive dress and customs.

During three days, two sessions were held each day, which enabled all the Saints who desired to do so to participate in the dedication. As it was anticipated that this temple would serve chiefly the Polynesian Saints in the South Pacific, the Prophet's dedicatory prayer included an expression of gratitude for the descendants of Father Lehi, who, he said, had been guided to these islands. Always conscious of the import of his words on others and of the need to cement relationships with all governments, President McKay said in his prayer: "We are thankful for the liberty existing in other free nations, especially in New Zealand, so that this great temple could be built."

Having dedicated the temple, which was the main reason for this trip into the Pacific, the Prophet turned his attention to a secondary reason for his visit—the dedication of the Church college at Hamilton, which was already in use. The campus boasted twenty academic buildings and twenty residences. Present for the dedication were hundreds of Saints along with local civic and government leaders, including the prime minister, Walter Nash; L. F. Ensper, superintendent of Auckland schools; Dame Hilda Ross, member of the New Zealand legislature; Francis H. Russell, United States ambassador to New Zealand; and George F. Fennemore, United States consul.

Traveling from Auckland to Suva, the president dedicated a chapel described by Sister McKay as "one of the most beautiful church edifices I have yet seen." What gave the building its special charm were the coral that had been tastefully imbedded in the cement, the polished wood hewn from New Zealand timber, and the beautiful landscaping, which featured the luxuriant greenery and the profuse floral offerings found on the island.

The simple yet impressive dedication ceremony was attended by the colonial governor, Sir Ronald Gawey, and other civil officials, who seemed impressed with President McKay's dedicatory sermon, entitled "Men's Hearts Can Be Changed." The Prophet spoke optimistically of the power of the gospel to change even the most hardened and obdurate heart, and he explained the effort of the Church to promote such change through aggressive proselyting and the establishment of permanent communities of Latter-day Saints around the world like the one to be served by the chapel being dedicated.

En route home from Suva, President McKay made a brief stop in Hawaii to inspect the work on the Church college then being constructed near Laie on Oahu. There he spoke to a large group of students who were then using the buildings that already had been completed.

Satisfied with the progress of the work in the Pacific, President McKay turned his attention again to Great Britain, where the London Temple was rapidly nearing completion. Learning that an early September date for the dedication was feasible, the Prophet began to plan for another trip eastward. Recognizing that by then he would have reached his eighty-fifth birthday, President McKay thought it advisable—as did his solicitous doctor-son, Edward—to undergo another thorough physical examination. David O. was elated when on June 2 Doctor Viko advised him, "President McKay, I think you are indestructible." That medical appraisal did not mean, however, that the Prophet was immune from physical problems, as a week later he underwent eye surgery under the hand of Doctor Richard W. Sonntag for the removal of a cataract from his right eye. Such an operation at that day was not the comparatively simple procedure that improved skill and technology have since made of it. Therefore, President McKay did not expect that it would meet with overnight success. At the same time, he did not anticipate the more than two months of discomfort and apprehension the surgery produced. He was hospitalized for six days; and it was almost two weeks before the stitches were removed. By the twenty-seventh of June, when it was expected he would be returning to normal, he recorded gloomily: "Not so well today. Very nervous and tired. Eye sore and inflamed. Hard to see." Later, he received a new lens in his glasses, which created new problems and upset him. By July 12, however, things began to look up: "Each day I am a little better able to see with my operated eye." And finally, after another month of experimentation and adjustment, this happy entry on August 11; "Went to Doctor Richard Sonntag's office for an eye examination. He says I have 20-20 vision in my operated eye with glasses. He gave me permission to drive and go about my business as usual."

While this cleared the way for the Prophet to leave for England the first week in September to dedicate the London Temple, the unexpected illness of Sister McKay would make it impossible for her to accompany him. She was hospitalized the last day of August with a deep-seated lung congestion and was therefore unable to go with her husband two days later. The loneliness David O. felt in leaving his sweetheart behind is apparent from this diary entry of September 2: "For the first time during twenty three years on a trip of any length, I was deprived of the loving companionship of Sister McKay. Although feeling better, she does not feel equal to make this brief, busy trip to attend dedicatory services of the London Temple."

And it was a brief and busy trip. After flying to New York City, the Prophet deviated from his other flights across the Atlantic by stopping first at Shannon, Ireland, and thence to London. With him were President and Sister Joseph Fielding Smith and A. Hamer Reiser. At London, the Prophet's party was met by Elders Henry D. Moyle, Richard L. Evans, Hugh B. Brown, and Gordon B. Hinckley; Bishop Thorpe B. Isaacson; architect Edward O. Anderson; and mission president Clifton Kerr. The wives of these brethren and the Prophet's sister Jeanette and her daughter Jeanette later joined him for the temple dedication, which began on September 7. Before the first session, President McKay, feeling the need for special spiritual enlightenment and strength, sought out a quiet room in the temple, where he implored the Lord for guidance. "I had a few minutes in secret prayer and sweet communion with Him whose house we are dedicating," he recorded of the incident. And the spirit that descended upon the Prophet on this occasion carried into and permeated the six dedicatory sessions that extended through September 9. It was a time of great rejoicing for the Latter-day Saints in the British Isles, representing a culmination of the hopes and dreams they had nurtured for many decades.

It was in the midst of these sessions that David O. McKay celebrated his eighty-fifth birthday. On the evening of September 8, members of the official party and other close associates gathered in the Claridge Hotel to honor the Prophet. At the right moment a marzipan-topped birthday cake, adorned with a single candle, was placed on the table. As the guest of honor blew it out, he said simply, "The years do pass quickly; but I feel young in spirit today." (DN, September 9, 1958.)

Following the dedication, President McKay and his sister and niece, accompanied by Brother Reiser, made a quick trip into Wales, where at Merthyr Tydfil David O. took great pleasure in showing the party, and especially his sister Jeanette, the birthplace of their mother, Jennette Evans McKay. The sight of the humble dwelling where their parent had been born kindled anew feelings of gratitude and awe for the astonishing effect on their lives, and their whole family, exerted by two anonymous elders who had called there over a hundred years before.

As the Prophet prepared to depart from London for his fifteenth crossing of the Atlantic, someone asked him when he would return. "If you double the membership of the London branch in two years," he answered, "we'll build a chapel here." (DN, September 16, 1958.) As we shall see, a beautiful chapel was begun in London in less than two years from that date, and two and a half years later, President McKay returned to dedicate it—and to perform an act that in September 1958 seemed improbable.

Arriving home September 15, President McKay's first question was, "How's Mother?" He was pleased to find Emma Ray much improved and busy counseling with Lawrence and Mildred about a belated family birthday party that was held two days later. There Papa Dade was introduced to his newest great-grandchild, Rebecca, the daughter of grandson Richard L. McKay and his wife. He blessed the child in the Yale Ward chapel on October 5. That the family patriarch took the time to perform this loving service in the midst of complex preparations for general conference indicates where his priorities lay. The kind of schedule eighty-five-year-old David O. McKay kept during this period is suggested by the following entry of October 2: "Awoke at 3 A.M. and at 4 A.M. began the day's work by studying on conference matters. Also gave thought to the special authorities meeting to be held this morning." It was at this meeting that the announcement was made of the call of William J. Critchlow, Jr., and Alvin R. Dyer as General Authorities. During the conference, these two were sustained as Assistants to the Twelve whose ranks had been further augmented six months earlier by the addition of Elders Gordon B. Hinckley and Henry D. Taylor.

As the October general conference ended, the Prophet turned his attention to numerous matters that had accumulated during his absence and to the plans for yet another trip abroad before the end of the year. This one would take him into the Pacific again for an event that he had antici-pated thirty-seven years before.

Meanwhile, a second eye surgery was scheduled to take place before his departure. This entailed the removal of a cataract from his left eye. Remembering that it required al-most two months for healing after his first cataract surgery, President McKay arranged with Doctor Sonntag to perform this second operation in mid-October so he would be fully recovered for a trip to Hawaii in mid-December.

The surgery was performed October 17. Fortunately, this operation, and the convalescence from it turned out much better than the first, so that by December 4 the pa-tient was fully recovered and his vision was better than it had been for years.

During his convalescence from this surgery, at a First Presidency meeting held in his home, the Prophet ap-proved the recommendation of his counselors to move Ricks College from Rexburg, Idaho, to Idaho Falls, Idaho. As will be seen later, this decision created an unfortunate and stressful dilemma for President McKay that would agi-tate him, his administration, and the residents of south-eastern Idaho for several years.

President McKay left for Hawaii on December 15. Two days later, he dedicated the Church College of Hawaii at Laie. "The school is the fulfillment of a project conceived 37 years ago," noted a reporter, "when President McKay, then a member of the Twelve, visited a small school in Laie taught by Mormon missionaries." (DN, December 20, 1958.) In the intervening years, David had often recalled the im-pression he received in Hawaii during his world tour about the need for an advanced school in the Islands to serve the Polynesian Saints. And now, years later, he saw this dream come to fruition, fulfilling the long-held desire of a man whose yearnings and aspirations were centered in educa-tion, whether temporal or spiritual.

As he fulfilled a dream in dedicating the college in Hawaii, he fulfilled a pledge twenty-six months later by returning to London to dedicate the new Hyde Park chapel. An extraordinary growth in the Church in England during the ensuing period had fulfilled the condition set during his September 1958 visit, and the Prophet was pleased to keep his promise. So on February 22, 1961, he left Salt Lake City for London with members of his family (Sister McKay, son Edward, and daughter Emma Rae); Elder Hugh B. Brown of the Twelve; Elder N. Eldon Tanner, Assistant to the Twelve, who had been appointed president of the West European Mission; and A. Hamer Reiser, the Prophet's traveling secretary. The party was met by Elder Alvin R. Dyer, Assistant to the Twelve, who had been laboring in Europe.

President McKay's arrival in London created a stir among members of the press, who were intrigued by the man whom his followers revered as a prophet of God. He responded to questions on a variety of subjects at a press conference on February 24. When asked about the main differences between the LDS Church and other churches, he listed four: a belief in divine authority; Church organization; the principle of tithing and fast offerings; and a belief in the eternal nature of covenants and ceremonies essential to salvation. As to the greatest threat or challenge facing the Church, he named "Communism with its Godless ideology, its complete subjection of the individual to the state and its complete materialism." (DN, February 25, 1961.) In reference to the chapel he had come to dedicate, the Prophet said: "This is a great opportunity to dedicate the chapel in London, a great event in the British Mission, one which I have been looking forward to for a hundred years—well, eighty-seven years." (Ibid.)

The surprise action the Prophet took in conjunction with the dedication of the Hyde Park chapel was the organization of the London Stake with Donald W. Hemingway as the stake president. Both events took place on February 26, 1961. When placed alongside the dedication of the London Temple in September 1958 and the organization of the Manchester Stake in March 1960, these two events at the Hyde Park chapel signaled an important milestone in President McKay's quest to plant the Church firmly in all nations. The process of expanding and solidifying this base in Great Britain continued unabated throughout the remainder of President McKay's administration. Its success in terms of the objective growth of the Church is clearly evident from the burgeoning baptismal statistics and the proliferation of new buildings. And the subjective perceptions of the people is suggested by the first area general conference, held in Manchester a few months after President McKay's death, where the closing musical number was a hymn composed by a Britisher entitled "This Is Our Place."

Providing music for meetings held during this trip to Great Britain were the Relief Society Singing Mothers, who presented a formal concert in the Royal Albert Hall on February 27, which the Prophet attended and enjoyed immensely. In the four days that followed, he held meetings with the missionaries in Manchester, Ireland, and Scotland, where, according to his usual custom, he inspired, entertained, and pricked the consciences of the young missionaries, who could not match the zeal and dedication of their eighty-seven-year-old leader.

Before returning home, President McKay made a side trip to Wales, where he broke ground for a new chapel at Merthyr Tydfil. There he indicated that if the necessary arrangements could be made, he would return when it was completed.

After dedicating a plaque that marked the birthplace of his mother, the Prophet left Great Britain, arriving home on March 4. On the sixth he and Ray drove to Huntsville to inspect and to spend their first night in a new home that had been built there across the street from the old family dwelling. This modern facility would provide a comfortable hideaway for them during the remaining years of their lives.

It took over two years to complete the chapel at Merthyr Tydfil. Toward the end of August 1963, when the Prophet received word it was ready for dedication, he prepared for still another trip to Great Britain to complete the cycle of his initiatives to establish the Church abroad. As Sister McKay was unable to accompany him, President McKay took Edward along as his traveling companion. With them as they departed on August 22 were Gus Backman, Salt Lake civic leader and longtime friend of President McKay; and Mrs. Backman. Gus Backman's purpose in accompanying the Prophet was to represent the Salt Lake business and professional community in formally presenting an organ for the Merthyr Tydfil chapel at the time of the dedication. The close relationship between this pair is indicated by a diary entry President McKay made on August 9 following a telephone conversation with his friend when he quoted Gus Backman as calling him "you old Galavanter." The comment was prompted by President McKay's recent return from a quick trip to Florida.

By now, the Prophet was almost ninety years old. He

President McKay relaxing on the family farm at Huntsville, Utah, October 19, 1957.

was still active and alert and as productive as he had ever been. But an accident three months before had shaken him profoundly. And in retrospect, it was this accident that started him toward the long series of illnesses that marked his final years. Ironically, the accident occurred at his beloved Huntsville. On May 7, he and Llewelyn went there for a horseback ride. As the saddle blanket was placed on Sonny Boy, the horse became frightened and bolted. "I was knocked down and pulled along the ground for about a block," wrote the Prophet. "However, he stopped and I was not hurt. We finally saddled him and he was his usual self and I had a very good ride on him which I enjoyed thoroughly." When David O. returned home, he was silent about the incident, not wanting to trouble Sister McKay, who, he was certain, "would have worried a great deal about it."

Any worry the horseman spared his wife at the time was merely deferred, as this entry of June 27 implies: "I was so tired when I got home that I alarmed members of the family who were there. I could hardly talk and they became very much concerned." Then, for the first time, we perceive a hint that David O. McKay had discovered his mortality. "I know that I have used up my reserve energy," he wrote, "and that it is foolish for me to go on this way, working such long hours without rest and sometimes without food."

This appraisal was confirmed by Doctor Viko, who gave the Prophet a thorough physical examination three days before his departure for Great Britain. After recording that the physician had given him a clean bill of health, President McKay noted in a postscript: "However, he advised me not to plan for any more long trips such as I am planning for at the present time."

As we shall see, the Prophet heeded this counsel, refraining from any trips abroad during the remaining years of his life. So when he and his party boarded the plane on August 22, this world citizen–traveler had begun his last overseas trip, the last of a series of journeys unequaled by any apostle in any dispensation.

This entire trip was tinged with a sense of nostalgia. Arriving in London on August 23, President McKay and his party traveled to Cardiff by train the next day, and then motored to Merthyr Tydfil in a drenching rain, "through the beautiful countryside and winding roads of Wales." As he inspected the distinctive little chapel, neat and clean and ready for dedication, his mind reverted to an incident forty years before when he presided over the European and British missions. The Prophet recalled that the city council had voted to reject the request of a member of the Church to hold services in the home he rented from the city. "That was the spirit of Cardiff in 1923," President McKay observed. In contrast, the head of the Church was now received by the local officials with great courtesy and deference. The old enmities and prejudices had been replaced by cordiality, even of pride in the fact that a person of such international prominence as David O. McKay was the son of one of Merthyr Tydfil's own.

Elder Mark E. Petersen of the Twelve, who then presided in Britain, nearly exhausted his ingenuity in preparing for the dedicatory service. In addition to republishing the first issue of the *Millennial Star*, as already mentioned, he had brought distinguished musical talent with him from London. The organist was Robert Cundick, who was then serving temporarily as the organist at the Hyde Park chapel and who is now the chief Salt Lake Tabernacle organist. And the vocal soloist was Annette Richardson Dinwoodey, internationally famed contralto, who was then living in London with her husband, Clinton Dinwoodey, an oil-company executive. When in visiting with her the Prophet asked Sister Dinwoodey about the absence of her husband, she explained he was in London making a living and taking care of his duties as the bishop of the Hyde Park Ward. "That's exactly where he should be, and what he should be doing," the President answered jovially.

As the dedicatory service progressed, President McKay was caught up in a nostalgic reverie. The laudatory words of his friend Gus Backman, made when he presented the organ, and Annette Dinwoodey's rendition of "I Know That My Redeemer Lives" so touched the Prophet that he was unable to speak. Seeing this, Elder Petersen asked the vocalist if she had another number to sing. During the rendition of this unscheduled solo, President McKay was able to regain his composure. When he stood to speak and to offer the dedicatory prayer, he was in full control of his emotions, so much so that it is doubtful that anyone in the chapel, other than Elder Petersen and the singer and her accompanist, knew of the struggle through which the speaker had passed.

Given the circumstances, it is not surprising that the Prophet's remarks on this occasion were more informal and intimate than was customary for him in speaking at public gatherings. In this setting it was natural and easy for him to reminisce about his mother, who claimed Merthyr Tydfil as her birthplace. And he could not have found an audience more appreciative of his confidential disclosures about Jennette Evans McKay than the Welch townsmen who assembled for the dedication. Among the anecdotes the speaker related, this one seems best to illustrate the loving relationship between mother and son and to show Jennette's jovial and spunky personality: "I [am] reminded of a visit I made home when I was in college," he told the audience. "Mother was sitting on my left where she always sat at dinner and I said 'Mother, I have found that I am the only member of your children whom you have switched.' She said, 'Yes, David O., I made such a failure of you I didn't want to use the same method on the other children.' "

Despite his age and the warnings he had received about his health, it is doubtful that the aged Prophet realized that this return flight from London would be his last crossing of the Atlantic—or of any other ocean for that matter. As we view it through the perspective of time, it marked the close of a significant chapter in his life and ministry, a chapter filled with culminating ceremonies denoting the completion of projects and programs conceived and commenced in the dawn of his prophetic ministry. And in this is seen the most significant contribution and achievement of President David O. McKay during his service as the head of the Church. Phrased in his own words, this consisted of "making the church a world-wide organization."

Chapter Twenty-Four

Priesthood, Personalities, and More Politics

L ike his predecessors, President David O. McKay frequently had to deal with political issues, which presented themselves in varying forms and with changing personalities. One such issue that created a special challenge for the Prophet was the service of Elder Ezra Taft Benson in the cabinet of President Dwight D. Eisenhower. Elder Benson accepted this appointment only after he had been told by President McKay, "If the opportunity comes in the proper spirit, I think you should accept." The Prophet gave him unqualified support, which included agreement with Elder Benson's strong views about the dangers of international Communism, an agreement that continued without change until the time of his death and that included encouragement for his associate to continue to speak out on the subject.

Yet the active participation of a member of the Twelve in the political arena created special concerns for the head of the Church, not the least of which was a widely held public perception that President McKay's support of Elder Benson, a conservative Republican serving in a Republican administration, meant that the Prophet, and therefore the Church, frowned on or opposed the Democratic Party. This perception, which, incidentally, has not been limited to that day, troubled President McKay, who, as the head of an organization that was establishing its international identity, recognized that the Church could not be seen as tied to a single political party in the United States. He found a golden opportunity to negate that false perception in the summer of 1958. On July 8, Elder Hugh B. Brown, who had been sustained as a member of the Twelve at the previous general conference, conferred with President McKay about an unusual request he had received. That was to give the keynote address at the Democratic state nominating convention later in the summer. The request was unusual, as it had been many years since a General Authority had played such a key role in the power structure of a political party. Because of Elder Brown's certified credentials as a Democrat, the head of the Church saw in this invitation an opportunity to make an important statement in answer to the charge that the Church was biased against Democrats: "Since some think we are one-sided in politics," wrote the Prophet, "it might be a good thing for him to accept this assignment and let the members of the church know that both political parties are represented in the church."

While Elder Brown's participation in the Democratic Convention that summer doubtless convinced some of the Church's neutrality in political matters, its effect was neither complete nor lasting. This is apparent from a troubled comment made to President McKay on November 16, 1961, by David S. King, prominent Democrat and Church leader. Congressman King had complained that there was "partiality" in the Church in respect to politics. The Prophet answered this charge convincingly: "The action of the President of the Church in choosing two democrats for counselors [Henry D. Moyle and Hugh B. Brown] should be sufficient indication that the democrats have a definite place in the church."

As the 1960 presidential campaign moved into high gear, President McKay faced something of a dilemma because of the political involvements of Elder Benson and Elder Brown. On September 13, he resolved that, however, when he suggested that neither of them actively participate in the campaign, a suggestion both of them followed without hesitation. This decision was especially difficult for Elder Benson, who was still a member of President Eisenhower's cabinet; and vice-president Richard M. Nixon, with whom Elder Benson had served in the Eisenhower administration, was the Republican presidential candidate. Moreover, this presidential contest held a special personal interest for Elder Benson, who earlier in the year had been widely discussed as a possible presidential candidate himself. On March 5, 1960, he and his son Reed had aired this possibility with the Prophet. At that time, President McKay suggested that his fellow apostle make no overt attempt to seek the presidency; but he did not preclude him from running if a ground-swell of support independent of his own efforts should develop. A month later, Elder Benson discussed the matter again with his leader. Since there had been no change in the circumstances during that interval, he received the same counsel. This practically ended any prospect of Elder Benson being nominated, as it was improbable that he could gain his party's nod without making an extraordinary personal effort to do so, something he was unwilling to do in view of President McKay's counsel. Brother Benson was, therefore, unable to participate in the important 1960 presidential contest, either as a candidate or as a campaigner, so that he and his associate in the Twelve, Elder Hugh B. Brown, were consigned to watching it from the sidelines.

And what they saw was the usual parade of candidates and their supporters come to visit the head of the Church. Of the candidates, the first to come was John F. Kennedy, who paid a courtesy call on September 23 to renew an acquaintance the senator had been assiduously cultivating for three years. Mr. Kennedy first came calling on President McKay on November 12, 1957, when a group of Utah Democrats introduced him to the Prophet as their party's next presidential candidate. On meeting him at that time, President McKay said, "You are younger than I thought." Senator Kennedy came calling again on January 30, 1960, when he brought with him several well-known Utah Democrats, including prominent Church members Briton and Oscar McConkie.

During the September 23, 1960, visit, President McKay allowed his picture to be taken with the candidate. And that evening, the Prophet went to the Tabernacle to hear Senator Kennedy speak. Richard M. Nixon was extended the same courtesies during his visit on October 10. After Mr. Nixon's visit, President McKay received several critical letters complaining that he had "wished Mr. Nixon success." As to these criticisms he noted ruefully: "When Senator Kennedy was here, many letters were received claiming the church had turned democratic," ending with this philosophical comment: "It is now up to the people."

These main players were followed by lesser lights of the campaign when on October 27 Democratic vice-presidential candidate Lyndon B. Johnson came calling with his friend Senator Henry Jackson; and four days later came former Democratic New York governor, Averill Harriman. That the Republicans sent none of their top brass to see President McKay other than Mr. Nixon implies the confidence they had in carrying the state, a confidence that was not misplaced.

The election of John F. Kennedy began an eight-year Democratic reign in Washington, D.C., that would extend through all but one of President McKay's remaining years. And during that time he enjoyed as close if not a closer relationship with the two Democratic presidents who occupied the White House as he had with their predecessor, Dwight D. Eisenhower.

In September 1963, when the drums heralding the 1964 presidential campaign had begun to beat loudly, John F. Kennedy, then the president of the United States, scheduled a special trip to Utah to deliver a major address. Following the usual protocol, he was invited to speak in the Tabernacle. The Prophet and Sister McKay met the president in the General Authorities' lounge beneath the Tabernacle choir loft before the address and then sat on the stand while he delivered it. In his address, President Kennedy acknowledged that hard questions remained as to Vietnam, Cuba, and Laos, but said that during the past two years the Communist offensive had been "thwarted and turned back and that the whole theory of the inevitability of a communist victory" had been shattered. (*Salt Lake Tribune*, September 27, 1963.) He also denounced isolationism, and, without mentioning any names, "He hammered away at the basic philosophy advocated by Goldwater and the conservative right." (*DN*, September 27, 1963.)

The next morning, President and Sister McKay hosted President Kennedy at breakfast in their Hotel Utah suite, where the hotel's Chef Gerrard treated the diners to one of his specialties—mountain trout. Other guests included the secretary of the interior, Stewart L. Udall; President Hugh B. Brown and Senator Ted Moss and their wives; and the McKays' daughter, Emma Rae. In this intimate setting, President McKay came to know and to better understand the country's chief executive. On this account, he was doubly shocked when he learned of President Kennedy's assassination on November 22, 1963. "All are shocked and stunned at the news," President McKay recorded in his diary, "as it was only a few weeks ago that it was our privilege to entertain the President in our apartment; and now to think he is gone is unbelievable."

The relationship the Prophet had with John F. Kennedy's successor was of a more intimate nature than it had been with the assassinated president. It began two months after Lyndon B. Johnson was sworn in as president when, on January 25, 1964, he called the Prophet to say, "I need some strength from you, President McKay. Could you come to Washington for an hour's consultation with me alone some time next week at your convenience?" Even though he had suffered a mild stroke in early November and had not fully recovered, President McKay heeded this request and five days later flew to the nation's capital with his son Lawrence and Brother N. Eldon Tanner. Greeting them at the airport was President McKay's granddaughter

*President and
Sister McKay with
Lyndon B. Johnson,
president of the
United States.*

Joyce, the wife of Robert F. Bennett, who presented Papa
Dade with still another great-grandchild, Julie Bennett.

At the White House the next day, President Johnson first
conducted the Utahns on a tour of the historic building,
pointing out and commenting on items of unusual importance or interest. In the Cabinet Room, they met Secretary
of Defense Robert S. McNamara and Sargent Shriver, head
of the Peace Corps. Later, following the private interview
between the Prophet and President Johnson, the entire Utah
congressional delegation, senators Wallace F. Bennett and
Ted E. Moss and congressmen Sherman Lloyd and Lawrence Burton; Idaho congressman Ralph Harding; and Utahn
Esther Peterson, assistant secretary of labor, were invited
to meet President McKay.

On first greeting him, President Johnson elaborated on
why he had asked the Mormon leader to come to Washington. "President McKay," he said, "I feel just like a young
boy who would like to put his head on his mother's breast
and seek comfort and encouragement from her. I need ad-

vice and strength." Later in the private interview, he mentioned the events that were "crowding in on him": Cyprus, Vietnam, and what he perceived to be a weakening of the moral fiber of the nation. These and many other stressful issues that had been thrust upon him had, he explained, caused him great concern and had prompted him to seek President McKay's advice.

How does a layman counsel the head of the most powerful nation on earth, without prior briefing or preparation, about global issues of the greatest complexity? "Let your conscience be your guide," the Prophet advised President Johnson. "Be true to yourself and your philosophy. Let the people know that you are sincere and the people will follow you."

This advice was typical of President McKay's approach to counseling others. There was no attempt to impose his own will or to advise about specific problems as to which he was uninformed. His admonition that President Johnson rely on his own conscience reflected his belief that through the Light of Christ everyone has constant access to the source of heavenly inspiration. He was confident, therefore, that if Mr. Johnson would consult that source, he would know what he ought or ought not to do in any situation. And the admonition to "be true to yourself" suggested the need for persistence in pursuing the course his conscience might dictate.

That a close, personal relationship had been established between this pair is suggested by the bantering statement President Johnson made shortly before the Prophet and his son Lawrence left the White House: "I think we had better break up before President McKay dismisses us," said the host good-naturedly. This referred to an incident at President Eisenhower's dinner where President McKay was a guest of honor, an incident that apparently had become almost legendary at some levels of Washington society. Toward the end of the evening, President McKay, sensing that President Eisenhower was tired, suggested that the guests leave so as not to wear out their welcome. At that, the host said jokingly that it was his, not President McKay's, prerogative to indicate when the festivities were at an end.

Knowing of his sharply honed political skills, a skeptic might suspect that this invitation to the Prophet was merely a ploy of President Johnson to advance his political fortunes, especially in view of the crowd of Latter-day Saint legislators and officials he assembled at the White House to greet him and to pose for pictures. And this thesis would find support in the series of visits President and Mrs. Johnson made to Salt Lake City later in the year prior to the presidential election. On August 15, for instance, Lady Bird Johnson, the president's wife, who was on tour, ostensibly to advance the interests of her environmental projects, paid a courtesy call on the McKays in their hotel suite. President Johnson himself made an unscheduled stop in Salt Lake City on September 17 en route to Sacramento. The visitor gave the Prophet a medallion bearing Mr. Johnson's likeness as a memento, commenting at the time on how good President McKay looked. "I haven't an ache or a pain," the ailing Mormon leader answered, "I am just plain sick." Then on October 29, just a few days before the election, Mr. and Mrs. Johnson visited the Prophet at the same time, enjoying breakfast with the McKays in their apartment. That evening, the president of the United States spoke in the Tabernacle, warning that "we must not underestimate the dangers of Communism." At the same time, he counseled that we should not "underestimate the danger to all the world if nuclear power is unleashed and we don't move toward peace."

But the overtures to President McKay did not end with Lyndon B. Johnson's landslide victory in early November 1964. On November 29 he called President McKay from Washington merely to inquire about the Prophet's health. And on January 20, 1965, he called again to say that President McKay "was in his thoughts during his inaugural address" and to express appreciation for the singing of the Tabernacle Choir. A month later, after President McKay had been hospitalized, the president of the United States sent him two and a half dozen carnations to brighten his sickroom. And on May 3, 1965, President McKay received from the nation's chief executive an American flag that had flown over the capitol during the inaugural ceremonies.

And so went the relationship between two unusual leaders, so different in style and tone, yet so alike in their enthusiasms and in their mastery of the skills upon which success in their respective fields depended.

While President Johnson played out his highly visible role of personal politics, cajoling, arm-twisting, and charming the voters into supporting him with large majorities at the ballot box, another politically related drama, played at a different level, absorbed the interest of many who were concerned about the failure of some of those in government to recognize the dangers of international Communism. To remedy this, several private organizations were brought into being to alert the uninformed to this danger. One of the most prominent of these was the John Birch Society, which was and is unremitting in its attacks on Communism. Many who were concerned about the Communist threat were attracted to this organization, including Elder Ezra Taft Benson. While he was not a member of the society, Elder Benson subscribed to its views; and his son Reed Benson became actively involved, ultimately being appointed its Utah coordinator. Before his son accepted this position, however, Elder Benson discussed the matter with the Prophet. During a conversation on the subject held on October 26, 1962, President McKay told the apostle, "It is up to you and Reed as to whether or not this position is accepted."

Because Elder Benson subscribed to the views of the John Birch Society and because his son was its Utah coordinator, many Latter-day Saints reached the unwarranted conclusion that the Church had officially endorsed the society. This created misunderstandings among members, many of whom contacted Church headquarters to ascertain the true position of the Church. The result was a First Presidency statement published on January 3, 1963, which affirmed that there was no alignment between the Church and the John Birch Society. While denouncing Communism, the statement questioned the approach of the society in opposing it. Local leaders also were instructed about restrictions on the use of Church buildings for other than Church purposes.

This action of the First Presidency swung the pendulum the other way, causing some to assume erroneously that the Church opposed the John Birch Society. President McKay sought to allay this false perception in letters sent from his office answering numerous inquiries about the subject. In his diary entry of March 6, 1963, he quoted an excerpt from those letters that affirmed "that members of the church are free to join anti-Communist organizations if they desire and their membership in the church is not jeopardized by so doing. The church is not opposed to the John Birch Society or any other organization of like nature. However, it is definitely opposed to anyone using the church for the purpose of increasing membership in private organizations sponsoring these various ideologies."

The Prophet hoped this would neutralize the issue by making it plain that while the Church opposed Communism, it did not endorse the John Birch Society, although members were free to join anti-Communist organizations like the John Birch Society if they wished to do so. But this hope was not fully realized during the life of President McKay. The issue would not die. It was too fraught with significance and emotion merely to fade away. And the Latter-day Saints on both sides of it—members of goodwill who had differing perceptions of the problem and its solution—felt both free and obligated to press their views, as long as doing so did not run afoul of the doctrines of the Church or the directives of the Prophet.

President McKay occupied the middle ground on this important issue. He concurred in Elder Benson's outspoken criticism and concerns about Communism. And on one occasion, he gave Elder Benson his permission and encouragement to accept an invitation to speak at a testimonial dinner for Robert Welch, founder of the John Birch Society. Yet he had some concerns about the John Birch Society. President McKay was unwilling, however, to draw a rigid line, leaving the Brethren free to express their views and speaking out himself as he felt impressed to do—and as he did at the general conference in April 1966. At that time he made one of his strongest statements about Communism and the different groups that were fighting Communism. That this statement was the product of careful deliberation is evident from President McKay's diary entry of January 11, 1966. In reference to a discussion he had had with his counselors, he commented: "I said I think the time has come for the First Presidency to make a statement as to the church's attitude regarding Communism; that this, however, should have nothing to do with the Birch Society and should be a message from the First Presidency of the church." He noted that his counselors agreed and concluded that he was "the one who should prepare it."

The statement, which was read by the Prophet's son Robert at the general priesthood meeting on Saturday, April 9, first affirmed the Church's policy of political neutrality. "We have no intention of trying to interfere with the fullest and freest exercise of the political franchise of our members," it stated. It also affirmed that "the position of this church on the subject of Communism has never changed," noting that this ideology was the greatest threat to the advancement of "peace and prosperity and the spread of God's work among men." As to the question being asked about the Church's attitude toward various patriotic groups that were speaking out on the subject of Communism, it read: "Our immediate concern . . . is not with parties, groups, or persons, but with principle. We therefore commend and encourage every person and every group who is sincerely seeking to study constitutional principles and awaken a sleeping and apathetic people to the alarming conditions that are rapidly advancing about us." (CR, April 1966, p. 109.)

Consistent with the decision of the First Presidency on

January 11, this statement made no reference to the John Birch Society, reflecting President McKay's desire to separate the Church's position on Communism from the unfortunate controversy that had arisen about the John Birch Society. This desire was shown in action taken shortly before the April general conference when the Prophet refused to allow his picture to appear on the cover of the April 1966 issue of the *American Opinion Magazine*, which was published by the John Birch Society. Reflection convinced the president that some would wrongly infer that his picture on that magazine meant that he, and therefore the Church, endorsed the John Birch Society.

During all the years President McKay wrestled with this problem in the glare of public controversy and debate, there fermented an issue of potentially greater importance that, for the most part, was discussed only within the high councils of the Church. This related to interesting and unforeseen stirrings among certain tribes and individuals in Black Africa. It began in the early 1960s when letters began arriving at Church headquarters from persons in Africa— chiefly from Nigeria and Ghana—seeking information about the Church and requesting that representatives be sent there to baptize those who had been converted and to establish the Church locally. From the outset there had been uncertainty as to how to respond to these letters. It was easy to satisfy the requests for information by sending Church books and pamphlets, which was done. It was quite another thing to comply with the requests for representatives and for the establishment of the Church there. The problem was not one of teaching and baptizing blacks, as that had gone on intermittently through the years, although not to any significant degree. The problem rather was the establishment of the Church in a black society when the policy then in effect precluded blacks from holding the priesthood. That policy would have prevented an organization established there from being anything more than a teaching and social unit without authority in the male members to administer the usual priesthood ordinances—baptism, confirmation, the sacrament, and so on. The alternative, equally unacceptable, would have been the creation of a Church unit led by nonblacks brought in from the outside. For these reasons, the answers given to these pleading letters were friendly and were responsive to the requests for literature but noncommital about sending representatives or about establishing the Church there.

The dilemma the Prophet faced and the ultimate answer to it are suggested by this journal entry of October 4, 1960, about a letter he had received from W. Grant Bangerter, mission president in Brazil, as to whether the priesthood could be given to those with mixed blood: "I said to tell President Bangerter," wrote President McKay, "to preach the gospel to them, but for the present, until the Lord gives us another revelation, those who have negro blood are not to receive the Priesthood." He then referred to a similar instruction he had given during his tour of South America.

And the magnitude of the Prophet's dilemma is indicated by these two entries he made in midsummer 1961, when the pressures created by the correspondence from West Africa had begun to mount. On June 30, he wrote in reference to a discussion about sending Church representatives to Nigeria: "The Lord will have to let us know; and when he is ready to open the door he will tell us." The next day, after having discussed this with the Twelve, he recorded: "I spoke to the brethren about the importance of a problem that is almost as serious as the one that was faced by Peter, James and John." President McKay then referred to the practice of the early apostles of withholding the gospel from the Gentiles; to the vision of Peter at Joppa when the ancient apostle was thrice told, "what God hath cleansed, that call not thou common" (Acts 10:15); and to the later baptism of the gentile Cornelius and his household after the Holy Ghost came to them, as to which Peter had said, "Can any man forbid water, that these should not be baptized, which have received the Holy Ghost as well as we?" (Acts 10:47.)

So frustrating was the problem in the absence of a clarifying revelation that President McKay merely marked time for a year following these entries, with nothing being done other than to acknowledge the numerous letters from West Africa and to send requested literature and supplies. By March 1962, however, word of a new development was received that cried out for further action. By then some of those in West Africa who had accepted the gospel had begun to use the official name of the Church. This foreshadowed their action in officially recording the name under the laws of Nigeria. By October of that year, it was reported that there were four thousand who held themselves out as members of the Church, though they had not been baptized.

These events prompted President McKay to place West Africa under the jurisdiction of the West European Mission, where Elder N. Eldon Tanner presided. And in mid-summer 1962, it was decided that Elder Tanner and Lamar Williams of Salt Lake City would travel to West Africa to appraise the circumstances there. On November 21 President McKay set Brother Williams apart for this purpose. Two couples were also designated to go there to work under him. However, when efforts to obtain their visas failed, the Prophet instructed Elder Tanner to go there alone en route to Salt Lake City from England, where he was scheduled to assume his duties as a member of the Twelve, a position to which he had been called at the October 1962 general conference.

On January 10, 1963, Elder Tanner made a detailed report to President McKay of his visit to Nigeria, advising that while there he had dedicated that land for "missionary work to be conducted as directed by the Lord through the Prophet." The impression this newest member of the Twelve made on the Prophet at that time doubtless was an important factor in his selection nine months later to serve as a counselor in the First Presidency. "After listening to Elder Tanner's report," wrote President McKay, "I was deeply impressed that it was most fortunate that I ap-

385

pointed Elder Tanner to go to Nigeria to look into the opening of the work there. I don't know of another man who could have met the conditions so favorably and intelligently as Brother Tanner did."

Parenthetically, it seems more than coincidental that less than six weeks before receiving Elder Tanner's report, President McKay interviewed a young leader who would be called to fill the vacancy in the Twelve caused by N. Eldon Tanner's call to the First Presidency. It was November 30, 1962, that President McKay made this significant entry: "Brother Thomas S. Monson, formerly President of the Canadian Mission, came in by appointment and reported to the First Presidency his presidency of the Canadian Mission. I have never heard a more excellent report from any mission president. His work among the Catholics in that mission has been very successful. Many of them have joined the church. I was very impressed with Brother Monson and remarked to my counselors, 'We must keep our eye on that man. He is very choice and capable.' "

It was not until August of 1965 that Lamar Williams finally received a visa to visit Nigeria. By that time the attitude toward establishing a proselyting mission there had changed, and Brother Williams was authorized merely to study the situation without making any commitments, and to report back. He submitted his findings to President McKay and his counselors on November 10, 1965. Thereafter, no action was taken with respect to West Africa during the administration of President David O. McKay, other than to respond to the many letters sent from there to Church headquarters and to send literature and other materials as requested. The ultimate resolution of the dilemma involving West Africa was to await further revelation from the Lord, which was not to come until more than eight years after the passing of President McKay. That revelation, received in 1978 by President Spencer W. Kimball would, like the vision given to Peter of old, dissolve the difficulties and uncertainties that President McKay and his predecessors had faced with respect to priesthood and the blacks and the work of the Church in Africa.

Chapter Twenty-Five

Administrative
Challenges
and Complexities

L ike colored threads in a tapestry, there were numerous issues and problems interwoven with those touched on in the previous chapter that intermittently claimed President McKay's attention over a period of several years. Two of the most important and controversial of these were the proposed transfer of Ricks College from Rexburg, Idaho, to Idaho Falls and the proposal to establish a network of junior colleges as branches of the Brigham Young University.

The Ricks College issue, which undoubtedly was one of the most stressful problems President McKay faced during his administration, was foreshadowed by a letter Arthur D. Browne wrote to William F. Edwards on December 31, 1953. In it the writer expressed the opinion that in terms of transportation routes, employment, housing opportunities for students, and other considerations, "there is little question that Ricks should be moved to Idaho Falls." He astutely observed, however, that the main obstacles would be "the cost" and "the delicate public relations involved." Subsequent events would prove that these two obstacles were insurmountable, although there were times during the interim when the ultimate outcome was in doubt.

The issue was actually joined in April 1957 when on the sixteenth the Church Board of Education unanimously approved moving Ricks College to Idaho Falls. This action was preceded by a special meeting of the First Presidency held on April 8, during the general conference, and attended by President Ernest L. Wilkinson of Brigham Young University; John L. Clark, president of Ricks College; and the stake presidents from the Rexburg-Idaho Falls areas. At that meeting, President Wilkinson made a detailed presentation of the facts supporting the proposed move. Of the results of this meeting, President McKay merely noted, "No decision was reached on this problem," indicating either that he was not convinced at that time of the need or wisdom of the move, or that any action had to be taken by the entire board of education.

Almost immediately after word of the board's decision was circulated, strong opposition to it began to surface. On April 25, 1957, President McKay received a telephone call from Steven Meikle, the president of a bank in Rexburg, who expressed concern about the financial problems that would be created if Ricks College were to be moved to Idaho Falls. "People planned on making payments on homes from rents to college students," the caller told the Prophet. Later the same day, President McKay received a call from his friend Orval Adams, a Salt Lake banker, who advised that 217 new homes had been built and 82 new businesses had been started in Rexburg in the previous five years. He told the Prophet that "a lot of this was done on the strength that the college would remain in Rexburg." Five days later, Steven Meikle and several stake presidents from the Rexburg area made a presentation to the First Presidency showing why the college should not be moved.

So concerned was President McKay about this issue that he made special trips to Rexburg on May 21 and June 1, 1957. On the last-mentioned visit, a lengthy meeting was held with fifteen stake presidents and several local civic officials where the pros and cons of the issue were aired in detail. Among the speakers was Ernest L. Wilkinson, who made a three-hour presentation to support the transfer decision. After considering the evidence from both sides, President McKay decided on July 11, 1957, that the move would not be made, a decision that was approved by the First Presidency and the Church Board of Education. President McKay was concerned that if the move were made, the buildings at Rexburg "would be left standing as ghosts," an irritating reminder of the lost cause. This and other critical factors caused him to conclude that it was not "worth the cost to move Ricks College from Rexburg to Idaho Falls."

But, like Banquo's ghost, this issue would not stay down. On October 29, 1958, fifteen months after the decision had been made to leave the college in Rexburg, five stake presidents from the Idaho Falls area wrote to the First Presidency advising that there was a movement afoot to establish a state junior college in Idaho Falls. The stake presidents argued that the transfer of Ricks to Idaho Falls would mean four times as many students as at Rexburg and would give the Church more influence in educational matters throughout the state. They also strongly implied that Latter-day Saints residing in Idaho Falls would overwhelmingly elect to go to the state junior college in their community rather than to travel to Ricks in Rexburg.

This matter was brought to President McKay by his counselors two days later at a special meeting held in the Prophet's home. It was held there because he had undergone cataract eye surgery a few days before and had not yet returned to his office. The patient had recorded on October 27 that he was then in "the most miserable stage of the eye operation," adding that "the stitches are very irritating to the eye." It was under these circumstances that David O. McKay reluctantly followed the advice of his counselors and reversed the decision not to transfer Ricks College. Predictably, this touched off another round of appeals from Church and civic leaders in Rexburg. On November 15, at a large meeting held in Rexburg, these leaders rejected the idea that a state junior college would be established in Idaho Falls. Meanwhile, they industriously prepared and circulated a pamphlet detailing the background of the controversy from their perspective and criticizing the role of

David O. McKay

Ernest L. Wilkinson in advocating the transfer. A copy of this pamphlet was given to President McKay and his counselors at a meeting they held with the presidency of the Rexburg Stake on February 10, 1959. The First Presidency showed their displeasure with the tone of this instrument through an editorial in the *Deseret News* three days later that sharply criticized the pamphlet.

Here the matter remained at rest for over a year with no overt action being taken to move the school. And by June of 1960, President Ernest L. Wilkinson could see the handwriting on the wall. On the twenty-fifth, President McKay told him in a private conference that he had "never felt good" about the transfer. Five days later, the Prophet made a complete report of the Ricks affair to the First Presidency and the Twelve in which he indicated his dissatisfaction with the decision to transfer the college, stating that he "could not feel right about moving the school from Rexburg to Idaho Falls and spending seven million dollars in building a new school, leaving standing at Rexburg at least three new buildings on campus."

Although no formal action was taken by the Church Board of Education on the matter, this date, June 30, 1960, marked the end of any viable prospect that the move would take place. Still, hope remained among the advocates of the move as there had been no formal announcement of a change in attitude on the part of President McKay and the other high leaders of the Church. So on September 7, 1960, representatives of the pro-move faction contacted the Prophet to ask why the construction of buildings at Idaho Falls had not commenced. And again on December 2, 1960, another delegation from Idaho Falls called on President McKay, urging that action be taken to implement the prior decision to move the college.

Although formal action to rescind the decision to move the college to Idaho Falls was never taken by the Church Board of Education, advocates of the move finally realized that their efforts had failed when in April 1961 it was announced that a new library, gymnasium, and other buildings would be constructed on the Rexburg campus. Not even the most sanguine advocates of the move could ignore the implications of this announcement. Instead of being moved to Idaho Falls, Ricks was to be planted even deeper in Rexburg. And the extent of that planting is suggested by the fact that by 1975, seventeen million dollars had been expended in renovating and enlarging Ricks's physical plant.

In tandem with the debate over the proposed move of Ricks College was an equally contentious argument of whether to establish a network of Church-operated junior colleges subordinate to Brigham Young University. The supporters of this proposal, again led by Ernest L. Wilkinson, reasoned that the anticipated growth of the Church would make it impossible to accommodate all LDS college students at BYU and that to provide the desired moral atmosphere and religious instruction for those students would require the establishment of junior colleges in outlying areas. The members of the board found this persuasive, and on December 5, 1957, they authorized the purchase of tracts of land in Salt Lake City and Los Angeles, California, for this purpose. At the same time, an enrollment cap of 15,000 was placed on the size of the BYU student body and approval was given to investigate the availability and price of possible junior-college sites in Phoenix, Arizona; San Francisco, California; Portland, Oregon; Spokane, Washington; and Boise-Caldwell, Idaho. By the summer of 1960, the Church had purchased approximately 1,650 acres of land as junior-college sites in five states at a cost of over eight million dollars. It was proposed that each junior college in the system would have a maximum enrollment of 5,000 students.

As the number of proposed junior-college sites multiplied and as the potential cost of constructing and maintaining buildings on them and bearing the heavy, continuing cost of administration and faculty salaries became apparent, serious doubts about the feasibility of the entire project took root among members of the board. The alternative plan, urged by the opponents of the junior-college concept, was to enlarge the Church institute program. This, they believed, would make it possible to provide religious instruction for LDS students on university campuses while, at the same time, providing Church-sponsored social activities and, in many instances, enabling LDS students to remain at or very near home. Moreover, the cost of this option, it was pointed out, would be far less than to gear up for a massive construction program on many widely scattered campuses and for the recruitment and continuing maintenance of large, expensive administrative and faculty staffs whose efforts would be devoted largely to the administration and instruction of subjects beyond the scope of the LDS religion.

One of the leading exponents of this alternate plan, and one whose opinion President McKay valued highly, was George Romney, president of the Detroit Stake and the chief executive officer of American Motors, who expressed his concerns to the Prophet in a letter dated February 2, 1959. He questioned whether the Church could afford to provide secular as well as religious instruction for all its college-age students. He raised an alarm also about sending young students away from home: "As Michigan parents," he told President McKay, "some of us would rather see our young people stay home for their undergraduate education." And he endorsed the institute program as providing a means to resolve the questions he raised while offering special religious instruction to the church's maturing young adults.

As a professional educator, the Prophet clearly understood the competing considerations on both sides of this issue. He had approved the decision of December 5, 1957, although his counselors, Stephen L Richards and J. Reuben Clark, and President Joseph Fielding Smith of the Twelve had actually spearheaded the move for approval. As time wore on, however, and as the issues and attending problems came into clearer focus, he began to move away from the junior-college concept. Two main factors, both growing out of the same root, account for this shift in position. The root cause was the rapid growth of the Church internationally. The financial demands this entailed, arising from the exorbitant cost of new buildings, had created serious cash-flow problems. "Until the income of the church will justify the junior college program," President McKay noted on September 21, 1960, "it should not be undertaken." By July 1962 the financial status of the Church had worsened to the point that on the twentieth President McKay gave instruction that "every effort should be [made] to increase our revenues." He also "instructed that the expenditures of the building committee should be reduced to a minimum."

Meanwhile, as the membership ranks swelled in countries far less affluent than the United States, a concern grew that it would be unwise and inequitable to expend the vast sums the junior-college program would require for the education of Latter-day Saints in the United States while ignoring or short-changing those in economically depressed countries. A chief exponent of this view was Elder Boyd K. Packer, then an Assistant to the Twelve, who is also a professional educator. In a letter dated February 18, 1963, Elder Packer suggested that Church educational funds could be better spent teaching illiterate members in Mexico rather than building up a vast educational structure in the United States. He therefore recommended a reevaluation of the junior-college proposal.

In less than a year from the date of this letter, the junior-college proposal was moribund. Three intervening events had practically assured its demise. First, on July 3, 1963, at a joint meeting of the Church Board of Education and the BYU Trustees, it was decided that the institute program be extended, that consideration be given to the educational needs of members in foreign countries, and that thereafter, if the funds of the Church would warrant it, the junior-college program should go forward. Second, in September 1963, William F. Edwards, a financial advisor to the First Presidency, expressed the opinion that the Church could not meet its existing commitments without dipping into its reserves. On this account, the budget committee decided that construction on the junior colleges would have to be delayed. And third, in January 1964, Ernest L. Wilkinson resigned as the president of BYU to run for the U.S. Senate. As he had been its prime advocate, President Wilkinson's departure sealed the doom of the junior-college program. However, because of the other deterring factors already mentioned, it is highly doubtful that this program would have gone forward even had President Wilkinson remained at BYU.

While the abandonment of the junior-college program was a great disappointment to those who had sponsored it, the time, effort, and expense it entailed were not wasted. The land purchased for the campus sites was later sold at greatly increased prices. And the hours of research, analysis, and preparation devoted to the development of the concept helped President McKay and his associates to reevaluate educational goals and procedures of the Church and to chart a course that harmonized with the demands made by a rapidly growing, international organization.

These and other educational matters that intermittently claimed President McKay's attention were an extension of his prophetic role as the presiding high priest of the Church, ultimately responsible for the training and motivation of its members. And, as in the cases of Ricks College and the junior-college proposal, the issues involving that role were usually given wide publicity. On the other hand, his many activities connected with his role as the corporation sole, in which he directed the financial, business, and other temporal affairs of the Church, received little publicity. The stock in the Church-owned or Church-controlled corporations was held in the name of the corporation sole, and was voted by the Prophet, who in legal contemplation was the corporation sole, for the election of their boards of directors. These, in turn, elected the officers who then managed their business affairs according to rules and procedures established by the articles and by-laws of the companies, or by their boards of directors. The ultimate control was, therefore, vested in the Prophet, who held and voted the stock. In addition, however, he had a direct hand in the management of many of them through service as a board member or officer. At various times during the active years of his administration, President McKay served as a board member, executive committee member, president, or chairman of the board of these companies, including Zion's Savings Bank and Trust Company, Zion's First National Bank, Hotel Utah, ZCMI, Heber J. Grant Company, Layton Sugar Company, Beneficial Life Insurance Company, Utah Home Fire Insurance Company, Utah-Idaho Sugar Company, Deseret Ranches of Florida, KSL Corporation, and Bonneville International Corporation. In addition, during most of his presidential tenure, he served as chairman of the Church Board of Education and of the Brigham Young University Board of Trustees. He was also the chairman of the Church Committee on Expenditures and presided over the Council on the Disposition of the Tithes, which controlled all Church finances and expenditures. The various and continuing meetings of these companies or organizations made substantial demands on the time and energies of President McKay, and his diaries are honeycombed with references to his involvement in them. It is true that he had much expert assistance in handling these matters and that through delegations he was able to distribute and therefore to lighten the load. Still, the weight and complexity of these accumulated responsibilities, even after delegations had been made, were such as to create a sense of wonderment in those who observed him in action. Some inkling of the pressures his mountainous duties generated, and the perceptions of those close to the Prophet who watched as he shouldered them, can be gained from a letter written to him under date of November 9, 1962, by Elder Richard L. Evans of the Twelve. The apostle, who called his communication a "fan" letter, stated in part: "A week ago Thursday I was in your office at about 7:30 A.M. . . . and Friday at about 8 A.M. with Arch Madsen, presenting problems and decisions to you pertaining to the Tabernacle and other KSL matters. Then, Tuesday morning I was with you [and] Brother Lee early and long, on matters involving a complex correlation program—and then Wednesday I was with you [and] Brother Mark Petersen, as we presented the World's Fair program—and then watched you go through nearly a two and a half hour BYU meeting with complex problems and weighty financial matters and decisions, and the meeting with the Twelve and Presidency yesterday, and this morning with the auxiliary heads—and when I see how wisely and considerately and patiently you handle all problems and personalities—and know that you do it early and late, day after day, I marvel at it. It is beyond comparison and almost beyond belief. . . . I know that what you accomplish is in fact a miracle." (DOMP.)

The import of Elder Evans' comments is even more significant when it is remembered that the writer was speaking of a man who was already in his ninetieth year and that his contacts with President McKay over the week he described represented only a small part of the Prophet's agenda during that period.

The role President McKay played as to the Church owned or controlled corporations was not a passive one. He was actively involved and interested in what transpired at the meetings he attended. And his voice was heard and heeded. Moreover, outside the formal meetings he attended, his influence, prestige and personality exerted a powerful and positive influence on the direction and activities of the companies. Not the least of his contributions in the realm of personal influence and diplomacy was his role as a personnel recruiter. Those whom President McKay invited to participate in either church or business affairs ordinarily responded with enthusiasm and alacrity. In late 1956, for instance, Zions First National Bank, of which President McKay was chairman of the board, was searching for a new president. A prime candidate was David M. Kennedy who was a vice-president of the Continental Illinois National Bank and Trust in Chicago. As the Prophet had planned a trip to inspect the Church ranching properties in Florida, with an intermediate stop in Chicago to spend Thanksgiving with Lou Jean and Russell Blood, he wrote Brother Kennedy on November 20, requesting an interview on the 23rd, a Friday. When he discussed the matter with the Chicago banker, who was a prominent and active member of the Church there, President McKay learned that the announcement of Brother Kennedy's appointment as the President of Continental was to be made the following Monday, November 26. (Memo from D. M. Kennedy to Author, Sept. 5, 1984.) An indication of the Prophetic influence and of the banker's willingness to do what was asked by his Church leader is shown in David Kennedy's statement to President McKay that if desired he would rescind his agreement to serve as Continental's president and would instead accept the presidency of Zions in Salt Lake City. On learning the facts, the Prophet urged his friend to remain at Continental from where, years later, he was recruited to serve as the Secretary of the Treasury in the United States cabinet and afterward as the U.S. Ambassador at large. More recently, David M. Kennedy has served as a Special Representative of the First Presidency, rendering vital service in delicate negotiations around the world, with heads of state and other high government leaders, to smooth the way for the growth and development of the Church.

In Florida, the Prophet spent four days riding over the ranch owned by the Church near Deer Park, examining with a practiced eye the livestock and improvements on this 210,000-acre spread. He was pleased with what he found, and, accustomed to the comparatively small acreages the McKays had managed near Huntsville, he was amazed at the enormous size and complexity of this Florida ranching operation.

President McKay intermingled several Church matters with the temporal affairs that had beckoned him to Florida. On November 25, he dedicated a new stake center in Jacksonville; and the following day he inspected a new branch chapel under construction in Orlando. He was displeased with the small size of this building, so he "called the church architect immediately" to give instructions to "enlarge the rooms." On the thirtieth, after completing his inspection of the ranch properties, he engaged in what for him was a once-in-a-lifetime diversion. He went deep sea fishing! Elder Henry D. Moyle, who had been involved in the development of the Florida Ranch, had made arrangements with the Phillips Petroleum Company for the use of its seagoing yacht. "Within an hour," President McKay noted with some excitement, "we had hooked a sail fish. I was handed the line to drag him in. But I knew that Brother Moyle had waited five years to catch a sail fish; so I handed the line to him and within fifteen minutes he had pulled him in." This modern Peter, fisher of men, then noted with some pride: "He weighed 42 pounds and was seven feet one inch long. I caught two bonitos and a king fish."

Chapter Twenty-Six

The Counselors

Within less than three years from his one and only deep-sea fishing experience, President McKay extended an unexpected call to Henry D. Moyle, to whom he had unexpectedly handed the line with which the apostle landed his gigantic sailfish. On June 11, 1959, President McKay made this significant journal entry: "Elder Henry D. Moyle came to my office following a council meeting to take up some welfare matters with me. Following our conversation on welfare problems, I told Brother Moyle that I had chosen him to be my second counselor." The following day he extended the call to President J. Reuben Clark to serve as the first counselor in the reorganized First Presidency, quoting President Clark as having said in response, "I don't want you to feel obligated to take me; but I feel honored by being asked. And I pledge you my whole hearted support; and all that I have I want to give to the cause and to the support of the church and the First Presidency; and I pledge my allegiance to you." Later the same day, President McKay presented his choice of counselors to the Twelve, who promptly ratified it. And six days later he set them apart. "I am sure and bear testimony," the Prophet wrote of the event, "that after the experience of the last week or two that the Lord's will was done when President Clark and President Moyle were set

David O. McKay

The First Presidency, April 5, 1961. Left to right: J. Reuben Clark, first counselor; David O. McKay, president; Henry D. Moyle, second counselor.

apart this morning as first and second counselors in the First Presidency."

These changes in the presiding quorum of the Church were made necessary by the death of President Stephen L Richards on May 19, 1959. The departure of this loyal friend was one of the chief sorrows of David O. McKay's entire administration. The understanding between this pair was almost perfect. Their personalities and styles were complementary, and their long relationship had created a special bond that was never duplicated outside the Prophet's family. It was based upon mutual respect, trust, and understanding and an awareness of the different yet interlocking roles they played and of the varying duties and prerogatives inherent in those roles. They seemed to understand instinctively the unseen and unspoken, yet real, boundaries that set them apart as individuals and Church officials. And they meticulously observed the gentlemanly rules of conduct and procedure governing that relationship.

It is no wonder, then, that when President McKay learned of the death of his friend, he broke down and wept. "The news of his passing was a terrible shock to me," he wrote. "He was as dear to me as a brother. A true and loyal friend. A wise counselor with one of the greatest minds in the church. Oh! how I shall miss him."

The sense of desolation this statement implies never quite left the Prophet during the rest of his life. He had many friends and acquaintances but few confidants. The other counselors who served him were able and dedicated men who possessed extraordinary skills and who were anxious to serve the president. But none of them had the unusual combination of abilities and characteristics found in Stephen L Richards that made him so valuable to a man whose leadership skills were intensely personal and charismatic. President McKay was, in a sense, the antithesis of the traditional "organization man." The essence of his leadership lay in the commitment, enthusiasm, and industry he generated among the Saints through his words and example. It did not lie in the structure and direction of vast and complex organizations and programs. If a chapel were needed, his most likely direction would have been "Build it," not "Prepare plans and specifications for review and consideration." His directive would have necessarily implied the requisite planning and follow-through; but his chief interest would have been in the result, not in the elaborate steps leading to the result. It was the role of detailed follow-through and wise counseling that Stephen L Richards played so well, never attempting to run ahead of or at cross purposes with his leader, always subordinating his desires to those of the Prophet, while, at the same time, providing sound advice as to the course being pursued, but in a kindly, diplomatic, and nonthreatening way.

It was a boon to President McKay and the Church that a man of Henry D. Moyle's experience and ability was called to the First Presidency at the death of Stephen L

David O. McKay

Richards. He was a vigorous seventy-year-old, having been a member of the Twelve for a dozen years and before that having rendered distinguished service as a stake president and as one of the early leaders of the welfare program. He was an attorney who had combined his legal expertise with a flair for business enterprise, which had brought him considerable wealth and a wide range of business and professional acquaintances. His style was almost diametrically opposite that of Stephen L Richards. Where President Richards had been scholarly, reticent, and low key, Henry D. Moyle was an outspoken, driving activist. To him the main criteria by which administrative success could be measured was results. And to get results, he was prone to cut through red tape and to disregard what he considered to be needless bureaucratic restrictions. With the harvest of converts beginning to crest as the result of President McKay's expansionary initiatives, and with an accompanying increased demand for physical facilities, it was essential that there be a driving force at the highest level to keep the cycles of growth in proper sync. With President McKay, who was in his upper eighties, being heavily occupied charting the course and providing overall leadership; and with President Clark, who was nearing ninety, being physically unable to carry a heavy administrative burden, this driving force was provided chiefly by President Henry D. Moyle. On the one hand, his strong influence was felt in proselyting when he was made chairman of the Missionary Executive Committee; and on the other hand, he played a key role in Church finances and construction. During the four years of his service in the First Presidency, from 1959 to 1963, there was a greater numerical growth in Church membership than during any previous comparable period in Church history. And during 1961, the Church for the first time had a membership growth of over 100,000. With this, of course, came a corresponding increase in budgets, buildings, and expenditures.

Such extraordinary growth exerted powerful pressure on the general leadership of the Church, which was already stretched paper thin. To provide some relief, it was decided in June 1961 to ordain some members of the First Council of Seventy high priests so as to enable them to handle organizational matters when they filled stake assignments. So on the eleventh of the month, Elders Antoine R. Ivins, S. Dilworth Young, Milton R. Hunter, and Bruce R. McConkie of that council were ordained high priests at the direction of President McKay. And, eleven days later, the Prophet took action to alleviate administrative pressures at the highest level of the Church when Elder Hugh B. Brown of the Twelve was called to serve as a third counselor in the First Presidency. The rapidly declining health of President J. Reuben Clark and the rapidly accelerating pace of Church growth and activity made this action imperative. Symbolic of the need to shore up the foundations of General Authority leadership is the fact that on the same day Elder Brown was called to the First Presidency, a special meeting was held with 150 stake presidents to instruct them in policies and procedures governing stake missionary work, the implementation of which, it was expected, would further fuel the already booming growth of the Church.

President Brown had experienced a meteoric rise in the hierarchal order of the Church, having arisen from an Assistant to the Twelve in 1953 to the First Presidency in 1961. Perhaps because of that, he remonstrated with President McKay about his call, suggesting that there were at least eleven other men more qualified than he to fill that high position. In the answer he received, the new counselor gained an important insight into his status and into the preeminent role of the eighty-eight-year-old prophet: "I remind you, Brother Brown," President McKay told his new counselor, "that the right of nomination does not rest in you, but in me; and you are the nominee!"

The seventy-seven-year-old third counselor was eminently qualified for his new position. A lawyer by profession, President Brown had served in the Canadian Army as a young man, attaining the rank of major; had served on the faculty of the Brigham Young University; and at various times had been engaged in government service and business enterprises. In the Church, before becoming a General Authority, he had served as a stake president, mission president, and the coordinator of LDS servicemen. He was tall, personable, and dignified, and was an articulate and persuasive speaker. Such a wide range of experiences and abilities provided President McKay with an important resource as he pursued his presidential goals.

Hugh B. Brown's tenure as a third counselor was short lived, as President J. Reuben Clark passed away on October 6, 1961, less than four months after Elder Brown was called to the First Presidency. Six days after President Clark's death, Henry D. Moyle was installed as the first counselor and Hugh B. Brown as the second counselor.

The First Presidency, April 20, 1962. Left to Right: *David O. McKay, president; Henry D. Moyle, first counselor; Hugh B. Brown, second counselor.*

The death of President J. Reuben Clark ended a career of twenty-eight and a half years of continuous service as a counselor in the First Presidency, except for a few days following the deaths of Heber J. Grant and George Albert Smith while the First Presidency was disorganized. No other counselor has even approached this record, except George Q. Cannon, whose service spanned twenty-eight years; but the continuity was interrupted for approximately five years while the First Presidency was disorganized after the deaths of Brigham Young, John Taylor, and Wilford Woodruff. And except for the first eighteen months of his service as a counselor, President Clark had served in the First Presidency with David O. McKay. So for twenty-seven years these two powerful, strong-minded men had toiled side by side in the presiding council of the Church. During that period, untold thousands of issues were presented to the First Presidency for decision. It would be fanciful to assume that the views of these two men always coincided. They did not. Given differences in personality, training, and perception, this was inevitable. But these differences never affected the warmth of their relationship nor the depth of their love and admiration for each other. More important, any differences they may have had while an issue was under discussion were always concealed afterward by their commitment to the principal of apostolic unity: once a decision has been made by the presiding authority, the decision is given the unqualified support of all members of the council, who are silent thereafter about any contrary opinions expressed during the discussion.

President McKay and President Clark were meticulous in observing the restraints imposed by this principle. Nor did they ever by word or action indicate any public disagreement with policies adopted by the First Presidency or with each other. As far as they were concerned, they and the First Presidency were one without difference or distinction—at least one in unity and purpose.

Under these circumstances, it is curious that some observers, unacquainted with the inner workings of the

Church hierarchy, have attempted to picture this pair as representatives of two opposite camps among the high leaders of the Church, alluding to them by the generic terms "McKay men" and "Clark men," and implying that they sought different objectives and were working at cross-purposes. Such an erroneous view impugns the integrity of both men, questions the validity of the principle of apostolic unity, and attributes to them qualities of ambition and self-seeking routinely found among leaders in secular organizations but wholly inconsistent with their roles as apostles of the Lord Jesus Christ. One may wonder whether the appraisals of those who hold such views are more self-portraits than an accurate portrayal of the men about whom they write or speak.

The fact is that there was an immutable bond of love, understanding, and admiration between David O. McKay and J. Reuben Clark. This was never more evident than during the last few weeks before President Clark's death. On September 1, 1961, the Prophet called at the Clark residence to wish his counselor a happy ninetieth birthday. And on the twenty-third, thirteen days before President Clark's death, he called again to ascertain the counselor's view about reorganizing the presiding Bishopric with John H. Vandenburg as the new Presiding bishop and Robert L. Simpson and Victor L. Brown as counselors. "Whatever you brethren have decided, I approve," he told the Prophet. Of the conversation that took place afterward, President McKay said: "We went back to our school days. President Clark was very emotional as he recalled the school days and particularly the twenty-seven years we have stood shoulder to shoulder in the First Presidency. We caressed and bid each other good bye. I left the house with a heavy heart." And at the funeral services on October 10, President McKay said of his friend and counselor: "A truly great man has gone back to his creator. He will be able to say truly as Paul said to Timothy: 'I have fought a good fight, I have finished my course, I have kept the faith.' "

Two days after President Clark's funeral, the First Presidency was reorganized with Henry D. Moyle as first counselor and Hugh B. Brown as second counselor. The ensuing year was one of extraordinary activity and achievement for the First Presidency and the Church. All three members of the presidency were well and active. The Prophet continued with his heavy travel schedule, and the counselors turned to their duties with enthusiasm and vigor. During 1961, the Church experienced a growth of approximately a hundred and thirty thousand, and in the following year this was increased to a hundred and forty-two thousand, an all-time high. Much of this growth was attributable to the dedicated work of President Henry D. Moyle, who, in order to increase skills and results, had begun to tour extensively, holding special instructional and motivational meetings throughout the Church with missionaries, mission presidents, and other leaders. Accompanying and participating with him on these tours was Elder Gordon B. Hinckley of the Twelve, who served under President Moyle's direction in the counselor's capacity as the chairman of the Missionary Executive Committee. While the results attest to the effectiveness of this procedure, some aspects of it gave pause to some members of the Twelve. Of principal concern was the fact that this approach short-circuited the customary channels in proselyting, since the Twelve was and is the General Missionary Committee of the Church. This concern prompted two ranking members of the Twelve to discuss the matter privately with President McKay on August 7, 1962. The visitors apparently convinced the Prophet that any beneficial results of this procedure were outweighed by negative considerations, because he broached the subject in a First Presidency meeting held two days later. At that time he indicated to President Moyle that the meetings he had been conducting with missionaries should be discontinued. "I indicated that the brethren of the Twelve are subject to the President of the Twelve," he told President Moyle, "and should go out under the direction of the Twelve and not under the direction of the First Presidency." This instruction to his counselor was formalized on January 31,

1963, when President McKay reorganized the Missionary Executive Committee, appointing Joseph Fielding Smith as the new chairman; Harold B. Lee as vice-chairman; and Marion G. Romney, Gordon B. Hinckley, and Boyd K. Packer as members. While this action released President Moyle from his leadership of the Missionary Executive Committee, he was instructed by the Prophet "to keep his hand on the situation."

Such a change for a man of Henry D. Moyle's energetic, driving propensities—from a role of aggressive, executive leadership to one of a somewhat passive, advisory nature—was difficult to accept. But he did so with good grace, although not without some regret and upset.

President Moyle passed away on September 18, 1963, at Deer Park, Florida. He died in his sleep, unexpectedly and peacefully, while on one of his many visits to inspect the progress of the Florida Ranch.

The passing of this able man was a terrible blow to President McKay, particularly because it was only four months before that the ninety-year-old Prophet had been injured when he was dragged by his horse, Sonny Boy. In the interval, he had suffered a temporary loss of speech, which had alarmed his family and the Brethren. His physical condition was very much on the Prophet's mind the day after President Moyle's death. Discussing the future with the Brethren, he said, "I am looking forward to more years. I said that I expected I would be here until the Lord says I am ready to go and that I would work as long as I can. I said that my legs are lazy but otherwise I feel fine."

Funeral services for President Moyle were held on September 21, when President McKay and the other speakers extolled his character and achievements. On the same day, the Prophet made this appraisal of his friend: "President Moyle was a very active, energetic counselor; always willing to respond to any call that was given to him. He was able, intelligent and untiring in his duties relating to the First Presidency."

Who could replace Henry D. Moyle? Sarah Tanner,

wife of N. Eldon Tanner, asked herself the same question at the cemetery after President Moyle's funeral. Because it was raining, she had remained in the car while her husband had gone with the other General Authorities to the grave site for the dedicatory prayer. As she reflected prayerfully on the events of the day, the question was formed in her mind: "Who could replace President Moyle?" Almost immediately the shocking answer came: "Your husband." She kept this revelatory thought to herself until it had been embodied in fact.

There was at least one other living person to whom this spiritual insight was given—the Prophet David O. McKay. "By appointment, Elder N. Eldon Tanner came into my private office," President McKay recorded on October 3, 1963. "At this time I told him that I should like him to be the second counselor in the First Presidency of the church. Brother Tanner was greatly overcome. It was hard for him

The First Presidency, October 10, 1963. Left to right: Hugh B. Brown, first counselor; David O. McKay, president; N. Eldon Tanner, second counselor.

to understand why the youngest in point of service should be selected. I told him that it is the Lord's will. With tears in his eyes, he accepted it with all his heart and said that he would do the best he could."

Later the same day, the Prophet called Hugh B. Brown as his first counselor and Thomas S. Monson as the new member of the Twelve, filling the vacancy created by Elder Tanner's call. President McKay's interview with Elder Monson was especially poignant: "I told him of his call as an apostle of the Lord," he wrote of his meeting with the thirty-six-year-old printing executive. "He seemed stunned for a moment. . . . My heart melted with his as I remembered the call I had come to me in my youth. I was thirty two years of age so I could fully sympathize with Elder Monson in the great obligation that has come to him."

These calls, which were ratified by the Twelve and the general conference, added significant strength to the presiding councils of the Church. Of special importance to President McKay at the moment was Elder Tanner's call to the First Presidency. In him the Prophet found a man of strength and integrity who had demonstrated administrative skills in Church, government, and business affairs in Canada. Though he had come to the presiding councils of the Church in 1960 at the comparatively advanced age of sixty-two, he had been well known to the General Authorities for many years and was uniformly admired and respected by them. On June 1, 1956, for instance, President Tanner received an honorary doctorate from Brigham Young University at commencement exercises presided over by President McKay. It was a coincidence that Hugh B. Brown, then a comparatively new Assistant to the Twelve, delivered the baccalaureate address at this commencement.

President Tanner, who, coincidentally, was President Brown's nephew, took over most of the duties that had been performed by President Moyle, including principal responsibility for financial and business affairs. Those were the areas of his special expertise and interest. President Tanner was deliberate, meticulous, and precise. He was a man of few words with great analytical skills and the ability to reduce a problem to its most basic elements or to summarize a lengthy discussion so as to omit all nonessentials. He was, therefore, an ideal headquarters man, organized, diligent, and prompt.

As already noted, the unfortunate accident at Huntsville involving the Prophet's horse, Sonny Boy, which seemed to trigger a series of physical problems, occurred just a few months before Hugh B. Brown and N. Eldon Tanner were installed as first and second counselors. While these problems did not disable President McKay, they slowed him down so that he was unable to carry the heavy load of administrative responsibility he had once carried with such ease. With the rapid growth of the Church, which inevitably increased the work load of the First Presidency, and with the preoccupation of the counselors in handling their responsibilities, President McKay, very soon after the death of President Moyle and the onset of his physical problems, began to reach out to others for assistance. At first, the one he turned to principally was Elder Thorpe B. Isaacson, Assistant to the Twelve and former counselor in the Presiding Bishopric. There had been a close working relationship between them since 1946 when the latter was sustained as second counselor in the Presiding Bishopric.

Elder Isaacson had had wide experience in business, educational, civic, and Church affairs. Before his call as a General Authority, he had been a successful insurance executive. He had served as a director of the Heber J. Grant Company; the Bank of Ogden; the Metropolitan Water Board; the Utah Symphony; the University of Utah Board of Regents; and the Utah State University board of trustees. As to the latter, he was elected as president of the board for seven consecutive terms. Later he became a consultant to the U.S. commissioner of education and a member of the Utah Little Hoover Commission. Elder Isaacson had also filled a special assignment for the federal government inspecting foreign-aid operations in the Near East and other foreign countries in connection with which he visited France, Italy,

Israel, Lebanon, Turkey, and Iran. He had served as president of the Utah Valley Hospital, the Ogden Dee Hospital, and the Logan LDS Hospital and as a board member of the LDS Hospital in Salt Lake City; as chairman of the Historic Sites Committee; as a director of the Beehive Clothing Mills; and as a member of the Church personnel and retirement committees.

These, then, were some of the qualifications of the man whom President McKay began to call upon for assistance soon after the First Presidency was reorganized in October 1963. The Prophet was frequently in touch with him about special matters in which he was interested. On February 25, 1964, for instance, President McKay recorded that he had conferred with Elder Isaacson "about several important items." Soon after, on March 17, 1964, the Prophet advised Elder Isaacson that he wanted him to occupy the office in the northwest corner of the main floor of the Administration Building. Being the office that President J. Reuben Clark had occupied for so many years, this placed him strategically close to the Prophet's office, with only the First Presidency's council room separating the two. Over the months that followed, the extent to which President McKay intended to use Elder Isaacson clearly emerged. On April 8, he was invited to meet with the First Presidency to discuss matters pertaining to the Church's Florida properties; on July 23 the Prophet appointed him to the board of Nauvoo Restoration, Inc.; and five days later, he represented President McKay at a ceremony in Washington, D.C. On October 21, 1964, the Prophet assigned him to work on a sensitive problem involving Church properties in San Jose, California; on November 30, Elder Isaacson was appointed to the board of the Hotel Utah and several months later was placed on the executive committee; on December 15, he was appointed to the board of station WRUL, and he was instructed by President McKay to study and make recommendations about the reorganization of the Church Building Committee.

It soon became apparent therefore that President McKay was using Elder Isaacson as his executive assistant in matters as to which he had retained administrative responsibility. In effect, he became the Prophet's eyes and ears, reporting to and receiving instructions from him directly.

By autumn 1965, President McKay realized that the procedure followed in using the services of Elder Isaacson had its deficiencies, as much of what he did was based upon instructions given or reports received outside the meetings of the First Presidency. So, in order that the counselors would be fully apprised of all actions being taken, and to provide for a complete record through the minutes of its meetings, he decided to bring Elder Isaacson into the First Presidency. At the same time, he decided to call President Joseph Fielding Smith as another counselor. These actions were approved by the Council of the First Presidency and Quorum of the Twelve on October 28, 1965, and the new counselors were set apart the next day.

The first meeting of the expanded First Presidency was held on November 9, at which time the Prophet elaborated on the reasons and the historical precedent for calling the additional counselors: "I welcome you as counselors in the First Presidency," he recorded in his diary, "and acknowledge with hesitancy that I am not so well as I used to be and called you brethren as counselors in the First Presidency to help carry the work. I pray the Lord's blessings to attend us in this quorum of the First Presidency. It is nothing new in the church. The Prophet Joseph Smith had several counselors; President Brigham Young had seven at one time I think; and this will constitute the quorum of the First Presidency. I should like to meet regularly with you and take up matters . . . as the occasion requires."

According to instructions given to him by the Prophet at the time of his call as a counselor, President Joseph Fielding Smith retained his position as the president of the Twelve. Such a division of his efforts, coupled with the fact that he was then in his ninetieth year, made it impossible for Elder Smith to carry much of the administrative load of the First Presidency. His chief role was to provide counsel—and continuity in the event he succeeded to the prophetic office. President McKay looked to Elder Isaacson to play a key administrative role and continued to assign him new responsibilities, as when, on January 19, 1966, he appointed him to the board of trustees of Brigham Young University, where, it was anticipated, his long experience on the boards of the University of Utah and the Utah State University would be invaluable. But President Isaacson's usefulness to the Prophet and the First Presidency suddenly ended nineteen days later when on February 7 he suffered a massive stroke that robbed him of his speech and his ability to walk. And it robbed President McKay of an able assistant who had served him in a personal way the other counselors could not duplicate because of their separate and heavy responsibilities. The Prophet lamented the loss of his friend's service; and when it became apparent that President Isaacson's disability was irreversible, he began to consider the possibility of bringing someone else into the First Presidency to fill his niche. In noting his sense of loss, he confided to his diary on April 15, 1966, that he "would have to appoint another counselor."

It is interesting and perhaps more than coincidental that on this same day, Elder Alvin R. Dyer reported to President McKay on certain matters pertaining to Missouri. This was the first time Elder Dyer's name had found its way into the Prophet's diary. "I told brother Dyer," President McKay recorded, "that he should proceed at once to obtain needed property and that I hold him responsible to see this is done and that he is to look after the project as a whole, keeping me advised of developments."

This initiated a series of contacts between the Prophet and Elder Dyer about affairs in Missouri. And by degrees, this led to an expansion of the areas of common interest between them. By June 1966, this relationship had developed to the point that on the fourteenth, the Prophet asked Elder Dyer to represent him at the Pleasant Grove Strawberry

Days parade. And on August 22, 1966, he asked Elder Dyer to work with Bishop Robert L. Simpson to study and report on the demonstrations that were then being conducted on college campuses and elsewhere in protest of the Vietnam War.

By January 1967, President McKay had seen enough of Elder Dyer and his work that on the eighteenth, as he gave further consideration to another counselor, he said of him, "He is one I have been thinking of. He is a man of good judgment and dependable."

Meanwhile, following a pattern he had adopted with Elder Isaacson, he began to give him progressively heavier assignments with the request that he report and make recommendations about what he had seen and heard. Among others, Elder Dyer became heavily involved in matters pertaining to Nauvoo Restoration, Inc., and Deseret Management Corporation, a holding company of the Corporation of the President. On April 21, 1967, the Prophet held a lengthy meeting with Elder Dyer when these matters were discussed along with problems pertaining to the Missouri lands and the Church real-estate department. The next day they met again when President McKay questioned Elder Dyer about his family and background.

By August 1967, following many months of frequent meetings about a variety of matters, the Prophet was ready to take a positive step toward formalizing their relationship. On the seventeenth, before Elder Dyer's departure for South America, the Prophet told him, "I am giving you notice now that I am calling you to be one of my assistants." He asked, "Did you know I have been watching you for a year now?"

Alvin R. Dyer returned from South America on September 18, 1967; and three days later President McKay presented his name to the Twelve for ordination as an apostle. He was sustained in that office at the general conference on September 29 and was ordained by President McKay on October 5. Following the ordination, the Prophet told the new apostle he wanted him to attend "every meeting I hold

with my counselors, including those held in the Temple."
This was affirmed at a meeting held with the counselors on
October 12 when he advised that Elder Dyer would attend
the meetings as "an assistant to the President."

The new apostle was soon functioning as if he were a
counselor in the First Presidency, fulfilling numerous assignments as directed by President McKay. He was appointed
to the BYU board of trustees, became heavily involved in
building and personnel matters at Church headquarters,
and was assigned to work with Elder Mark E. Petersen on
plans for a visitors' center in Independence, Missouri. By
January 1968, the Prophet felt the need to have Elder Dyer
physically closer to him, and so, after clearing the matter
with President Isaacson, he arranged on the fifth for him to
occupy the office in the northwest corner on the main floor
of the Church Administration Building. And by April, President McKay felt the need for him to be installed as an official
member of the First Presidency. On the sixth, therefore,
Alvin R. Dyer was sustained as a fifth counselor in the First
Presidency, thus giving him official status in that quorum.

The First Presidency, as constituted following Elder
Dyer's induction into that quorum, included President
McKay and five counselors: Hugh B. Brown, N. Eldon Tanner, Joseph Fielding Smith, Thorpe B. Isaacson, and Alvin
R. Dyer. And this group would serve together as the presiding quorum of the Church during the remainder of President McKay's life, with President Isaacson's participation
being almost nonexistent because of his stroke.

Chapter Twenty-Seven

The Last Years

T he last few years of President McKay's life, after the accident with Sonny Boy, were marked by a series of illnesses and hospitalizations. The mild stroke he suffered in November of 1963 resulted in a weakness in his legs and a slight impediment in his speech. And intermittently medication prescribed by his physician tended to make him drowsy and lethargic. But his mind was not impaired. His perceptions and mental faculties were such as to enable him to perform ably the essential role of his Prophetic office—decision-making. Through delegations of authority, the counselors were able to handle the ongoing affairs of the Church. But in matters that represented a departure from established policies or procedures, only the Prophet could and did decide. And even in matters that might have been regarded as administratively routine, the president was not reluctant to, and did on occasion, reverse decisions made by the counselors when he felt they were wrong or ill advised. So, despite the annoying ailments with which he was afflicted from time to time, David O. McKay remained very much in charge of Church affairs during these last years, although his active participation was curtailed in many things, and his voice was muted.

Beginning in midsummer 1959, Sister McKay suffered a series of illnesses that culminated with a slight stroke in February 1960. Because of the physical impairment she suffered, the McKays found it necessary to give up their much-loved family home on East South Temple. On August 4, 1960, they moved into a comfortable apartment in the Hotel Utah, where they lived during the rest of their lives. The apartment had a well-appointed study for the Prophet; and it was here, following his stroke, that he often held meetings of the First Presidency or received callers. Later, President McKay arranged for the construction of a modern cottage across the street from the Old Home in Huntsville, and it was to this retreat that they went intermittently for a change of scene.

As his mobility diminished, especially during the two years between President Isaacson's stroke and Alvin R. Dyer's call to the First Presidency, the Prophet relied more and more upon staff assistance. The member of the staff whom he called on most frequently was his personal secretary, Clare Middlemiss, who had served him dutifully for

President McKay at 92 years of age, October 1, 1965, with his four sisters. **Left to right:** *Mrs. Joseph R. Morrell (Jeanette), Mrs. George R. Hill (Elizabeth), Mrs. Joel E. Ricks (Katherine), and Mrs. Thomas B. Farr (Anne).*

418

three decades. Such was his confidence in this efficient woman that he entrusted her with many matters far beyond the normal scope of clerical responsibility. All correspondence received in or sent from the office of the president passed under the gaze of Clare Middlemiss. Knowing the mind and will of her employer as few people did, she was able in many instances to draft suggested answers to letters for the Prophet's consideration before he had even read the correspondence being answered.

Such competence and experience was a vast aid to President McKay and relieved him of a heavy burden of administrative detail. And it greatly facilitated the efficient handling of the ever-increasing flow of administrative matters in and out of the president's office. But it also created some unintentional problems of an inconsequential nature. These traced to the historic differences between line and staff personnel and to the hierarchal nature of the Mormon priesthood.

Notwithstanding his physical disabilities, President McKay continued with his usual round of activities during the remainder of his life, though on a diminishing scale. He met intermittently with his counselors, the Twelve, and other General Authorities. Until 1966, he continued to speak at general conference, although at the October conference that year, his legs were so weak he sat on a high stool to deliver his talk. Thereafter, members of his family read the talks for him. He attended most of the general conferences, although on the advice of his physician, he watched some of the sessions in his apartment.

President McKay continued to participate in ceremonial and entertainment functions and to enjoy outings to Huntsville almost to the very end. In the first week of January 1965, for instance, he dedicated the new Deseret Gymnasium in Salt Lake City, and six months later he attended the opening of the Valley Music Hall in Bountiful. Shortly before Christmas that year, he saw *Peter Pan* at the Valley Music Hall, enjoying it immensely. And he regularly participated in the July 24 parades. His last one, July 24, 1969, was especially memorable as he was made an honorary member of the Royal Scots Pipe Band. The band serenaded him as he came down from his Hotel Utah apartment and was just behind his car during the parade, jauntily attired in their colorful kilts and piping the Scottish airs he loved so much.

Huntsville never lost its magnetic attraction for the Prophet. He visited there often with Ray during the spring, summer, and early autumn months, staying in their comfortable cottage and transacting any pressing business by phone or in person when necessary with associates who drove up from Salt Lake City. Following a visit there for the customary July 4 celebration in 1968, he wrote, "It seemed wonderful to see my beloved home town after many weeks of absence."

The last full year of President McKay's life was preceded by a signal honor that revealed the extent to which his character and achievements had seeped into the public consciousness. On December 29, 1968, Dr. George Gallup published the results of his poll about the world's most admired men. The question posed by the poll taker was, "What man that you have heard or read about living today in any part of the world do you admire most?" In the field of religion, President David O. McKay was named second only to Cardinal Cushing. Others on the list included Norman Vincent Peale and Bishop Fulton J. Sheen. It is significant that the leader of a comparatively small church (then about two and a half million) headquartered in the Mountain West would have ranked that high in a random national poll.

Reverend Peale, one of his co-honorees, who was an ardent admirer of President McKay, wrote a tribute to him on the occasion of his ninety-second birthday, focusing on an aspect of the Prophet's character that gave him a special appeal to the public. Dr. Peale identified this as his "tremendous zest for life." As the author left an interview with the Prophet in company with his wife, he said to her, "You know, I think he is one of the happiest men I ever met." (IE, September 1965, pp. 767-68.)

This quality in his character surfaced repeatedly throughout his life, even at the threshold of death. On November 7, 1969, two months before his passing, the Prophet received a visit from his sister Kits and her husband Joel Ricks. During their visit, President McKay said to them, "I do love life; I do love life." And indicative of his positive, forward-looking attitude, even at such an advanced age, he told them he had made an appointment with Henry A. Smith, editor of the *Church News*, for an interview on September 8, 1973, his one-hundreth birthday!

But this was one of the few earthly goals this energetic prophet did not achieve. He passed away quietly on Sunday morning January 18, 1970, in his Hotel Utah apartment. Present at the moment of death were Emma Ray and five of the six living children. Word that the ninety-six-year-old head of the Mormon Church had passed on was immediately flashed around the globe. Television, radio, and newspaper outlets picked up on the story and flooded the media with pictures and biographical data about the man who was an oddity in the modern world—a prophet of God.

Although death was not unexpected, given his advanced age and the physical ailments he had suffered, the reality of President McKay's demise sent shock waves of sorrow and disbelief among members of the Church everywhere. Well over half of the almost three million Church members had never known another leader. To many of them, especially those who lived in distant places and who had never seen him in person, David O. McKay was an immutable constant like air and water. He had always been there, with his beaming countenance and assuring words. Now the great man, to whom so many had clung for encouragement and guidance, was gone. To some it was a personal, irreplaceable loss, akin to the loss of an earthly father and mentor.

The depth of the grief into which so many were thrown by President McKay's death, and the mark of the respect his followers and friends had for him, are suggested by the throngs who came to the viewing. Beginning Tuesday af-

David O. McKay

ternoon, January 20, and continuing to Thursday morning, the twenty-second, the day of the funeral, tens of thousands filed by the bronze casket in the foyer of the Church Administration Building. The line of mourners, three abreast, waiting their turn to view the body, wound out of the building through the South Temple entrance, down the wide granite steps, and thence east past the Lion House and Beehive House to State Street. During peak hours, the viewing line grew until it almost girded the entire block, wending its way north on State Street to North Temple, then west to Main Street past the Relief Society Building, then south to the Hotel Utah and around that corner to South Temple again, reaching toward the Church Administration Building from the west.

An air of solemnity filled the Tabernacle as the Saints assembled to pay their respects to the deceased prophet and his family. Seated on the stand were all the General Authorities who were well enough or near enough to Salt Lake City to attend. Even though Brother McKay's death had automatically dissolved the First Presidency, the Twelve, under whose direction the funeral was held, had recognized all the former counselors by inviting them to sit on the top level of the five-tiered stand. In the front center rows facing the stand and the Prophet's flower-draped bier were members of the McKay clan led by Sister McKay, her children, and their companions. Sisters and brothers-in-law and numerous grandchildren, great-grandchildren, nieces, nephews, and cousins were there to join with thousands of Saints and nonmember friends to offer a final salute to the deceased prophet.

President Hugh B. Brown conducted the services. The Tabernacle Choir sang three of President McKay's favorite hymns: "I Need Thee Every Hour," "Crossing the Bar," and "I Know That My Redeemer Lives." President Alvin R. Dyer and Elder Ezra Taft Benson offered the prayers. And Joseph Fielding Smith, Hugh B. Brown, N. Eldon Tanner, and Harold B. Lee spoke. The speakers focused on the dedication and quality of President McKay's service as an apostle of the Lord, a service of sixty-three years, nine months, and nine days, longer than any other apostolic tenure. They also extolled his fine character, his zest for living, and his love for family and fellowmen.

President Joseph Fielding Smith, who had known the deceased longer than any of the Brethren and who would succeed him in the Prophetic office, offered this fitting and perceptive tribute: "I thank God for the life and ministry of this great spirit who came here to preside in Israel. He did his work well and has just returned clean and perfected to the realm of light and joyous reunion."

It was cold at the cemetery, high on the east bench of Salt Lake City, where the associates, family, and friends of the Prophet assembled for the final rite performed in his honor. There his protégé and fellow apostle Richard L. Evans offered the prayer dedicating the grave that would hold his mortal remains. But the body laid to rest there was not David O. McKay, but was merely the earthly shell that for a time had housed his immortal spirit, a spirit that, as President Smith indicated in his eulogy, had gone to a joyous reunion with his heavenly parents and with members of his earthly family who had preceded him in death, there to await the resurrection.

In a sense, however, President McKay has never left us. He has remained on the earth through the medium of his words and his works, which are a constant reminder of the nobility of the human spirit and of the power and influence of God manifested through the life of one of His chosen servants. And these are also a constant goad and reminder to those who would emulate his example of happy, zestful, and productive living—especially to those of his priesthood brotherhood who would build upon the foundation he and his prophetic predecessors laid, looking toward the time when the Savior will return to reign personally over His kingdom that will govern the entire earth.

Bibliography

Books, Monographs, Compilations

Brigham Young University, The First Hundred Years. Edited by Ernest L. Wilkinson. 4 volumes. Provo: Brigham Young University Press.

Cannon, Hugh J. "David O. McKay's World Tour," unpublished manuscript, copy in possession of author; furnished by Adrian Cannon.

Clark, James R., comp. *Messages of the First Presidency of The Church of Jesus Christ of Latter-day Saints.* 6 vols. Salt Lake City: Bookcraft, 1965-75.

Evans, Richard L. *A Century of Mormonism in Great Britain.* Salt Lake City: Deseret News Press, 1937.

McKay, David O. *Cherished Experiences.* Compiled by Clare Middlemiss. Salt Lake City: Deseret Book Company, 1955.

―――. *Gospel Ideals.* 2nd printing. Salt Lake City: Improvement Era, 1954.

―――. *Man May Know for Himself.* Compiled by Clare Middlemiss. Salt Lake City: Deseret Book Company, 1967.

―――. *"My Young Friends . . . " President McKay Speaks to Youth.* Compiled by Llewelyn R. McKay. Salt Lake City: Bookcraft, 1973.

―――. *Pathways to Happiness.* Compiled by Llewelyn R. McKay. Salt Lake City: Bookcraft, 1966.

―――. *Stepping Stones to an Abundant Life.* Compiled by Llewelyn R. McKay. Salt Lake City: Deseret Book Company, 1971.

―――. *Treasures of Life.* Compiled by Clare Middlemiss. Salt Lake City: Deseret Book Company, 1962.

425

————. *True to the Faith.* Compiled by Llewelyn R. McKay. Salt Lake City: Bookcraft, 1967.

McKay, Donald D. *Memories of Huntsville and Its People.* Published privately, 1960.

McKay, Emma Ray Riggs. *The Art of Rearing Children Peacefully.* Provo: Brigham Young University Press, 1952.

McKay, Llewelyn R. *Home Memories of President David O. McKay.* Salt Lake City: Deseret Book Company, 1956.

Morrell, Jeanette McKay. *Highlights in the Life of President David O. McKay.* Salt Lake City: Deseret Book Company, 1966.

Selected Articles about David O. McKay

Adams, John Q. "Samoa's Love and Affection." *Improvement Era* 26 (May 1923) : 644-50.

"Apostle David Oman McKay." *Millennial Star* 68 (1906) : 498-99.

Appointed Principal of the Weber Stake Academy. *Millennial Star* 64 (May 1902) : 298.

Benson, Ezra Taft. "Heritage of Freedom." *Improvement Era* 61 (December 1958) : 954-57.

————. "Of One Blood." *Improvement Era* 61 (June 1958) : 433-34.

Brown, Hugh B. "God Makes a Giant Among Men." *Improvement Era* 73 (February 1970) : 88-91.

————. "President David O. McKay." *Improvement Era* 65 (September 1962) : 639-41, 665-66.

Cannon, Hugh J. "China Dedicated for Preaching of the Gospel." *Young Women Journal* 32 (April 1921) : 221-24.

Clark, J. Reuben. "Our Tribute to President McKay." *Improvement Era* 56 (September 1953) : 641.

"David O. McKay." *Improvement Era* 61 (November 1958) : 842.

"David O. McKay: Highlights of His Life and Works." *Improvement Era* 66 (September 1963) : 736-45.

"David O. McKay Becomes Ninth President of the Church." *Improvement Era* 54 (May 1951) : 324-25, 363.

Durham, G. Homer. "Man for the Hour." *Improvement Era* 54 (July 1951) : 482, 523.

"Elder David O. McKay in Glasgow." *Millennial Star* 83 (1921) : 826.

Bibliography

"Elders McKay and Cannon in Liverpool." *Millennial Star* 83 (1921) : 795-96.

Evans, Richard L. "David O. McKay: Portrait of a President." *Improvement Era* 54 (June 1951) : 400-403, 458.

———. "Fields of McKay." *Improvement Era* 46 (September 1943) : 530-31, 573-75.

———. "Highlights in the Life of President David O. McKay." *Improvement Era* 54 (June 1951) : 459.

———. "Reaffirmation: 'We Thank Thee O God for a Prophet'." *Improvement Era* 61 (December 1958) : 942-45.

"Felicitations: From the Auxiliaries." *Improvement Era* 56 (September 1953) : 630.

Green, Doyle L., and Albert L. Zobell. "President David O. McKay Visits Europe." *Improvement Era* 55 (September 1952) : 632-35, 658, 660, 662, 664.

———. "President McKay at Eighty-five." *Improvement Era* 61 (September 1958) : 643-49, 686-88.

Hanks, Marion D. "The Soul of a Prophet." *Improvement Era* 71 (September 1968) : 3-5.

"He Has Always Lifted People Up." *Church News*, January 24, 1970, pp. 6-7.

Hinckley, Bryant S. "David O. McKay." *Improvement Era* 35 (May 1932) : 389-91, 443-46.

Hinckley, Bryant S., et al. "Tributes to President David O. McKay." *Improvement Era* 66 (September 1963) : 746-49.

Hinckley, Gordon B. "God's Kingdom Is Here." *Improvement Era* 61 (December 1958) : 924-25.

"His Life's Work: Telling Church Story." *Church News*, September 12, 1981, p. 4.

Hunter, Howard W. "Prophets in This Dispensation." *Improvement Era* 66 (December 1963) : 1098-99.

"Inspirational Stories from the Life of David O. McKay." *Improvement Era* 69 (September 1966) : 768-72.

Josephson, Marba C. "At Home with the McKays." *Improvement Era* 56 (September 1953) : 644-45, 680, 683.

———. "President and Acting President of the Council of the Twelve." *Improvement Era* 53 (November 1950) : 872, 935.

Lee, Harold B. "He Lighted the Lamps of Faith." *Improvement Era* 73 (February 1970) : 93-95.

McKay, David Lawrence. "Keeping a Promise." *Instructor* 105 (August 1970) : 275.

McKay, Llewelyn R. "The 'Auld Hous'." *Improvement Era* 56 (October 1953) : 747-48.

McKay, Robert R. "A Son's Tribute to the Prophet." *Improvement Era* 70 (June 1967) : 79-80.

Middlemiss, Clare. "With the President in Europe." *Improvement Era* 58 (November 1955) : 799-800.

Monson, Leland H. "David O. McKay Was a Deacon, Too." *Instructor* 97 (September 1965) : 298-99.

Morrell, Jeanette McKay. "Ancestry of President David O. McKay." *Relief Society Magazine* 40 (September 1953) : 574-78.

———. "Boyhood of President David O. McKay." *Relief Society Magazine* 40 (October 1953) : 656-62.

———. "Life of President David O. McKay." *Relief Society Magazine* 40 (November 1953) : 730-37.

———. "Life of President David O. McKay." *Relief Society Magazine* 40 (December 1953) : 813-20.

Moyle, Henry D. "President McKay—Exemplar of Missionary Service." *Improvement Era* 64 (July 1961) : 511-12.

Murdock, Franklin J. "President David O. McKay and the South Seas Missions." *Improvement Era* 58 (April 1955) : 223-25.

———. "With the President: Patience and the Clasp of a Hand." *Improvement Era* 58 (March 1955) : 143.

Nibley, Preston. "When David McKay Went on a Mission." *Improvement Era* 64 (April 1961) : 218-22, 278.

Peale, Norman Vincent. "A Man with a Secret." *Improvement Era* 68 (September 1965) : 767-69.

Peterson, Willis S. "Our Prophet, David O. McKay." *Instructor* 100 (September 1965) : 357.

Pinnock, Florence B. "Our First Family." *Improvement Era* 66 (September 1963) : 792-94.

"President David O. McKay: Over the Years." *Improvement Era* 67 (September 1964) : 716-29.

Bibliography

"President McKay and the *Era's* Editors." *Improvement Era* 54 (May 1951) : 317-18.

Reiser, A. Hamer. "Eleven Days with President McKay in Europe." *Instructor* 88 (November 1953) : 324-25, 348-49.

———. "President David O. McKay: A Tribute." *Improvement Era* 63 (September 1960) : 623-25, 666-68.

———. "Sunday School Pioneer." *Instructor* 101 (September 1966) : 334-36.

Richards, Stayner. "Tribute to President David O. McKay." *Improvement Era* 55 (December 1952) : 910-11.

Richards, Steven L. "On the Eightieth Birthday of Our President." *Improvement Era* 56 (September 1953) : 640.

Rogers, C. Wayne. "Impressions." *Improvement Era* 44 (September 1941) : 521, 575.

"Significant Dates and Events in the Life of President David O. McKay." *Improvement Era* 66 (September 1963) : 750-51.

Smith, George Albert, George F. Richards, and The First Presidency. "Editorials." *Improvement Era* 48 (June 1945) : 335.

Smith, Joseph Fielding and Levi Edgar Young. "Birthday Greetings." *Improvement Era* 56 (September 1953) : 704.

Stapley, Delbert L. "Faith and the Polynesians." *Improvement Era* 61 (December 1958) : 926-29.

Tanner, N. Eldon. "True Exemplar of the Life of Christ." *Improvement Era* 73 (February 1970) : 91-93.

"University of Utah Honors President David O. McKay." *Improvement Era* 56 (September 1953) : 663.

Wahlquist, John T. "David O. McKay: A Holy Man." *Instructor* 91 (September 1956) : 264.

Wallace, John M., and John Rosenblatt. "President McKay Honored." *Improvement Era* 66 (February 1963) : 82-85, 111-12.

Widtsoe, John A. "What Can We Learn from President McKay's Recent Tour of Europe?" *Improvement Era* 55 (October 1952) : 710-11.

"Worth of a Soul." *New Era* 2 (January 1972) : 55-60.

Zobell, Albert L. "President David O. McKay Is Honored for 50 Years of Devoted Service." *Improvement Era* 59 (April 1956) : 224, 281-82.

———. "President McKay Visits Missions in Latin America." *Improvement Era* 57 (April 1954) : 228-29, 285-87.

———. "President McKay Visits South Africa." *Improvement Era* 57 (March 1954) : 144-45.

Selected Articles by David O. McKay

"Christmas Letter" from David O. McKay to his brother Elder Thomas E. McKay. *Improvement Era* 59 (December 1956) : 899, 977.

"Church and Missionary Work." *Improvement Era* 26 (December 1922) : 185-89.

"Church and the Present War." *Improvement Era* 45 (May 1942) : 276, 340-42.

Correspondence (about ship running into an iceberg). *Millennial Star* 61 (September 1, 1899) : 604.

"Counteracting of Pernicious Ideas and Subversive Teachings." *Improvement Era* 54 (December 1951) : 874-76.

"Effect of Revelation on Man's Creed." *Improvement Era* 23 (April 1920) : 506-14.

"Exemplar to All Men." *Improvement Era* 53 (April 1950) : 267.

"Faith Triumphant." *Improvement Era* 50 (August 1947) : 507, 562-63.

"Greatest Responsibilities: The Greatest Honor." *Improvement Era* 54 (June 1951) : 406-7.

"Honoring the Utah Pioneers and Lasting Values." *Improvement Era* 50 (May 1947) : 270-71, 345-48.

"How to Teach." *Improvement Era* 20 (December 1916) : 179-80.

"Joseph Smith, Prophet, Seer, and Revelator." *Improvement Era* 45 (January 1942) : 12-13, 54-56.

Letter from Glasgow. *Millennial Star* 45 (February 12, 1883) : 173.

Letter from Huntsville. *Millennial Star* 45 (May 29, 1883) : 410-11.

Letter from Scotland. *Millennial Star* 43 (November 15, 1881) : 747-48.

"My Mother." *Improvement Era* 61 (May 1958) : 303.

"Nearness of Our Father." *Improvement Era* 55 (September 1952) : 629-30.

"Nobility of Character: Essentials to a Great Nation." *Improvement Era* 46 (May 1943) : 270-71, 313-14.

Bibliography

"President Grant: The Benefactor." *Improvement Era* 44 (November 1941) : 655.

"President Grant Still Young at Eighty." *Improvement Era* 39 (November 1936) : 661.

"President Heber J. Grant." *Improvement Era* 48 (June 1945) : 334, 361.

"President McKay Explains Policy in Choosing Aides." *Improvement Era* 54 (June 1951) : 464-65.

"Prophet Joseph: On Doctrine and Organization." *Improvement Era* 48 (January 1945) : 14-15, 45-47.

"Reaching the Souls of Men." *Improvement Era* 23 (November 1919) : 18-22.

"Righteousness: Key to World Peace." *Improvement Era* 58 (June 1955) : 395-97.

"Some Characteristics of 'The Kingdom'." *Improvement Era* 57 (August 1954) : 557-58.

"Sylvester Q. Cannon." *Improvement Era* 46 (August 1943) : 465, 509-10.

"Testimony." *Improvement Era* 68 (September 1965) : 799.

Testimony from David O. McKay. *Millennial Star* 60 (1898) 747.

"Testimony of the Gospel." *Millennial Star* 83 (1921) : 177-79.

"Transforming Power of Faith in Jesus Christ." *Improvement Era* 54 (June 1951) : 406-9, 478.

"Tribute to John A. Widtsoe." *Improvement Era* 56 (January 1953) : 20.

"Whate'er Thou Art Act Well Thy Part." *Improvement Era* 62 (October 1959) : 726-27, 770.

Index

Commercial corporations. *See* Corporations, commercial
Commission, Utah Centennial, DOM as chairman of, 240-42
Commissioner of Education, DOM called as, 97-98
Committee, Missionary Executive, 407-8
Communism, 207, 258, 315-17, 365, 380-82
Conference: Scottish, DOM presides over, 46-47, 49; Glasgow, 53; Spanish-speaking, 233-34
"Conference House," 42-43
Cook Islands, DOM travels to, 114
Coombs, D'Monte W., 345
Coombs, Mark V., 115
Corporations, commercial: DOM involved with, 163, 394-97; Church reorganizes, 192-93
Courtship of DOM, 56
Cowles, Leroy, 244
Cowley, Matthias F., 66-67, 167-68, 329-30
Cummings, Byron, 29
Cundick, Robert, 369

Daily Record, 47
Deacons quorum, DOM as president of, 20
Dedication of China, 107-8
Dedications, DOM speaks at, 34-42, 419-20
Denmark, DOM travels to, 297-98
Depression, the Great, 158
Dinners, family, 221-22
Dinwoodey, Annette Richardson, 369-70
Diplomacy of DOM, 296
Drama, 140-41
Dunn, James, 304

Duties of DOM as prophet, 282
Dyer, Alvin R., 414-16

East Central States Mission, 145
Eccles, David, 49, 83
Eccles, Marriner, 310
Eck, Samuel K., 254
Economic problems, DOM discusses, 154-55
Edling, Wilford G., 127
Education: in Huntsville, 8; of DOM, 24; of McKay children, 27-28; DOM called as commissioner of, 97-98; role of Church in, 342, 391-93
Edwards, John T., 46
Effort, war, DOM assists in, 93
Egypt, DOM travels to, 118-19
Eighteenth Amendment, 150-51
Eisenhower, Dwight D., 313, 316-17, 351-52
Elizabeth II, Queen, 306
Embolism, DOM suffers, 247
Empress of Japan, 102-3
England: DOM as missionary in, 39; DOM as mission president in, 123-24; DOM travels to, 295, 306-7, 323, 365-66
Epidemic, influenza, 95, 96
Europe: DOM travels to, 122, 292; WW II affects missions in, 184-85; chapels in, 128, 293-94, 365-67
European Mission: headquarters of, 40; DOM called to preside over, 123; DOM reports on, 129
Evans, Jennette, 3. *See also* McKay, Jennette Evans
Evans, Richard L., 181-82, 329
Evans, Thomas B., 58

Fame of DOM, 263-64, 283-84
Family home evening, 143-44
Family life of DOM: 76, 130-31,

Index

in, 20; DOM as, board
member, 58-59; DOM writes
article about, 64; DOM in
general superintendency of,
83-84; curriculum for, 85;
DOM supervises, 134
Surgery, DOM undergoes, 352,
361, 364, 389
Sweden, DOM travels to, 298
Swiss Temple, 309, 323, 354-56
Switzerland, DOM travels to,
295-96, 303, 323, 354-56

Tabernacle, Salt Lake, 86, 90-91
Tabernacle Choir, 351, 353-55
Taft, Robert A., 314
Tahiti, DOM travels to, 113-14,
346
Talk, DOM gives first, in
Tabernacle, 86-88
Talmage, James E., 29, 85, 127,
148-49
Tanner, N. Eldon, 409-11
Taylor, George S., 114
Taylor, John W., 66-67
Teacher training, 84
Teaching: accreditation of DOM,
25-26; job accepted by DOM,
55
Teasdale, George, 70
Telecast of general conference,
329
Temple: Idaho Falls, 163-64, 194,
230; Hawaii, 202; sites,
acquisition of, 307-8; Swiss,
309, 323, 354-56; London, 321,
323, 354, 361-62; work,
committee supervises,
329-31; ceremony, DOM
studies, 342-43; New
Zealand, 349; Los Angeles,
356-58
Tenyo Maru, 109-10
Testimony of DOM, 17-18,
48-51, 256

This Is the Place Monument,
250, 252-53
Thurso, Scotland, 1-2, 52, 293,
295, 323
Tithing, DOM learns, 21-22
Tonga, DOM travels to, 115,
345
Tonsillectomy, Emma Ray
undergoes, 144
Tornado, 290
Tragedy at Winter Quarters
(sculpture) 166
Truman, Harry S, 228, 312-13

University, Brigham Young, 25,
31, 141, 266-67, 312
University of Utah, 29, 31
Uruguay, DOM travels to, 336
Uruguay Mission, 259
Utah Centennial Commission,
182-83, 240-42. *See also*
Centennial celebration
Utah Council on Child Health
and Protection, 135

VanDam, Donovan H., 296
Virginia, 94
Vision of redemption of the
dead, 96

Waddoups, William M., 111,
165
Wales, 52-53, 223-24, 305,
362-63, 366-70
War effort, DOM assists in, 93
Ward, Huntsville, 14
Washington, D.C., DOM travels
to, 157, 351-52
Weber Stake Academy: DOM
attends, 24; DOM teaches at,
55; DOM as principal of,
59-60, 82; financial problems
of, 83
Welfare program, Church. *See*
Church welfare program

Index